"Captain Power-Waters brings an understanding and appreciation of Air Traffic Control from two perspectives: as a pilot operating within the system; and as someone who possesses a vast knowledge of the ATC's work."

—William F. Faville, Jr., President,
National Air Traffic Controllers Association, MKC.
Eighty-five percent of the controllers are members.

"If you are interested in the training of an airline captain, if you think your airline is safe, or if you think the FAA is totally interested in your safety, this is the book for you."

—Carl Butterworth, Senior Captain, American Airlines,
retired Brigadier General, Air National Guard.

"You obviously have done an extensive job researching this topic, and more importantly, it is clear you have lived the issues. I congratulate you on your effort."

—Robert Roach, Jr., General Vice President, International
Association of Machinists and Aerospace Workers.
We represent over 14,000 mechanics and flight attendants.

Is It Safe?

$33.50

Is It Safe?

Why Flying Commercial Airliners Is Still A Risky Business ... And What Can Be Done About It.

This Book May Save Your Life!

Captain Brian Power-Waters XIII
Author of *Safety Last*, and *Margin for Error: None*,
and *93 Seconds to Disaster*

250101

iUniverse, Inc.
New York Lincoln Shanghai

Is It Safe?
Why Flying Commercial Airliners Is Still A Risky Business ... And What Can Be Done About It.

Copyright © 2008 by Brian Power-Waters XIII

iUniverse books may be ordered through booksellers or by contacting:

iUniverse
2021 Pine Lake Road, Suite 100
Lincoln, NE 68512
www.iuniverse.com
1-800-Authors (1-800-288-4677)

Because of the dynamic nature of the Internet, any Web addresses or links contained in this book may have changed since publication and may no longer be valid.

The views expressed in this work are solely those of the author and do not necessarily reflect the views of the publisher, and the publisher hereby disclaims any responsibility for them.

ISBN: 978-0-595-49015-8 (pbk)
ISBN: 978-0-595-60931-4 (ebk)

Printed in the United States of America

For my children
Lisette, Laurette, Linette, and Lanette

My parents, Alma and Pierce, and sister, Pat.

Last, but by no means least, my beautiful wife, Kay,
who put up with so much while I was writing this book

Contents

▼

Foreword

▼

I have been interested in aviation since the age of seven. I have been extremely lucky in life because I have spent over 50 years doing something I would have gladly done for nothing: fly.

I first soloed at age 16 and earned my private license a year later. Because I was a British subject, I was not permitted to train as a U.S. pilot during World War II, even though I had lived in this country since the age of five (I became an American citizen in 1949). In 1943, I joined the Royal Canadian Air Force and entered initial training ground school. There, I was confronted with two of my least favorite subjects: math and physics. Because of a shortage of barracks, we were posted in private homes near Toronto, Canada. Here, we were on our own, coming and going as we pleased. I am ashamed to admit that I let my studies take a back seat to the great enjoyment of chasing girls. I already had my pilot's license and I really thought I had it made.

My ground school professor, on the other hand, grew tired of giving me failing grades and trying to keep me awake in class. He warned me that I would be eliminated from pilot training. I was devastated and pleaded for another chance. I was then told that I could pick any other crew position in the aircraft. My response to them was that if I could not fly the plane, I did not want to ride in it! My wishes were granted. For over a year, I was on general duties that consisted of scrubbing pots and pans in the enlisted men's mess hall.

Finally, I came to my senses. I applied and was accepted for flight engineer training. I would be trained for the Mark-5 Halifax bomber in which the engineer's position is similar to that of a co-pilot on an American bomber.

After the war, I pursued my first dream: to be an Air Force pilot. I graduated as a pilot in the U.S. Air Force in 1950 and served on active duty for five years. I transferred to the Air Force Reserve and Air Guard where I continued to fly fighters until 1981.

In 1954, I became an airline pilot for Mohawk Airlines and later, following an airline strike, Allegheny Airlines absorbed my company and changed the name to USAir (later USAirways). I checked out in one of their BAC 1-11 (similar to a DC-9, only better). I was fortunate to have made the transition from co-pilot to captain in 18 months, something unheard of today. I have been a captain with USAirways for over 28 years and have accumulated over 30,000 hours in the air.

I am a qualified flight instructor on everything from gliders to jets. I have an ATP (Airline Transport Pilot, the highest U.S. rating) on the DC-3, Martin 202, Convair 240, 340, 440, Martin 404, and BAC-111. I have commercial privileges on the single-engine Land, Sea, Glider, C-45, C-46, C-47, C-54, B-25, B-17, P-38, F-86, F8F, T-28, T-6, PT-19, PT-12, UC-78, Schweizer 222 and 126, Moyes ultralight, and various hang gliders. I also have flown the P-51 Mustang. I am an FAA ground instructor, flight engineer, senior parachute rigger with 40 jumps to my credit, and I am a hot air balloon driver. Three years ago, I completed the most demanding course I have ever taken: I obtained my Aircraft Mechanics Certificate with airframe and power plant ratings.

I am a member of the International Aerobatic Club (IAC), Chapter 11, in Washington, D.C. I fly a home-built Pitts SIS that is an open cockpit biplane. I participate in a half-dozen aerobatic contests each year. A few year ago, I placed third in Canada and seventh in the United States.

Pilots are considered god-like beings by many people, but I know better. Personally, I have always admired air traffic controllers. They have the destiny of dozens of aircraft in their hands: pilots have only one. For this reason, I felt particularly honored when, in 1976, I was awarded the Professional Air Traffic Controllers Organization Presidential Citation. PATCO's then-president, John Leyden, invited my family and me to come to its convention in San Diego, California, as the guest of honor. The citation on my plaque reads: "To Captain Brian Power-Waters who, in his role as an airline captain, has done so much in developing a continuing dialogue and relationship between pilots and controllers. [This award is] for his many contributions throughout the years in his furtherance of aviation safety and particularly the assistance and friendship he has extended to PATCO officers and PATCO controllers during its formative years."

During the 1981 PATCO strike, I was the only pilot who defended the controllers and what they were fighting for. This cost me my job as captain with USAirways. I could afford to be brave: I was near retirement anyway. But mostly, I had no desire to pilot a plane through unsafe skies.

—BP-W

Preface

▼

Now as to why I wanted to write this book. I have been gathering notes and anecdotes for decades. If I saw something that was dangerous, I would report it. There was barely a trip that I would fly when I didn't find some sort of safety discrepancy. These notes grew and grew until I believed I had the makings of a great book on air safety.

In reality, it takes a pilot to write about air safety: laymen are not sufficiently knowledgeable about what is really wrong within the system. For example, when an outsider goes to a control center and says he is getting material for a book, he is immediately confronted by a supervisor who will be sure that the author departs with erroneous information. The supervisor will show the author only traffic sectors that are fully staffed and equipment that is operating perfectly. He will arrange interviews with controllers who dare not say anything derogatory about the system.

Exactly the same scenario will take place when the author visits a maintenance base or an aircraft factory. The truth can be found only by visiting union headquarters or by talking to shop stewards who are not afraid of their company. As for getting an airline pilot to admit that the system is flawed, that would be next to impossible. Most pilots are worried about saying anything that might disrupt the all-important pushing of that large, money-filled wheelbarrow to the bank.

The vast majority of airline pilots are great at what they do: driving airplanes. If you ask them about something over and above their six-month check requirements, they don't know or care. And, by law, they don't have to possess any diversified knowledge.

This book is not written to produce fear. It is hoped that it will alert the reader to safety issues in the airline industry. The stories depicted in this book actually occurred and every person referred to is, or was, a real person. Many of the anecdotes in this book were incidents that actually happened to me. I did not have to interview a pilot who was afraid to speak up. I was there.

Over 70 percent of this book touches on subjects that have never before appeared in similar books or other publications. *Is It Safe?* does not simply rehash old crashes but explores entirely new subjects. Even though the United States usually has the best of everything regarding aviation, even we are still a long, long way from having the safety standards that could—or should—prevail.

All you have to do is turn on the TV or pick up a newspaper to realize that airline safety is no better today that it was 30 or even 10 years ago. If anything, it seems as though the airline disasters we heard about in the late 1990s are more horrifying and kill more people than ever. From dangerous airports and poor plane maintenance to overworked air traffic controllers and enraged passengers, there are hazards in the skies for every one of us who flies. It may want you to believe otherwise, but the Federal Aviation Administration, the government agency responsible for making air travel safe, is not doing all it can, not even remotely. Taking your next commercial flight may, indeed, be your last.

I should know. I was a USAirways captain for 28 years. When my two earlier books on this subject—*Safety Last* (Dial Press) and *Margin for Error: None* (Pierce)—were published some years ago, they and I became a cause celebre. I was interviewed by Larry King and Morley Safer of "60 Minutes." I was featured in everything from *The Wall Street Journal* to *Harper's*, from the *New York Daily News* to *Publishers Weekly*. In headlines that screamed "Veteran Pilot's Book Takes on the FAA" and "Pilot's Book Blasts Airlines and the FAA," stories about me and my books flooded the airwaves and the newspapers. I pulled no punches in my books. They cost me my job with USAirways but they won me the undying respect and admiration of pilots and air traffic controllers everywhere. I was even awarded a special commendation by PATCO.

I wish I could say that more than two decades later, my efforts, and the efforts of other concerned airline insiders, have made a difference, and that planes today are relatively safe and trouble-free. But I can't. If anything, conditions are worse than ever. This is why *Is It Safe?* is so needed right now. In it, I uncover those frightening conditions in detail certain to cause FAA officials many sleepless nights. In addition, I describe exactly what the airlines as well as you and I—the everyday person who flies for business or pleasure—can do to minimize those risks and make those skies above us friendly instead of deadly.

Is It Safe? is the first book to uncover all-new facts about the inner workings of the commercial airline industry, facts it would just as soon you didn't know. It is written for the typical concerned traveler, but like my earlier two books, *Is It Safe?* will be equally fascinating and eye-opening to the seasoned senior airline captain.

Acknowledgments

▼

Many thanks to all the people who helped me with this book. I had the input of more people than I can mention. Further, the identity of some must remain anonymous so they can retain their jobs.

American Airlines Senior Captain Herb Hamilton and Captain/General Carl Butterworth (Air National Guard, Retired), American Airlines Captain Tony Vallilloo, Air Canada Captain Bob Pearson, and USAirways' Captains Ron Barnhart and Jerry Clark, along with Captain Mark Darrow, United Airlines.

Of the National Air Traffic Controllers Association: Will Faville, Muskegon, MI; Joseph Bellino, Chicago Il; Michael Coulter, Denver, CO; Richard Sullivan, Boston, MA; Richard Sawyer, Washington, D.C.; Mike McNally, Washington, D.C.; Jane Clancy, Washington, D.C.; and Bryan Thomson, controller and editor of The Voice.

Of the International Association of Machinists (IAM): Robert Roach, vice president, Bill Upton, and Joe Tiberi.

Of the Air Line Pilots Association: Pierie Huggins, Jerry Wright, Rick Kessell, and Gary Dinumo.

My thanks also to Glen Moore (congressional research), Chuck Frinfrock, Captain David B. Gwinn (wind shear expert), Major David Arrington and Dr. Richard A. Dolber (bird strike experts), Bob Schwartz (FAA engineer), Dr. Ralph Libby, Dave Smith, Bob Hudson (Safe Flight), Barkley and Mike Bloomgarden, Ben Knight, Steve Goodman, George Crumb, Steve Bollinger, Jim Burke, Vern Kemp, Linda Konner, George Brosan, and Lawrence Brosan.

Thanks also to my wife, Kay, and daughters Lisette, Laurette, Linette, and Lanette for typing and correcting my manuscript. I only write in long-hand, and my family took sections of the book and typed it into the final manuscript.

CHAPTER 1

▼

THE MAGIC PENCIL

When a pilot is checked out in a simulator, he must fulfill a 25-hour training period in the real aircraft before he becomes a fully qualified captain. This training time is supervised by a check captain on a regularly scheduled flight.

Fifty-eight year old Captain Richard E. Boddy had just completed his check out in the Eastern Airlines L-1011 simulator. He was anxious to be free of being watched by a check airman, and today's flight would add to the required 25 supervised hours. Captain Boddy had logged a total of 12,045 hours flight time of which 13 hours were in the Lockheed-1011.

Before his training flight, Captain Boddy was busy reading his aircraft log and checking for open items (those not signed off). His crew included Captain Steve C. Thompson, 48, who would be check riding and fulfilling the duties of co-pilot; Dudley H. Barnes, 44, who would be riding "side saddle" in the engineers seat; and senior cabin attendant Shirley Alexiou, who would be supervising the six other cabin crewmembers.

The weather at Miami International Airport was cloudy with the first deck of broken clouds at 2,300 feet with two higher decks. The temperature was 68 degrees and the visibility was seven miles. The wide-bodied L-1011 was fueled with 46,000 pounds of jet fuel: takeoff weight was 327.367 pounds, and there were 162 passengers on board. The destination weather at Nassau in the Bahamas showed rain showers, 500-foot scattered clouds, 1,000-foot broken clouds, and visibility of four miles.

At 08:56 A.M., Eastern Airlines Flight 855 lifted off Runway 27R and headed out over the ocean for Nassau. This would be a nice 27-minute trip to the tiny island of New Providence. As they passed 1,500 feet, the flight engineer called the company to give the out off and arrival times to dispatch. Engineer Barnes continued to monitor his panel and no discrepancies were noted.

At 0908:14, Captain Boddy leveled the plane out at 23,000 feet, adjusted the power, and flicked on the altitude hold. Seventy miles away from their destination, they received a descent clearance from Nassau approach control. As Flight 855 descended through 15,000 feet, Captain Boddy turned to his engineer and said: "Say Dudley, the No. 2 pressure light is on for No. 2 engine."

Engineer: "My panel shows No. 1 and No. 3 have about 15 quarts with pressure in the green (acceptable range), but No. 2 indicates a quantity of only 8 quarts, and the oil pressure is fluctuating between 15 and 25 psi" (minimum operating pressure was 30 psi).

Captain Boddy: "Shut down No. 2 engine."

This quick decision was the key point in averting a major catastrophe. The auxiliary power unit (APU) was started as a precautionary measure. The flight was now only 38 miles from Nassau, and the good book says that with an engine out, you should land at the nearest suitable airport. It was decided, wisely, that it would be better to reverse course and land back at Miami. This decision was tempered by the fact that Nassau doesn't possess a proper instrument landing system (ILS), the weather was deteriorating, they had to follow a light plane ahead of them, and there was no radar at the destination airport. Engineer Barnes keyed his mike:

"Miami Center, we've, ah, we've had a precautionary shutdown on No. 2 engine."

Center: "Okay. You need any special handling?"

Engineer: "Negative, sir."

Center: "Okay."

Engineer: "Miami Center Eastern, ah 855, ah, we have, ah, some rather serious indications, ah, we have an indication of all three pressures on all three engines, ah … ah … down to zero. We believe it to be faulty indications, ah, since the chances of all three engines having zero oil pressure and quantity is almost nil. However, those are our indications in the cockpit at the present time."

Center: "Okay, fine. Why don't you turn right about 15 degrees? We'll give you direct to Miami, maintain Flight Level 20, whatever altitude you want to maintain, and we're just going to have the equipment (crash crews) standing by anyway for you."

Engineer: "Eastern 855 proceeding direct to Miami Airport."

Flight Engineer Barnes was extremely busy monitoring the radio and his complicated instrument panel. Presently, he was devoting all his time to performing the No. 2 engine shutdown checklist that took about four minutes. While running the shutdown check, he had no time to monitor engines 1 and 3, and the two pilots had their hands full up front. This will give you some insight into why it's wise to have a crew of three. The newer jets today have eliminated the all-important engineer.

At 09:28, the No. 3 engine failed. The crew reluctantly had to admit that the oil quantity gauges were not at fault and that they were truly running out of oil. They were now descending through 16,000 feet with Miami still a long 80 miles away. Engineer Dudley Barnes called the senior flight attendant, Shirley Alexiou, to the cockpit and said,

"Shirley, you had better prepare the cabin for a ditching."

She wanted to stay on the flight deck to obtain further information, but she could see the crew was extremely busy, so she wisely returned to the cabin. After briefing her cabin crew, she gave explicit instruction on how to don the life vests when removing them from their stowed pockets under the seats.

Even though the cabin crew instructed the passengers in a step-by-step demonstration there was still a turmoil. Many passengers became tangled in their vests and had to be assisted by the crew. The parents of small children had a special problem. Adults put their life vests on over their head whereas children step into them. This difference is not depicted on many of the airline passenger briefing cards.

Some of the male passengers refused to assist the flight attendants and would not be responsible to man a safety exit. Some were too drunk to know what was about to happen. Perhaps they were better off.

At 09:29, Second Officer Barnes transmitted, "Ah, Eastern number Eastern 855. We've just lost our No. 3 engine, sir."

Center: "Oh, losing No. 3. You still got two turning?"

Engineer: "Negative, we only have one now, and we're going to restart No. 2."

Center: "Okay. Fine, we're listening. Okay. Cleared direct. Miami's altimeter 29.89 and you can descend at your discretion at any altitude you need. You're clear of traffic."

At 0933:20, the last operable engine failed and Flight 855 became a wide-bodied glider. At an altitude 12,000 feet, air speed of 225 knots, distance to Miami 60 miles, and the descent rate increased from 600 feet per minute with one engine operating to a whopping 1,600 feet per minute with all engines out, there would be no chance to make it to Miami.

Captain Boddy was doing his best to conserve the precious altitude without getting slow enough to invite a stall. Engineer Barnes picked up the mike to the cabin and reluctantly said "Ditching is imminent."

When the passengers heard this fearful announcement, the ones that were close to panic began to scream in terror. The cabin crew responded like the professionals they were, and after assuring the most nervous people, began their final check to ensure all were in the braced position.

Miami Center alerted the Coast Guard District Headquarters, and a Coast Guard Falcon jet and chopper departed immediately from their base at Opa Locka, Florida. At 09:36, another chopper and a C-130, both of which were already airborne from USCG Station in Clearwater, were diverted to aid Flight 855. One Coast Guard cutter and five patrol vessels were standing by at sea.

Captain Boddy would not have considered the loss of one engine as routine, but with all engines gone it looked like he would get to try his first water landing, a thrill he could do without. All that was left now was to complete the ditching checklist and to keep trying to start an engine.

They were now down to 13,000 feet and Miami was a long 50 miles away. The crew had no way of knowing that the No. 1 and No. 3 engines were so internally torn up that the disconnection of the drives to the engine-driven fuel pumps were the cause of the flameouts. Their only chance for a relight would be No. 2 engine. Captain Boddy cautiously had shut this engine down before all the oil was depleted. The captain tried to restart No. 3 and No. 1, but again was unsuccessful. A wet landing looked imminent. The crew could see the Coast Guard planes and boats all flying close to the crippled giant.

Now they were down to 4,000 feet, and land was still over 20 miles away. With a prayer on his lips, Captain Boddy tried for another start. He activated the No. 2 start switch and to everyone's joy, the gauges sprang to life and the instrument needles started their journey into the green area. They now had one engine running. That would be sufficient for a downhill glide.

A grateful engineer pressed his mike button and spread the good news to Miami Center, "We have an engine going; now we believe we can make the airport, well, we believe we've got it made."

At 0946, Flight 855 made a perfect landing on Runway 27L at Miami International Airport. Once again, an experienced, dedicated aircrew had cheated gravity and lived to tell about it.

You have seen how a well-trained flight and cabin crew acted in an extreme emergency. Now it's time to examine the disgraceful cause of this near-fatal tragedy.

Each of the three giant Rolls Royce RB-211-22B engines are equipped with a small one and one-half by two-inch master chip detector located in the bottom of each engine. This plug is cylindrical and has two grooves in its center that are normally filled with two one-inch diameter O-rings (similar to a rubber washer that goes in the end of a garden hose). These plugs have a magnetized end that pick up any metal chips the engine might lose during its normal operation.

These units are usually removed on each overnight service, or at least each 40 hours of engine operating time. If a master chip detector is inserted into the oil system without O-ring seals, an oil leak will commence as soon as the engine is started. The No. 1 and No. 3 engines were checked on landing and the oil quantity was zero. No. 2 engine was nearly ready to shut down because the oil quantity was almost nil.

The night before the near disastrous flight, two highly skilled mechanics, Lynn Burris and James Sunbury, were given the task of replacing these tiny master chip plugs. One of the mechanics went to the foreman's office to get the three replacement master chip detectors. For years, mechanics had always obtained these chips from the foreman cabinet with the two O-rings already in place. On this particular evening, and for the first time, these chip detectors had to be drawn from supply. Each of the three detectors was packed in a semi-transparent plastic bag with a serviceable parts tag attached to each package. This tag signified that the part was ready for use as is. The aircraft was parked in a dark area of the Eastern ramp, and it was necessary for the mechanic to aim the headlights of his truck at the No. 1 and No. 3 engines in order to see anything.

The inside of a jet nacelle (outer covering of the engine) is dark even in daylight. So at night, these men had to replace the master chip plugs by feel; they couldn't see what they were doing. They installed all the plugs and never checked to ensure that the all-important O-rings were in place.

The rest is history. There were no O-rings on these detectors and it only took about 35 minutes of flight time before the oil had leaked out of all but one of the engines.

How could such an important item as 1-inch rubber bands be treated in such a careless fashion? Who is to blame?

The mechanics are partially to blame, but the management of Eastern and the FAA are entitled to the lion's share of this fiasco. Eastern Airlines kept a record of in-flight engine shutdown per 1,000 hours of operation but only for the Rolls Royce RB211 engines. Eastern utilizes many other types of engines that are not included in this survey.

In 1981, eighty-three engines were shut down for various mechanical failures. In 1982, a rise in shutdowns brought the number to a staggering record high of 123.

In 1981, after three L-1011 aircraft experienced in-flight shutdowns because of oil loss, Eastern issued special training procedures (STP) 49-81. The new check was supposed to eliminate chip detector problems. After replacing the chip detectors, the engines had to be turned over in order to check for leaks under pressure. No specified motoring time was ever stated. The mechanics who replaced the magnetic chips on Flight 855 said that they did motor the engines for a period of 10 seconds each, not nearly long enough to check for a faulty plug leak.

At the time of the incident, the new procedure was placed on a bulletin board for all to read, if they were so inclined. Both mechanics in question said that they had never seen the new STP and knew nothing about it.

Immediately after the incident on Flight 855, master chips would not be issued with O-rings installed, thereby requiring that each mechanic personally affix the O-rings. And the engines had to be motored, turned over for 30 seconds to two minutes.

From September 2, 1981, until May 5, 1983, the date of the Flight 855 incident, Eastern Airlines had experienced 12 engine shutdowns because of faulty or missing O-rings and chip detectors. The mechanics union, the International Association of Mechanics (IAM), also saw a dangerous situation brewing, and they told the Eastern management that the magnetic chip problem was out of hand. So two years prior to this incident, both Eastern and the FAA were fully aware that they had a problem.

Eastern was the only carrier that had to shut down an engine because of a master chip detector; other carriers used the same L-1011, but had no chip problem.

Eastern's FAA principal maintenance inspector (PMI) was fully aware of all the incidents concerning the Eastern master chip problem, but he didn't think it was important enough to fuss over. "He did not consider the problem with master chip detector and O-ring seal installations a major system problem, and did not assign a special surveillance priority to it." After the Flight 855 incident he changed his tune.

In my opinion, inspectors with such a cavalier attitude toward safety should be horsewhipped.

When the FAA originally certified the L-1011, ditching tests were performed using a model of a Boeing 707. This test was performed in a tank by the National Advisory Committee for Aeronautics in 1955. Regulation test 25.801—Ditching states, in part, that "The probable behavior of the airplane in a water landing must be investigated by model tests or by comparison with airplanes of similar configuration for which ditching characteristics are known."

The Boeing 707 is a narrow-bodied, four-engine jet with two engines mounted under each wing. The Lockheed L-1011 is a wide-bodied, three-engine aircraft with one engine in the tail and two under the wings. Talk about apples and oranges. Anything to save a dollar.

The probable cause hearing by the National Transportation Safety Board (NTSB) had this to say, in part, concerning the failure of the three engines on the L-1011: "The repeated failure of supervisory personnel to require mechanics to comply strictly with the prescribed installation procedures, and the failure of Eastern Airlines management to assess adequately the significance of similar previous occurrences and to act effectively to institute corrective action. Contributing to the cause of the accident was the failure of the FAA maintenance inspectors to assess the significance of the incidents involving master chip detectors, and to take effective surveillance and enforcement measures to prevent the recurrence of the incident."

At Eastern Airlines, the job of the full-time maintenance inspector was considered to be one of their links to safe operation. These inspectors were former line mechanics who received a prescribed training course, and were required to assimilate vast amounts of daily reports and regulations. Since deregulation has forced cutbacks in nearly all maintenance departments, the full-time inspectors at Eastern have vanished.

Now the company had an agreement with the FAA whereby any mechanic can be designated as a temporary inspector. The tour usually lasts for a period of thirty days. These temporary inspectors receive no formal training regarding the all-important inspection procedure.

When a pilot or a mechanic identifies a mechanical malfunction in the aircraft log (called "squawking"), it must be repaired or assigned as a carried over item, deferred item (CI) in the aircraft's log. An airworthy item must be repaired before the aircraft is released for flight. But many non-airworthy items, when combined with other carry-over items, can be potential dangers. Because of the rapid aircraft turnaround time, it's not uncommon for a plane to traverse many maintenance bases without ever being repaired.

When a crew squawks a certain item such as the number one communications radio, a mechanic must sign off the squawk. The fastest way is to unscrew two bolts and replace the unit. This might take a maximum of 10 minutes. A few days later, this same aircraft might have a similar write-up again. The quick "fix" is to change the same black box again.

This scenario might continue until a conscientious captain reviews the log and sees that the radio problem stems from a write-up two weeks previous. He may then decide that he wants the problem traced, and to discontinue the changing of the black box. If the departure time is too close to properly troubleshoot the system, the maintenance supervisor will tell the mechanic to "sign off" that he has found the problem, even if he hasn't. Most mechanics never sign their names to work they don't feel comfortable with. What happens now? If the item isn't signed off by a qualified mechanic, the plane cannot move.

This is where the maintenance supervisor earns his keep. Since he is considered management and he is not protected by a union, he will do his "thing" or be replaced. His "thing" consists of signing off items in the aircraft log when a mechanic doesn't believe that the squawk is properly repaired. The captain checks his logbook and sees that all discrepancies are signed off, so he is home free. Nothing could be further from the truth. More than one accident has been caused by "the magic pencil" of the supervisor. It took me years to find this glaring fault in the system, and under the ever-present pressure of on-time departures, it's the bad guys who cause delays.

I am not a union lover, but it becomes a necessity to be unionized if you work for a shady employer. If it weren't for unions, there would be many more aircraft accidents. If a mechanic is pressured to perform unsafe maintenance, he can always threaten his supervisor with union reprisal. It gives the worker a "big stick," and he becomes a partner to safer operation. Nonunion mechanics that service the penny-pinching carriers must do as they're told, or else.

The FAA should require that supervisors' signatures be made readily recognizable by requiring them to use a red pencil, or some means, so that the unsuspecting aircrew could not be goaded into trying to fly a faulty machine. Remember that maintenance supervisors do not normally repair aircraft. Any time a supervisor's signature appears in a logbook, it means only one thing: potential danger.

If you think I am the only pilot concerned about faulty maintenance sign-offs, listen to this.

A few years ago, I was a panelist on "The Joan London Show." The subject was airline safety and the studio audience was filled with striking Eastern Airline crewmembers. Edward Murphy, a maintenance supervisor at JFK Airport in New York was asked by Joan, "Don't all aircraft discrepancies have to be signed off?" Edward Murphy replied "Maintenance managers often sign off write-ups. The FAA should get in there and find out why a regular mechanic did not sign the item off." Joan asked "Are you saying that there are aircraft signed off that are not legal?" Ed replied "You better believe it."

While Eastern was operating, there were regular C checks performed that required jacking up the airplane so that a gear retraction test could be observed. Dozens of planes went through this C check. Only one problem existed. JFK did not have any gear retraction jacks. Who signed them off? Maintenance supervisors; certainly not mechanics.

After the Alaska Airlines MD-80 crashed into the Pacific, there was a lot of government investigation on the Alaska Airlines property. They are still digging for answers but a brave young maintenance man named John Liotine had this to say about sign-offs: He had inspected the same aircraft that crashed into the Pacific two years before the accident. He stated that the tail jackscrew was worn out and should be replaced. He wrote it up in the aircraft log and never thought much more about it until that same aircraft crashed because of a faulty tail jackscrew. He investigated this two-year-old write-up and found to his dismay that it had been scratched out and signed off by another mechanic.

If the faulty jackscrew had been replaced as John Liotine requested, two years before the crash, there would be 88 people alive today. The mechanic that overrode Liotine's write-up should be subject to manslaughter charges.

The stabilizer, or elevator, on the tails of all aircraft is by far the most important flight control on the plane. It enables the pilot to command the plane to climb or descend. Such a vital component requires constant mechanical scrutiny. Let's hope that the FAA gets it right before another one goes in.

United Airlines was experiencing problems with their mechanics. It seems the technicians were trying to make the aircraft airworthy, but management had other ideas. "Management's out there second-guessing everything we do" said George Davis, a senior mechanic who was fired. "They're always arguing over what can be deferred or not. They are intimidating some mechanics who are then afraid to write things up."

In December of 2000, USA Today had a great piece on United's maintenance department. Mechanic Davis had this to say concerning a faulty tire on a United B-727. "Denver is one of the worst stations for delays. I felt the heat and had it out with management a few times. I think the tire was the last straw." He says the tire he cited the previous month was replaced after the flight captain asked Davis' opinion. When Davis again recommended the change, the captain refused to take off, despite the maintenance supervisor's insistence that the tire was safe. Three hours later, Davis was placed on leave without pay. Shortly after, he was fired.

Thank God for a dedicated captain and mechanic. Davis' union, the IAM, appealed his case. As a result, Davis and nine other mechanics were rehired.

You can see a strong case for the existence of unions. Without their vast strength, may more airliners would be burying themselves into the ground.

The FAA should insist on a standard method of numbering aircraft parts. Airlines are bitter rivals on fares, but they are most congenial when it comes to borrowing aircraft parts. The manufacturer puts his number on every item he produces. When the part gets to an airline shop, that airline puts its special number on the item. If another airline borrows a component, it, too, puts a number on it. There are far too many numbers on the various parts, and many times a piece ordered for a 727 arrives as a part for an L-1011.

Pilots know of only one aircraft logbook. So when they check the book and find the squawks have all been rectified, they will probably take the aircraft up. If they are wise enough to question why a supervisor signed off an item, that's great; but there is another shady deal that I only found out about while researching this book. It's called the supplement sheet.

When a mechanic performs a certain check on an aircraft, he makes a notation to the effect that he checked what was required. If he finds a discrepancy in the aircraft, he simply states in the logbook "check complete, see supplement." This supplement sheet is supposed to be part of the aircraft log, but it usually is conveniently misplaced.

For example, items on this sheet are required to be entered into the computer so that Eastern's main base in Miami is fully aware of all maintenance discrepancies. This is not always done. When an aircraft arrives at a maintenance base, the aircraft logbook is quickly ushered into the maintenance supervisor's office. Here it becomes more difficult for mechanics to write up any discrepancies on aircraft. To do so, they must speak to the supervisor and it's usually a losing battle to write up a squawk that might delay departure.

In 1982, the job of outside gate agent at Eastern was eliminated. This gate agent was the baggage handler who checked the final boarding of luggage and freight. Now the cargo is checked inside the building and is driven out to the aircraft to be loaded. Where there used to be a crew of seven men to load an L-1011, now, thanks to deregulation, there are only three.

Many times a truck will pull up on the ramp with mail or freight, and the loaders will put the cargo on the aircraft and close the baggage doors.

The added cargo is never accounted for, and when the pilot wonders why the takeoff roll was so long, it might have been because he was a few thousand pounds over (assumed to be aircraft weight).

Checked luggage is figured on an average weight of 24.5 pounds per item. With this average baggage weight, there is no way that an accurate take-off weight can be calculated. Accurate weight is essential for a truly safe operation.

From 1981 to 1983, Eastern experienced 243 flameouts (engine shutdowns) on their L-1011 aircraft. From 1979 to 1985, the following engine shutdowns were also recorded: DC-9, six; B-727, fifteen; B-757, two; and the Airbus 300, two.

On May 25, 1979, American Airlines Flight 191, a wide-bodied DC-10, was poised at the end of Chicago's O'Hare Runway 32L headed for Los Angeles. There wasn't a cloud in the sky and the visibility was over 15 miles.

Fifty-three-year-old Captain Walter H. Lux was in the left seat, but on this leg, he would perform the duties of first officer and his co-pilot, Jim Dillard, would fly the aircraft. The final checklist was run and the elevator trim was set at 5 degrees, flaps were at 10 degrees, the takeoff weight was 379,000 pounds, V1 speed (the speed at which the plane is committed to takeoff) was calculated at 139 knots, and the V2 speed (minimum safe climb speed) was 153 knots. The O'Hare tower local controller broadcast, "American 191 heavy cleared for takeoff."

Captain Walter replied, "American 191 under way."

The throttles were smoothly advanced and 379,000 pounds of dead weight started its journey down the 10,000-foot runway. All gauges were in the green (operating normally), and as Captain Lux saw the airspeed indicator passing 139 knots, he called out V1.

Just prior to the V2 call, the instrument panel lights started flashing, resembling a high score on a video game. There was a serious problem but the crew had no way of knowing its magnitude. Only seconds past the decision speed (whether to abort or continue), the left engine and its pylon separated from the aircraft. It traveled up over the wing and fell to the runway. At this time, unknown to the crew, the leading edge slats on the left wing retracted due to loss of hydraulic pressure. This failure could not have happened at a more critical time. From the cockpit, the engine is not visible, and even if it was, there was no time to check it. The commit speed had been passed; all that remained was to continue the roll until rotation speed was reached. As the air speed indicator hit 145 knots, the captain called out "Rotate."

The first officer applied backpressure to the yoke (control column) and the troubled DC-10 became airborne. Engineer Udovich was doing his best to detect the problem. He knew that No. 1 engine had quit, but he had no idea that it was lying back on the runway. The Captain and First Officer were both on the controls, but for some reason, the aircraft wanted to bank to the left. As they reached 300 feet, they were both fighting the controls, trying desperately to level her out. As the bank reached the vertical position, there was no way the crew could overpower the high lift caused by the operable leading edge slats (a high lift device) on the right wing. They had no knowledge of the inoperable slats on the left wing. The asymmetrical forces of the wing devices gave the right wing a high lift while the left wing's lift was greatly reduced.

With No. 1 engine gone and the left slats retracted, control at this speed was impossible. When the engine tore loose, it also knocked out the slat disagreement indicator in the cockpit. The crew performed a textbook "engine out" procedure, but there was no way they could fight a poorly designed aircraft.

At an altitude of 325 feet, she started down. The left wing hit the ground first and the aircraft exploded, scattering debris into an open field and an adjacent trailer part. Two hundred and seventy-one people on board were killed instantly, along with two people on the ground. In addition to the human loss, a hangar, a mobile home, and several automobiles also were destroyed by the faulty giant.

This was the worst single plane disaster in the history of U.S. aviation. I would like to be able to praise the FAA for something, but when you examine the evidence, I believe you will have to agree that they are, once again, the culprits by not requiring more stringent rules concerning the manufacture and maintenance of the Douglas DC-10.

Within hours of the crash, FAA Chief Langhorn M. Bond ordered all 138 DC-10s operated by U.S. Airlines to be grounded immediately. He wanted all engines and their pylons to be inspected for signs of damage or defective components.

The problem with the American DC-10 started at the Douglas factory when it was first built. They manufactured 23 engine pylons that required shims in the top of the upper flange. They were experiencing spacing problems that began with fuselage No. 15 and continued to No. 36. The American fuselage was No. 22. The McDonald Douglas Company admitted that the clearance problem was caused by a tooling malfunction. They also produced 31 aircraft with faulty pylons with loose or missing fasteners. One of these aircraft was sold to United where the cracking of the upper spar web caused the failure of 26 fasteners.

In May of 1975, McDonald Douglas issued DC-10 service bulletins 54-048 and 54-59, respectively. Service Bulletin 54 called for the replacement of the engine pylon forward bulkhead's lower and upper spherical bearings, and they issued specific procedures for the various airlines to accomplish this mandatory maintenance. They strongly recommended that the engine first be detached from its pylon because the mating clearances were small and it would be safer to detach the engine first.

It is interesting to note that the manufacturer of an aircraft has no authority to approve or disapprove the maintenance practices of its customers. Likewise, the FAA has little to say until something drastic happens. The carriers are primarily on the honor system. The FAA has the honor, and the company has the system.

In 1977, American Airlines agreed to modify four of Varig Airline's DC-10s engine pylons. Larger carriers, such as American, frequently do heavy maintenance work for lines that are technically or financially unable to do the work themselves. American's engineering department devised a way to remove the engine and pylon without disconnecting them. This technique saved 200 man-hours per aircraft; it also saved a large number of electrical hydraulics and fuel "disconnects," from 79 down to 27.

After checking with Douglas concerning the critical center of gravity of the pylon and engine combination, an engine stand and a forklift were set in place. Douglas was against this procedure but had no authority to stop it, and the FAA was somewhere in hiding. The work was completed in record time and no discrepancies were noted.

Since American already had eight pylon removals to their credit, they decided to utilize the same procedure on their own DC-10s, even though they were slightly different models than the Varig Airlines aircraft.

On July 28, American issued engineering change order (ECO) R-2693 to establish a new pylon forklift change sequence. The engineer who developed this ECO gave specific rules as to which of the pylon bolts were to be removed, but failed to stipulate the proper sequence. The mechanics who worked on this project removed the rear bolts first, contrary to what the engineering department had planned. It required a steady hand on the forklift controls because a fraction of an inch could crack a flange.

United Airlines was performing the same maintenance on their DC-10s, but they were doing it properly, by first disconnecting the engine and using a hoist.

On December 19, 1978, Continental Airlines used the same removal method as American. One of their mechanics heard a loud "pop" when they removed a pin from the flange. The crack was discovered and repaired; American was not as lucky.

It is important for one carrier to alert another when they experience a maintenance problem. Unfortunately, many of them don't, and the FAA does not require them to.

Now that you have an idea of how McDonald Douglas, American Airlines, and the FAA all had a hand in killing 273 people, let's look into exactly what the crew of the ill-fated DC-10 had to contend with.

The engine and pad assembly were never checked after they were mated to the aircraft, so the fatigued metal cracks were never discovered. The whole maintenance procedure was riddled with faults and it was done contrary to the manufacturer's desires.

On the Lockheed-1011 and the Boeing 747, the other two wide-bodied craft that were competing with the DC-10, both had far safer construction. All three aircraft have leading edge slats, but only Douglas failed to put a restrictor in the slat control lines so that the slats on one wing could not differ greatly from the slats on the other wing.

The American aircraft crashed for only one reason: not because it dropped off an engine (it can climb and fly nicely on two engines) but because it had slats extended on the right wing and none on the left wing. When the engine ripped off from the wing, it took with it the means of extending the left leading edge slats. The warning light that informed the pilot the slats were out of sync became inoperable due to the damaged wing, and the wing is located so far behind the cockpit, there was no way for the captain to see it. If he had any idea that those all-important lift devices were inoperable, he most certainly would have aborted the takeoff. Regardless of the speed or what the book says, there was no redundancy in the warning system, and he was committed to go.

What did the FAA do after the accident to ensure that such a tragedy would not happen again? In a word, nothing. They did require an inspection of all U.S. DC-10's pylons, but that was it. Such a freak accident would never happen again, so what's the fuss?

On September 22, 1981, two years after the American disaster, an Air Florida DC-10 experienced practically the same mechanical problems. The Air Florida was on the takeoff roll but not quite up to commit speed when suddenly its No. 2 engine blew up. The crew was able to abort the takeoff and stopped well within the confines of the runway. The problem that would never happen again did.

When the engine blew, it sent 30 pieces of shrapnel through the wings and nacelle. One of them managed to sever the slat follow cable and caused the wing tip slats to retract. If this engine had blown a few seconds later, there would probably have been another catastrophe to add to the long list of DC-10 accidents.

This one awakened the FAA. Five months after the Air Florida incident, and four years after American's crash, the leading edge slats were modified so that they would remain in their proper position regardless of how many hydraulic lines were severed.

McDonald Douglas was fined $300,000 by the FAA for manufacturing defective pylons and fasteners. While agreeing to pay the fine, McDonald

Douglas did not admit to any FAA violation. Where have we heard that before?

A federal judge in Chicago ordered American Airlines to pay over $200,000 in penalties for withholding various internal reports concerning maintenance practices, and the FAA fined them $500,000, the largest penalty to date. The combined legal suits filed by the families of the crash victims was in the billion dollar range.

In January of 1985, the FAA caught American using bogus parts on some of their aircraft and fined them $375,000. By now they certainly must have learned their lesson regarding the all important wing slats. Not so. It seems that mechanics had installed a plastic pulley in the slat mechanism instead of the proper aluminum one. Three DC-10s were repaired improperly.

On September 14, 1984, while a DC-10 was on final approach to Dallas-Fort Worth International Airport, a 200-pound slat fell from the wing and landed harmlessly in a yard. When an airline fails to learn by past experience, there isn't much hope for it. Luck can't last forever.

Between June 15 and July 1, 1985, an American Douglas MD-80 flew 79 flights with a faulty left engine. It was written up numerous times by aircrews, but was not repaired until it failed during a takeoff. On several occasions, aircraft had to return and land because the gear pins were not removed (pins that are inserted in the wheel struts to prevent inadvertent gear retraction) while the aircraft is parked. A mechanic who had no DC-9 training failed to insert a pin on a wheel he was changing. The aircraft flew to Chicago and when the landing was completed, the wheel "popped" off the axle.

By now, we are all aware of the important part played by O-rings. Eastern nearly lost a plane because of them, seven astronauts were killed because of them, and now another problem was caused because of the lack of the O-rings. This time the culprit was the faulty O-rings in an American 727 toilet. Believe it or not, the faulty toilet caused the destruction of a jet engine.

In April of 1985, an American Boeing 727 jetliner was over New Mexico on a trip from Dallas to San Diego. Because of a faulty O-ring in the plumbing, four gallons of blue fluid quickly turned to ice in the rarified cold atmosphere. The ice mass grew too heavy to stay with the fuselage and it dropped off. The speed of the aircraft quickly propelled this chunk of ice into one of the rear engines. The intense shock of the ice on the engine blades was more than it could stand. It tore loose from the aircraft and fell to the ground.

The aircraft landed safely and there were no injuries except to the embarrassed maintenance crew of American. For the sake of a $2.00 O-ring, a million dollar engine was lost. This discrepancy was written up for five months prior to the incident but it was never properly repaired.

A month after the O-ring incident, a piece of a DC-10 cowling fell off as an aircraft climbed out of New York. The aircraft made a successful landing and there were no injuries.

To show the FAA that American was on top of the maintenance problems, they hired over 200 new mechanics but it still would not get them off the FAA hook. American was already the highest fined airline for its DC-10 accident in Chicago. Now the fine would be three times as large, $1.5 million. And from 1979 to 1985, American Airlines, for mechanical reasons, was forced to shut down 35 engines while in flight. There were 22 on DC-10s, 13 on B727s, and one on the MD-80.

In spite of all the discrepancies found in American's maintenance procedures, FAA's former administrator, Admiral Engen, had this to say concerning the inspection of American: "... confirms the essential integrity and soundness of the company's maintenance and airworthiness functions."

At TWA's line maintenance stations (not major maintenance base), they have discontinued the maintenance supervisor position; instead, the line mechanic answers to a ground operations supervisor. With the advent of deregulation, cost cutting became a must. Many of the mechanics were offered the position of supervisor but there were very few takers. Supervisors are management and have no union to protect them. TWA has stooped so low as to hire people off the street to fill their diminishing ranks of the men with the "magic pencil."

The only requirement to fill the job now is prior experience at handling subordinates. The job previously required an aircraft and power plant (A&P) license, an ability to recommend solutions to problems, familiarization with TWA's mechanics contract, and the ability to manage subordinate lead mechanics. Now, TWA is paying less, so they are getting less. At the major maintenance bases such as Kennedy and Kansas City, there are specialty craftsmen, electricians, metal benders, and hydraulic and engine experts. Some of these men are not licensed but they have many years of experience and their work seldom fails to be signed off by licensed mechanics. However, at out-of-the-way line maintenance stations it's a totally different picture. Here the mechanic is expected to perform any and all maintenance on every aircraft. And at major maintenance bases, the airline Captain is king. Maintenance literally bends over backward to rectify discrepancies in the aircraft log. But at line stations, the atmosphere is quite a bit different.

If a pilot is on the ball at TWA, he can fathom work quickly with the payroll number. Aircraft inspectors sign with their initials, and the bad guys sign with their full signatures. With this knowledge, it's not as easy to "sell" a pilot an aircraft (pawn off a broken one).

At a major maintenance base, TWA management was desperately in need of a supervisor. None of the mechanics would take the bait, so the powers that be decided to give the job to a building maintenance man, a janitor, who years ago worked as an A&P mechanic but had not turned a wrench on an aircraft during the past 12 years. He didn't want the job, but pressure from higher up forced him to take it. Now we had an inexperienced TWA supervisor signing off maintenance faults because an experienced mechanic believed the repair wasn't airworthy and would not sign for it.

A TWA 707 needed a mach trim coupler because the one on the aircraft was inoperable. The mechanic contacted Kansas City to locate the whereabouts of a new part. He learned that one was available at a nearby airport, so he got a driver to go and pick it up. In the meantime, the supervisor got wind of the delay that a "fix" would cause, so he signed off the squawk and sent the plane out in a non-airworthy condition.

At Newark, New Jersey, one of TWA's 727s experienced a dangerous running fuel leak and was in the process of being repaired. A new panel would arrive at 6:00 a.m. for a 6:45 a.m. departure. The supervisor came over to check the progress and decided that by waiting for the panel to arrive, he would be held responsible for a delay. He decided to put some fuel tank sealer in the faulty seam instead. For this to adhere properly, it would take at least an hour to dry. When the aircraft was fueled for its scheduled departure, the leak started again. The mechanic refused to sign off such a disgraceful "fix." Out came the supervisor's magic pencil and the departure left on schedule.

I talked about the crash of an Alaska Airlines MD-80 into the Pacific that killed all 88 people earlier in this chapter. The stabilizer jackscrew appears to have been the problem, but I would place faulty maintenance as the key culprit.

For more than a year, prior to the crash, federal law enforcement agencies were investigating supervisory maintenance personnel for falsifying maintenance results. At a hearing, the mechanics of Alaska Airlines composed a statement concerning sloppy maintenance practices. A draft of the letter said workers were directed to do this, "specifically contradicting" federal aviation regulations, and stated that they had been "pressured, threatened, and intimidated ... in the daily performance of our work."

In a recent report on an MD-80, mechanics said that they were told not to replace warn parts. Robert Falla, chief of Alaska's Seattle maintenance base, was ordered on administrative leave, according to the report.

Airline maintenance is a self-policing agenda. There just aren't enough FAA inspectors to go around, with the result that when an airliner crashes, the FAA descends on the faulty carrier in force. The jackscrew problem with the Alaska MD-80 stabilizer initiated the government requirement to check all stabilizers on MD-80s, MD-90s, Boeing 717s, and DC-9s, all variations of the same basic design. Twenty-one aircraft were grounded when their stabilizer jackscrews were not up to snuff.

Why must passengers die before the FAA gets into the act?

Prior to deregulation, it was a TWA standard procedure for a mechanic to meet each in-bound flight. One mechanic would start his walk around the aircraft checking for leaks, tears, dents, or any number of other discrepancies. Another mechanic would board the aircraft and talk to the crew to see if they had any squawks. That was the old procedure. Now, with many of the maintenance men furloughed, this check is no longer performed. Presently, it's up to the outbound flight engineer or pilot to check for any discrepancies.

A TWA 747 experienced numerous bird strikes and it was written up in the aircraft logbook. A lead mechanic assigned two men to check for any damages. The supervisor came onto the scene and ordered both mechanics to work on other aircraft; he would check out the bird damage himself. He checked nothing; all he did was write it off in the log. "Visually checked for bird strikes. Okay for service."

The following is one of the shadiest deals I have ever heard of. A crew brought an aircraft in and wrote up the fact that there was an abundance of oil and hydraulic fluid leaking out of one of the engines. The supervisor sent a mechanic out to wash the engine down. Not to check out the leak, just to wash it down. When the mechanic returned after completing the task the supervisor directed a different mechanic to go out and check the leaking engine. The second mechanic quickly returned and said the engine showed no signs of leaks and that it was clean. "Shifty" then gave him the logbook and had him sign off the crews' write-up.

There are some mechanics that are "gold bricks;" any way to get out of work is fine with them. They have learned that if they are told to repair something and they can stretch it out so there will be a departure delay, the supervisor will put the item on a carry over or just sign it off as repaired.

From 1979 to 1985, TWA crews were required to shut down 30 engines for mechanical reasons. The breakdown is as follows: 14 on the L-1011; 6 on the 727; 5 on the 747; and 2 on the 707 and the Boeing 767.

There are a series of four maintenance checks that all narrow-body jets must receive in order to stay airworthy:

A checks: Every hundred and fifty hours; involve engines, air frames, and avionics

B checks: Every seven hundred hours; landing gear checks, fluid checks, oil and lube

C checks: Every three thousand hours; a more detailed inspection of accessories, engines, and airframes

D checks: Every twenty thousand hours; the aircraft is nearly completely disassembled, cleaned, and refurbished (this check can easily take over a month)

Some airlines are more concerned with safety than others. United has been replacing turbine spacers for the past two years, and TWA is replacing spacers during their normal overhauls. Northwest Orient Airlines is the only carrier that has nearly completed its retrofit that began years ago.

On August 22, 1985, a British Airtours Boeing 737 was on takeoff roll at Manchester, England, when the left engine exploded without warning. The aircraft was brought to a stop on the runway, but the devastating explosion severed some fuel lines and the ensuing fire burned 54 people to death. Prior to the disaster, the faulty engine had numerous write-ups. It is believed that there was a faulty combustion chamber that caused the massive explosion and fire. Once again the JT8D engine was the culprit.

FAA airlines maintenance inspectors have far too many new carriers to inspect. These inspectors are devoting the lion's share of their time on the new "cockroach" airlines (substandard airlines) and their normal inspection duties cannot be performed. Between 1980 and 1985, the FAA was required to certify 76 new airlines and 233 new commuters; they utilized approximately 27,000 man-days just qualifying the new entrants. It becomes clear why so many routine items are being neglected; there just aren't enough inspectors.

In order to spread the small inspector force over a larger area, some of the men from the Flight Standard District Office (FSDO) have been cross trained to handle large airliners. This, I believe, is a costly mistake. It takes a lot more than a few weeks' training to teach an inspector who has handled Cessnas and Beechcraft all his life to properly inspect a 747.

The General Accounting Office (GAO) complied an excellent report concerning the aircraft maintenance inspection force.

One airline informed its flight crews that all equipment failures listed on the (minimum equipment list (MEL) could be deferred automatically for 30 days because of lack of manpower and spare parts availability. If at the end of the 30-day period the airline was still experiencing manpower or spare parts problems, the failure could be deferred for an additional 30 days. Another airline recently put out a memo to its flight crews that "maintenance would be conducted on deferred items only if it didn't disrupt service."

A few years ago, 29 air carriers received no avionics inspection, four carriers received no FAA operations inspections, and two of the airlines received neither an operations nor an avionics inspection. There are no specified rules as to the number of checks an airline will receive each year, but the ones where the inspection is "unannounced" produce the lion's share of discrepancies.

Air carrier inspectors spend the greatest amount of time indoors checking the airlines' paperwork and logbooks. A lot more could be gained if they performed more aircraft inspection and checked for supervisor sign-offs that were never completed.

I checked with six of the largest carriers, and their mechanics all had this to say about the FAA inspectors: most of them really don't know what to look for in the shops or out on the ramp; they just haven't got that much knowledge about airliners.

The latest national safety inspection report of US airlines produced a much higher degree of maintenance noncompliance than was previously suspected. Inspectors discovered safety infractions in one out of every three checks and a shocking level of serious violations.

Six retired inspectors compiled a safety report and they found that of the 13,624 inspections conducted on 327 airlines, 64 airlines were dangerously below standard.

On August 12, 1985, Boeing Aircraft Co. was confronted with one of their most costly maintenance blunders of all times. A Japanese Airline 747 crashed, killing all 520 people on board. Months prior to the fateful accident, the same 747 aircraft experienced a hard landing that caused some damage to the rear pressure bulkhead.

The JAL people wanted their 747 inspected and repaired by the people who knew it best. So Boeing sent their technicians over to supervise the repair of the faulty pressure bulkhead. They failed to notice some existing cracks that went undetected because of a covering. The repairs were completed and the aircraft was returned to service. The 747 rear pressure bulkhead, the one that Boeing repaired, blew out and Boeing's faulty "fix" killed 520 people. In April of 1991, Boeing and the surviving relatives of the crash came to an out-of-court settlement of close to a million dollars per victim. It's a pretty sad state of affairs when the people who build an airliner lack the knowledge of how to repair it properly.

On June 10, 1990, a British Airways sleek twin jet BAC1-11 climbed out of Birmingham, England for a flight to Malaga, Spain. At 17,000 feet, 13 minutes after liftoff, Captain Lancaster pointed to the town of Abingdon and said to his co-pilot, "There's my house." No sooner had he made that statement than there was an explosion and he was partially sucked out of the windshield into the 320-mph slipstream. The cockpit door was propelled forward and crashed into the cockpit console. The No. 3 steward, Nigel Ogden, rushed forward to grab the captain by his legs before he was sucked completely through the 2- by-3-foot windscreen frame. The co-pilot made a successful touchdown and the captain remained half-in and half-out throughout the landing. He was severely frost bitten, but within a few weeks he was back on the good old BAC1-11.

What caused the explosive decompression? The British accident investigators stated that maintenance had replaced 84 of the 90 bolts that secured the windshield with smaller diameter bolts than required for the captive nuts onto which they were installed.

On May 9, 1990, a Boeing 737 was up on a training flight over West Germany. The co-pilot was flying when to his great surprise the control wheel came off in his hands. After further checking, Boeing found that six similar incidents had occurred on Boeing 737-300, 400, and 500 aircraft. It seems that someone at the factory had failed to insert a locking device called a cotter pin.

On August 27, 1990, a United Boeing 747-400 experienced nose gear problems. After a low pass by the tower, a second pass, and a touch-and-go landing, the nose gear still remained in its well. The crew of the 747 made a successful landing on Runway 25R at Los Angeles International Airport. This aircraft was turned out by the factory only six months prior to the incident. It seems that quality control at Boeing was not up to par because a vital nut and cotter pin were missing, allowing a bolt to "partially back out."

Boeing checked on other undelivered 747s at their factory and found another nut without a cotter pin.

In July of 1991, a Canadian chartered DC-8 was readied for its Nigerian departure. There were 264 people on board who had no idea that 12 minutes after takeoff, they would all be dead. What went wrong is a shocking revelation concerning a maintenance sign-off that was never performed.

As the aircraft started its taxi to the runway, two of its ten tires failed, then disintegrated, preventing the individual wheels from rotating. The crew continued to taxi to the runway and before long, the locked up wheels began to burn. The tower reported to the flight crew that there seemed to be smoke coming from the landing gear. This warning was disregarded by the crew. The takeoff completed, the landing gear was selected to go up and the burning wheels were retracted into their wells in the wings. It was only a matter of seconds before the fire from the faulty wheels ignited the fuel in the wings. The crew asked the tower for a return emergency landing. By now the fire was so intense, the fuselage was completely burned through. On final approach, passengers were seen falling from their fiery tomb, and within seconds, the hulk hit the ground, killing the few remaining passengers who had not yet burned to death.

The Canadian Transport Safety Board did a marvelous job of reconstructing this needless tragedy. The battered aircraft log was recovered and through numerous tests, the smudged unreadable pages began to produce the answer to the cause of the crash. The normal tire pressure was supposed to be 185 psi. The log showed 160 and 155 for two of the main tires. A mechanic who ran this check was aware that two of the tires, No. 1 and No. 3, were below the approved pressure. He did not have time to pump them up so he put checkmarks after each faulty tire to show the "fix" was not completed. There was not sufficient time to fill the tires to their proper readings so the maintenance supervisor changed the 160 reading to 180, and the 155 reading to 185.

For the sake of a maintenance delay, 264 people met a fiery death.

In January of 1999, a former employee of the Strandflex Company blew the whistle on her previous employer.

Strandflex manufactures cables, some of which is used on military and commercial aircraft to enable the crews to control the engines and landing gear. The cables were supposed to be precisely constructed and tested to exacting specifications. For years, this company had sold cables in the aerospace industry without testing their integrity.

The FAA was alerted as well as the military. Military officials immediately tested the cables and discovered that they would break at only half the load they were supposed to support. The Air Force immediately began replacing all the faulty cables (one of the aircraft with the bad cables installed was the back-up jet for Air Force One).

In direct contrast, the FAA performed no cable tests, and waited a year before they decided to tell the airlines that they might have a potential problem with some of their cables. The FAA did not consider the cable a real problem and merely alerted the carriers but did not make a cable check mandatory. They said that the cables were not a critical component of the aircraft and that cable failure could not cause an accident.

Any part of an aircraft has the potential to cause an accident and the FAA's handling of this potentially dangerous discovery was in keeping with their motto, "Don't Rock the Boat."

After the crash of Alaska Airlines MD-80 on January 31, 2000, the FAA inspectors descended on the airline like a plague of locusts. Once again, the FAA took action after the crash. Paul Takemoto, an FAA spokesman, stated that all carriers flying the MD-80s, MD-90s, Boeing 717s, and DC-99s would have to inspect their tail assembly within the next 30 days.

Since the inspection started, twenty-one aircraft have been grounded because of tail problems. Alaska Airlines had the most tail problems followed by four Delta jets, three at Northwest, and two at Air Tran; and one each at Hawaiian, Continental, and American.

One FAA inspector recommended that Alaska Airlines be fined $8.7 million for falsifying records. But, as to be expected, top FAA bras reduced the fine to $44,000. Mr. Nick Lacey, the FAA's director of flight standards, stated that the FAA surveillance of Aloha Airlines "could have been managed more vigorously." That's putting it mildly.

The FAA allowed Alaska Airlines to inspect their tail jackscrews far less frequently than other airlines.

Eight months after the Alaska crash, an Alaska captain was forced to make an emergency landing because of jackscrew problems. And on August 3, 2000, Alaska Airlines pulled 17 of its MD-80 aircraft out of service to check faulty tail sections.

And so it goes.

The following is a direct quote taken from a NASA Latest Call Back publication:

One-Size-Fits-All Maintenance Problem

In the past year several incidents have been reported to ASRS in which Boeing 737-100 and -200 wheel bearings were incorrectly installed on the series -300 aircraft. Now here's a Captain's report that describe the installation of a B-757 wheel bearing on a B-737-300 wheel—with potentially catastrophic results:

Shortly after departure from Runway 34L the Tower controller informed us we had lost a wheel on the takeoff. In a very short period of time, we were told we had lost either the right outward main gear wheel, the right inboard main gear wheel, or even both right main gear wheels. I elected to stay in the local area and reduce fuel to an acceptable level (weight) for landing. The B-737-300 does not have fuel-dumping capabilities.

Since I did not know the integrity or even existence of the remaining wheel on the right side, I wanted to reduce the aircraft weight as much as possible for landing. We held outside the [airport] area for two hours. I realized that if we held for an extended period, we would be making an emergency landing, and quite possibly a passenger evacuation after sunset. With this consideration, I held until the time we could make a low pass, get a visual inspection from the Tower and return for landing just prior to sunset.

The low pass was conducted and the ATC personnel, as well as company mechanics, reported the right outboard wheel was intact, and inboard was missing. After the visual inspection, we returned for landing … the approach and landing were uneventful. The aircraft was towed to the maintenance hangar where it was discovered that the main wheel bearing on the right inboard wheel had failed. The wheel departed the airplane, leaving the axle and the brake assembly intact on the landing gear … there was absolutely no indication on the takeoff roll that the wheel had failed. In fact, when the errant wheel was located, it too was intact and even still inflated.

The B-737-300 wheel apparently will accept B-737-100, -200, and B-757 bearings and look like a correct installation. The underlying problem is that part numbers on the bearing race are normally covered with grease. Unless maintenance technicians take time to verify the B-737 part numbers, the wrong bearing may be installed on the wheel."

It is interesting to note that whenever an engine or a component malfunction is discovered, it is not torn down by the FAA. So where does it go? To the manufacturer. But it is extremely difficult for the original designer to find faults with its products, so it will lay blame on the maintenance people at the carrier or other suppliers. You can bet that the original factory will find little or nothing wrong with what they have produced.

Aircraft Mechanics

The unsung heroes of the airline industry are the maintenance technicians. The vast amount of knowledge that a mechanic must remember and continually update is impossible to comprehend. These fine people have to work under very harsh conditions. At outlying stations where there are no hangars, these technicians can be found atop stands in the bitter cold and wind working feverishly so that your flight departs on time. They must be prepared to work on numerous aircraft and a variety of systems.

I have nearly all the flying ratings, but I was always interested as to exactly what it entailed to be an aircraft mechanic. In order to get my mechanics license, I had to contend with classes four days a week for two years at a local junior college. I had to pass a test every two weeks as well as semester tests. If I failed a test twice, I would have been out of the program. After taking three final exams on each phase of the course, I had to pass similar tests at the FAA office. With these tests under my belt, I was again tested by an FAA designate examiner. After the oral exam, I spent two days in a hangar answering questions put to me by the examiner. I had to manually prove my worth by riveting, checking manuals, and finding out what various components could legally be installed on different aircraft.

By comparison, in order to be eligible for an airline captain's license, one must have 1,500 hours of pilot in command time. A Bachelor of Science degree requires an average of 127 college credit hours but a licensed mechanic must cover 43 subject areas and be in school for 1,900 hours. A mechanic also must supply his own tools that can cost a minimum of $3,500.

All repairs that a mechanic performs must be signed off, but that signature can cost him or her a job or time in prison if the work done causes an incident or accident. And after two years of study, the starting salary of a mechanic is equal to that of a person working in Burger King. Airlines pay their technicians a decent wage, but it isn't that easy to get an airline job. A good mechanic stands by his convictions and is not intimidated by a supervisor to sign off any non-airworthy items.

Air carriers offer technicians a starting salary between $20,000 and $27,000 for a 40-hour week. Within five years, a mechanic's salary should increase to between $35,000 and $45,000 a year. A general aviation (small plane) mechanic will receive a starting salary of $18,000 to $24,000 a year. Scheduled airlines employ approximately 50,000 mechanics. General aviation employs approximately 37,000 technicians.

It is interesting to note that the FAA has no maximum time that mechanics are on duty. Their skills keep airplanes from falling from the sky, but they can be on duty indefinitely.

Maximum on-duty time for a pilot is 16 hours, but the Air Transport Association (ATA) is trying its best to get the time back to no limit at all.

It doesn't matter whether you call them grease monkeys, mechanics, or aircraft technicians; they are a great bunch of people, and I am mighty proud to be considered one of them.

The Service Difficulty

Air Carrier Weekly Summary

FAR 121.703 mechanical reliability reports state that each airline must submit mandatory reports: "Each report of occurrences during a 24-hour period must be mailed or delivered to that office within the next 72 hours."

The Airline must report such discrepancies as fire during flight, false warnings, engine shutdowns, fuel dumping, landing gear malfunctions, faulty brakes, cracks, and any aircraft structure that requires major repairs.

These reports are very informative and really do a great job of keeping pilots on top of any maintenance trends. Unfortunately, the reports are on the honor system. By that I mean the carrier is expected to voluntarily file these reports. We have seen before, and we will see again, airlines that do not speak the truth. You must be objective concerning the following statistics.

I have picked reports for the months of September, October, November, and December of 1993 as examples. During these four months, thousands of reports were filed and most airlines were honest. But I find it hard to believe that Aloha, with its proven shoddy maintenance practices, filed only nine reports.

AIRLINE	REPORTS FILED
Aloha	9
Hawaiian	48
TWA	72
American	161
United	167
Alaska	202
American West	315
Continental	319
USAir	4,811
Delta	1,377
Northwest	1,545

Let's take a look at the various types of aircraft and see how they compare to each other. Remember that there are far fewer MD-11s flying than there are Boeing 727s.

TOTAL DISCREPANCIES BY AIRCRAFT TYPE IN A FOUR-MONTH PERIOD SEPT-OCT-NOV-DEC 1993

TYPE	DISCREPANCIES	TYPE	DISCREPANCIES
Air Bus 300	58	Douglas DC-10	159
Air Bus 310	100	Douglas DC-8	701
Air Bus 320	100	Douglas DC-9	1,429
		Douglas MD-11	25
		Douglas MD-88	331
Boeing 727	2,310	Fokker F-28	165
Boeing 737	1,421	Lockheed 1011	448
Boeing 747	568		
Boeing 757	251		
Boeing 767	113		

I would like you to see exactly how the airlines compose their discrepancy forms that they submit to the FAA.

PART

MAKE	MODEL	SERIAL #	OPERATOR	ATA	NAME	COND	DATE
DOUG	DC1040	46750	NWAA	7200	ENGINE	FAILED	931027

"During cruise (CLA) FL330, No. 2 engine began experiencing a loss of oil quantity and was shut down. The aircraft diverted to GLA where an uneventful two-engine landing was made. No fuel was dumped. The aircraft was ferried to MSP for an engine change."

PART

MAKE	MODEL	SERIAL #	OPERATOR	ATA	NAME	COND	DATE
DOUG	DC-9	48066	CALA	7200	ENGINE	FAILED	930917

"DSM FLT 0400—aircraft vibration was felt during cruise flight and was followed by the NR1 engine oil pressure dropping to zero with oil temperature rising to approximately 130 degrees. A precautionary shut down of the No. 1 engine was performed and aircraft diverted to DSM where it landed without incident. The No. 1 engine was removed and replaced."

PART

MAKE	MODEL	SERIAL #	OPERATOR	ATA	NAME	COND	DATE
BOEING	747	19731	CALA	7250	BLADE	FRACTURED	930102

"HNL-FLT 0001—The NR1 engine gave off a loud report with EGT rising rapidly off scale approximately two hours into flight. The NR1 engine was shut down and aircraft was returned to HNL where it landed without further incident. The NR1 engine was removed and replaced. Investigation revealed that the primary cause of engine failure was due to the fracture of a second stage high pressure turbine blade."

PART

MAKE	MODEL	SERIAL #	OPERATOR	ATA	NAME	COND	DATE
BOEING	747	25278	UALA	8200	BIRD	STRIKE	931025

"No. 2 engine ingested a bird which caused an in-flight shutdown. Returned to field under amber alert."

These are just a few of the engine problems during the four-month period. Following are the actual engine problems with 13 major of the major carriers.

AMERICAN AIRLINES

10-16-93	767 R. Engine
10-22-93	727 No. 2 Engine
10-27-93	727 No. 1 Failed
11-02-93	DC-9 No. 2 Failed
11-07-93	727 No. 3 Failed

CONTINENTAL AIRLINES

09-17-93	DC-9 No. 1 Shutdown
10-09-93	A-300 No. 1 Shutdown
10-14-93	B-727 No. 2 Shutdown
10-24-93	L-1011 No. 3 Shutdown
10-25-93	DC-9 No. 2 Shutdown
11-09-93	DC-9 No. 1 Removed
11-10-93	DC-10 No. 3 Shutdown
11-11-93	DC-9 No. 2 Shutdown
11-18-93	DC-9 No. 1 Shutdown
11-19-93	DC-10 No. 3 Flameout
11-22-93	DC-10 No. 3 Shutdown
11-24-93	DC-9 No. 2 Shutdown
11-26-93	DC-9 No. 1 Flameout
11-29-93	727 Flameout

NORTHWEST

10-27-93	DC-10 No. 2 Shutdown
10-30-93	747 No. 1 Shutdown
11-12-93	747 No. 1 Shutdown
11-20-93	747 No. 4 Flameout
11-23-93	747 No. 3 Flameout
12-02-93	747 No. 1 Flameout
12-03-93	747 No. 1 Engine
12-05-93	747 No. 3 Shutdown
12-08-93	747 No. 1 Engine replaced
12-11-93	DC-9 No. 2 Comp. Blade

UNITED

09-29-93	DC-10 No. 1 Failed
10-25-93	747 No. 2 Shutdown
11-02-93	757 No. 1 Shutdown
11-12-93	DC-10 No. 2 Shutdown

USAir

09-24-93	757 L. Engine
09-28-93	DC-9 L. Engine
09-28-93	737 R. Engine
10-18-93	737 L. Engine
11-03-93	DC-9 R. Engine
11-07-93	737 L. Engine
11-22-93	737 R. Engine

DELTA

10-04-93	MD88 No. 2 Engine
10-20-93	767 No. 1 Engine
11-27-93	MD11 No. 1 Engine

AMERICA WEST

09-14-93	757 L. Engine
09-31-93	757 L. Engine
11-16-93	737 R. Engine

The year 1994 had its share of engines that were shut down. They may have been stopped as a precaution, or a fire, or they may have shut themselves down because of lack of thrust. At any rate, in 1994 there were at least 278 failed engines. In 11 months of 1995, there were 244 power plants that failed. These reports are only directed to airlines; there were many more failures on aircraft other than airliners.

This looks like an appropriate spot to insert a quote from David Hinson, the former FAA Administrator, in a speech given at the National Press Club in Washington, DC, on October 16, 1996:

"We essentially have removed engine failure as an issue. Now it does happen; you can read about it. But it is so good that most airline pilots today will never, ever experience an engine failure in their career if they start today. That's how reliable power plants are."

Oxygen Masks

You hear the flight attendant announcing: "In the unlikely event of cabin depressurization, a compartment over your head will automatically open and an oxygen mask will deploy."

If you are flying on Northwest Airlines and you have a decompression problem, you had better take a deep breath because there is a chance that the compartment over your head has an improper hose, the door will not open, or if it does, there may not be an oxygen mask in that overhead compartment.

During the last four months of 1993, the only airline out of my list of 13 to file a Service Difficulty Report regarding oxygen was Northwest Airlines. They more than made up for all the rest because during the survey period they submitted no less than 38 discrepancy reports. Either Northwest is very honest or the rest of the carriers failed to check these all-important emergency devices. At any rate, following are just three of Northwest's 38 reports.

10-21-93 Boeing 747—"During passenger oxygen system check, found 34 seats where hoses were not properly installed; 10 where masks were missing; 6 seats where masks were damaged; 5 seats where masks failed pull test."

10-31-93 747—(This one really takes the cake.) "During passenger oxygen system check, found 60 seats where oxygen masks were missing; 3 seats where pin clips were missing; and one where oxygen mask failed pull test."

10-27-93 747—"During passenger oxygen system functional check, found 11 seats with the oxygen hoses improperly installed; 11 seats with streamers missing; 11 seats with improper number of masks installed; 8 seats with masks that failed pull test; 2 seats with masks that failed to deploy; and 1 kinked hose."

1-29-94 Northwest DC-10 N046758—"During passenger oxygen system functional check, found four seat generators failed to fire and one generator previously failed. Replaced generators and re-rigged per MM."

Also on the same date, another Northwest DC-10 N046761—"During passenger seat oxygen system aneroid drop function check, found passenger oxygen mask failed to deploy. Rigged system per E02520-1170. Operational check okay."

Maintenance Fines

In 1998, maintenance fines averaged eight per working day. The number of fines rose from 283 in 1996 to 664 in 1998. A fine can be imposed for a minor paperwork violation up to a major FAA violation.

American West Airlines paid 2.5 million for operating 17 jets over 41,000 times without performing required inspections.

Alaska Airlines was fined $338.000 for operating a Boeing 737 on over 9,000 passenger flights "in an improperly altered state."

Continental was fined 3.4 million in 1990 for FAA violations.

From 1994 to 1998, Continental was the leader of the enforcement cases at $5.6 million, Delta $4.9 million, American $4.7 million, US Airways $3.1 million, United $2.9 million, Northwest $2.9 million, Southwest $2.1 million, TWA $1.8 million, and Alaska was the lowest with $1.3 million.

In the case of Alaska Airlines, I believe their low status will change after the findings of their recent MD-80 crash are revealed.

Since October of 1998, the "feds" have charged America West, the nation's ninth largest airline, for over 19 maintenance violations. Southwest Airline has only had one violation. The FAA found that 13 America West planes were flying in a non-airworthy condition.

In December of 1995, 500 mechanics were fired by America West and it began farming out its heavy maintenance in order to save money.

Captain Roger Cox, a Boeing 757 pilot for America West, stated, "A famous expression around here was 'Don't gold-plate the airplane'." That was a code for "Only do the minimum, just do the least amount of maintenance work possible."

In 1998, FAA maintenance inspection teams were considering a fine of $5 million. However, FAA inspector Lacey reduced the penalty to $2.5 million. Before this agreement was signed, America West's maintenance department had a list of between 1,500 and 1,700 items a day. That's a very large amount.

Between July of 1999 and June of 2000, a Boeing analysis discovered that 737s and 757s were grounded more than any other airliner.

Referring to shaky maintenance, FAA inspector Jim Pratt said "More airplanes will fall out of the sky."

"For the big carriers, there's too much watering down of unit penalties," says Billie Vincent, a former FAA director. "There's good reason some of them are dropped, but when the final amount is 25% of the original fine, something is wrong with the whole process. Then one has to wonder whether the deterrent value is there."

Airlines are not the only culprits when it comes to maintenance violations. The FAA has proposed a penalty of $392.000 against the Boeing Commercial Airplane Group. The penalty is for failing to report a defect on the B-757 airplanes and their fuel shutoff valves. When the valves were installed, they were misaligned, and when fuel was selected off, it continued to flow. This could be a major hazard if fire was detected in one of the engines. Between 1992 and 1995, Boeing constructed about 200 B-757s with misaligned valves. The company was required to report this defect to the FAA within 24 hours of discovering it. Allegedly, Boeing discovered this defect in May of 1995 but kept quiet until June of 1996.

In November of 1999, Boeing halted delivery of 5 aircraft models because of an improperly assembled unit that could allow moisture into the cockpit. Hundreds of 747s, 757s, 767s, 777s, and their newest model, the 717, all are flying passengers with "nonconforming" drip shields that prevent condensation from entering a vital area of the cockpit containing wires and instruments. The delivery of 34 planes has been curtailed until the FAA or Boeing figures out what to do.

On August 1, 2000, the Boeing Aircraft Company agreed to pay $61.5 million to settle a lawsuit by whistleblowers who accused Boeing of selling non-airworthy parts for the CH-47D Chinook helicopter. Brett Roly, an engineer for Speco Corporation, which manufactured the parts, claims that Boeing knew that the gears might develop cracks.

Fire Warning Systems

Every airliner has a system that alerts the crew to a fire in various sections of the aircraft. There are two or three different means to this end, but all require a certain amount of wiring to warn the cockpit crew to a fire somewhere in the airplane. These systems usually employ a bell and a light that illuminates whenever there is a fire.

There are usually two systems; a primary system and a back-up, and both must be tested and functioning properly before a takeoff is permitted. Warning systems are certainly necessary, especially in and around the engine nacelles (engine covering). Unfortunately, these systems give more false warnings than they do real ones. Most of the time a pilot cannot see all his aircraft's engines, so it's nice to have a few sensors out there to warn of impending fires.

Nearly all of the pilot's manuals state that when a fire warning sounds in the cockpit, it should be treated as a real fire and the engine shutdown checklist completed. However, there have been takeoff aborts, unscheduled landings performed, and lots of fuel dumped to prevent an overweight landing when the warnings were false. These are some of the carriers during the survey time that have experienced false fire warnings:

CONTINENTAL	HAWAIIAN	
12-8-93 737	11-9-93 DHG	
12-11-93 737	11-10-93 L-1011	
12-16-93 737	11-15-93 L-1011	
	11-17-93 DH	

NORTHWEST	USAir	DELTA
11-11-93 747	9-17-93 F28	10-20-93 767
12-13-93 747	11-30-93 757	11-3-93 727

Following are some actual discrepancies reported by various airlines:

CONTINENTAL 737 8-7-93

"DLN Flt 0562—The APU fire warning sounded on final approach during APU start. The APU fire procedure in the quick reference handbook was followed and the aircraft landed safely. Maintenance inspected the APU area and found NO EVIDENCE OF FIRE" (capitals mine).

CONTINENTAL 737 12-8-93

"FLT NR100l-LAH—The NR2 engine overheat light illuminated followed by activation of the fire warning on climb-out of LAH. A fire bottle was discharged and the fire warning ceased. The NR2 engine was shut down and the aircraft was returned to LAH where it landed without incident. Maintenance found NO EVIDENCE OF FIRE" (capitals mine).

CONTINENTAL DC-9 12-11-93

"FLT 0316—DEN—The NR2 engine fire-handle flickered momentarily in flight and was accompanied by illumination of the fire detection loop light. The NR2 engine was shut down after landing and shortly afterwards the fire-handle came on, steadily accompanied by oral warning. Maintenance found NO EVIDENCE OF FIRE" (capitals mine).

There have been potentially hazardous takeoff aborts that could have easily ended in disaster, not to mention the potential hazards of having to shut down a perfectly good engine. These emergencies cost the carriers thousands of dollars each year. You would think they could come up with a more reliable system. Or perhaps a few more close inspections would be in order.

In 1994, there were 60 false fire warnings. In 11 months of 1995, the airlines experienced 68 bogus warnings.

There are hundreds of cases where wires have chafed and caused potentially dangerous false warnings. There is always vibration in an aircraft. The reciprocating engines are responsible for the lion's share of vibrations; jets are relatively smooth. But those wires, if they are not routed properly and inspected thoroughly, are going to cause problems.

A few years ago, a Boeing 737-300 was being pushed back in preparation for takeoff. The APU was supplying the electricity for the aircraft. It was believed that faulty wiring in the center tank float switch caused a spark that prompted an explosion that killed eight people and injured 30 more.

Boeing was fined $200,000 for improperly wiring some of their aircraft. The FAA initiated a mandatory repair that involved the following discrepancies: crossed wiring on a B-737 that could cause the fire extinguisher for the wrong engine to operate; crossed wiring on a B-757 that could cause a misdirected charge to go off; and crossed wiring on a B-757 that could give an overheat warning for the wrong engine.

Faulty Wiring

Experts agree that faulty aircraft wiring is the main source of many disasters. There are over 140 miles of wiring on a modern jet airliner. It has been found that the wiring is the first part of a plane to deteriorate long before the designed life of the aircraft is reached.

At various times, all wiring bundles must be visually inspected for wear and security, a task that is near impossible. Over seventy percent of the wiring on an airliner cannot be seen. It is hidden behind sections manufactured when the aircraft was first constructed. Some panels are removed, but there is still an abundance of wires that go unchecked for decades.

The wiring on forty percent of airliners is shielded by a substance called Kapton. This insulation is as thick as four human hairs, not nearly thick enough to withstand the vibration in an aircraft but it does save weight. Excessive heat can reverse the reason for insulation and can turn it into a conductor instead of an insulator.

Kapton coated wires are very susceptible to breakage and cause electrical explosions and fires, yet many airliners still have miles of these potentially lethal wires winding endlessly through the airframe.

Gill Gasper, a wiring expert who works for TWA, has stated many times to Lockheed and Boeing that Kapton wire is a fire waiting to happen.

Both companies decided to stay with Kapton. Here are just a few of the results.

A British Airways 757 was nearly brought down by Kapton wiring that failed and interrupted the flight system.

May 11, 1990—A Philippines Airlines 737 caught fire on the ground. Eight died.

March 17, 1991—A Delta Airlines Tri Star had to make an emergency landing.

November 24, 1993—A Copenhagen Airlines MD87 caught fire on the ground.

There is strong evidence that faulty wiring caused both the TWA Flight 800 and the latest Swissair crash into the ocean, killing hundreds of passengers.

Recently, in 1998—a British Airways 747 caught fire on the ground.

A United Airlines 747 had just departed Honolulu and was climbing through 22,000 feet when a cargo door blew off, sucking nine people out of the aircraft. It was initially thought that a mechanic had failed to close the door properly, but the father of one of the victims proved that faulty wiring caused the door to open in flight.

Saudi Airway flight 163 Jal-1011 caught fire after takeoff. The flames from the cargo hold spread to the cabin and over three hundred people died. Kapton wires were the direct cause of the accident.

All electrical wires on aircraft have a circuit breaker that should pop when the electrical current flow reaches a dangerous level. It is a standard practice for pilots to reset a circuit breaker one time. That might be all it takes on a Kapton wire to cause it to explode and spread fire until it reaches the power source.

Hats off to the U.S. Navy. They discovered that Kapton wires were not safe for their aircraft and they grounded all planes with these faulty wires. In addition, they refused to accept any new aircraft that contain Kapton coated wires.

Where is the FAA during all this turmoil? No where to be found. They could have caught the faulty wiring at the factory where the aircraft was fabricated, but you know how it is: they hate to make waves.

The F-16 fighter is truly a design marvel. It is flown by electronics and the control stick only moves about a quarter of an inch to give full movement of the flight controls. The wiring on this beauty had better be correct because the pilot is completely dependent on it.

However, many Air Force aircraft are wired with wires covered in Kapton. Again, this is a very thin insulation, mainly to save that all-important weight. There have been over 50 fires directly caused by the use of Kapton. Each F-16 has 11 miles of wire going just about everywhere, and chafing also has been a major problem.

Captain Ted Harduva was up on a training flight. Flyers close to the lead said he was seen going inverted and diving straight into the deck. His crash was called pilot error, but his courageous wife had other ideas. She spent years researching the real cause of this tragedy. She brought out the fact that General Dynamics was experiencing wiring problems. She found a video tape put out by the manufacturer warning the maintenance technicians that there are numerous places where wire chafing could be a problem. This video was the deciding factor in clearing her husband's name.

The Air Force Times states "F-16s accomplishments have come at a price: 243 aircraft have been destroyed in crashes and 65 pilots have lost their lives. Fourteen F-16s crashed in fiscal 1998, a 28% increase over the 1997 rate." Yet the Air Force says that the F-16 is the safest single engine fighter ever built.

On the Airbus, there have been numerous autopilot disengagements just as the airplane is flaring for landing. There have also been many unwarranted rolling and pitching movements. The Airbus has experienced three crashes with no specific probable cause. We are, indeed, getting into the age of glass cockpits where we are completely dependent on electronic gadgetry and computers talking to each other.

Just a word of advice about the latest model Airbuses. The passengers are not the only ones sitting there going where the aircraft takes them.

At times, the crew has little power over this fly-by-wire beast and they go where the airplane is programmed, like it or not.

With so many old airplanes still flying, it's going to take a lot more nondestructive testing and much closer inspections by experienced maintenance technicians before airliners really will be safe.

Knock-off Artists

On September 8, 1989, a Convair 440 airliner was boarding passengers at Oslo, Norway. This was charter Flight No. 394 en route to Hamburg, Germany. The aircraft was certified airworthy by a United States' government approved repair station. Thirty minutes into the flight, it disappeared from the radar screen and 50 people perished in the North Sea. There were no distress radio calls, and the weather was excellent. Why did it crash?

The wreck was discovered and raised to the surface for an extensive examination. Piece by piece, the wreckage was reassembled. The only glaring discrepancy was that the tail section was discovered miles from the main wreckage. There was no reported turbulence in the area at the time of the crash. This left only one feasible reason for the tail section to break away; structural failure. The bolts that held the tail to the fuselage were not serviceable parts. They were manufactured in Florida and were not up to aircraft quality. Some how these bogus bolts were installed and were the direct cause of the deaths of 50 innocent people.

I could not uncover any incidents in the United States where bogus parts were the cause of any fatalities. As usual, crashes that happen in other countries cause little or no concern to the U.S. Federal Aviation Agency.

In 1990, Department of Transportation Inspector General Mary Schiavo started intensive investigations concerning the bogus parts problem. Only a few months had passed since the start of her investigation and she had this to say: "We have more leads and allegations than we would ever be able to prosecute."

Any person can become an aircraft parts broker. All you need is a telephone, fax, and a computer, and you could be on your way to making millions by selling bogus parts. There are no licenses required, and nearly any one who is unscrupulous enough to be a "forger for profit" can start his or her own company.

One of the leading brokers in England was Gerald Web who ran the Jet Air Company. He sold parts to most of the major carriers in the United States, England, and Africa. One of his clever tricks was to purchase an authorized part from Eagle Aircraft, an FAA-licensed repair shop located in Florida. When he received the part, he promptly opened the package and located the Certificate of Conformance that must accompany it. Now he had a legal document from a reputable FAA repair station with its name and license number. He blanked out all the writing that described the part he had purchased, went to a local print shop, and had hundreds of copies made. Now the stage was set for his illegal operation. Whenever he sold a part, he would fill in the blanks and watch the money start rolling in.

In Miami, Gabriel Kirsh ran an FAA-licensed repair station but he did not run it legitimately. He had the golden opportunity to tag bad parts for good ones. He sold numerous jet starter motors that contained an abundance of corroded parts. Instead of an approved spring, he used one that came from a box spring mattress company. Most of the innards of these starters were comprised of unserviceable parts. But when his shop got through assembling, painting, bagging, and yellow-tagging them, no one could tell the difference. The only way an airline could check these starters would be to completely disassemble them. That would take a lot of time, and time is money.

In one year, Kirsh sold over $3 million in bogus parts to various airlines worldwide. Mr. Kirsh was finally apprehended and when interrogated, he was asked, "How good is the system of regulations in the United States?" Kirsh replied with a smile and a chuckle, "It's a joke." How often did the FAA inspect your repair station? "They came in twice a year, had a cup of coffee, tried to pick up my secretary, and left."

The FBI stated that George Lisenko and his partner, Danny E. Rudd, supplied unapproved parts, mostly bearings and bushings, to James S. Daniels, operator of D.C. Air, Inc., San Clemente, California. Rudd and Lisenko both pleaded guilty to one count of wire fraud. Rudd received seven months in prison and Lisenko was sentenced to six months; both were fined $5,000. Mr. Daniels was sentenced to a 25-year prison term and was fined $250,000. An additional fine was imposed on Daniels' business property and inventory that could be as high as $15 million. The FBI stated that Daniels sold over $4 million worth of unapproved parts from 1990 to 1994. The FBI cited wire orders for parts from World Airway, Mitchell Aircraft, Algonquin, and Continental Airlines.

The bogus parts industry has flourished for decades. Millions of dollars have been made by unscrupulous individuals. It is an extremely complex industry and it is sometimes very difficult for a mechanic to know if he or she is installing a "bogus" or serviceable part or component.

Some of the following is taken from the FAA 1993 approved Part's Program Reference Material: parts and components of unknown origin, or from aircraft that were involved in crashes are available to the aircraft industry as replacements. Many of these parts or components can be of questionable serviceability (airworthiness).

Let's look at some of the disqualifying categories that can affect salvaged parts. Many parts are non-airworthy because of the following:

A. Parts may have been subject to intense heat that could have a direct affect on dimension and strength.

B. Corrosive liquids can take their toll on aircraft parts. Some crashes that are recovered from the sea are dismantled and parts are sold off.

C. Any parts that are taken from an aircraft that has experienced a ground accident could be of permanent questionable serviceability.

D. Ex-military aircraft that were utilized by civilian-type certificates can create problems, especially when the original manufacturer has discontinued production.

During the Gulf War, a British Airways jet that was destroyed on the ground by gunfire was "parted out" by unscrupulous people in order to make a quick buck. The insurance company that covered the airliner demanded that all parts be destroyed or cut into small pieces. This was not completely accomplished, and barrels full of useless turbine fan blades made their way into the airline industry. Some blades that were cracked were welded together, polished, and sold as serviceable surplus with the all-important bogus yellow tags in place.

Some manufacturers are bidding on their own parts that they originally classified as "bogus." At military surplus sales, they bid on lots of parts that they originally sold for 10 times the price they are paying for them now.

Here's a real kicker: the Inspector General says that an audit of the FAA's own aircraft parts inventory revealed that over 88% of their parts were not airworthy.

The FAA is not the only government agency with bad parts in their stockroom. The Department of Defense (DOD) has an even higher percentage. Special Agent John F. West, in charge of the Defense Criminal Investigative Service (DCIS) had this to say regarding the purchases of the DOD: "Seventy-eight percent of the parts purchased in the undercover capacity with the vendors knowing they were going to the Defense Department were defective."

The March, 1995, issue of *Aviation Week* had this to say about bogus parts: "A 12-count indictment returned by a San Antonio, Texas, grand jury on March 8, charged two companies and two individuals with conspiring to manufacture bogus parts for Boeing 727 aircraft. The U.S. Justice Department names Arthur Stewart and Gary Aerospace Corp. of Honda, Texas, and Joseph L. Mendiola and JLM Aviation International, Inc., of Nuperville, Illinois, as defendants. Mendiola was arrested on March 13th. All defendants are charged with conspiracy, mail fraud, and wire fraud in connection with manufacturing counterfeit, defective, and fraudulent document parts for use on civil aircraft. Mendiola and JLM told customers the parts were genuine airworthy Boeing-made parts."

The Daily News, a San Francisco Valley-based newspaper, made the following report regarding consolidated aeronautics: "The President of Consolidated was sentenced to six months and a fine of $300,000 for selling 'faulty' jet parts to the military. The company was also fined $2 million. Consolidated was selling defective and used parts for USAF fighters. "They stripped old jets and sold the parts out the back door to the

U.S. Government.' Many of the parts came from the government's aircraft bone-yard at Davis-Monthan in Tucson, Arizona."

A government investigation found that a disturbingly large percentage of FAA-approved repair stations, 23 out of 25, performed illegal repairs on air starters. Inspector General Mary Schiavo had this to say: "We shopped a part at repair stations as part of the investigation. We went around with a box full of components that needed to be assembled into a larger component. They needed repair, needed improvement. A lot of parts were life-limited and beyond their time. Only two repair stations turned them down, and 23 actually did the work."

While performing routine maintenance on a United Airlines jet engine, a mechanic was alert enough to discover a potentially dangerous situation. He found a counterfeit spacer on a JT8D engine. It was marked as a Pratt & Whitney part. The surface was bronze-colored but it lacked the bright, machined silver color associated with a serviceable P-W spacer. The mechanic put the spacer through a Rockwell hardness test and it failed to pass.

Pratt & Whitney tested the spacer further, decided it was definitely a bogus part, and alerted operators of the 14,000 JT8Ds worldwide. The FAA immediately dispatched an airworthiness directive to all JT8D operators. The feds ordered all pertinent carriers to make a one-time inspection for these bogus spacers.

The JT8D engine is used on more airliners than any other. It powers DC-9s, MD-80s, 727s and 737s. Several operators confirmed that they had found bogus spacers in their stockroom. The "feds" said that the six bogus spacers they checked were masterpieces in counterfeiting. And they predicted, "the unapproved spacers will result in rapid deterioration of seal elements and that failure is anticipated to occur within 600 hours time in 'service.'"

The alert mechanic who discovered the bad spacer may have averted a potential crash. He should have been given a medal, but I would be quite surprised if he received any official recognition at all.

To obtain a mechanic's license a person must master many facets concerning airframes and power plants. However, how to distinguish an approved part from one that is not has never been part of a technician's course. Picture, if you will, the thousands of parts that make up a modern jetliner. When a mechanic goes to the stockroom to pick up a necessary part or component, he is entirely responsible for ascertaining that the unit he is replacing is indeed an approved part. I firmly believe that each carrier should have a person in charge of confirming that every item in the stockroom is an FAA-approved part. This would take some of the weight off the shoulders of the aircraft mechanic.

As we have seen previously, the "knock-off artists" manufacture documents and package their units so skillfully that it often takes a legitimate manufacturer to ascertain if a part is approved or bogus. Often, the mechanics are prodded to complete a task as rapidly as possible. Why? Because if they don't, they might fear that dreaded word in the airline industry, "delay." Mechanics are expected to examine a part or component before installation, but are not expected to check each piece under a microscope.

"Approved parts" are not necessarily airworthy parts. Approved parts must meet at least one of the following standards:

1. Parts produced in a foreign country with which the United States utilizes a bilateral agreement

2. Parts manufactured under a technical standard order (TSC)

3. Parts manufactured by the original aircraft manufacturer (PAH)

Unapproved parts fit into two categories: undocumented or counterfeit.

1. Counterfeit parts are copies of the original. They may or may not possess the same level of strength as the original

2. Undocumented parts are probably more abundant than any other bogus parts

Used parts, salvaged parts, or overhauled parts are all in this category. If a part lacks documentation, there is really no way to determine if the unit is serviceable or not.

On March 17, 1995, AD 95-07-0l was issued to 6,000 owners of aircraft with specific Lycoming engines. This AD temporarily grounded all 6,000 aircraft until their engines were torn down and examined to determine if bogus bolts were used to secure the connecting rods.

These bogus bolts came to light when a small plane pilot made a forced landing after his engine malfunctioned. It was torn down and the bad bolts were discovered. It was determined that the bolts were imported from Europe and shipped to Superior Air Parts, a reputable parts dealer. The crafts distributor in Europe started shipping bolts in factory sealed boxes. And as the United States dealer saw no problem with these factory boxes, bogus parts were gradually introduced to each order.

The FAA's Airworthiness Directive had this to say concerning the bad bolts: "The traceability of these bolts is extremely difficult, and the FAA has determined that the vast majority of the bolts distributed cannot be recovered, nor can they be identified by a routine records search of engines which have been overhauled since February 15, 1994."

The FAA concluded that all engines that may have been overhauled using these connecting rod bolts must be visually inspected for the installation of unmarked connecting rod bolts. This means all of the 6,000 engines must be torn down to run a visual check on those bolts. The 50 people who died in the North Sea on that charter flight never had a chance.

Another example of bogus parts has to do with Air Force One. In 1995, it was discovered that the fire extinguishing system on the 747 contained illicit parts. If there had been an emergency on the President's plane, you could be sure the government would put "bogus" parts on a high-priority list.

I think you will agree that the "bogus" parts industry is indeed a serious problem. So far, there only has been one fatal crash that killed 50 people. There are presently numerous bogus parts on aircraft, and more are being installed daily. We have a major problem at hand and very little is being done to stamp it out.

In November of 1996, it was revealed that US Airways—at the time it was called US Air—was fined $450,000 for maintenance violations between 1990 and 1996. And, America West Airlines was sighted by the FAA for various maintenance and operational practices. Aircraft were flying passengers with discrepancies such as a vital tail component not serviced properly, cargo-hold webbing not installed correctly, and seventeen Airbus A 320s "overdue for significant structural inspections."

At a recent congressional committee hearing, the former FAA administrator Hinson made this statement: "The use of unapproved parts in the aviation industry is 'just not a real problem.'" Tell that to the loved ones of the 50 people that died in the CV 440 crash.

CHAPTER 2

▼

CAUTION!
BOEING 737 IN FLIGHT

It was September 8, 1994, and USAir's flight 427 was flying in clear, smooth weather less than thirty minutes away from its destination at Pittsburgh International Airport.

Cleveland Air Traffic Control Center transmitted the following to the crew of 427: "USAir four twenty seven, cleared direct to Akron, rest of route unchanged. Give me the best forward airspeed in-trail spacing."

Crew: "Best forward, you got it. Four twenty seven USAir."

The cockpit door opened and a pretty flight attendant entered. "You guys need drinks here?"

Captain: "I could use a glass of something, whatever's open. Water, uh, water, a juice."

First Officer: "I'll split a water, a juice, whatever's back there. I'll split one with him."

Flight Attendant: "Okey-dokey." Do you want me to make you my special fruit juice cocktail? You wanna try it?" She left the cockpit and got to work on making her special drinks.

Cleveland Center: "US Air four twenty seven. Cross CUTTA one zero thousand two five zero knots now."

Crew: "Ten two fifty over CUTTA, US Air four twenty seven."

USAir was now less than ten minutes from Pittsburgh airport. The air was still smooth and the visibility was fifteen miles.

The cockpit door opened and the flight attendant appeared with her freshly made drinks.

Flight Attendant: "Here they are. If you don't like them, I didn't taste 'em and I don't know if they came out right.

First Officer: "That is different. Be real, real good with some dark rum in it."

Captain: "There's a little grapefruit in it." There was the sound of laughter.

Flight Attendant: "Cranberry orange and diet sprite."

First Officer: "Really nice."

Their conversation was interrupted by an air traffic control transmission.

Cleveland Center: "US Air four twenty seven. Descend and maintain six thousand.

Crew: "Cleared to six. USAir four twenty seven."

Cleveland Center: "US Air four twenty seven, turn left heading one zero zero. Traffic will be one to two o'clock, six miles, northbound jet stream, climbing out of thirty three for five thousand."

Crew: "We're looking for the traffic, turning to one zero zero, US Air four twenty seven."

First Officer: "That sun is gonna be just like it was taking off in Cleveland yesterday. You holler when it looks like we're close." A sound of laughter that would soon be changed to a more serious mood as three distinct thumps were heard.

Captain: "Sheeez."

First Officer: "Zuh."

Another loud thump was heard.

Captain: "Whoa. Hang on!"

The aircraft started a bank to the left and then leveled out to wings level attitude as it approached the 100 degrees heading assigned by approach control. The aircraft again started a left bank, steepening from less than

8 degrees to more than 20 degrees. The recorder picked up the sound of engine noise increasing and an additional thump followed by two "clickety-click" sounds. The aircraft continued its erratic flight. Now the bank angle increased to over 42 degrees. The aircraft descended from its assigned attitude of 6,000 feet and the air speed had decreased to a dangerously low level.

The crew was fighting for control of an aircraft that had a mind of its own. The captain transmitted to ATC: "Four twenty seven EMERGENCY." The aircraft's stick shaker (stall warning device) started its death rattle.

Captain: "What the hell is this?"

The aircraft rolled nearly vertical and started a rapid descent.

Ben and Wendy Knight were playing golf on a nearby course. Just as Ben was about to tee up, he heard a weird whining sound that got louder and louder. They both looked up in amazement as an airliner was screaming earthward toward certain destruction.

Captain: "Oh God! Oh God. Pull!"

First Officer: "Oh."

Captain: "Pull, Pull!"

First Officer: "God!"

The sound of screaming was recorded just before the $30 million 737 buried itself and all 132 occupants into a wooded hillside just a few miles short of its destination.

If you think that what you have just read is shocking, wait until you read about the cause of this unnecessary disaster.

The NTSB report that was completed in March 24, 1999, had this to say concerning the US Air crash: "The probable cause of the US Air flight 427 accident was a loss of control of the airplane resulting from the movement of the rudder surface to its blow-down limit. The rudder surface most likely deflected in a direction opposite to that commanded by the pilots as a result of a jam of the main rudder power control unit servo valve secondary slide to the servo valve housing offset from its mounted position and over travel of the primary slide."

How the Rudder Works

The pilot's control wheel directs hydraulic pressure to controls that can make the aircraft climb, descend, and bank in either direction. The primary use of the rudder, the vertical moveable panel at the end of the tail, is to steer the nose left or right. The method of control movement is through two rudder pedals located on the cockpit floor. Push on the left pedal and hydraulic pressure turns the nose left. Right rudder pedal input makes the nose go to the right. The rudder control is probably the least important of all the flight controls. Most modern jets can be flown the vast majority of the time with the pilot's feet on the floor, but should an engine stop, the rudder becomes paramount in keeping the plane from turning into the dead engine and possibly over on its back.

Aircraft with wing-mounted engines need a more powerful rudder than planes that have engines mounted on the fuselage. Power plants attached to the wings have much more force to turn an aircraft than those attached at or near the fuselage. Large transport-category airplanes such as McDonald Douglas, Lockheed, and Airbus all have split rudders and numerous hydraulic backups. The NTSB says that Boeing's 737 is the only large transport airplane designed with a one-panel rudder and a single hydraulic actuator.

The hydraulic actuator for the 737 Rudder is called the power control unit (PCU). When the cockpit rudder pedals are depressed, hydraulic fluid is sent to the PCU that commands the unit to send fluid in the proper direction to actuate the rudder. When you turn your automobile wheel in either direction, you are sending hydraulic fluid into a steering box that aids in making the car turn. The PCU in the 737 works the same way, only it turns the aircraft rudder right or left.

How would you feel if you were driving down the highway in your car and you turned the wheel to the right but the car turned to the left? Rather frightening, but you can always apply the brakes and stop. Now picture the crew of the USAir 737 who were pressing on a rudder pedal to stop a turn and the turn continued in the same direction and steepened. They never had a fighting chance.

Problems with the 737 Rudder

In March of 1991, United Airlines flight 585, a 737, was rolling out of a right turn on final approach at Colorado Springs when it yawed and rolled, pitched down, and crashed, killing all 25 people on board. Rudder reversal was the culprit.

On July 16, 1992, during a ground control check of the rudder, a United 737 crew noted that when the rudder pedal was depressed, it jammed in the depressed or forward position.

On March 8, 1994, a Sahara India Airlines 737 was on a training flight when the crew lost control just after takeoff. The aircraft crashed, killing all on board and five others on the ground. The cause was a faulty rudder.

On June 1 and June 8, 1996, an Eastwind Airlines B-737 experienced rudder anomalies. And on June 9, 1996, Captain Brian Bishop was in command of Eastwood flight 517 that was cruising at 5,000 feet near Richmond, Virginia.

Captain Bishop stated, "As the aircraft descended out of 5,000 feet, I felt a brief rudder 'kick' or 'bump' on the right rudder pedal but the pedal did not move." At 4,000 feet, the aircraft yawed fiercely to the right followed by a roll. Captain Bishop applied maximum pressure to the opposite rudder. The first officer stated, "the Captain was straining to depress the left rudder and fighting, trying to regain control."

Examination and testing of the aircraft by the NTSB and Boeing revealed that wiring from the yaw damper couples that control the rudder was chafed, and "infiltration of fluid was consistent with, but not conclusive evidence of, an electrical fault." Much more, later on, concerning moisture in the electronic bay and how it got there.

Captain Eastwood has been flying for many years, and he had this to say about the incident: "It was the sickest feeling I have ever had in over twenty years of flying."

On August 13, 1998, A Delta Airlines B-737 experienced a yaw/roll event while cruising at 33,000 feet. The rudder pedals "pulsed" for the remainder of the flight.

These were only a few of the numerous rudder problems on the B-737 prior to the first United Airlines crash caused by rudder reversal.

A New Rudder PCU Is Designed

In 1998, four years after the US Air crash, the FAA finally got moving on correcting the faulty rudder on the B-737. The FAA told Boeing that a new PCU must be designed.

The second rudder PCU was designed and installed on numerous 737s. This new unit was going to eliminate any more rudder problems. But cracks were discovered on many of the newly improved units that had to be replaced. The new design was not getting off to a very good start.

On February 23, 1999, a US Airways 737 Metrojet was cruising at altitude when the crew reported to ATC that it was experiencing control problems. The crew noticed that the right rudder pedal was fully displaced and that it moved without any control input from the crew. The Captain pushed the left rudder but found it stuck. After moving the hydraulic "B" switch, to standby rudder position, the rudder pedals returned to their neutral position. The crew landed safely but not without a few more vicious rudder kicks on final approach.

Since 1980, ten years before the United crash in Colorado, the NTSB has investigated over one hundred events involving the faulty rudder components on the B-737. In spite of all the documented rudder problems, the FAA is still "pussyfooting" around, and being nice to the aircraft companies and the airlines. Instead of requiring a positive fix for the rudder, here's what they did.

Don't Fix It; Try To Live With It

Two years before the US Air crash in Pittsburgh, the NTSB requested the FAA to require upset training to air carriers' flight crews. The "feds" said that the airline simulators were not geared to give such violent training. After the US Air crash, the FAA stated that upset training might be a good idea and they set out guidance for air carriers to give VOLUNTARY training. So far, only thirteen U.S. carriers are implementing these life-saving maneuvers. That means over two-thirds of U.S. B-737 operators are not teaching their crews how to cope with an uncommanded rudder hard-over.

AD96-26070 Airworthiness Directives from the FAA were issued December 23, 1996, two years after the US Air crash, and included procedures that would enable pilots to take "appropriate action to maintain control of the airplane during an uncommanded yaw or roll condition," and "correct a jammed or restricted fight control condition." This AD was in written form to be inserted in the pilots' operational manual.

At the time of the US Air Pittsburgh crash, no flight crews had received any training in unusual attitudes. In other words, the aircraft could be tossed about in vertical banks and possibly inverted because of weather, jet wake, or a controls malfunction, and the crew wouldn't have the slightest idea of how to guide the aircraft back to level flight.

Years ago, in the propeller era, all crews were tested on unusual attitudes. Since jets came on the scene, and not until after the US Air crash, have crews been trained to recover from violent upsets. Does this sound like the FAA is really interested in your safety?

Flight Data Capabilities

United flight 585 and US Air flight 427 were equipped with inferior flight recorders that recorded fewer than thirteen flight parameters. At the time of the US Air accident, recorders existed that could report on dozens of important parameters. Lives could have been saved if the newer recorders had been mandatory equipment aboard the numerous aircraft later subjected to rudder anomalies.

In July of 1997, the FAA issued its final rule requiring all air carriers to install the latest flight data recorders by August 19, 2001.

Hats off to Southwest Airlines. It was the only airline installing new FDRs on their fleet long before it was mandated. At a cost of $70,000 per aircraft, its fleet of 248 B-737s was equipped with the new recorder by December 1999, a year before the FAA requirement. Some people just know how to run an airline.

The Rudder is Not the Only Problem

The Cabin Roof Blew Off

April 18, 1988, an Aloha Airlines B-737 was in cruise flight at 24,000 feet. An explosive decompression took place and 18 feet of the cabin ceiling blew out, along with one of the flight attendants. The cause of this accident was the use, by Boeing, of a cheap method of bonding the aircraft skin. And Aloha's maintenance department was lax in its inspections. Fortunately, the aircraft landed without any further problems.

Fatigue Cracks

An FAA airworthiness directive was issued April 26, 1999 concerning cracks in the rear pressure bulkhead of some 737s. If these cracks are not detected in time, an explosive decompression could result. A similar bulkhead on a Japan Airlines 747 blew out in flight, making the control of the aircraft impossible. It hit a mountain and hundreds died. This accident was caused by Boeing, which repaired a broken aircraft and did not do the job properly.

Blue Water

The 737 forward lavatory is located on top of the electrical/electronics (E/E) compartment which contains the electronic brains of the aircraft. It is a place where liquid is not welcome.

In 1995, Boeing established an assessment team to investigate fluid contamination of electrical and electronic boxes. The team reviewed 653 Boeing 737 E/E bay service reports from January 1984 to February 1986. Fluid contamination was noted in 111 of these reports. The team also reviewed 13,905 repair station records pertaining to electrical boxes. Three hundred sixty-six of these reports showed that leaking toilets were the culprits. The primary causes of the toilet leaks were failed gaskets, cracked toilet tanks, and damaged dump valves.

Some of the electrical components in the E/E bay are electrical links to the flight control systems through the autopilot. The rudder trim and yaw damper are in this compartment. The 737 is equipped with fluid barriers designed to contain or prevent liquids from reaching the vital E/E bay. These barriers can be damaged during service, allowing fluids to enter the E/E compartment. It's pretty frightening to think that an airliner could be downed by a leaky toilet.

Electrical Problems

In May of 1998, the FAA issued an airworthiness directive (AD) requiring older B-737s be inspected for damage to the fuel pump electrical wires found in each wing. This AD affects the 100–200 series aircraft of which there are 118 domestic and 282 worldwide.

This AD was orchestrated after a pinhole fuel leak was discovered on a Continental Airlines B-737. The leak was found inside one of the wings. This same problem is what was believed to have caused the TWA 747 to explode in mid-air. Two days after the AD was issued, thirteen of twenty-six main fuel pump wires showed insulation wear. The FAA said that one wing wiring brindle on a B-737 "showed clear signs of arcing in one location, and a second spot where bare wires were already exposed."

Before a new model airliner can fly in passenger service, it must pass FAA certification tests. Since the FAA only oversees about five percent of the design and construction of any new model, it allows the aircraft company to get away with murder.

The following is a quote from the NTSB US Air 787 accident report: "During the initial certification of the 737-100 series, FAA Certification officials expressed concern about the airplane's single-panel, single-activator rudder system and recognized that possibility of undetected latent failure in the servo valve, thereby negating the system's redundancy. The rudder system's history of service difficulties (some of which still remain unresolved, particularly the servo valve's history of jamming) validates those concerns."

The FAA, this time, was entirely on the right track. If they had only used the power that they possess, the faulty rudder design could have been nipped in the bud, and one hundred and fifty-seven passenger deaths would have been averted.

The NTSB Findings section of the US Air 737 crash had this to say concerning the poorly designed rudder system:

"The dual-concentric servo valve used on all B-737 main rudder power control units is not reliably redundant." And "the training being provided to many Boeing 737 flight crews on the procedures for recovery from a jammed or restricted rudder (including a rudder reversal) is inadequate."

Boeing stands behind this aircraft no matter what. It did, however, acknowledge that a rudder hard over on 737s during the most critical phase of flight—takeoff and/or landing (which Boeing estimates at 60 to 90 seconds per flight)—would be catastrophic. Another quote from the NTSB concerning Boeing: "The 737-G, the combination of a jammed servo value with a loss of engine power during takeoff would be catastrophic only using a seven-second window from VI through liftoff."

What's seven seconds? That's not much time, but it could be enough to kill you.

Takeoff in an aircraft is probably the most critical part of the flight. Pilots do not need the added worry of applying full rudder to counteract a failed engine only to have the rudder reverse and cause a fatal crash.

The only way a pilot knows which way the rudder is moving is by looking out the window and watching the nose go left or right. On all airplanes, except the B-737, when a pilot looks down at his feet and sees that both pedals are neutral, he knows that there is no rudder movement. On the 737, this is not the case. Neutral rudder pedals signify nothing. The rudder could be full left or full right, and the pilot would be completely baffled.

The latest B-737s have a rudder direction indicator in the cockpit. Since B-737s have a history of rudder horrors, it behooves the FAA to require cockpit rudder position indicators on all Boeing 737s, new or old.

Let's review the record. It has taken eight years for a "fix" to the rudder problems and these modifications have proven useless. The safety conscious Air Line Pilots Association (ALPA) is continuing their investigation concerning the B-737 rudder anomalies. They have already spent over $781,000 of member dues to try to make the B-737 a safe aircraft.

For and Against Boeing

For Boeing

FAA: The FAA does not believe sufficient evidence exists to establish rudder system failure as a cause of the accident.

Boeing: There is no data to indicate that the Eastwood Flight 517 event, the United Flight 585 accident, and the US Air flight 427 accidents were caused by a common airplane malfunction.

Parker Hannifin: The manufacturers of the faulty rudder PCU stated there is no evidence that the main PCU from flight 427 malfunctioned or was other than fully operational.

There have been over 100 documented rudder anomalies, and yet these three bedfellows say there is no rudder problem.

Against Boeing

US Air: "A mechanical malfunction of US Air flight 427 rudder PCU resulted in a rudder reversal or uncommanded deflection that caused flight 427 to depart controlled flight and crash.

ALPA: "ALPA believes more strongly than ever that the cause of the accident was a rudder anomaly.

NTSB: The accident was caused by a loss of control of the airplane resulting from the movement of the rudder surface to its blow-down limits. The rudder surface most likely deflected in a direction opposite to that commanded by the pilots.

The Boeing 737 is the most popular airliner ever built. There are 2,705 flying worldwide including 1,115 in the United States. In fact, every seven seconds there is one climbing out of an airport somewhere in the world.

Sure, the 737 has a great safety record, but when a known problem has existed for nearly ten years, something drastic should be done to make the 737 not only the most popular but the safest airliner in the sky.

The Safety Board notes that "737 flight crews continue to report anomalous rudder behaviors, and it is possible that another catastrophic 737 upset-related accident could occur."

On July 25, 2000, an Air France Concord crashed and burned, killing 113 people. The next day, the French government grounded all Concords. The exact cause of the crash is not yet known but a blown tire is suspected. The French only needed one crash and they put the Concord on the ground.

The Boeing 737 has had two crashes killing one hundred and fifty-seven people. There are known rudder problems and there have been hundreds of documented cases confirming the problem. The PCU in the tail was redesigned and it proved to be useless. In September of 2000, the FAA demanded that Boeing try once again to redesign the killer rudder. Boeing said that it would take until 2006 to complete the project. In the meantime, let's keep our fingers crossed.

CHAPTER 3

▼

LOOK OUT BELOW!

Captain George D. Gill, age 44, began his flying career with the Royal Canadian Air Force in August of 1954 and flew C45, Harvard, DC-3, and T-33 aircraft. In 1966, he joined Air Canada and flew Viscounts, DC-8s, and Douglas DC-9s. Gill was promoted to Captain in May of 1979.

On September 17, 1979, Captain Gill was commanding Air Canada's Flight 680, a Douglas DC-9, operating from Boston, Massachusetts to Yarmouth, Nova Scotia, Canada. The takeoff and climb-out were relatively uneventful. At 1226 EDT, prior to leveling out at 25,000 feet, the tail cone section cracked and dropped from the aircraft. The tremendous force of the decompression ripped the cockpit door from the hinges, and the crew could look down the length of the cabin and see blue sky streaming in through the gaping hole in the rear of the fuselage. Atlantic Ocean fish now have a vital part of a jetliner to call home. The passenger oxygen masks dropped down, as advertised, and the crew quickly donned their masks and called Air Traffic Control.

Crew: "Boston Center, Air Canada 680 is doing a rapid emergency descent. Clearance back to Boston, we're out of 23,000 descending."

Boston Center: "680 turn right and proceed direct to Boston. Descend and maintain 14,000. Boston, altimeter 30.24. Are you going to need assistance?"

Crew: "Boston Center we are leaving 20,000 and requesting 9,000 feet."

The Center cleared Air Canada to descend to and maintain 10,000 feet. At 1228.24 the crew responded: "Roger, we are just leveling now and the back end of our tail is blown completely off. If you could have some emergency crews standing by."

The flight attendants were comforting the passengers, but the engine and air noise was nearly deafening. The flight was now cleared to 9,000 feet. At this time, First Officer Long went into the cabin to check on the passengers and crew. The Lead Cabin Attendant advised him that all was well except for an attendant who had received a bump on her head. At 1231, the crew again requested the emergency equipment.

Boston Center: "They've got the equipment out and 33 left."

Crew: "Roger, understand 33 left."

At 1239:38, Boston Center: "680 are you having any control problems?"

Crew: "Negative."

A visual approach was made to 33L and a good landing was executed without the aid of the left engine reverse that was inoperable.

On the ground, a visual inspection was made to determine the extent of the damage. The rear section of the fuselage was damaged. Structurally, the drink cart, tail cone, aft cabin pressure bulkhead access door, and the lavatory water supply tank were all missing. Unusable flight controls included the horizontal stabilizer indicating control, the rudder trim, and the right elevator trim.

During the investigation, the NTSB became concerned that the crack in the bulkhead that caused the accident had gone undetected for over four months. During a routine X-ray of the bulkhead in question, four months prior to the mishap, a fatigue crack was clearly in evidence but was not caught by the inspectors.

This time, for a change, the FAA moved rapidly. A day after the accident, an AD was dispatched to seven air carriers that used DC-9 aircraft. Out of 119 aircraft inspected, cracks were found in 33.

On September 22, 1981, 58-year-old Captain Adam C. Kagel was in command of Eastern Airlines L-1011 flight 935 from Newark, New Jersey, to San Juan, Puerto Rico. Takeoff and climb from Runway 22L was normal until reaching an altitude of 800 feet. Here, the airborne vibration monitor (AVM) began to flash for the No. 2 engine. At 1,000 feet, the normal power reduction was made and the instruments read in the green (normal).

At 2,000 feet, the oil filter pressure warning light illuminated, indicating a potential blocked filter. The power was reduced on No. 2, and as the wide-bodied transport reached 10,000 feet, the crew heard a loud explosion followed by heavy aircraft buffeting.

"It jolted me right out of my seat, just about" Kagel says, "And the shaking ... I was stunned."

Within seconds, the cockpit panels resembled a winning game at a video arcade. The engineer called out that No. 2 engine had failed, and that hydraulic systems A, B, and D were, simultaneously, all lost. No. 2 was immediately shut down, and the fire extinguisher discharged as a precautionary measure.

"I was scared," Capt. Kagel says. "You're not only thinking about saving the airplane and the people; you are also thinking about saving yourself."

The crew requested and received an immediate clearance to JFK with appropriate headings so that they could dump fuel because they were too heavy to land. The engine explosion jammed the nose wheel steering and the rudder pedals. Now the crew would have to skillfully use the ailerons (banking controls on the wings) and differential engine thrust to try and "pinch hit" for the useless rudder.

The airport emergency equipment was ready, and a smooth and skillful landing was made on Runway 22L. After the crash, the crew examined the plane for leaks or a fire. It was taxied to the gate, and 201 grateful people were delighted to be back safely on the ground. Because of Captain Kagel's airmanship, flight 935 was not another statistic on the death rolls of America's air disasters.

An inspection of the aircraft revealed that a part of No. 2 engine's low pressure compressor, including the blades, disc, and a 26-inch section of the fan shaft, had dropped from the engine and landed harmlessly in the ocean. The disintegrating engine parts left their presence on the aircraft skin before falling to the ground. As the fan module separated, it cut a path through the inlet duct and hit the left side of the fuselage. Before the module's energy was spent, it punctured the body, leaving a clear crucifix-type impact mark. The top surface of the horizontal stabilizer center box resembled a B-17 that had been shot up over Berlin. There were perforations in the forward cargo web, and the port stabilizer contained 18 holes in the top and 2 holes in the bottom.

Just so the DC-10 won't feel slighted, it is only fitting to include a horror story about her.

If Captain Boyd Roger Lofgren, a 49-year-old veteran with over 16,000 hours, had any idea of what was in store for him on his next trip, he would probably have called in sick.

January 31, 1981 was a great day for aviating.

The weather at Dulles International Airport was clear, 20 miles visibility, and the temperature a crisp 20 degrees. Northwest Airlines Flight 79 was in the process of taxing to Runway 01L. They were filed IFR and launched at 1801 EST. Dulles Departure Control cleared them directly on course to the Martinsburg VOR to climb to 7,000 feet. I know you have heard this before, but I must tell it like it was.

Leaving 6,000 feet, the crew was startled by an explosion, accompanied by very heavy buffeting. First Officer Patrick T. Donlan exclaimed, "No. 3 engine has failed."

Simultaneously, the No. 3 electric and hydraulic systems became inoperable. This also caused the F/O instrument panel lights to go dark. The Captain requested immediate return to Dulles. Forty thousand pounds of fuel was jettisoned to reduce the weight below maximum landing weight and the flight was given vectors for a landing on Runway 12.

If you have any kind of emergency, having Dulles below you is a reassuring feeling because it is one of the best airports in the world. A delaying 360 degrees turn was made on the base leg (last leg in pattern before turning final) because the landing gear had to be lowered by use of the emergency landing gear extension procedure. At 1825, the crew made a skillful landing, and, after being inspected by the crash crew, taxied to a regular parking spot. The No. 3 engine was minus the No. 30 turbofan blade, the entire nose cowl assembly, and the fan containment case.

On January 31, 1981, the nose cowl was recovered from the back yard of a residence in Leesburg, Virginia, with only very slight ground impact damage. And on February 24, 1981, the fan containment case was recovered in a creek about 300 feet from where the first piece was discovered.

In May of 1983, an 18-inch man-made meteor came scalding into the back yard of the Wick's family in Dallas, Texas, landing with a loud bang. Judith Wick recalled that "The house shook, and I heard a loud bang, and I looked outside and saw this white smoke."

Dave Wick stated, "The object hit not far from the swing set where the kids play. It's a good thing it was nap time."

FAA spokesman Tom Geaves stated that the aircraft from which the object fell was never identified. The part was from a General Electric engine, and it definitely would have been the cause of an engine failure.

In Hull, Massachusetts, September 1983, after a nonstop flight from Los Angeles, a United DC-10 made a safe landing at Logan International Airport. On the approach to the field, the DC-10 shed a six-inch landing gear bolt that crashed through the roof of a house, narrowly missing its occupant, Maureen Peacock. She said she was sitting in the living room when she heard a thud on the porch roof. She investigated and soon discovered the cause of the disturbance: there was a bolt lying on the porch floor and a gaping hole in the ceiling.

In May of 1985, an American Airlines 727 was in cruise flight when, without any warning, their No. 3 engine seized and fell from the aircraft.

In September of 1984, American Airlines was fined $375,000 by the FAA for the installation of bogus parts in the wings of three of their DC-10s. The agency was alerted to the allegedly improper practices when a 200-pound slat (an airfoil device on the wing) fell from a DC-10 while on final approach to Dallas-Fort Worth International Airport.

Major Peter Clark from Dover Air Force Base, Delaware, made a startling statement concerning the C5A Galaxy, the world's largest transport. Over 45 parts had fallen from this model aircraft during the last two years. The largest piece was a 353-pound door that fell from an altitude of 6,000 feet.

According to a computer printout from the FAA, between 1983 and 1985, there have been over 410 items that have fallen from aircraft during takeoff, cruise, and landing. This list is only concerned with large transport style aircraft; commuters, general aviation, or military aircraft are not included.

05-12-1983 Boeing 747 American

Remarks: Arrived with right-hand slide door open and slide missing.

05-12-1983 Boeing 747 American

Remarks: Right wing escape door on in-flight. Door opened slide departed aircraft.

06-15-1983 Boeing 747 American

Remarks: Lost slide during landing.

11-30-1983 Douglas DC-10 Pan American

Remarks: Crew advised something fell from aircraft. Found forward fairing of LH outboard sporter missing.

01-05-1984 Douglas DC-9 Eastern

Remarks: Found No. 2 engine upper cowling missing.

01-04-1984 Boeing 767 United

Remarks: No. 3 wheel and tire departed.

02-06-1984 Lockheed 1011 Eastern

Remarks: Parts of core cowling came out of No. 1 engine.

05-01-1984 Douglas DC-10 American

Remarks: Portion of No. 3 engine cowling missing.

05-08-1984 Boeing 747 Pan American

Remarks: Flight returned due to loss of No. 1 engine cowling.

05-08-1984 Boeing 747 United

Remarks: Flight returned due to vibration. Found 20 x 60 inch panel missing.

09-12-1984 Boeing 757 Eastern

Remarks: Left outboard flap, inboard track fairing missing.

04-03-1985 Boeing 757 Eastern

Remarks: Escape slide over wing deployed during climb-out.

04-08-1985 Boeing 757 Eastern

Remarks: First officers windshield wiper arm came off and was ingested in No. 2 engine, causing Exhaust Gas Temperature to climb to 877 degrees

04-22-1985 Boeing 727 American

Remarks: No. 3 engine fell off.

06-12-1985 Douglas DC-10 American

Remarks: Cabin decompressed at 17,000 feet. No. 3 core cowl departed aircraft, creating a 2 x 2 foot hole in fuselage.

In October of 1987, an All-Nippon 767-200 lost a large portion of its outboard flaps. This piece fell off on a Tokyo-to-Hakodate flight during the first flight of a brand new aircraft.

On December 5, 1987, a US AIR 737 was climbing through 4,000 feet when the cockpit warning lights came on. Three cone-shaped engine mount bolts and a steel strap that secured the No. 2 engine let go, depositing the engine in a field nine miles southwest of Philadelphia.

In 1989, a British Airway Concord supersonic transport was flying from Christchurch, New Zealand, to Sydney, Australia. After landing at Sydney, it was discovered that a 6 x 5 foot section of the rudder was missing.

In December 1991, a 747 freighter crashed in Taiwan. A year later, another 747 freighter crashed in the Netherlands. The culprit in both cases was a dropped engine due to faulty pylon bolts.

In April of 1995, the students of a Chino, California, high school were taking notes as their French teacher left his desk and proceeded to the blackboard. No sooner had he reached the front of the room than a loud bang was heard and a three-foot object broke through the roof and shattered the teacher's desk. What could this strange object be? Since it came from the air the FAA was summoned. They found it was a ball of blue ice and waste from a passing airliner's toilet.

On October 18, 1995, in Woodinville, Washington, Leroy Cinnamon and his wife, Gerri, were watching the Seahawks-Raiders football game. The game was exciting, but not nearly as chilling as what was about to happen. At 3:00 p.m., something came crashing down through their living room ceiling. This thing from out of space shattered into baseball-size pieces of bluish ice. It hit a few feet from where they were sitting. Terrified, the Cinnamons dialed 911. Rescue workers, wearing protective clothing, roped off the area, fearing that the object might be a radioactive meteorite. The Cinnamon family was driven to a local hospital where they were scrubbed down.

"I was sick to my stomach with fright because I had picked up a piece. I didn't want the dogs to lick it."

After being reassured that the stuff was non-radio active, the Cinnamons returned to their home and stashed the blue ice in their freezer so that they could show their insurance adjuster. A few days later, an FAA investigator confirmed the identity of the material to be human waste combined with blue disinfectant.

The "feds" traced down the guilty airline and found it to be United flight 461 from Chicago to Seattle.

"It's a good thing none of us was killed," states Leroy Cinnamon. "What would you put on the tombstone?"

So far, there have been no fatalities from parts raining from the skies, but only time will tell.

CHAPTER 4

▼

SURROGATES OF FAA

On May 26, 1991, a Lauda Air Boeing 767-300ER crashed northwest of Bangkok, killing 223 passengers and crewmembers. For a change, the probable cause was not pilot error; it was FAA error.

Before introducing a newly designed aircraft into service, a manufacturer must obtain FAA certification that the new craft meets certain safety standards. It usually takes about five years for the manufacturer to supply the FAA with exacting analysis as well as a prototype of the newly planned aircraft.

All FAA certification activities are channeled through its Aircraft Certification Service in Washington, D.C. The service is composed of four branches that certify airworthiness of small airplanes, engines, rotorcraft, and transports. Because the two main large aircraft builders are on the west coast, the FAA's main airline division is in Renton, Washington.

As of March 1993, there were 118 engineers and test pilots assigned to the Seattle and Los Angeles Aircraft Certification Office (ACO). These people are the watchdogs for the FAA at the various aircraft factories around the country. There are not nearly enough FAA personnel to oversee all facets of a newly designed aircraft, so what do the "feds" do about that? They allow the manufacturer to appoint surrogates for the FAA in examining new aircraft designs. There are, of course, certain criteria that must be followed before the manufacturer is allowed to utilize the services of a surrogate, and it makes sure the engineers it picks will have no problem being approved by the FAA. When an employee of a factory is designated as an FAA spy, he or she is called a designated engineering representative (DER).

Now, let's go over that again. Because the FAA is short on engineers, and especially engineers who know what's going on, they allow factory-employed engineers who are picked by the manufacturers to oversee the building of a new aircraft. It does sound ludicrous but that's the way the FAA operates. If you were employed as an engineer for an aircraft factory, do you think you would last long if you turned down too many of your employer's designs?

Throughout the years, the FAA's role in certification has grown less and less. What percentage of the certification process do you think the FAA is actually performing itself? Fifty percent or seventy-five percent would be acceptable figures, but they are not even near that mark. Believe it or not, ninety five percent of all the lengthy certification process is performed by company representative DERs. Today, there are approximately 1,300 DERs doing the FAA's work.

Between 1980 and 1992, the number of designees rose from 299 to 1,287 (430%). The FAA designated ninety-five percent of all certification activities for the new Boeing 747-400 aircraft. A quote from the GAO had this to say regarding FAA competence: "Another internal review found that the staff were not sufficiently familiar with the Boeing 747-400 flight management system to define requirements for testing it or verifying regulatory compliance."

In 1991, a contractor hired by the FAA found that their engineering training was inadequate. "Over half of the engineers with primary responsibility in the certification of the Boeing 777 have never participated in a major certification project."

Another quote from the September 1993 GAO report of Aircraft Certification: "Because FAA has increased delegation over the last 13 years, its ability to effectively oversee or add value to the certification process as well as understand new technologies has been questioned by internal reviews and FAA industry officials." The report continues: "FAA identified a need for 23 experts but has staffed only 8 positions. Between 1990 and 1992, only 1 of the 12 FAA engineers responsible for approving aircraft software attended a software-related training course. FAA officials acknowledged that inadequate training over the last decade has limited the certification staff's ability to understand such areas of dramatic technological advancement."

The rates of DERs to FAA staff were 3 to 1 in 1980 and increased to 11 to 1 by 1992. Several FAA officials were interviewed. They stated that continuing to increase technical delegation was a great concern because the agency would lose competence in "understanding the systems it is responsible for certifying." Another great quote from the GAO had this to say about FAA engineers' competency: "An internal study by the Transport Airplane Directorate found that the FAA engineers delegated to DERs approved the entire flight management system."

This operates the navigational system and monitors the performance of other systems. The FAA was not sufficiently familiar with the system to provide meaningful inputs to the testing requirements or to verify compliance with the regulatory standards. As a result, FAA allowed Boeing to conduct the certification activities without the FAA staff members understanding the system. Similarly, because FAA engineers had minimal knowledge of ten other systems, including the aircraft's braking system, the agency delegated to DERs key analysis of those systems analysis that on previous certification projects FAA had reserved for its own staff.

As of 1993, the following is a list of important engineering positions that were never authorized by the FAA.

Aircraft systems safety analysis

Flight loads/aeroelasticity (rotorcraft)

Fuel systems

Hydromechanical systems

Tanking gear systems

Nondestructive testing

Performance (fixed wing aircraft)

Performance (rotorcraft)

Propeller design

Rotorcraft drive systems

There is a position for flight environment (ICING) but it has been vacant since 1987. While all of the above are extremely important positions, there have been hundreds of lives lost because of the effect of icing on an airplane. Yet the FAA has no interest in examining the effects ice may have on a newly designed aircraft, at least not until it crashes. This is ludicrous with a capital "L".

The knowledge of the FAA engineers is considerably less than the manufacturer DERs, the people they are supposed to be supervising.

Concerning the certification process, a director of the FAA had a few words to say about certification. In 1985, FAA admitted that certification training was "a mess." At FAA schools, the training of engineers was mostly concerned with automation of office work and courses in the operation of word processors. Of the 31 courses offered, only twenty-nine percent were technical. The rest were not related to the certification process. According to GAO reports, nontechnical courses are becoming more important so the FAA can effectively manage and oversee DERs' work.

Let us now return to the beginning of this chapter concerning the crash of a Boeing 767. You have, I am sure, noticed the loud engine noises after your airliner has landed. This is the work of the thrust reversers doing their thing. The engine rotation does not reverse, rather a method is used to direct the air from the rear of the jet engine to reverse its flow forward. This procedure greatly reduces the landing roll. However, these devices are only activated by the pilot, and only on the ground. If one engine accidentally goes into reverse by itself during flight, bad things happen.

The following quote from the GAO sums up neatly why 223 people lost their lives in this tragic accident. "In May of 1991, a Lauda Air Boeing 767 crashed in Thailand after an engine thrust reverser accidentally activated in flight. Two hundred and twenty-three people were killed."

During the certification of the Boeing 767 in 1982, FAA, in approving the thrust reverser as safe, required Boeing to, among other things, address the effects of an in-flight deployment. However, the agency relied on

Boeing DERs to approve the failure analysis of the device. The documentation Boeing submitted to obtain certification was simply a statement that an in-flight deployment had been CONSIDERED (author's capitals) and that the aircraft would operate safely. During the certification process, FAA did not review the actual analysis or the assumptions made; rather it asked Boeing DERs to recommend the approval of the failure analysis. The FAA approved the analysis on this recommendation."

If the FAA knew what it was doing, and had the smarts to understand the potential for a faulty thrust reverse system, two hundred and twenty-three people could be alive today.

Not only was the FAA at fault for not fully testing the thrust reverse system; it was equally guilty in the testing of other systems. The "feds" do not require aircraft to be tested in a myriad of different conditions such as ice, snow, wet, rough, and short runway conditions. This is left to the line pilot in his day-to-day operation of airliners.

When the FAA certifies a new aircraft's braking system, they do so in a strict environment. The runways used in these tests are much longer than an average airline airport. Wind conditions are near calm, tests are performed during daylight hours on a dry runway (tests are not required on wet runways), use of a brand new aircraft with new tires and brakes, a test pilot who has more time in it than any other pilot, and a crew that has had adequate sleep. These criteria are about as much like line flying as night and day.

The FAA test pilot does not need to be over the end of the runway because the runway they use in these tests is many miles long. The pilot is only checked when he is fifty feet above the runway. He must establish a high rate of sink and flare to a descent rate of less than ten feet per second. An FAA test pilot who was performing these tests with the Douglas DC-9-80 did not react properly and landed hard. The fuselage cracked into two pieces.

If the test pilot fails to land properly, he can always try it again. If a line pilot landed his plane similar to the way the test pilot did, he would be referred to his chief pilot for remedial training, but the FAA still persists in testing aircraft in an unreal environment.

I have only touched on two of the many FAA faults concerning certifying and testing a new aircraft. Between 1983 and 1992, there were 173 "hull loss" accidents. One hundred twenty-two of these accidents have been officially identified: 68.9 percent were caused by pilot error and 13.1 percent were caused by a failure of the aircraft's design, structure, or system.

That 13.1 percent of aircraft design failures could be reduced to zero if only the FAA knew what it was doing.

CHAPTER 5

▼

TOO OLD TO FLY

On April 28, 1988, an Aloha Airlines Boeing 737 was scheduled for a series of inter-island flights. There were 89 passengers and 6 crewmembers on board. As flight number 243 leveled out at 24,000 feet, the crew heard a loud "clap" and a "wooshing" sound, followed by a loud wind noise.

The captain turned around in his seat and was astonished to find that the cockpit door was missing and he could see bright blue sky where the first-class ceiling had been. For some reason, the aircraft had experienced an explosive decompression (the cabin literally exploded because of a faulty skin). The number one flight attendant was sucked out, along with 18 feet of the top and both sides of the fuselage. An emergency descent was initiated, and at 10,000 feet the aircraft was slowed to 210 knots. They went directly to Maui, the nearest place to land. To add to the emergency conditions, the left engine fuel and throttle cable were broken, causing the engine to shut down.

In 1987, one year prior to this incident, Aloha Airlines discovered that a carbon steel thrust control cable had corroded and frayed. Only five of the seven strands remained intact. They reported this to Boeing who issued a Service Letter (SL) 737-SL-76-2-A on August 25, 1987, eight months before the incident, advising their 737 customers to replace the cable with one made of stainless steel. The Boeing Company advised changing the cable, but the airline that initiated the discrepancy did nothing about it.

Forty-five-year-old Captain Robert L. Schoinstheimer did an excellent job. He earned his lifetime salary in thirteen minutes. The approach speed was kept up to 170 knots, which was well over the normal speed. This was necessary, because when speed was reduced and normal flaps were dropped, the craft became unstable. This landing would be made with only five degrees of flap, and only one engine.

How this airframe stayed together is a miracle in itself. The aircraft skin and substructure were completely missing from just aft of the main cabin door to just forward of the wings. The only structure left in the area was the floor, and it was extensively damaged.

Prior to this flight the aircraft maintenance log showed no discrepancies, and all regional FAA directives were shown as accomplished. Why then did this supposedly airworthy aircraft break up in flight?

The NTSB did an excellent job researching this accident. There were only a few points that they could have developed more completely, but to see the FAA bear the brunt of this case was gratifying. The following is the NTSB's probable cause.

"The probable cause of this accident was the failure of the Aloha Airlines maintenance program to detect the presence of significant separation or debonding and fatigue damage which ultimately led to failure of the lap joint at S10L and the separation of the fuselage upper lobe. Contributing to the accident were the failure of Aloha Airlines management to supervise properly its maintenance program and to assess the airlines inspection and quality control deficiencies; the failure of the FAA to require Airworthiness Directives 87-21-08 inspections of lap joints."

To begin this saga, we will have to go back to the construction methods used by Boeing on their first 291 production 737 airplanes. Then we'll peek into how well the FAA is taking care of the traveling public.

When the Boeing Aircraft Co. first produced the 737, the method of joining the metal covering of the aircraft was with a "cold" bond. The adjacent skin panels were joined longitudinally by overlapping the edge of the upper panel over the lower panel. Prior to this overlapping, the skin was cleaned and an epoxy impregnated "scrim" cloth was placed between the overlap sections. In addition, the panels were joined by three rows of countersunk rivets. This process was performed at room temperature and Boeing used this inferior method for two reasons. Lighter panels could be used and it was considerably cheaper than the preferred hot bond (cured at 250 degrees at 45 psi).

The service history of this cold bonding was not good. The early models of the B-727 and B-747 also were constructed with this technique. One of the reasons for this gluing method was to keep moisture out, but when the glue debonded, it invited moisture to enter the joint and caused dangerous corrosion. This process was discontinued in 1972.

In May of 1970, Boeing issued its first service bulletin concerning "Sealing of Cold Bonded Structure For Corrosion Protection." A service bulletin does not require a mandatory compliance; it is primarily an advisory notice. In October of 1972, it was updated and a revision was reissued in February of 1974, stating that thirty aircraft reported serious debonding or separation. Things really started getting touchy as more and more Boeing customers complained about corrosion. So in August of 1987, the above service bulletin was elevated to an airworthiness directive (AD): compliance in this case was now mandatory. This directive read in part, "(AD) 87-21-08 to prevent rapid depressurization as a result of failure of certain fuselage top splices, accomplish the following ..." (instructions followed). In essence, this means when the 737 was first introduced Boeing charged five million dollars for its airworthy masterpiece. When they found that they made a small mistake gluing it together; they expected the customer to repair the fault.

Since the FAA leaves 95 percent of the certification process up to the manufacturer, Boeing decided that full-scale fatigue testing of the 737 fuselage would not be necessary. Instead, they tested a half fuselage model but tested it to two lifetimes. Two in-flight breakups of the 737 aircraft proved this method of testing to be in error.

Boeing designed the 737 for an "economic service life" of twenty years, to include 75,000 cycles (takeoff and landing), and 51,000 hours. The Aloha aircraft were purchased new in 1969. That put them five years above their useful life. Flight 243 was 14,680 cycles over the maximum and had the second highest number of cycles of any existing 737-200. Aloha's fleet consisted of eleven 737 aircraft. Four of their planes were considered to be high time, in excess of 60,000 cycles; and one of the fleet had the highest time of any 737 in the world.

In August of 1981, a Far Eastern Air Transport Ltd. Boeing 737-200 was cruising at 24,000 feet near Taiwan. A skin panel separated in flight and internal pressure of the cabin caused the plane to disintegrate, hurling 110 people to their deaths. Boeing was glad that this accident did not happen in the United States where it would have been hard to keep a lid on it.

The Aloha accident that occurred six years later was caused by the same faulty construction. Luckily this time, the aircraft held together for a safe landing.

You might wonder why I am discussing accidents that happened many years ago. It's because there are still hundreds of aircraft in service with cold bonded fuselages, and I wanted to give you the proper background history for another potential disaster.

According to Boeing engineers, when the epoxy between the lap joints debonds or separates, the load transfers to the three rows of countersunk rivets that mechanically keep the skin panels together. The countersink for the flush rivet heads traverses the entire thickness of the skin panel. A sharp edge is created at the bottom of the hole where stress could concentrate. The continual flexing of the cabin skin, caused by thousands of pressurization cycles (belly of the aircraft literally moved in and out at each pressurization cycle) ultimately causes disastrous fatigue cracking.

Here is a sample of how well the FAA is watching over the airline maintenance program. In December of 1986, five years after the first disintegration of a Far East 737 and some fifteen months before the Aloha incident, an FAA report concerning cracking was distributed to interested parties. Here is a sample of the report.

"Conclusion at this time the team sees no evidence that any of the aircraft included in the assessment are operating unsafely because of multiple site damage (MSD). It is the judgment of the team that aircraft have been designed to sound damage tolerance principles to ensure safe operation."

Since the FAA only oversees five percent of the aircraft certification process, do they really know?

Following the Aloha incident, the FAA inspection team descended on the airline and inspected the remainder of the fleet. Aircraft number N73712, which had the highest number of cycles of any 737 in the world (over 87,000) was the first to be inspected. What did they find? After a thorough—for a change—corrosion/fatigue inspection it was determined that the aircraft was far beyond economical repair. It was dismantled on the spot and sold for scrap.

The next aircraft, number N73713, had accumulated 83,488 cycles. A seven and one-half-inch crack, in the same area as the Aloha Airlines incident aircraft, was discovered along with other discrepancies. This aircraft also was dismantled on the spot and sold for parts. If these discrepancies continued, Aloha would not have any serviceable aircraft to use on their routes.

The last of the non-airworthy aircraft was number N73717. It had accumulated 68,954 cycles and was parked for over five months awaiting final disposition. It was finally flown to an independent overhaul facility for refurbishment. This aircraft remained out of service for about a year. It was then put up for sale.

It should be understood that the above three aircraft were all in service with little or no discrepancies in the aircraft maintenance logs. Aloha was going to continue to utilize them in scheduled service. Were it not for the Aloha incident, they would probably all still be flying.

How it is possible for any airline to have such substandard maintenance? Airlines are put on the honor system. By that I mean the manufacturer and the FAA both oversee a new carrier when it begins service. After the maintenance manuals and personnel are in place, the airline is supposed to operate on the honor system. It does not look like that system is working.

The FAA is represented by a principal maintenance inspector (PMI) at all the major carriers. His duties, among others, are to provide guidance in development of required maintenance manuals, determine if the air carriers' training complies with the federal air regulations (FAR), and monitor all phases of the air carriers' maintenance.

The smaller carriers can expect infrequent visits from their PMI because of the numerous other carriers and maintenance facilities under their jurisdiction.

The PMI assigned to Aloha Airlines was also in charge of eight other airlines and seven repair stations. His route covered the Pacific basin (Taiwan, Hong Kong, Singapore, the Philippines, and Hawaii). His was an impossible task, but to make matters worse, he was not trained in the maintenance field. He was trained, and worked, as an air carrier inspector. This lack of training in the maintenance fields gave the carriers he was in charge of a great chance to pull the wool over his eyes. I am sure that many of them did.

In September of 1987, seven months before the Aloha incident, Boeing selected 35 airlines they would visit to update them on aging aircraft and corrosion control. Following are some of their suggestions directed to Aloha maintenance department.

1. They recommended that some of their fleet should be grounded. "Put present airplane down for a period of 30 to 60 days and totally strip and upgrade the structure." This was not done.

2. Conduct complete structural inspections on N73712, N73713, N73717 and N73711. This was the aircraft that the roof blew off. This was obviously not done.

3. Conduct a detailed S-4 lap slice inspection on all aircraft over 40,000 flight cycles. This was not done.

When Boeing completed its inspection and discussed its findings with Aloha's management, the FAA's PMI was not allowed to attend that meeting. I wonder why?

The first inspection that a mechanic performs when checking for cracks, damaged rivets, or corrosion is a visual one. At Aloha, he simply gets out there on top of the fuselage and has a safety rope tied to a rafter in case he slips. Most airlines have appropriate scaffolding to accomplish this work. The mechanic is armed with a high-powered magnifying glass and a flashlight. Since the aircraft skin is fastened with thousands of rivets, it is a time-consuming and boring job. If any areas seem suspicious, the mechanic performs a high-frequency eddy current inspection by shooting a current into the skin with a small probe to check for cracks. This method of searching is known as nondestructive testing (NDT) because the mechanic doesn't need to dismantle the section he is working on. The field of NDT is one that requires many weeks of study. At Aloha, their maintenance inspectors received little or no training in this vital subject. In fact, Aloha asked Boeing if they would provide NDT training to their maintenance personnel.

I can speak from experience when it comes to NDT. About three years ago, I completed a two-year aircraft mechanics course. During those two years of intensive study, only two hours was devoted to NDT, and no eddy instruction whatsoever. In fact, some schools do not even have the necessary equipment to teach this all-important subject.

There are four specified times when maintenance people perform their main checks. Below are those times for A, B, C, and D checks. The first column shows the nationwide fleet average; the second column depicts Aloha Airlines that averages over twice the time between their aircraft cycles checks.

	737 FLEET	ALOHA
A Checks	160 cycles	500 cycles
B Checks	630 cycles	2,100 cycles
C Checks	2,970 cycles	8,100 cycles
D Checks	20,500 cycles	40,500 cycles

Not only did Aloha perform their checks half as frequently as the rest of the industry, but also they did so with fewer mechanics than any of the other carriers. The total mechanical force at Aloha was approximately 165, or about 17 technicians per aircraft. The rest of the U.S. carriers average 27 mechanics per aircraft.

Before we get into the main thrust of this chapter, I believe we should review some of the reasons that the Aloha Airlines Boeing 737 nearly killed 94 people.

1. The Boeing 737-200 was not constructed properly.

2. The FAA only oversees five percent of the aircraft's certification process.

3. Aloha Airlines had no engineering office to oversee their maintenance inspectors' work.

4. The FAA PMI was not trained to be a PMI.

5. Aloha's maintenance inspectors were not trained in some of the work they had to certify.

6. The line mechanics were not properly trained.

7. There were no spare aircraft so that the night maintenance crew could complete the work they had started. Every morning those aircraft had better be ready to fly.

8. You could not find a location that produces more corrosion than in the middle of the Pacific Ocean.

Once again, a serious mishap got the attention of the FAA. A month after the Aloha incident, the FAA convened an International Conference on Aging Airplanes. Approximately 400 representatives of manufacturers, airlines, and regulatory authorities from twelve countries participated. The conference made over twenty-six recommendations to the "feds" and the industry. One of their best recommendations was the fact a visual inspection was not the answer. When the manufacturer detects a problem with its fleet, it issued instructions on how to check for the discrepancy, then how to repair it. These directives are usually followed by the airline, but they are not mandatory. If the discrepancy continues and the manufacturer and the FAA deem it necessary, they issue an AD. If this AD is not complied with to the letter, the aircraft must be grounded. If some of the SBs were upgraded to ADs, it would cost the airlines millions. Boeing estimates that it would cost at least $600,000 per aircraft and $800 million for the fleet.

McDonald Douglas estimated repairs would run $269,000 per aircraft, a total of $563 million for the fleet. The conference also recommended that the FAA should conduct more hands-on inspections rather than sifting through aircraft logbooks that might be filled with bogus write-offs.

Even though Eastern Airlines is no longer in existence, they did manage to pull off quite a maintenance coup. A hands-on inspection would have disclosed that one Eastern 727 made over 10,000 flights while not in an airworthy condition. Another 727 flew over 8,900 flights while not in compliance with an identical AD. Eastern also operated for nearly a week, with thirty-seven aircraft on 1,100 flights, without compliance with an AD that required a hands-on inspection for cracks. The "feds" caught Eastern and fined them 9.5 million dollars.

In October of 1989, the industry's second aging conference was held in Baltimore, Maryland. More important issues were brought to light. Over thirty-one percent of the airliners in use exceed the design goals originally set by the manufacturer. Today, sixty-four percent of the worldwide fleet is over twenty years old. The average cost of a new airliner is about $55 million whereas the cost of a major overhaul for a 727 is over $2 million and between $4 and 20 million for a 747.

Following the Aloha incident, there have been several times when fatigue cracks have been detected on other aircraft. A mechanic was walking around a United Airlines Boeing 727 discovered a five-inch crack in a row of rivets in a lap joint. Closer examination revealed that the crack extended for nineteen inches. This particular lap joint was of the cold-bonded variety similar to Aloha's. This time, the FAA issued an AD, not one of those "good old boy" service bulletins.

The FAA aircraft inspector is given a free hand as to how and when he inspects airliners. The inspector might decide to check for completed ADs or for non-AD-related items. The FAA does not know the extent of compliance with ADs. This should be brought to a halt. If there is one thing the FAA should want to know, it is how many of their directives have been carried out by the airlines. Since the FAA issues approximately 200 ADs every year, you would think they would be most interested in just how many of their directives are properly accomplished.

Every week, the FAA prints an eighty-page booklet that lists approximately five hundred airline maintenance discrepancies. It is known as the Service Difficulty Report (SDR). It is an excellent means of checking maintenance trends on different aircraft. Each week, every airliner in the

U.S. is listed as to type of equipment and the discrepancy that it encountered. The yearly listing is approximately 19,000. While the FAA has been printing these reports for over two decades, it fails to use this valuable tool to enhance safety. Because of insufficient staffing and data quality problems, this excellent system is not consulted for maintenance trends. Since about 1,400 of the 4,100 large airliners registered in the U.S. are considered to be "aging aircraft," any publication that could aid in keeping them safely flying should be thoroughly examined. According to an FAA official concerning SDR reports:

1. "The system's products are untimely." They most certainly are timely issued weekly.

2. "Contain too much unnecessary information." Each discrepancy is followed by a very short paragraph.

3. "Lack enough detail to be useful." Each discrepancy is written so that you know exactly what the problem is. If more information is needed, the FAA knows which airline to contact.

I have been receiving the SDR for about six months, and what do you suppose the dominating discrepancy of all airlines is? Cracks and corrosion. The time limit for the airlines to repair their aging fleet was four years, starting in 1990. As of 1994, the clock ran out.

The FAA mandatory structural ADs are the single most expensive item with which the airlines have ever had to cope. The total cost for all the airlines to restructure their aircraft is in the neighborhood of $2 to 3 billion dollars. Just the cost of pulling an aircraft out of service could be from $25 to $100,000 per day, depending on the aircraft type and usage.

Not only were the airlines confronted with massive maintenance; they also had to decide what to do concerning the stage three noise standards by December 31, 1999. There have been so many complaints about jet noise, the FAA demanded that the airlines put hush kits on their engines, or replace them with newer and quieter power plants. It could cost between $2 and $8 million per aircraft to convert to the quieter power plants.

There are three major drawbacks to refurbishing the aging airline fleet.

1. A scarcity of hanger space
2. Insufficient qualified maintenance technicians
3. A scarcity of parts

The lack of parts is the biggest drawback.

In April of 1991, only 28 aircraft out of 1,300 had completed renovation. The requirement for another 705 was partially met and the 1994 deadline was not met. Carriers typically order parts for scheduled maintenance just prior to the repair date. But some manufacturers may require as much as two years' notice. Parts are so scarce that some of the suppliers are rationing their kits, making them available for a few selected aircraft. Boeing and Douglas are only supplying kits to airlines that are in need of them in order to fly.

New hangar space also will have to be constructed. A 75,000 square foot building, large enough to house a 747, recently cost $6 million. And graduates from aircraft mechanic schools will require at least two years of on-the-job training before they are of any use to the airline.

Here is a list from the GAO of the average age of the aircraft in service for nine of the major air carriers.

	AVERAGE AGE IN YEARS	PERCENTAGE OF FLEET 20 YEARS OR OLDER
TRANS WORLD	17.06	43
NORTHWEST	15.88	43
CONTINENTAL	14.05	28
U.S. FLEET	13.92	34
FED EX	12.17	29
UNITED	11.96	24
USAir	9.64	16
AMERICAN	9.59	15
DELTA	8.79	6

The FAA, so far, has no definitive means of tracking airliners that must be repaired to comply with the aging aircraft ADs. The FAA said that their aging aircraft ADs must be complied with before 1994 or they would start grounding the faulty aircraft. Since the FAA has a two-fold existence, to regulate and promote aviation, this has recently been modified. I still wouldn't hold my breath waiting for the groundings to take place.

CHAPTER 6

▼

THE INSPECTORS

Unfortunately, for the airline passenger, airlines are on the honor system. That is, they are supposed to police themselves. As of 1994, there were approximately 2,600 aviation inspectors, not nearly enough to oversee the more than 6,500 commercial airliners, 4,439 repair stations, 547 pilot schools, 177 mechanics' schools, 641,477 current pilots, and 274,884 general aviation aircraft.

The GAO aviation safety report dated March 1992 did a great job of pointing out the inadequacies of the FAA inspection system.

Every large scheduled carrier has at least three FAA inspectors assigned to their main base of operation. They oversee avionics (electronics, radio, radar, etc.) airworthiness, (airframes and power plants) and operations (pilot proficiency). All of these FAA inspectors are supposed to be extremely knowledgeable in their chosen field. The FAA has a school in Oklahoma City to keep these inspectors up to date; unfortunately, the FAA finds it very difficult to entice qualified instructors to teach the various courses. If you are a new inspector, you might attend a good course and then again, you might not.

Before you become an inspector, your qualifications must be top drawer, and you should have many years or hours at your trade. Pilots must have a specified number of hours and ratings before they are accepted. When an

FAA pilot is assigned to an air carrier, he or she must attend the carriers captain's checkout school, both ground and simulator, before being allowed to oversee the line pilots. The GAO report stated: "Our analysis of inspector training showed that 63 percent, or 495 of the 786 operations inspectors assigned to flight-check duties, had not received recurrent flight training during the six month period ending December 31, 1988. However, FAA often waved this training requirement, and many inspectors continued to make flight checks even though they were not fully qualified to do so."

If an air carrier captain is caught flying the line without receiving recurrent flight training at prescribed intervals (approximately every six months), the carrier and the captain both could lose their licenses. Yet it is all right for an unqualified inspector to check pilots, even though his experience is usually about one-fourth that of the person being checked.

The GAO report continues: "In some cases, the region found that inspectors held ratings for aircraft types that no longer operated in their district. Other cases were found where inspectors had received training during the past six months for aircraft on which they had not performed any flight checks during the past year."

The FAA requested that their academy in Oklahoma City develop six new training courses in avionics (electronics). The academy fell short on instructors with the result that only three new courses were developed. In addition, the inadequate number of qualified instructors caused the cancellation of over 70 percent of the planned avionics courses.

There are certain prescribed inspections that the avionics and airworthiness inspectors must perform annually. They must check operations, avionics, and airworthiness at least once each year per carrier. In fiscal year 1990, 36 percent received no check at all. When we talk about maintenance checks, you might picture an inspector up on a scaffold checking a tail, or perhaps moving panels to have a look inside. You are looking at the wrong picture. Inspectors do not get their hands soiled. What they do check is maintenance logbooks and may be getting only half the story.

When a pilot or mechanic finds a discrepancy, it is written up in the aircraft log. If it is an airworthy item, it must be signed off by an A&P mechanic before the aircraft can be flown. However, there are unscrupulous supervisors who will sign off discrepancies, whether or not the item was properly repaired. So what are FAA inspectors checking? Mainly to see if the logbook write-ups have been signed off. Well! The sign-off might be in the book, but the only way to be sure it was a real fix, and not one on paper, is to go and physically check the aircraft.

In 1990 the airlines were allowed a voluntary disclosure program that extended amnesty for penalties if the airline reported and corrected their own violations. The carriers thought it would be a lot cheaper to fix their mistakes rather than be fined by the FAA. Now the "feds" can levy fines ranging from $1,000 to $10,000 per occurrence.

The March of 1992, GAO report stated that numerous airlines voluntarily disclosed their own violations. Here are a few of them.

"Two Boeing 737s operated with overdue airworthiness inspections.

Cabin door evacuation slide overdue for overhaul by sixty-seven days.

Three Boeing 757s operated for 1,437 hours without required cable inspections.

Incorrect maintenance procedures, leading to over torqued bolts on 11 DC-9 aircraft.

Aircraft operated for 18 days with emergency slide deactivated.

Aircraft continued in service while failing to comply with an AD.

Crew of 19 pilots used on 272 flights without completing required recurrent training.

Wheel chock left in aircraft landing gear causing diversion of flight.

Two aircraft operated for eight months with non-airworthy elevator spar.

One crewmember used on 17 flights with a lapsed flight engineer proficiency check.

And last, but not least (Author's statement), A DC-10 aircraft operated for 292 flights with a blanket and seat cushion in the fuel tank."

The airlines were running scared. If the "feds" caught these discrepancies, the fines could be in the thousands, so they confessed to a few of their malpractices. An FAA review of 56 voluntary disclosures report showed that 93 percent were maintenance problems and seven percent were concerned with flight operations. Nearly all of the reports came from large airlines. Does it look like they are policing themselves, or running scared?

The FAA is finally entering some of the air carrier discrepancies into a computer. However, they must be using an old one that is cheap, outdated, and totally useless.

They have little or no training in computer programming with the result they have no idea how to follow-up when unsatisfactory conditions are identified. The "feds" have little idea what their inspectors are looking for, and have no way of knowing if they ever follow up on their identified discrepancies. In fiscal year 1990, inspectors discovered 9,115 problems that were, or had the potential to be, in noncompliance with a federal air regulation (FAR). The "feds" did not know how many of the 9,115 problems were corrected because inspectors were not required to account for the disposition of the discrepancies they had uncovered. What a way to run a company!

Because of an overweight takeoff, Alaska's Ryan Air Service crashed and killed eighteen people. Were the FAA, principal operations inspectors (POI), and regional council aware of this violation? You bet they were. Whistleblowers at the airline advised them of the dangerous violations; all they wanted to do was sweep it under the rug. FAA inspectors were so concerned about the airworthiness of Ryan Air that they refused to fly on them, yet they allowed ticketed passengers to fly on these aircraft. What are you and I paying these people for?

There were over 185 separate maintenance violations discovered on all ten of the carriers' aircraft, yet it took weeks before the "feds" finally grounded the fleet. The FAA initially fined Ryan $250,000 in civil penalties. Then it was reduced to $25,999, next to $16,500, and finally the penalty was waived under a consent order between Ryan and the FAA.

There was a congressional hearing concerning the crashes in Alaska. Honorable James L. Oberstar, Former Chairman of the Subcommittee, was right on the money when he stated. "That is just astonishing. It is as though this regional counsel was in cahoots with Ryan Air to protect them and keep them flying at all costs."

The "Chicago Convention"

In 1944, representatives from fifty-two countries convened in Chicago to create a framework for international cooperation regarding civil aviation. They created the International Civil Aviation Organization (ICAO) to look into such fields as security, environment protection, communications, meteorology, and airworthiness. As of September 1992, 173 different countries had signed up to uphold the "Chicago Convention." Keeping all those countries happy was a very ticklish situation. When foreign air carriers enter the United States, they must meet or exceed the existing FARs. Likewise, U.S. carriers must qualify with foreign standards before they are permitted to land on foreign soil.

Only 2 percent of the 2,600 inspectors must determine the airworthiness of all foreign airliners, another nearly impossible FAA task. It is estimated that about 300 carriers from 94 different countries were permitted to fly into the U.S. about 900 times a day.

Three different cases involving three different aircraft from three different carriers concerning corrosion and cracks. The "feds" tried to remove these aircraft from service, but made no attempts to check other planes operated by the same carrier. A quote from a 1992 GAO report describes the kid gloves necessary in these cases.

"FAA advises its inspectors to use tact and diplomacy when inspecting foreign carriers due to the sensitivities involved in foreign relations."

In January, 1992, the Canadian Transport Ministry suspended the operation of Transport Aereas Ejectivos (TAESA) Boeing 727 aircraft because they were "being operated in such a manner that an immediate threat to safety exists."

Between February and April 1992, TAESA flights experienced four safety problems.

1. At a NY airport, they hit a passenger walkway.

2. The crew failed to follow ATC instructions and lost normal separation with head-on traffic.

3. At a NY airport, nearly ran out of runway while making a takeoff.

4. Nearly hit the trees after liftoff.

In April of 1992, the Canadians suspended all operations of TAESA because they neglected to repair previous deficiencies.

In January of 1992, the Canadian government notified the FAA concerning TAESA faulty 727 aircraft. The "feds" contacted its Dallas/Fort Worth Flight Standards District Office, the primary office responsible for this Mexican carrier. TAESA continued to fly into Pittsburgh, Seattle, Cleveland, Las Vegas, and New York.

The "feds" Dallas/Fort Worth office should have alerted other FAA offices throughout America, but it took two and a half months after the initial Canadian suspensions.

Between January and May, the "feds" identified eighteen safety-related problems on TAESA. Between January and April of 1992, TAESA invited both the FAA and the Canadian inspectors to fly with them to observe their operation. The Canadians accepted, the "feds" declined. They said that route checks should be performed by the Mexican government.

The Canadians have forbidden TAESA to fly into Canada, but the U.S. still permits their dangerous operations.

A few years ago I spotted a good article in the San Jose Mercury News. It seems that an FAA plane crashed and the "feds" found 409 FAR violations. Here are just a few.

1. Unmarked parts.

2. Incomplete and outdated manuals.

3. Pilots flying with expired licenses.

4. Deferred mandatory pilot training.

I wonder what fines the "fed" levied on itself?

CHAPTER 7

▼

AMATEUR EXPERTS

Let's blame the crew; they are all dead. Far too often, the NTSB team keeps this theme in mind when they are sifting through the ashes of a downed airliner. Well over one-half the air carrier accidents are attributed to the ever-famous "pilot error," and the National Transportation Safety Board uses this phrase in the majority of their accident reports. Aircrews can be most thankful that the Air Line Pilots Association is in their corner and that they are relentless in their quest to bring out the true facts of an airline disaster.

The NTSB has a dual role under the 1966 statute that created it, and the act that conferred its complete independence in 1974. It is not only the federal government's transportation accident investigator; it is also a federal "watchdog" of all transportation safety. The safety board has the difficult task of investigating nearly all accidents that occur in civil aviation, marine, rail, pipeline and highway. The NTSB is also the Supreme Court for deciding the fate of airmen's certificate action.

The NTSB is located in the Department of Transportation building in Washington, D.C., but it functions as a completely autonomous agency. The board must not only determine the cause of an accident, but also must formulate safety improvement recommendations. The board investigates all air carrier accidents, mid airs, and general aviation crashes that involve at least one fatality. All other aviation accidents may be assigned to the FAA.

Due to government cutbacks, the board has shrunk from 401 employees to 325. There are eleven small field offices around the country but the main one is in Washington, D.C.

The board is unique in several ways. First, the safety recommendations that the board suggests are not mandatory. The board has no power to demand regulations changes. They can only recommend. Second, the board must make public all of its recommendations. This is their big stick to shame the offenders into proper safety procedures. Enforcing new regulations is the job of the lip service FAA.

When an accident is reported, the board is ready within a few hours to send members to the disaster site. Most members carry a "beeper" when they are out of the office so that they can be contacted around the clock. The go-team members do not keep a suitcase packed because they don't know if they will be investigating a crash in the snow or in sunny Florida. They do, however, keep an oversized briefcase ready with the tools of the trade: a camera, notebook, magnifying glass, tape recorder, and a flashlight, just a few of the necessary items. Depending on the person's specialty, he or she also will carry a set of wrenches, range finder, transit, and pocket-sized compass.

Team members are assigned from Monday at 1701 hours to the following Monday at 1700 hours. The team's mode of travel to the accident site is by the most rapid method, usually aboard a government aircraft or in the jump seat of an airliner. The specialty team consists of about 10 aviation experts (supposedly). Some of these specialties include meteorologists, air traffic controllers, power plant engineers, structures (airframe), systems (instruments, electrical, hydraulic), human factors (survivability, injury causes), and operations (history of flight). One member of the five-man board is in charge of the total operation.

Once the team members reach, the scene, they become the head of a cooperative investigative effort three or four times larger than the go-team itself. The FAA, ALPA, Flight Attendants Union, Flight Engineers Union, Flight Dispatcher Association, Air Traffic Controller Union, and the manufacturer of the aircraft and its engines are all represented. An organizational meeting will form "working groups," each for a specific area and each headed by a specialist from the board. These groups may stay in the accident area for as little as a few days to as much as three weeks, depending on accident circumstances.

One of the greatest assets to solving the cause of an accident is the two famous "black boxes;" in reality they are orange. The aircraft's flight recorder, encased in a tough protective outer shell, relates all parameters that the aircraft was subjected to prior to the crash. A thick aluminum foil strip records the plane's airspeed, vertical speed, altitude, heading, and "G" forces. The time for all of the above movements having occurred is also accurately recorded. Newer FRs record over 100 parameters.

The other black box is known as the cockpit voice recorder. This name is really not quite correct. I believe it should be called a sound recorder because it records all sounds, whistles, bells, beeps, and the like, as well as all transmissions over the radio, intercom, public address system and all normal conversation on the flight deck.

If the aircraft wreckage is scattered, the structures group's initial action is to locate as many sections as possible and plot their precise position on a wreckage distribution sheet. The airframe experts may reconstruct the various pieces of wreckage in a full mock-up. This may range in complexity from a loose layout of several broken parts to a complex reassembly of all the available pieces wired in position to a full size framework of timber and chicken wire.

When the go-team returns to Washington, each specialty team writes its report and submits it to the board for approval. Far too often, the safety board members request that changes be made concerning technical matters where they have little or no expertise. In this way, they can and do control the outcome of the probable cause that takes between 8 and 12 months to compile.

The board submits hundreds of safety recommendations to the FAA for their approval. Most of their requests are well done and deserve to be considered by the feds. However, their methods for arriving at the probable cause of an accident leave much to be desired.

When I flew for Mohawk Airlines, one of our BAC 1-11s crashed in Pennsylvania. A good friend of mine was on the investigating team representing the Air Line Pilots Association. He told me that when they examined the electronics gear at the accident site, the engineer from the NTSB did not even know the basic difference between a communications receiver and a navigational black box.

I have been told of one case in which an NTSB engineer, when writing up the fatal crash of a Cessna, literally sat down with the Cessna factory representative and completed the accident report form in accordance with the Cessna representative's suggestions.

Aviation Consumer magazine recently had a most interesting article about "Chuck" Miller who previously was director of the NTSB's Bureau of Aviation Safety. He is presently a top-notch air safety consultant. Miller relates: "Talk about evidence being lost. Remember that Air Illinois crash a couple of years ago where both generators go out and the guy lost electrical power and crashed in bad weather? There was a switching device in the electrical box, and there was a question whether it had operated correctly. Well, the switching unit disappeared. The NTSB called in outside police because they thought it had been stolen. Well, a few months ago they found the switching device under somebody's desk back at NTSB headquarters."

Miller continues: "There was an MV-2 crash in Ypsilanti, Michigan, four or five years ago that's a classic example where the NTSB's work wasn't done accurately and the FAA's work compounded the felony, so to speak. A couple of guys were coming in at night, both corporate pilots, lots of hours, but relatively new to the MV-2. Everything was fine until they hit 250 feet. The guy in the left seat says he doesn't see anything and is going around. He has been having trouble with the yoke mounted autopilot cut-off. He tells the co-pilot to cut the autopilot on the panel. Meanwhile, the pilot advances the throttles and pulls back on the wheel. From our own investigation, I believe they didn't get the autopilot off when they expected so when he pulled back on the yoke the trim went full down because the autopilot was still trying to compensate. Neither pilot knows exactly what happened after that but a few seconds later they hit the ground. Miraculously, both of them lived. In the course of the NTSB investigation, the autopilot was never looked at. This was at a time when there was a rush of MV-2 accidents. The aircraft handbooks hardly addressed the autopilot/trim issue at all. So a guy could be trained in the airplane, fly it normally, and never have this point driven home."

Miller also states: "These are the kinds of things we ran into that were never brought up by the NTSB. Now, this case was so flagrant that I came back and pointed it out to some people at the board. They told me the FAA was doing a certification review of the MV-2 based on their earlier recommendations and I should wait and see how they come out. Well, a year or so went by and the FAA finally says that the aircraft was properly certified, and that's as far as it went."

"I couldn't believe it," Miller stated. "When the engines are recovered from the crash site, where do you suppose they are shipped for tear-down and analysis? They go to the power plant manufacturer and their disassembly is seldom watched by a board engineer who probably would not understand what he was looking at anyway."

It will be a cold day in hell before a manufacturer admits to a faulty part or anything that would cast a shadow of doubt on their company. Wouldn't the insurance companies have a field day if the engine manufacturer were to admit any faults in his product?

My best friend, Captain Raymond Hourihan, crashed in mountainous terrain shooting a nonprecision approach. For a full week prior to the crash, Captain Hourihan's aircraft had been written up daily for faulty navigation equipment. The board said that these problems "did not constitute a trend."

The president of ALPA sent a critique to the chairman of the NTSB and requested a meeting to discuss the above tragedy. One of the statements that the chairman of the safety board made in his answer to ALPA was quite a shocker: "In conclusion, it is not essential whether we are precisely correct in the analysis of the facts, or the ultimate determination of cause, but that we have stated all the facts fairly, fully, and accurately and that the ultimate conclusions are reasonable and supported by the facts."

A senior captain at TWA, Vernon W. Lowell, who also wrote a fine book entitled Airline Safety is a Myth, was so disturbed by the board's antics that he was prompted to write a personal letter to the chairman of the NTSB concerning the crash of a TWA 880.

A TWA jetliner was making an instrument approach and crashed just short of the runway killing all on-board. For weeks prior to the accident, the airline was in the process of modifying the aircraft's pitot static system. This could directly affect the altimeter reading as well as a few other vital instruments.

This most pertinent fact was disregarded, and the usual pilot error was their answer. Several days prior to the public hearing concerning this crash, another TWA jet descended too low and flew through some electrical wires near O'Hare. The crew landed safely, but the incident was similar. The board would not allow any discussion concerning the second incident, even though it was nearly identical to the crash that they were presently investigating.

Following are some statements from Captain Lowell's letter to the NTSB:

"The board disbelieved and discounted a report by the airline (TWA) which stated that the information the pilots were seeing on their instrument panel was not what the aircraft was actually doing. Why should the board discard this expertise?"

The board stated in their report that "The cockpit crew conversations reflected a relaxed atmosphere in the cockpit until the last few seconds prior to impact."

I have seen this statement many times in the hundreds of reports I have read, and believe me, it only shows the complete lack of knowledge that the board has concerning airline cockpit management. Because of their lack of experience in airline operation, the board made another faux pas in their probable cause.

A Pacific Southwest Airliner collided with a Cessna 150 while approaching San Diego, California. It was one of the worst mid-airs to date and brought about some improved safety regulations. The usual probable cause was pilot error.

This is far from the truth. The captain on PSA was issued traffic at 12 o'clock. He looked out and saw a plane in that vicinity and stated that he had the traffic in sight. However, there were two aircraft at 12 o'clock and the one he had in sight was not the critical aircraft. There was another one directly below him that caused the collision. The tower made no mention of there being two aircraft in the same general vicinity. The tower was equipped with a low-level repeater radar called a "Brite" display. There wasn't one controller at Lindbergh Field who was qualified to use this unit. None of them had formal training on the use of radar equipment, but they were using it daily to separate traffic.

The board was aware of the untrained radar controllers, but their lack of knowledge of how the air traffic control system operates led them to label this accident pilot error.

A similar accident happened in Certitas, California, in August of 1986. An Aernoves De Mexico DC-9 was hit by a tiny Piper aircraft, and a total of 60 people died. This time the airline crew was not blamed but rather the all too faulty air traffic control system. This is one of the few times that the board blamed the FAA, something they don't do often enough. This same probable cause should have been recorded for the San Diego crash.

The Air Florida crash at Washington National in the District of Columbia was another of the board's bad calls. While I do agree that the captain was at fault, the board saw no problem with the following:

Aircraft on approach are supposed to be separated by three miles as long as they are outside the outer fix. The Air Florida was still on the take-off roll while an Eastern 727 was landing on the same runway. The local control position (tower) was in the hands of a supervisor. These people lost the feel of controlling aircraft years ago. These factors and more were definitely contributing to the cause of the accident, but they weren't even mentioned.

On September 11, 1974, an Eastern Airlines Douglas DC-9 crashed at the Charlotte Airport, North Carolina. Seventy-one people died and as usual, the crew was blamed. "The NTSB determines that the probable cause of the accident was the flight crew's lack of altitude awareness at critical points during the approach due to poor cockpit discipline in that the crew did not follow prescribed procedures."

Because of airport construction, the crew did not have the luxury of a precision approach that left them without a glide slope to follow. The approach lighting system was also inoperative. The board was correct when they said that the crew should have been more alert concerning their altitude, but when it comes to crewmembers who dare to converse about something other than checklists, they are way off base.

It is obvious that none of the board members knows anything about what goes on in an airliner cockpit. Most pilots have many thousands of hours, and shooting an instrument approach, even down to limits, is no "big deal." If the board had been witness to the things I used to discuss with my co-pilot, they would all have seizures. Time and again, I see the words in their reports concerning laxness in the cockpit. Up to a point, this is the only way to fly. A RELAXED COCKPIT IS A SAFE COCKPIT. There is no need to get up tight on an approach, and a crewmember with sweaty palms is the sign of a nervous, insecure pilot.

After the crash, the board plays the tape recording from the cockpit voice recorder. This tape only records oral signals, so there is no way of knowing precisely what transpired on the flight deck. This guessing game is compounded by a vital point that is seldom considered: humans often combine their voice with body language such as hand signals or facial expressions. All the board knows is what it hears on the tape. Most airlines require a command and response to the myriad of checklist items. It is written in the airlines operational manual that the pilot not flying reads off the various commands on the checklist, and he must receive a response to each item from the pilot who is flying.

Most airlines are shifting to aircraft that can be operated with a crew of two rather than having the safety of a flight engineer on board. Many times, the three-man crew has their hands full. With a crew of two, it could be close to "impossible." One way that pilots free themselves of responding to the checklist is by allowing their co-pilot to run the silent list and complete each item himself.

At US AIR, I was the number one captain on my equipment at my base in Washington, D.C. I flew the best trips, which meant I flew with the most senior, experienced co-pilots. I flew with one pilot for over three years. He had 15,000 hours and was highly capable. There was no reason not to trust him, so we ran a silent checklist.

What do you suppose the board would think if they failed to hear the command and response if they had to play my tapes? Being unfamiliar with the ways of the airline, they would immediately brand the crew as not following the prescribed procedures. So the failure to hear the checklist chatter on the tape could have little or no bearing on the fact that the checklist was, in fact, completed in total.

There are also numerous hand signals that are legal, in fact, are part of the required procedures. For instance, after takeoff before the wheels are retracted, the pilot flying gives a verbal "gear-up" to coincide with a thumbs-up signal. Now, if the captain only gives the visual thumbs-up signal, the gear is raised just the same, but the recorder would fail to register this vital response.

The same is true of landing crews working out various hand signals to lower the flaps. A captain may hold up one finger signifying to the co-pilot that he wants the first notch of flaps. Two fingers mean the second notch, and so on. None of these flap commands are recorded because they are silent, but the flaps are lowered just the same.

Another hand signal used extensively when taxiing is the thumbs-up gesture. Before a captain makes a turn, or perhaps is warned about having wing-tip clearance, he looks out his side for clearance, then calls to his co-pilot, "Clear, left?" The co-pilot usually simply signals back with a thumbs-up, and he may or may not announce the clear signal verbally.

Can't you just see the shocked look on the face of the board as they play the tape back after a ground mishap? "Well, Charlie, you can plainly hear the captain ask, 'clear, right?' but there is no response from the co-pilot."

When flying in a crowded terminal area, it is a godsend to be able to look out for conflicting traffic. Yet this is the very time that the checklist is used the most. It is a prudent pilot who allows his experienced co-pilot to run the list while he keeps a vigil out the window.

While a pilot is one of the few individuals required to listen to two radios (ATC and Company) at the same time, he is also expected to keep himself clear of conflicting traffic while both the pilots have their heads in the cockpit. In this day of electronic marvels, it is the crew's job to visually keep clear of other aircraft. In practically every report concerning mid-air collisions, the crew is blamed for not keeping a proper vigil outside, a difficult task when your attention is being utilized inside the plane. While the co-pilot is busy reading a list, and the captain is responding by pushing various knobs in the cockpit, no one is looking out the window; this could be the very time your day is ruined by having two planes meeting in mid-air. Perhaps the board would rather see some cross-eyed pilot up front; then there could be an eye in the cockpit while the other is scanning outside.

On August 2, 1985, Delta Airlines Flight 191, a Lockheed wide-bodied L-1011, crashed while approaching the Dallas/Forth Worth International Airport in Texas. This tragic crash took the lives of 163 people on board and two on the ground. The NTSB said that the crew should not have flown into a dangerous microburst. Once again, pilot error. I hope that after reading the following you will agree with me the crew was killed because of the inadequacies of the so-called safest system in the world. First, however, the probable cause of the accident:

"The National Transportation Safety Board determined that the probable cause of the accident was the flight crew's decision to initiate and continue the approach into a cumulonimbus cloud which they observed to contain visible lightning." They also stated that the lack of knowledge concerning wind shear was a contributing factor. Nevertheless, it was mainly the crew's fault. I hope that what you are about to read will shed some more light into the antics of the board.

Let's take a look at the experience of the crew. Delta is one of the finest airlines in the country and their crews are highly experienced. It's the system that is at fault, certainly not this valiant crew.

Captain Edward N. Connors, age 57, began flying for Delta in 1954. He had a total of 29,300 hours in the air, 3,000 of which were in the Lockheed L-1011. First Officer Rudolph P. Price, Jr., age 42, was employed by Delta on February 13, 1970. His log total was 6,500 hours, 1200 of which were in the L-1011. Second Officer Flight Engineer N. Nassick, age 43, began flying for Delta on October 19, 1976. His total flying time of 6,500 hours was mostly at the engineer's panel of the L-1011. All members were highly skilled, competent men. I hope to prove that even experienced crews can be killed in a very dangerous system.

Since this accident was directly attributed to horrendous weather, let's examine the weather forecast that was presented to the crew. Or perhaps the lack of information would be more apropos.

The 1600 National Weather Service (NWS) chart showed a weak stationary front about 60 miles north of the DFW Airport with "a slight chance of a thunderstorm. There were no CIGMET (weather warnings to the safety of all aircraft) in effect at this time. The weather report received by the crew was often relayed to them after they were already in trouble. In this case, there were four different weather facilities involved and among them all, the crew never got the word.

Delta Airlines' main offices are at Atlanta Hartsfield Airport in Atlanta, Georgia. Their weather department is staffed with 14 meteorologists. The man in charge of this Delta flight stated: "At the time of the accident, I would have placed these cells still some distance northeast of DFW. I was surprised when it became obvious the accident was thunderstorm related."

The weather radar station at Stephenville, which supplies weather information for the Dallas area, is located 72 miles from the DFW airport. The radar specialist on duty testified that he left his position at 1735 for dinner. At 1800 (the accident occurred at 1805:52), the specialist returned to his scope and detected a small cell that was barely a "pinpoint four."

Storm echoes are given various levels. 1 is the weakest, 6 is the strongest. This storm was in the vicinity of the airport, but he could not state a precise distance because there was no overlay to determine the location of the various airports. This weather station was primarily concerned with issuing information to the public via TV and radio; aviation weather was a sideline. What else is new?

At 1804 the specialist called the Fort Worth Forecast Office and advised of a strong echo with tops of 40,000 feet. The Fort Worth National Forecast Office serves the general public as well as the aviation community. The forecaster in charge at this time was also manning the aviation desk. He testified that no special training "with regard to aviation" was required before his assignment to the aviation desk.

This is a very sad state of affairs. Aviation weather is an exacting science, and a person not familiar with aviation and its myriad of weather requirements has no business working with pilots, especially at one of the busiest airports in the world. You might be wondering why in the world they didn't have a weather forecaster at the airport. Well, they did, but this office at DFW Airport is even a bigger joke than the downtown NWS office.

Surface weather observations at the airport are conducted by a contract weather person who has gone through a "quickie" course at the NWS. The airport weather observer's office is located on the second floor of the Delta maintenance hanger. From his office, only 50 percent of the sky is visible. Therefore, he had to go to the hanger roof or out on the ramp to observe the sky from the north through east. What a great place to put a weather observer. Since the control tower has a 360 degrees view of the sky, our weather observer often relies on reports from the control tower. Believe me, when the traffic rush is on, controllers don't have time to tell the paid weather observer what's happening on the north side of the airport, the very place that the crash took place.

At 1751, the airport forecaster transmitted the following via his electrowriter (an instrument that sends copies of the airport weather to various offices at the field). The weather system was developing so rapidly that he put out a special: "Thunderstorm began 1802, NNW and overhead moving slowly south, occasional lightning cloud to cloud, rain showers unknown intensity NNE, towering cumulus, NE-SW. Wind 070 degrees at 8 knots. Fifty-two seconds after this special was issued, the crew of the jumbo Delta still had not received notification regarding the intensity of the storm. They were a scant 52 seconds from another FAA-induced "smoking hole."

There were numerous aircraft on the ground witnessing one of nature's most destructive forces. Two captains reported seeing funnel-type structures inside the rainfall.

At 1803:32, one of the captains of a taxiing aircraft stated: "There was a tubular area between the sheets that I think, lead me to believe it was a tornado."

Another captain who was approaching DFW airport said that his radar was pointing a huge cell at the airport. He compared the rapid development of this call to "an atomic bomb explosion filmed in slow motion." The energy inside this treacherous piece of air had the potential for destruction that would make an atomic bomb seem like a minor explosion.

It is an FAA regulation that any crewmember observing weather that could be potentially dangerous to an aircraft must transmit their findings to an air traffic controller so that it may be broadcast for all to hear. Not one pilot even lifted his microphone.

The weather radar on the Delta jet was a Bendix model RFR-1F mono-chromatic system. When a storm is surveyed at a range of closer than two miles, the cell's radar return gradually disappears at the bottom of the scope. Also, when an aircraft is pointed down, as was the case on final approach, the screen picks up ground clutter that could completely eliminate any storm cells on the screen. Captain Connors was using his radar en route and he seemed to have a few complaints concerning its operation. Even though the aircraft log showed seven write-ups concerning the radar between June 6th and July 25, 1985, the last write-up was corrected seven days before the fateful flight. Electronic devices have a way of malfunctioning rapidly. It is quite possible that the radar was not used during this period and there is a possibility that it may not have been contouring (depicting bad storm areas) as it should, even though it functioned displaying relatively smooth areas.

While the operation of a radar set is quite simple, the only formal training given by airlines is an instruction book written by the manufac-turer and distributed to each crewmember. There is no formal hands-on training as there should be. The Ground School Manager at Delta had this to say regarding the operation of airborne radar: "It's largely something that has to be learned by experience."

Captain Connors was using the radar en route to the airport. It was picking up cells and he asked the air traffic controller for steers to avoid them. He was doing the safe thing even though it would make the flight longer.

At 1735:36, the crew of Delta 191 received the following ATIS Romeo (a broadcast from a facility at or near the airport that gives pertinent airport and weather information): "Listen DFW arrival information Romeo, two one four seven Greenwich, weather six thousand scattered, two one thousand scattered, visibility one zero, temperature one zero one, dew point six seven, wind calm, altimeter two nine niner two, Runway one eight right, one seven left, visual approaches in progress, advise approach control that you have Romeo."

The weather was VFR and there was no mention of a thunderstorm being at or near the airport.

At 1756:28, the DFW approach controller stated: "Attention, all aircraft listening except for Delta twelve ninety one is going to go across the airport; there is a little rain shower just north of the airport."

This transmission was the only call that the crew of Delta 191 received from the air traffic controller regarding weather. There was no mention of the boiling block of air that was out there waiting to cause headlines.

At 1804:18 (one minute and 5 seconds before impact) First Officer Price said "Lightning coming out of that one."

Captain Connors: "What?"

First Officer: "Lightning coming out of that one."

Captain: "Where?"

First Officer: "Right ahead of us."

This is the first statement made by the crew concerning weather while on final approach. It is nearly impossible to define the correct distance between you and a flash of lightning, especially when traversing a torrential downpour. I believe that you will have to agree that there has been a lot of discussion concerning the weather, but none of the pertinent weather facts ever reached the radio speakers of the Delta 191 cockpit.

On page 79 of the NTSB report; the board's conclusions concerning the accident, paragraph 18 stated that "The flight crew and the captain had sufficient information to assess the weather north of the approach end of Runway 17L. The lightning observed and reported by the first officer was adequate, combined with the other data (what other data? author) known to the flight crew and captain, to determine that there was a thunderstorm between the airplane and the airport."

The board, in their infinite wisdom concerning the cause of the accident, has already stated in part: "The probable cause of the accident was the flight crew's decision to initiate and continue the approach into a cumulonimbus cloud."

Page 64, paragraph 4, has an interesting statement concerning the latest Automated Terminal Information Service (ATIS) Sierra broadcast which should have contained vital information concerning the cumulonimbus (thunderstorm): "Given the timing of ATIS Sierra, Flight 191 never received Sierra; therefore, the Safety Board concludes that the omission of the cumulonimbus and towering cumulus from the message played no part in causing the accident." By the time Sierra was issued, Flight 191 was on a downwind leg for Runway 17L."

ATIS is a tape played continuously over a specified radio frequency. It contains pertinent pilot information concerning the weather, runway in use, altimeter setting, wind, and so forth. It has a maximum playing time of 30 seconds and it is updated whenever new information is required. When the weather conditions are potentially crucial, there is a special section used on the tape called "other pertinent remarks."

The weather office at DFW finally got around to the fact that there was a horrendous thunderstorm on the final approach, with tops to 40,000 feet thunderstorms with boiling clouds and vertical winds powerful enough to crush a giant airliner. These are necessary items to be transmitted to pilots approaching a runway.

The manager of the FAA's Terminal Procedures Branch stated that thunderstorms do not qualify as items required for inclusion on ATIS broadcasts. The controller assistant on duty in the tower when the thunderstorm weather report was received testified that it was not the facility's policy to include cumulonimbus clouds as "other pertinent in the ATIS because it's not pertinent information to the safety of a flight." That is one of the stupidest statements ever made. The FAA should make it mandatory that all potential dangerous meteorological conditions be issued to all crewmembers to enable them to decide if a safe landing can be made.

As in this case, I feel sure that the experienced crew of Delta 191 would most certainly have abandoned the approach if they were forewarned of the dangers ahead. This accident was caused by lack of proper, timely weather information that left Captain Connors at the mercy of the FAA's inaccurate weather discriminating process.

The microburst diameter was 3.4 kilometers, the horizontal wind shear traversing the microburst was over 73 knots, and the vertical currents were over 48 feet per second. The last reported wind that was issued to the crew was 090 degrees at five gusts to one five. This report was issued by the local controller at 18:04:01. Within two minutes, Delta was buffeted about with a wind shear of 73 knots; that's a rare increase of 58 knots. The crew was "sucked" into a portion of air with such vertical intensity that probably no pilot could have safely flown out of it.

At the time, DFW airport was equipped with the latest in wind shear detectors. Since the storm cell's southern edge was 2,000 feet short of hitting the nearest wind sensor on the field, no wind shear alarm was sounded in the tower until the storm had drifted over the airport. The first alarm sounded approximately 10 minutes AFTER the crash.

Sixteen years have gone by since the Delta crash. You would hope that the deaths of 165 people would be sufficient to "shake-up" the FAA so that a similar accident would not happen again. Wrong. Over a decade has gone by since this crash and it was caused by the lack of wind shear warning. There is still no Doppler radar at this airport that provides such warnings.

Let's delve into the air traffic control situation at the time of the crash. The board takes great pains to detail the experience and capabilities of the flight crews, but similar information pertaining to the air traffic controllers is usually quite sketchy. The board only lists the controllers directly associated with Flight 191. No mention is made concerning the required numbers of ATC as compared to the people who were actually on duty. Nothing was mentioned about the over-the-shoulder checks that each controller must complete. Perhaps there was a trend where a controller had problems with his checks, or had some "deals" (mistakes) that might be pertinent. It's always the pilot that is scrutinized the most, especially a dead one.

The radar utilized by all approach personnel is ancient and it is designed so that it cannot clearly portray an aircraft and a storm cell simultaneously. At the time of the accident, the ASR-8 radar was in the circular polarization mode as the controller's primary concern was to separate traffic away from each other, not to pinpoint hazardous weather. It would be prudent for the feds to install new equipment and safer procedures so that wind shear accidents could be greatly reduced.

Unfortunately for all concerned, the developmental (student) controller learns his craft while working live traffic. The workload was quite high at this time, and it would appear that all positions in the tower cab were not properly manned. Up until 1750:00, which by strange coincidence was close to the time Delta 191 came on frequency, a developmental controller was operating the Local Controller East (LCE) position. This person is responsible for maintaining proper spacing on final approach from about five miles out on the final leg down to the runway. Regarding the number of controllers on duty, it would appear that they were short by at least one man. FAA Facility Management Manual No. 7210, paragraph 75, regarding supervisors, states: "Efficient facility management requires supervision of each watch regardless of the number of people assigned to a watch."

The DFW airport had experienced a 24 percent traffic increase since 1981, yet it was 17 percent below its authorized crew compliment of 94 full-performance level controllers. One-half their supervisors were eligible to retire in 1986. They were bending the rules, as usual, because of the shortage of qualified journeymen; supervisors were required to work a position in order to keep the traffic moving. It is estimated that supervisors are required to work aircraft over 20 percent of their time on watch. On this watch, a supervisor was busy teaching a new trainee the ropes.

That is allowed, but a qualified journeyman should have taken over from the supervisor when he decided to discontinue training. A supervisor cannot oversee the tower cab if he is busy directing traffic. Supervisors, as a rule, are really out of the control business. They have lost their touch, and supervising is all they should be allowed to do. Would you like to fly in an airliner if the captain's flight time consisted of one short trip per month?

The LCE controller stated that at the time frame surrounding the crash, he made 44 transmissions to various aircraft. During a three-minute, eight-seconds period, he made 44 calls; that's about one call every four seconds. He classified his workload as moderate. I would hate to hear the number of transmissions it would take to upgrade the workload to heavy.

On page 62 of the NTSB report, it makes this statement regarding controllers. "The board found no evidence to indicate that any required duties had been omitted."

At 1803:46, Delta 191 was given an order by approach control to reduce his speed to 150 knots. He was evidently gaining on a Learjet preceding him to the airport. The controller's manual 7110.80, paragraph 1391 relates "Speed Minima": "Turbojet aircraft on a vector to intercept the final approach course or established on the final approach course—a speed not less than 160 knots IAS." Any adjustment to a lower speed must be prefaced with the phrase: "If feasible, maintain (specified speed) knots." The speed adjustment for Delta 191 was not accomplished in accordance with the above criteria. Traffic separation was not working well on this fateful afternoon. An experienced controller may cause an aircraft to break off his approach because he is too close to the craft ahead, but to have this happen twice in the same shift warrants some investigation. While the supervisor was working the position, he experienced an aircraft that was taking off and did not clear the runway in time, so a landing plane was forced to go around. A short time later, a landing aircraft failed to clear the runway as expected and another airliner was sent around.

This is not a normal happening. I have been flying airliners for a total of 30 years and I would say that I have had to go around because of traffic perhaps three times. I believe there is much more here than met the board's eyes. The Learjet immediately ahead of the Delta flight was slowing down and the normal spacing of three miles in trail was lost. It was determined by the board that the minimum spacing was down to two and one-half miles.

The board said: "The loss of separation did not contribute to the accident."

Perhaps the board members have been in such a situation, but I doubt it since none of them have ever been airline pilots. The fact that a controller is slowing you down because you are crowding the plane ahead is always a factor a pilot faces on an instrument approach. He has all his normal functions to perform plus an additional burden.

See how this strikes you.

The Learjet pilot just ahead of Delta 191 used about 25 knots more speed on close in final than he normally would. He was nearing the runway and lost all forward visibility. He decided to "stay high" and fly above the glide slope. When he broke clear of the rain and spotted the runway, he was "high and hot," and, therefore, landed long. Delta 191 was still steadily approaching the runway behind the Lear.

The controller was now getting worried about his spacing, as well he should. He asked the Learjet pilot if he could clear the runway at a high-speed turn off. He was still hot and rolled past the requested turn off.

The controller barked: "Expedite down to the next taxiway."

This transmission was answered by the Lear Jet pilot at 1805:53.

At precisely 1805:52, Delta had already made her first contact with the ground.

At 1805:56, four seconds after Delta had made the hit short of the airport, the tower controller told Delta 191: "Delta go around."

The time involved with the Lear clearing the runway and Delta making ground contact was only a matter of seconds. There's no way that traffic separation could have been any more than about a mile apart at the time of the accident.

Another point to be considered is the fact that controllers do not try to fly the airliners. If a pilot is diving at the runway or is too high, a controller might question it, but I have never heard the phrase "go around" used at any time other than when the traffic spacing is inadequate. The number of landing aircraft at DFW airport gave the crew of Delta 191 a false sense of security. After all, they were all coming down final and none of the pilots complained to the tower concerning the weather.

At 1805:19, Delta 191 encountered strong downdrafts. The first officer, who was flying, applied immediate nose-up control correction. At 1805:22, the aircraft entered very heavy rain and the captain warned his co-pilot to "Watch your speed." This statement was followed by "You're gonna lose it all of a sudden; there it is."

At this point, the airspeed decreased 44 knots. They knew they were in big trouble. These are the times when a pilot can earn a year's pay in a few seconds.

Captain Connors yelled, "Push the power up, way up, way up."

At 1805:29, the sound of the three giant engines speeding up could be detected on the tape. Not only would the ever-present gravity have to be overcome but also the treacherous pull of a torrential downdraft.

Whoop—whoop. "Pull up" came the command from the Ground Proximity Warning System. They were now 23 seconds from disaster.

Captain Connors, in a commanding voice, said: "TOGA."

This signified that he intended to get the hell out of there. The command bar that controls the aircraft's path was from 6 to 23 degrees. The crew had done all they could. What remained was to watch the altimeter and hope their maximum thrust and pitch would be sufficient to keep the 325,000-pound aircraft from becoming another wind shear statistic.

The downburst proved to be far too powerful and at 1805:52, Flight 191 became history.

To summarize:

Referring to the ATIS tape, the board stated "the omission of the cumulonimbus and towering cumulus played no part in causing the accident.

On the contrary, it was the direct cause of the crash. The crew had no idea of the treacherous weather ahead.

The board states: "The north side of the cell formation containing the thunderstorm was not masked from Flight 191 by any intervening clouds."

It is most difficult to see a cloud formation when you are flying through a vicious downpour. Aircraft weather radar would be showing mostly ground clutter this close to the airport.

At 1805:52, flight 191 made the first contact with the ground. At 1805:56, the tower operator told Delta to go around. That was five seconds after Delta hit the ground. No mention is made of this mistake.

The tower area supervisor was working a position in the tower, and he was also training a developmental controller. This meant that they were short one controller in the tower, and that there was no supervision because the area supervisor was working a position. This controller was required to ask pilots for reports concerning their approaches through a thunderstorm. He failed to make this transmission.

No mention was made by the board that there was no assigned supervisor in the tower. The supervisor who was working the LCE position caused two aircraft to go around because of poor spacing. The third go-around was going to be Delta 191. Unfortunately, it crashed.

The board states: "The three-mile separation was not maintained between Flight 191 and the preceding Learjet; the loss of separation did not contribute to the accident."

How would a group of amateurs possibly know what goes on in a captain's mind? The proximity of the Learjet most certainly was an added burden for the captain of 191. He was too busy to mention it, but believe me, it was an extra problem. The board makes no mention of the mistake that the supervisor made when he let Delta and the Learjet get closer then two and one-half miles. In reality, the Delta flight was touching down close to the runway while the Learjet was still not clear of the active strip. If Delta could have made it to the runway, he would most likely have landed on the near end of the runway while the Learjet was still looking for the taxiway at the other end.

The board also failed to find any fault with the large water tanks adjacent to the runway. In reality, one tank was the cause of the aircraft's break-up. If this area had been clear of obstructions, many more people would be alive today.

The Contract Weather Observer at DFW is located in a building that gives no view of 50 percent of the airport. Unfortunately, the view to the north, where the accident occurred, was completely blocked out. Can you imagine the FAA and the Weather Service allowing a weather reporter to occupy a room that fails to give him a complete view of the airport perimeters? I can.

No disciplinary action was given to the airline crews sitting on the ground watching the horrendous microburst developing. It was the crews' duty to report to the tower any unusual weather phenomena. They all failed to do this. If the tower didn't warn the Delta crew, the least that could be expected from fellow pilots would be a life-saving transmission over the radio. They just sat there and watched the demise of Delta 191.

Could this disaster have been avoided? Was the crew trained properly in wind shear penetration? Is the FAA to blame?

The flight director is today's answer to the WW2 artificial horizon. The instrument consists of a diamond-shaped device that is supposed to be flown into a set of command bars. These bars have various settings to enable a pilot to select different pitch altitudes. The maximum nose-up is 17.5 degrees and nose-down is 1.2 degrees. These units are computerized, and when operating properly, is a most helpful aid to the crew.

As we have already discussed, the TOGA made on Delta was set in anticipation of a go-around. The pilots were desperately trying their best to keep clear of the ground. The aircraft was violently rolling and pitching as the torrential rain hammered the windshield. They were, indeed, fighting for their lives in the bowels of a treacherous microburst. The prescribed procedure for penetrating a microburst is to trade all the air speed possible in exchange for altitude.

If the "feds" required a wind shear position on the command bars, lives could be saved. Other airlines have cautioned their crews against using TOGA during wind shear encounter; Delta has not.

Each year, airline pilots must spend two days in ground school. Here they learn all the latest information concerning flight safety, and perhaps even a little something about wind shear if they have time.

The safety board's accident report states on page 72, line 4: "The captain was familiar with this type of wind shear from recurrent ground and simulator training."

And on page 72, paragraph 3: "Based on his wind shear training and L-1011 simulator experience with wind shear encounters, the captain's decision to continue the approach was understandable following momentary stabilization of the airplane above 500 feet."

Page 53 of the accident report states in paragraph 3: "The instructor who administered the last simulator period with the captain and first officer of Flight 191 was unable to recall whether they had conducted approaches under wind shear conditions during those training periods.

The crew may or may not have received this vital training. Why then does the board persist in making potentially false statements?

After the crash, the Delta manual was changed as follows: "Delta's policy concerning wind shear continues to be that we must avoid significant wind shear."

Avoiding wind shear that is not reported by pilots or controllers is nearly impossible. There is no sure way to forecast it except by using the latest Doppler radar. Whenever there is a thunderstorm, potential wind shear is always possible. Therefore, the only sensible way to avoid disasters such as Delta 191 is to close the airport to all traffic until the storm has passed, especially if there isn't any Doppler radar on the airport. This would dip deeply into the airport's finances since each airliner that lands has to pay a landing fee to the airport authority.

This one is really a shocker. The charges made to an airliner are related to the actual weight of the aircraft as it touches down. An average fee is $1 per thousand pounds. Delta 191 weighed 324,800 pound when it crashed at Dallas. If it had made a routine landing, the airport management would have collected $325. I wouldn't be surprised if they charged them anyway.

As you can see, a large aircraft pays about $325 every time it lands. The smallest airliner, a DC-9, 737, and 727 might get by with a fee of around $100. At a busy terminal during peak periods, 80 landings per hour would not be unusual. Multiply the number of aircraft per hour by the landing weight and you can easily average over $15,000 per hour. The Dallas/Fort Worth Airport receives over $25,000 per day just from American airlines. Since money talks, that's one of the reasons airports are rarely ever closed.

Thunderstorms only last for a very few minutes but it is far better to have a live passenger complaining about delays rather than a dead one who costs the airline millions in settlement costs.

The death toll in this accident could have been greatly reduced if airports were not festooned with "airplane stopping" structures. The Delta 1011 was relatively intact when it first hit the ground. The deadly explosion and break-up were caused by a large water tank adjacent to the runway. Many times, structures close to runways are the causes for compounding accidents. Until the "feds" eliminate these potential dangers and close airports that are experiencing thunderstorms, the death toll will continue to rise.

It is really amazing how a board whose mission is "to make safety recommendations" can completely ignore the disaster-causing structures on and around our major airports. I can never recall in any of their reports where an airport structure was a contributing factor to a disaster.

Now you may have a better understanding of how the board functions. I hope you will agree that the NTSB was way out of line when they called this one pilot error. It should have been entitled FAA error.

The emphasis around air carrier accidents is the fact that they usually kill more people at one time than a small general aviation crash. A board member gets a lot of TV coverage when they investigate an airline accident. Because the general aviation crash isn't nearly as spectacular as a large carrier, the media coverage is localized to the immediate area of the accident. The death rate for airliners ranges any where from 0 in a good year to over 500 in a bad one. This in no way compares to the lives that are lost annually in those Cherokees, Cessnas, Beeches, and others. Approximately 100 people are killed every month in light planes, and these tragedies occur year in and year out, as regular as clockwork.

What does the board do about this? Well, since the public is not aware of the hundreds who die annually in private aircraft accidents, the board has only one person who is assigned to determining the causes of these numerous deaths.

The sole general aviation specialist at NTSB is an enthusiastic private pilot and aeronautical engineer named Paul Alexander. He has the task of analyzing over 3,000 "putt-putt" accidents each year that claim more lives in one year than five years of airline crashes. Excluding the military, there are over 220,000 aircraft registered in the U.S. Fewer than 2 percent or 3,000 of these are airliners.

The Crash of US AIR at Charlotte, North Carolina

US AIR Flight 1016A, Douglas DC-9, was preparing to depart Columbus, South Carolina, for its return trip to Charlotte, North Carolina. The highly experienced flight crew consisted of a captain with five years experience as an airline pilot with over 8,000 total hours, 1.970 in the DC-9-31. Not only was he experienced in airliners; he was equally at home in F-16 fighters that he flew for the 906th Reserve Fighters Group at Wright Paterson Air Force Base in Ohio. He was also a distinguished graduate from the Air Force Pilot Training School. His quick reflexes, necessary to fly fighters, would soon prove invaluable to US AIR. It requires far more skill to pilot a jet fighter than it does to drive an airliner.

His first officer held an airline captain's license with over 12,000 hours of total time, 3,180 of which was in the DC-9. Both crewmembers had first-class physicals with no waivers.

The DC-9-3 aircraft was in airworthy condition with no known major discrepancies noted in the aircraft logbook. The takeoff weight of 86,325 pounds was 13,075 pounds below the certificated maximum takeoff weight of 105,000 pounds.

Weather information provided to the crew by the US AIR dispatcher indicated that the Charlotte weather was similar to what they had encountered one hour earlier on their outbound flight, except for widely scattered thunderstorms in the area.

At 1823, flight 1016 was airborne with 57 souls on board, 52 passengers and a crew of five. The crew was in good spirits for their short 35-minute flight to Charlotte, North Carolina.

This was the first officer's leg to fly the aircraft, so the captain acted as the non-flying crewmember and dialed in the Charlotte ATIS, a continuous taped, updated weather, runway wind, etc., information advisory. This is what the crew heard: "Information Yankee 1751 EDT clouds 5,000 feet scattered, visibility six miles, haze, temperature 88 degrees Fahrenheit, dew point 67 degrees Fahrenheit, wind 150 at 8 knots, altimeter 30.01 inches HG, ILS approaches to runways 18L (left) and 18R (right), localizer back course to Runway 23 approach in use." THERE WAS NO MENTION OF THUNDERSTORMS.

At 1828.11, the captain made the following PA announcement: "Ladies and gentlemen, we're 40 miles from Charlotte, should be on the ground, safe and happy holiday. At this time, we'd like our flight attendants to please prepare the cabin for arrival."

1829.54 First Officer: "There's more rain than I thought. It's starting pretty good a minute ago. Now it's held up."

1829.56 Captain: "Yeah."

The previously smooth flight was starting to get some rumble of turbulence.

1833.19 Captain: "We're showing a little build-up at, uh, looks like it's sitting on the radial. Like to go about five degrees to the left, to the west."

1833.27 Charlotte Approach: "How far ahead are you looking 1016?"

1833.30 Captain: "About 15 miles."

1833:32 Charlotte Approach: "I'm going to turn you before you get there. I'm going to turn you in about five miles northbound."

1833:35: Captain: "Okay."

1835:21 Charlotte Approach: "US AIR 1016, Charlotte approach, maintain 4,000 Runway 18-Right."

1835:25: Captain: "Four thousand for the right side."

The preliminary landing checklist was "run." The intensity of the rain was beating a steady staccato on the aircraft as it neared Runway 18R at Charlotte Douglas Airport.

1839:43: First Officer: "Gear down."

A click on the gear handle is heard and the sound of rushing air can be identified, signifying that the gear is in transit.

1839:47 Charlotte Approach: "18-right. Cleared to land. Following F one hundred short final. Previous arrival reported SMOOTH RIDE ALL THE WAY DOWN THE FINAL." (capitals mine).

1839:49: Captain: "US AIR 1016, I'd appreciate a pirep (pilot's report) from the guy in front of us."

1840:42 Charlotte Approach: "US AIR 1016, company "FK" 100 just exited the runway, sir. HE SAID SMOOTH RIDE" (capitals mine).

The intensity of the rain was now so loud that you could barely hear yourself talking in the cockpit.

1841:54: Captain: "Here comes the wipers" (windshield wipers).

Flight 1016 was about 400 feet above the runway but that altitude was soon to diminish because of a previous downpour causing air to descend in a rapid velocity. Windshield wipers were turned to maximum and the first officer remained on instruments while the captain scanned through the torrential rain for a glimpse of the runway.

1841:58.9 First Officer: "There's, oh, 10 knots right there" (referring to his minimum safe approach speed).

1842:06.4 Captain: "Okay, you're plus 20."

It's the non-flying pilot's duty to keep vigilance outside the aircraft while the flying pilot stays on the gauges and waits until he hears "runway in sight," or "decision height." If the outside visual clues are not seen at this time, the only thing to do is go around (apply power and climb). This alert captain sensed weather problems and before he ever reached decision height (200 feet above the surface) he commanded his first officer:

1842:14: Captain: "Take it around, go to the right." 1842:17.7: "Max power."

1842:18: First Officer: "Yeah, max power."

1842:19.4: First Officer: "Flaps to 15."

1842:28.4: Sound of the ground proximity warning system: "Whoop— Whoop, terrain."

1842:35.6: The deadly wind shear had caught another victim in its web. Flight 1016 hit the ground first in a grassy field located within the airport boundaries. The right landing gear touched down first; 18 feet further, the left gear hit. Still traveling at over 100 knots, the plane sheared a group of trees as the passenger's cabin crushed three large oaks. The tail section and its two engines came to rest in the carport of a two-bedroom house.

The post-crash fire consumed most of the wing that contained the fuel. It was a miracle that all were not killed. Twenty occupants managed to make it out alive but 37 will never again be subjected to the disgraceful way the FAA allows aircraft to land at large airports without the state-of-the-art Doppler radar, a system that detects wind shear in a timely and accurate manner.

If you are not a pilot, you can easily surmise that this experienced crew did as they were supposed to do. If you are a pilot, you know that they performed admirably under such extreme conditions. The NTSB report that was copied in this section came from their April 4, 1995 report. They stated that the probable cause was as follows: "The National Transportation Board determined that the probable causes of the accident were:

1. "The flight crew's decision to continue on approach into severe convective activity that was conducive to a microburst;

2. The flight crew's failure to recognize a wind shear situation in a timely manner;

3. The flight crew's failure to establish and maintain the proper airplane altitude and thrust setting necessary to escape the wind shear;

4. The lack of real-time adverse weather and wind shear hazard information dissemination from air traffic control, all of which led to an encounter with and failure to escape from a microburst-induced wind shear that was produced by a rapidly developing thunderstorm located at the approach end of Runway 18R."

The NTSB is long on claiming pilot error, especially if the crew is dead and can't fight back, but very short on blaming other government agencies such as the FAA. As you have probably surmised by now, I find the NTSB's probable cause in this case to be highly inaccurate. I will attempt to prove to you, in detail, that the facts in this case do not indicate any pilot error, but rather numerous FAA failures.

This accident is quite similar to the Delta 1011 crash at the beginning of this chapter. We will compare them both in a short while.

Let's take the NTSB probable causes one at a time and see how inaccurate they are.

1. "The flight crew's decision to continue on approach into severe convective activity that was conducive to a microburst."

What the previous statement claimed, in simple English, was that the crew knowingly flew their DC-9 into a severe thunderstorm. The crew had no idea that there was a treacherous microburst waiting for them. Why should they? They were trapped into believing that the weather ahead was not as severe as it turned out to be.

At 1827:06, 15 minutes prior to the accident, the crew tuned in the ATIS "Yankee" which made no mention of the severe weather near the airport.

At 1835:18, seven minutes prior to the crash, the tower supervisor made the following statement to his controller: "It's raining like hell at the south end of the airport."

This was not relayed to the US AIR crew. The Charlotte Final Radar West controller observed on his ASR-9 radar a level 3 cell "pop-up" (just appearing on his scope) near the airport. This was not relayed to the US AIR crew.

At 1837:33, five minutes before the crash, the Local Controller East transmitted to a Piedmont airliner that was landing on a different runway: "Heavy rain on the airport now, wind 150 at 14."

This tower transmission was spoken on a different radio frequency than the one that US AIR was using, so it was not received by the DC-9 crew.

At 1839:12, three minutes prior to the crash, US AIR Flight 806 was on the ground near the approach end of Runway 18R. They remarked to the tower: "And 806 looks like, uh, we've gotten a storm right on top of the field here." The controller responded "affirmative."

This crew elected to delay their departure because of the intense storm at the airport. The crew of the ill-fated DC-9 never heard this transmission because he was not on their frequency at this time. How the crew of this company aircraft could sit there in the "blocks" (an apron next to the runway) and watch while their company flight was headed for trouble is more than I can fathom. They failed to warn Flight 1016 of the very storm that they were waiting out on the ground.

If a pilot sees any dangerous weather conditions he is, by law, required to broadcast a warning to any other aircraft that might be entering the hazardous conditions. There were two USAIR flights on the ground waiting for the storm to dissipate. One of the captains described the rain as: "Very heavy, with visibility reduced to almost zero." Another USAIR captain who was taxiing at this time had this to say concerning the weather: "heaviest rain he had been through in a long time." He described the precipitation as "wall of water."

Flight 1016 received no warning from their fellow pilots who were sitting in the blocks (the last stop before turning onto the runway) watching a potential disaster.

1840, 1 minute, 32 seconds before impact, the tower supervisor determined that the visibility had decreased to one mile. This he announced in a "loud voice" to his controller. However, the LCW testified that he never heard the supervisor's announcement concerning the lowered visibility, therefore, he could not relay this to Flight 1016.

AFTER the accident, it became mandatory for the supervisor to advise each controller personally of any weather changes. Shouting would not be sufficient.

It is interesting to note that the controller's handbook (ATP 7110.65) does not make the issuance of weather information mandatory. So if a controller spots a storm area on his scope; he need only describe it to the pilot as "there is some rain out there." What kind of world has the FAA created?

At this time, Flight 1016 received a message from the tower saying that a company aircraft that had just landed stated they had a "smooth ride," another reason for the crew to believe that all would be well.

1841:05, 1 minute, 30 seconds before the crash, the tower's Local Controller West made the following transmission: "Wind shear alert northeast boundary, wind 1903." He followed this transmission with: "Attention all aircraft wind shear alert the surface wind 100 at 20 northeast boundary, wind 190 at 16." Both of these vital reports were transmitted by the Local Controller East. Unfortunately, the DC-9 crew was tuned to the controller responsible for aircraft on the West side of the airport and this alert was not received by the crew of USAIR Flight 1016.

At 1842:14, the captain continued his vigilance outside the cockpit windscreen, hoping for some visual clues. They were now almost down to decision height (at this altitude if you don't see the ground you apply power and go around), and still no sign of the runway.

1842.14, the captain said to his F/O: "Take it around, go to the right."

The crew of USAIR 1016 was NEVER advised of the treacherous weather that they were about to penetrate.

In 1982, a Pan American 727 crashed after encountering a microburst shortly after takeoff from New Orleans. The NTSB report stated: "The airplane's encounter during lift-off and initial climb phase of flight with a microburst-induced wind shear imposed a down-draft and decreasing head-wind, the affects of which the pilot would have DIFFICULTY RECOGNIZING AND REACTING TO IN TIME" (capitals mine).

Why would a previous board say that the pilot would have a difficult time recognizing a wind shear, but today's board blames the crew of USAIR 1016 for "failure to recognize a wind shear situation in a timely manner?" Sometimes you just can't win.

If you are not in sympathy with the crew of 1016 at this time, read on.

The second statement from the NTSB concerning this accident is as follows:

> "2. The flight crew's failure to recognize a wind shear situation in a timely manner."

It is quite difficult to recognize a wind shear in flight. About all you have is an air speed indicator that may increase or decrease in speed. When you are penetrating a microburst and you are being tossed around the sky, it's probably too late to correlate the air speed indicator heading up or down the scale. Wouldn't it be nice if there were a device on the ground and in the cockpit that could ACCURATELY forecast wind shear? Well, those two dreams are a reality, but the equipment on the USAIR DC-9 and the sensors on the airport are not always accurate.

The system installed at Charlotte Douglas airport consisted of six wind sensor remote stations stationed strategically throughout the airport. This phase II system was the newest model of this ancient system (Low-Level Wind shear Alert System [LLWAS]). These devices are only a stop-gap measure until the latest Doppler radar can be installed. Doppler can accurately pinpoint microbursts; LLWAS cannot.

The LLWAS at Charlotte had numerous problems in the past, mainly false wind shear reports. It seems that sensor No. 2 (northeast boundary) and No. 6 (northwest boundary) were sheltered by obstacles that could deter from their accuracy. Since this "Mickey Mouse" system is not the greatest, you would think that the FAA would be meticulous about not having any of the units shielded from the wind. Well, the day of the crash, the LLWAS units did transmit to the tower that there was, indeed, a wind shear taking place on the airport. There was only one minor problem. They failed to alert the controllers in the tower until 1843:07, nearly a minute after USAIR 1016 had crashed.

Let's get into another reason why the crew of USAIR 1016 never got a warning from their wind shear alert instrument in the cockpit. This one should really get to you. In 1991, USAIR installed the Honeywell Standard Wind shear Detection System. This system is an approved "reactive" system designed to display warnings whenever a "severe" wind shear is detected. The USAIR pilots' handbook defines a severe wind shear as "A wind shear of such intensity and duration that it would exceed the performance capabilities of the particular airplane type and likely cause an inadvertent loss of control or ground contact."

This airborne detector is operated by a computer that integrates data from various aircraft sensors such as angle-of-attack (attitude), wing-flap position sensors, and N1 engine tachometers. There are two types of wind shear annunciations that are displayed in the cockpit. A flashing red light and an oral warning over the loudspeakers in the cockpit stating, "wind shear, wind shear, wind shear."

The flight crew of USAIR 1016 stated that they never received any warnings, either visual or oral, and the cockpit tapes verify this to be true. Why did this unit fail? You will find the answer difficult to believe. When this system was originally evaluated in a simulator, it was not tested while the wing flaps were in-transit. Well, it took the crash of USAIR 1016 to bring the FAA to its senses. The Honeywell wind shear system was never tested in the real world of flying, something the FAA has yet to master.

When an aircraft is in the landing or takeoff mode, the wing flaps are in motion a fair part of the time. So why wasn't this device tested with the flaps in-transit? The NTSB report stated: "The system was not evaluated with the flaps in transition; thus the evaluation process neither revealed the system's delayed activation when the flaps were moving, NOR WAS IT A REQUIREMENT OF THE CERTIFICATION TESTS" (capitals mine).

To repeat the second part of the NTSB probable cause: "the flight crew's failure to recognize a wind shear in a timely manner."

As you have seen, the crew never received any warning from the tower regarding the potential for a wind shear, mainly because of the lack of storm information, and because both the cockpit and ground wind shear alert system failed to operate until AFTER the DC-9 crash.

The proper wording of the above NTSB statement should read: the FAA failed miserably in certifying wind shear devices both on the ground and in the air.

The third statement in the NTSB report concerning the probable cause:

3. "The flight crew's failure to establish and maintain the proper airplane altitude and thrust setting necessary to escape the wind shear."

At USAIR, the go-around and wind shear escape procedures are identical. The company manual states that when a wind shear alert or the red warning light illuminates, a go-around be initiated. Power must be increased to maximum power along with a 15 degrees increase in pitch. This procedure is precisely what the crew of USAIR 1016 performed, and to their credit, they did it before decision height, and without the benefit of the cockpit wind shear alerting system that, at the time, was inoperative.

Recurrent flight training for captains usually requires a wind shear problem every six months, but first officers only get this training every two years. The last time the first officer received hands-on training concerning wind shear was about two years prior to the crash of 1016.

Let's just take a moment to compare the similarities of the Delta 1011 crash with that of USAIR 1016. The NTSB reporting capabilities have not changed since the Delta crash of 1985.

4. The lack of real-time adverse weather and wind shear hazard information dissemination from air traffic control, all of which led to an encounter with, and failure to, escape from a microburst. Induced

wind shear that was produced by a rapidly developing thunderstorm located at the approach end of runway 18R.

Both Delta and USAIR never received the vital information concerning a large thunderstorm sitting off the end of the runway.

ATIS: Both airlines received ATIS information that made no mention of thunderstorms at their airport.

Company Aircraft on Ground: Both crash sites had company aircraft on the ground in the blocks watching the storms developing but saying nothing to their company crews in the air. Some of the Delta crews made the statement that they thought they were witnessing a tornado. The USAIR crews on the ground stated that they were witnessing some of the greatest downpours they had ever seen. Thanks, fellows.

Smooth Rides: In both crashes, the aircraft preceding them down final approach reported a smooth ride.

Low-Level Wind shear Alert Systems: The LLWAS at the Dallas/Fort Worth Airport sounded the alarm, but 10 minutes after the crash. In the case of USAIR, the warning did not sound until one minute after the disaster.

Doppler Radar: This state-of-the-art weather radar can depict microbursts and wind shear, and should be standard equipment at all airline airports. This unit can SAVE LIVES. The Delta crash site still lacks this valuable unit. Charlotte has finally gotten a Doppler Radar system, but how well does it work? It has averaged two failures per month from several minutes to as much as four days

The all-important weather disseminate from the FAA has not changed in over a decade. The crews of both these crashes never had any wind shear warning. The Delta aircraft did not have a cockpit wind shear warning device; the USAIR had one that was faulty.

Safety Board Member Qualifications

What stringent requirements are necessary to enable a person to serve as a board member? Since they are the supreme court for all civil aviation, highway, marine, pipeline, bridges, and railroad accidents, they must surely be knowledgeable concerning all of these phases of transportation.

The Chairman of the Safety Board is James Evans Hall. He received his law degree from the University of Tennessee, College of Law, and served as council to the U.S. Senate Subcommittee on Intergovernmental Relations. He also is on the staff of U.S. Senator Al Gore, Sr. In addition, he was responsible for developing Tennessee's first antidrug efforts. He may be a fine lawyer, but he certainly knows nothing concerning air safety.

John Arthur Hammerschmidt became a member of the board in June of 1991. From 1974 to 1983, he was the CEO of the Hammerschmidt Lumber Company, Inc. He earned his Bachelor of Arts degree from Dartmouth College with a major in history. His current term expired in December of 1995. He is a licensed private pilot (certainly better than nothing), but not qualified nearly enough to pass judgment on complicated airline crashes.

Robert Francis II, who serves as vice-chairman, is another member of the board . He started his governmental career as a congressional relations officer for the FAA in 1977. His term expires on December 31, 1999, and he certainly is not qualified to pass judgment on highly technical airline crashes.

In August of 1995, John Goglia was confirmed as a board member whose term expired in December of 1999. He has over 30 years of experience in the aviation industry. He was instrumental in developing the Maintenance Resource Management Program for USAIR. He served as team coordinator of the International Association of Machinists accident investigation team and he has participated on the Aviation Rulemaking Advisory Committee that recommends changes regarding operational and safety regulations.

Goglia's career at USAIR spanned a wide range of responsibilities, from basic mechanic to lead mechanic and inspector. He received the 1994 FAA Aviation Mechanic of the Year Award. He is the first A&P mechanic to serve on the board, and he is highly qualified to pass judgment on aircraft mechanical failures. I only hope that he will not be swayed by his fellow board members to hang a pilot when the fault lies elsewhere.

Since appointments to the NTSB are made by the president, they are usually bestowed on people who have contributed to the presidential election WHETHER THEY ARE QUALIFIED OR NOT. As you can see, the only member of the board who is at all qualified to pass judgment on airline crashes is John Goglia. His expertise lies in human factors and maintenance that in no way makes him an expert on any of the other facets related to airline crashes. It really takes an airline pilot to know what goes on in the flight deck of an airliner.

It would seem appropriate, since one of the board members is a general aviation pilot, that more interest would be generated in the field of private aviation. Here is where their knowledge could be better utilized. All board members, most certainly, should be knowledgeable concerning transportation accidents. However, Public Law 97-309, 97th Congress states: "At any given time, no less than three members of the board shall be individuals who have been appointed on the basis of technical qualifications, professional standing, and demonstrated knowledge in the fields of accident reconstruction, safety engineering, human factors, transportation safety, or transportation regulations."

Why it is that only three of the five members of the board are required to be knowledgeable about transportation disasters is more than I can fathom. At any rate, there is only one member who comes near to fulfilling the public law, and that is John Goglia.

News Media

Have you noticed how rapidly the news media exposes the transcripts of the cockpit voice recorder, sometimes only weeks after a crash? By law, this vital transcript is not supposed to be released until the board's public hearing, or "in no event later than 60 days following the accident." A premature release is not only against the board's laws but also causes irreparable damage to the reputation of the flight crews, the manufacturers and the airlines.

On Monday, August 17, a day after the Detroit DC-9 crash, the cockpit voice recorder was taken to the NTSB headquarters in Washington, D.C. What a "scoop" it would be for a reporter to obtain a copy of this transcript. Well, some how, the contents of the CVC tape were given to a reporter for the New York Times. These types of shenanigans can only lead to false accusations and assumptions by the general public.

The Air Line Pilots Association considers its role in accident investigation so important that it has sent nearly 200 of its pilots through a special investigation course at the University of Southern California. These active crewmembers are infinitely more qualified than any of the board members, yet none of the safety board members are required to attend such an important school.

What Aviation Experts Have to Say About NTSB

Chuck Miller, a former director of the board's Bureau of Aviation Safety and an active air safety consultant, has few compliments about the way the board is run. One of his statements to the aviation consumer is as follows: "There are many cases of sloppy or incomplete NTSB investigations. The staff morale at NTSB these days is just terrible."

In recent years, many of the old timers, the really knowledgeable technicians, have left the board. Many went with the FAA or NASA, not because of better pay, but simply because they got tired of rewriting accident reports, ones that were accurate, simply to appease the board members.

When Miller was asked about Jim Burnett, the board's past chairman, he had this to say: "He came to the board with zero managerial or safety expertise. The standard joke is the closest he ever came to transportation was adjudicating traffic tickets back in Arkansas. The staff learns fast. They get sick and tired of writing up a report and getting called in and browbeaten by the board members saying this is the way it ought to be."

Dave Noland, a staff member at the Aviation Consumer Publication, sums-up his feelings: "In short, the NTSB has failed miserably to be an aggressive activist force to improve the safety of general aviation."

One of the Air Line Pilots Association's TWA jet captains, Vernon W. Lowell, an official accident investigator, made this statement: "I must denounce in the strongest terms possible the NTSB's accident reporting. Too often their reports are distorted, inaccurate, amateurish in their technical aspects, and yes, even dishonest."

Mr. Harold F. Marthinsen, director of the Airline Pilots Association accident investigation department was quite outspoken when it came to the NTSB. He has filed dozens of petitions with the NTSB for Reconsideration of Probable Cause. Board findings that he knows are inaccurate take years of badgering until the truth is brought to light. Mr. Marthinsen relates: "The quality of the NTSB staff is thin. There are people over there who really don't know what they are doing. That's a problem that goes back a few years. The NTSB staff is not geared to the technology of a microburst. Their meteorologists are not sufficiently knowledgeable to come up with the right answers.

The problems begin when the investigation team breaks up and goes back to Washington. Now you have people who were not involved in the investigation making decisions about what the analysis should be. It's amazing to see the things that come out in a report for which there's no basis for the analysis in relation to the specific accident. This is the part of the investigative process that gives ALPA heartburn."

Marthinsen continues: "I think the board does good work in a number of instances, but last week I was in the U.K. talking to their accident investigators, and it was like a breath of fresh air. They have a completely different philosophy and have so many innovating things going on.

Philip I. Ryther was in government service for 26 years. He headed the FAA's evaluation division and was one of the few managerial individuals in government who was totally dedicated to air safety. He wrote a great book entitled Who's Watching the Airways? The following is a quote from his book concerning the workings of the NTSB. Mr. Ryther wrote a scathing report concerning the FAA's unsafe practices. For this he was terminated, for doing the job he was hired to do. "And last, there was the National Transportation Safety Board. Its failure even to try to obtain a copy of my report could be put down as shear laziness. But it is entirely possible that the members feared they would not be reappointed if they appeared interested in challenging the FAA, a branch of the Department of Transportation. After all, the safety board itself is part of the DOT.

The lesson of all of this is clear enough. The bureaucracy, as led by political appointees, is unwilling to face up to undoing a poor performance.

The bureaucrats themselves are afraid to do anything that will reflect unfavorably on their peers. Each overseer of the bureaucracy has his own reason for failing to act, but it generally amounts to keeping peace with those to whom he owes potential favors, such as his job.

And so it is that those very agencies that are supposed to be the staunch guardians of our safety, the agencies that were created to keep the air lanes safe for you and me, turn out to be little more than a single incredible bureaucracy. Incredible, because it is a bureaucracy stalled by a lack of leadership, one that is frightened, ineffectual, and reluctant to the art. Its members are bound by political ties and past favors to those they regulate and to whom they owe their jobs.

On August 12, 1985, a Japanese Airlines 747 crashed killing 505 people. The report of the Japanese Aircraft Accident Investigation Commission was compiled by experts and it contains much more information than a similar NTSB report. For instance, many of the NTSB reports are about one-quarter the size of the Japanese report, and most of the U.S. reports have no pictures and graphs, as well as 300 pages of text.

Aviation writer Peter Garrison has this to say about the NTSB: "In a mishap involving weather, the NTSB can choose to blame the crew for making the decision to enter the area of bad weather, the National Weather service for inadequate forecasting or dissemination of information, the controllers for failing to inform the crew of a report from another airplane, or the manufacturer for some design features that failed. Because the NTSB findings can have an impact on the fortunes of such industrial giants as Boeing and McDonald Douglas, to say nothing of the airlines, the board is lobbied by manufacturers, airlines, and pilot's organizations, all trying to make sure someone else shoulders as much of the blame as possible. Consequently, NTSB findings of probable cause are often POLITICALLY COLORED AND STATISTICS BLURRED." (capitals mine).

Aircraft Owners and Pilots Association's (AOPA) past president, John Baker, was highly critical of the board. He was a former FAA association administrator for general aviation. He stated: "The national interests won't be served until the five members of the board are all technically qualified;

the lack of that quality on the board is bound to effect the staff that has the job of investigating accidents."

In America, the aviation industry is second only to the nation's number one industry, automobiles. It behooves the Congress to reinstate a separate aviation division, one that is staffed with experts, not political hacks.

CHAPTER 8

DANGER: FAA AT WORK

Strike, Strike, Strike, Strike, Strike. This was the defiant chant of 1,000 representatives of the Professional Air Traffic Controller Organization (PATCO) that filled the air at their last convention in New Orleans. It was 1981, and a year of great decision for the controller forces that numbered over 14,000. What was it that made 90 percent of the air traffic controllers so frustrated? They had a job that paid an average of over $30,000 (1980) per year plus a terrific pension.

In January of 1968, PATCO became the sole bargaining agent for controllers in labor relations with the FAA. FAA management and their unsympathetic dealings with controllers produced nothing but contempt.

Between 1960 and 1970, the controllers staged several "sickouts," and by-the-book "slowdowns" similar to the way traffic is normally handled today. Complaints from the controllers were similar then as they are now: working conditions, staffing levels, faulty equipment, poor management, and wages.

In early 1981, negotiations began for their contract that would expire on the 15th day of March 1981. PATCO listed 99 bargaining points, including a say in how the traffic would be routed, more up-to-date equipment, a 32-hour workweek, an increase in salary that would put them nearly on a par with an airline co-pilot, and management that "gave a damn."

For years the controllers had been carrying the weight of a faulty system on their backs; in 1999 they still are!

In 1968, a prominent lawyer and pilot, F. Lee Bailey, was asked by PATCO to advise them on their dealings with the government. He agreed to do what he could, and in one of his meetings with the past FAA administrator, General McKee, the General was quoted as saying: "Why the hell didn't you come along a year ago when I was still here? Together, we could have gotten some money out of those skinflints on the hill and kept pace with the expansion of air traffic."

The breed of FAA administrators has steadily gone downhill. This, coupled with management at the control facilities was the main reason for the unrest of the controlling force.

On October 20, 1980, presidential candidate Ronald Reagan wrote the following letter to the president of PATCO, relating all the benefits the controllers would reap if the membership would back his campaign.

> Robert C. Poli, President
> Professional Air Traffic Controllers Organization
> 444 Capital Street
> Washington, D.C.
>
> Dear Mr. Poli:
>
> I have been thoroughly briefed by members of my staff as to the deplorable state of our nation's air traffic control system. They have told me that too few people working unreasonable hours with obsolete equipment has placed the nation's air travelers in unwarranted danger. In an area so clearly related to public safety the Carter Administration has failed to act responsibly.
>
> You can rest assured that if I am elected President, I will take whatever steps are necessary to provide our air traffic controllers with the most modern equipment available and to adjust staff levels and work days so that they are commensurate with a maximum degree of public safety.
>
> As in all other areas of the federal government where the President has the power of appointment, I fully intend to appoint highly qualified

individuals who can work harmoniously with the Congress and the employees of the government agencies they oversee.

I pledge to you that my administration will work very closely with you to bring about a spirit of cooperation between the President and the air traffic controllers. Such harmony can and must exist if we are to restore the people's confidence in the government.

Sincerely,
Ronald Reagan

Much more to relate later concerning that letter.

Prior to the PATCO strike, the only way air traffic controllers could get any recognition from the public was to stage a by-the-book slowdown. This earned immediate recognition and hatred for the inconvenience caused to the traveling public. But at least the ATC became a real live person and not just a body behind a radar scope. The slowdown resulted in snarled traffic at most major terminals in the northeast. The press may not have been the best but at least the FAA was taking notice.

The controllers were not the only problem that was bothering the government. The postal workers were due for a new contract at precisely the same time as PATCO. There was a lot more at stake for the government than just 14,000 controllers. The 175,000 postal workers were much more of a threat to them than PATCO.

PATCO President Poli negotiated, in good faith, over 37 times with the FAA. Each time he came away from the bargaining table with nothing. He could see that there was little more he could do so he set a strike date of June 22nd. Subsequent negotiations made little or no progress. Agitation and resentment among the controller workforce increased. On June 21st, "the count" was started. All PATCO controllers were contacted to see just how many could be relied upon for "D" day. It turned out that the count was insufficient. Poli met again with Department of Transportation Secretary, Drew Lewis. He signed a contract that he knew would be unacceptable to his troops. Perhaps, he thought, this would be the turning point in recruiting more people to ensure a guaranteed strike. He was right. By now the controllers were unified and poised for an all-out work stoppage.

In the meantime, the postal workers extended their strike deadline to a date after the controllers. This way they could see what wrath the government had in store for them.

The PATCO strike was set for August 3, 1981. More than 14 years of neglect and bitterness resulted in some 11,000 Professional Air Traffic Controllers leaving their jobs. Air traffic was nearly brought to a standstill. Over 90 percent of all ATCs were on the picket line; what were left were the dregs and the supervisors. President Reagan announced that the controllers would have a 48-hour moratorium to return to work. After that they would all be fired.

All government employees are required to take an oath that they will not strike. This oath has been broken numerous times by other government workers and they were not fired. Our country was born by the breaking of an oath to the King of England. President Richard Nixon was a man who broke many oaths, yet he was pardoned by President Ford and has made a fortune with his books and speaking engagements. He received his full retirement at taxpayer's expense, and he was guarded around the clock by secret service agents.

Since 1950, there have been 22 federal sector strikes and at no time were the people fired. In 1978, at Newark, New Jersey, 9,000 postal workers struck. And in 1982, President Reagan allowed a settlement that let the postal workers return to their jobs. It looks like PATCO was the scapegoat for the postal workers union.

The scare tactic worked for President Reagan. He was exuberant at the flexing of his newfound presidential muscles. He decided to be a little nicer to the postal workers. In fact, he offered them a bonus of $700 if they would sign their contract. The President must have realized that he could scrape the barrel and replace the 11,000 PATCO workers, but he could never dismiss 175,000 postal workers.

Believe it or not, Ronald Reagan was a union man. He was president of the Screen Actors Guild for a number of years. In his book, *Where's The Rest of Me? The Ronald Reagan Story*, he had this to say regarding the Screen Actors Guild Strike, page 138: "Moreover, what I heard and read in the papers placed me on the side of the strikers. I was then and continue to be a strong believer in the rights of unions as well as in the rights of individuals. I think we have the right as free men to refuse to work for just grievances. The strike is an inalienable weapon of any citizen."

Page 278: "The strike lasted six months. It probably cost actors $10,000,000 in lost income and the studio five times that in lost production. And it really didn't have to happen at all. If only they had agreed to negotiate, they would have found out how reasonable our demands were. We settled for what we were always willing to settle for. Actually, the strike wasn't over amounts or terms but because they said, "We won't even talk to you." There is only so long you can keep knocking on a closed door."

The PATCO strike was devastating to the aviation industry. Airline schedules were cut to shreds and general aviation was nearly grounded. Supervisors at all the facilities were immediately pressed into control positions, something they had not done for years. Yes, they were qualified as far as the records show, but were they really?

A controller's job is one of the most demanding in the aerospace industry. He must be capable of thinking in three dimensions, similar to pilots. When he scans his scope, he must see his traffic not only in the directions of the compass, but also at different altitudes. This takes years of steady practice, something that supervisors do not maintain. When a controller checks out as an FPL (full performance level), he is really only licensed to perform his skills at his facility, and this takes years to accomplish.

The people now being pressed into service were not from the journeymen status. Still, the traffic had to be kept moving at all costs. Supervisors who spent a good part of their time in their offices were now required to work the airline traffic. Military controllers were hired into civilian facilities to help out. Prior to the strike, it took anywhere from three to four years for a raw recruit to reach journeymen status. Now, recruits were manning the scopes with only a few months training. The FAA made a mad scramble to save face. They said they could run the system with the few scabs (strike breakers) who failed to stand up and be counted. And they would use any devious means to achieve their goal. There are various skill levels in the ATC system. Just because a person has a controller's license and is currently checked out, it is not the sole criteria for safe operation. Managers who oversee the real workers seldom separate traffic. They get a checkout from another manager so they are legal on paper.

When the FAA touts the fact that a certain controller has 20 years of service and is one of the most senior men at a facility, look out! They may not be nearly as proficient as a new FPL who has only a few years of experience.

Here are a few facilities where the numbers of FPLs can be compared.

	July 31, 1981 FPL	August 28, 1981 FPL
Chicago Center	397	57
O'Hare Tower	89	17
Cleveland Center	468	131
Cleveland Tower	49	8
L.A. Center	222	104
L.A. Tracon	83	5
Y.Y. Center	411	54
N.Y. Tracon	175	12
Washington Center	381	212
Washington Tower	73	17
TOTAL	2,348	617

By September 27, 1981, the FAA had a patchwork system of nonstriking workers comprised of military controllers, reemployed annuitants, support personnel, and men who were medically disqualified from ever controlling again. Nearly all of the 2,271 supervisors were working the boards at a control position.

The FAA claimed that all were medically certified and qualified. There were over 60 retired controllers who were pressed into service, and approximately 800 military personnel were being worked into the system. Prior to the strike, if an FPL from Kennedy Tower were to transfer to O'Hare, his training time at the new facility could be as long as six months.

Now, we are talking about an FPL, not a recruit off the streets or a military controller. This being fact, how is it that Air Force controllers, men and women who had never worked civil aircraft, were checking out in a matter of weeks? Controllers who were medically retired for such things as coronary problems, high blood pressure, vision problems, nerves, and psychological and other disorders were given waivers by the same flight surgeon who previously failed them. One controller who lost an eye was observed working traffic at the Indianapolis Tower.

There were numerous controllers who could not hack the program. Some people could not check out in Level Five towers (highest level of complexity), so they were transferred to lower level towers (one or two) where the work was much slower and they didn't have to talk to air carriers. There were numerous cases where men were unable to qualify for radar positions at a specific facility. Those people were farmed out to a low traffic tower. Then they were reassigned to the high traffic facility, back to the place where they originally started but failed, only this time they were fully certified in the position in which they had previously failed to qualify.

Sectors were combined (a sector is a specified air space) so that one man might work the air space that was previously controlled by two. For example, the Atlanta Center combined 39 existing sectors into 28. Nearly all facilities made similar operational changes in order to keep the traffic moving.

Of the 17,295 prestrike workforce, 13,311 were FPLs and 2,939 were developmental (training status) controllers. The 11,400 PATCO strikers reduced the number of ATCs to 4,669, a reduction of over 68 percent.

The FAA closed down over 70 less active towers and transferred their inexperienced controllers into the high traffic facilities. The workweek of the controller was initially pegged at 60 hours per week. By September 6, 1981, 70 percent of the ATCs were scheduled for a nice easy week of only 48 hours. Workers were allowed the luxury of not being scheduled for more than two 10-hour days in a row.

The FAA relied heavily on the restriction of traffic in the system. This was done by the central Flow Control in Washington, D.C. As the name implies, they put out guidelines for all facilities that controlled all the traffic in the United States. Aircraft were kept on the ground at their departure points until there was sufficient space on the airways to accommodate them. In this case, the FAA did something right for a change.

Traffic between terminals is normally separated by 1,000 feet vertically and five miles horizontally. The vertical separation remained, but the lateral separation was extended to 30 or 50 miles. This way, the nonunion controller would work at a slower pace, and in-the-air holding would be nonexistent. The majority of the controllers at this time would not have the faintest idea of how to hold an aircraft in flight.

Prior to the strike, there was an abundance of friction between pilots and controllers. After the strike, this situation made a 180-degree reversal. Pilots and controllers were working together, the reason being that without those men on the boards, the planes would be grounded. So it was the season of "lets be nice to the controller" so that we can all keep earning those big bucks.

It wasn't only the pilots who were "apple polishing" the controllers. The airlines got into the act as well. The carriers made a practice of delivering food and beverages to the various control facilities throughout the country. This was to be part of their reward for staying on the job and keeping the traffic moving. The only fly in the ointment was the fact that it is illegal for a government employee to receive any gratuitous gifts (DOT 31USC 665 D). The supervisors knew that this bribery was a "no-no" but they permitted it anyway. The fine for this could be as high as $5,000 or imprisonment for not more than one year.

It seemed that just after the strike, the whole world was against the striking controllers. The press was down on them, the public, and the airline pilots all said they could operate nicely without those "underworked and overpaid prima donnas." If ALPA, the bargaining union for over 50,000 pilots, had backed the controllers in their time of need, the airline industry would have come to a resounding halt. It might have taken a maximum of two days of grounding before the government would have been forced to bargain in good faith.

At the time of the strike, the president of ALPA was J.J. O'Donnell. Sitting atop his ivory tower in Washington, D.C., he had the power to curtail flights that were being handled dangerously but he never did. ALPA set up a system whereby the ATCs could be monitored and all the findings would end up on J.J.'s desk. There were airline pilots assigned to every major airport in the United States. Their function was to record incidents that were fed to them by their fellow pilots. Each day produced pages and pages of incidents and errors. Let's just examine some of the highlights for one day, August 9, 1981. I have purposely only recorded the reports from ALPA even though I have hundreds of incidents from PATCO.

"Delta near miss 1,000 feet with light aircraft."

"Eastern near miss, Mobile, Alabama, with Coast Guard helicopter."

"Western near miss over Gotman, California, with military A-7."

"Tower closings nationwide announced by FAA, leaving many navigational aids unmonitored."

The ALPA air traffic control committee had this to say:

> "We have reports from our members of controller fatigue and believe this presents a safety hazard."
>
> "We have verified several near misses and incidents involving general aviation and air carrier aircraft and believe this presents a new safety hazard in the ATC system that did not exist prior to the disruption."
>
> "We have serious concerns based upon ALPA policy, pilots reports, airlines operating experience and criteria for establishment of FAA towers that a higher potential of danger has been introduced into the ATC system."
>
> "Arrival/Approach B727 lFR (instrument flight rules) VAL912 descending VFR Citation traffic given too late, missed by 200 feet."
>
> "VAL crew stated weather bad deviations were given by controller "edgy."
>
> "ALPA observers still not allowed into FAA facilities." [All licensed pilots are always allowed into FAA facilities. I guess they didn't want to scare the pilots by letting them into a house of chaos] (brackets mine).
>
> "About 25 percent of the reports being received referenced the ATC system operation indicate that the controllers are sounding tired and edgy, as well as reports voicing concern as to the quality of control."

National Officers
J. Bavis
J. Howell

The above is just a partial report concerning one day, August 9, 1981. Similar reports were compiled for weeks.

On August 19, 1981, Captain O'Donnell called a news conference. With hundreds of dangerous reports received from his own pilots, he nervously had this to say: "Our ATC monitoring procedures were showing no unsafe conditions. Already, we have some 300 members on or about to be furloughed, and the chance of a substantial increase in that number is likely. I can say without equivocation the ATC system in this country is safe. I think we have had 17 incidents since the strike occurred. [For one day only, August 9th, I counted 34 incidents] (brackets mine). If it were not safe, we would be the first to speak out, to direct actions to get it safe or take steps to protect the traveling public and our own members."

The airline flight attendants were differently motivated about the unsafe system and they had the courage to spend $26,000 for a full-page ad in the New York Times. August 14, 1981, President Reagan's letter to the head of PATCO, Bob Poli, was reprinted. At the bottom on the letter was the following statement:

"The primary concern of flight attendants throughout the United States is air safety."

"We urge President Reagan to honor his pledge to the air traffic controllers and return to the bargaining table with PATCO. President Reagan has an obligation to the nation's air travelers and in-flight workers; the public's safety and our jobs are at stake.

Respectfully,
Coalition of Flight Attendants
630 Third Avenue
New York, N.Y.

I have been an ALPA member for 28 years. I have always been proud of my membership and for what my association stood, but after seeing and hearing the manner in which Captain O'Donnell conducted himself at the press conference I had nothing but contempt for ALPA in 1981.

On August 11, 1981, I flew my first trip since the PATCO strike started. I was most apprehensive because I had been studying the system and I knew it would be "hairy." I was flying a BAC l-11 (a twin jet similar to a DC-9) from Baltimore, Maryland, to Boston, Massachusetts. To start with, as we taxied out, we had to call ground control three different times before they finally got the trip number correct. I had to hold in the run-up block (pad just adjacent to runway) until the plane ahead got 30 miles away. Normally, it's only five miles.

I finally got takeoff clearance and was told to climb to 9.0; there is no such number. Next, we were switched to Washington Center where we were cleared to FL 290 (29,000 feet) per our request. Well, the BAC l-11 is only permitted to climb to 25,000 feet and no higher. What's more, I never requested 290. Washington then changed us over to New York Center and said to go to 133.05. This was the wrong frequency so we corrected it ourselves. When we finally got to Boston's approach controller, he assigned the wrong runway. When that was straightened out, he never did clear us over to the local controller (tower).

We were now three miles out. I had to ask him if he wanted us to change over. He replied with a grateful "please do." The tower then cleared us to land with an aircraft sitting on the runway.

Well, I saw for myself that all was definitely not well in the ATC "never-never land." I had some time to ponder the situation because my next scheduled trip wasn't until August 18th. I attended some PATCO meetings and watched T.V. All you heard about was the ATC system and how safe the government was making it. I was hoping for good weather for my upcoming three-day trip. At least on a clear day you have a chance to get out of the other fellow's way. In the clouds, you're at the mercy of ATC.

The first day of the trip was relatively safe. Little did I know that on Wednesday, the 19th of August, I would be commanding my last flight on USAir. We were parked at the gate in Indianapolis. The passengers were boarded and we had copied our clearance to Baltimore, Maryland. There wasn't a cloud in the sky, we were the only airliner on the field and none were moving near the airport.

We stayed at the gate for over 15 minutes and the passengers were getting restless. The ATC situation was no secret to my passengers, so I thought it time to put a well-deserved plug in for PATCO. While I cannot remember the exact words, I made the following announcement:

"Good afternoon folks, I suppose you are wondering just why on such a great day we are still parked and not on our way. The main reason is that the people in the tower are not readily acquainted with just how to get us out of here. If the PATCO controllers were still on the job we would have been on our way long ago. I will keep you advised."

Well, we finally got airborne and made our stop at Baltimore. The next leg would be to Bradley field in Connecticut. As we taxied onto the ramp and contacted our company, I was told to come into operations. As I did, the agent told me to contact my regional chief pilot at Washington, a Mr. Sullivan.

"Hello, Jim. I understand you wanted to speak to me."

"Yes, I was told to relate a message to you from Mr. Ron Sessa (Vice-President, Flying). He says to tell you that when you complete your next leg to Philadelphia you are off the line" (grounded).

Well, this was quite a shock.

"Did Sessa say why?" I asked Jim.

"No, he didn't. He just said to tell you that you are to get off the trip and a reserve captain will take it from there."

I wasn't too sure of what dangerous deed I had performed in order to be grounded. All I could think of was that perhaps one of the passengers didn't like to hear the truth and reported me. Well, it's the law of all the airlines; you are guilty until proven innocent. I phoned my wife, Kay, to please drive to Philly to pick me up.

I should give you some more background on this matter. Prior to the strike, I had written two books. The first one dealt exclusively with airline safety, or better, the lack thereof. My last one was about controllers. Needless to say, USAir was less than joyful with my literary offerings, and they weren't backward about showing it. I imagine that Sessa thought that he had me where he wanted me and that the folks at the top echelon would give him a pat on the back. Of course, Sessa was in such a position that he could do whatever he wanted to, but could he make his vengeance stick?

On August 28, 1981, I received the following letter from Mr. Sessa (better known by pilots as "the snake"):

"Dear Captain Power-Waters:

This letter is to confirm you being held out of service, with pay, pending an investigation surrounding events associated with Flight 404 on August 18, 1981.

Sincerely,
M.R. Sessa"

The due process of the ALPA contract was unfolding, whereby I would have a series of meetings with Sessa and then on to the system board of adjustment. The first meeting in Pittsburgh with Mr. Sessa was most interesting. I was represented by my ALPA lawyer, J. Small, and Sessa was armed with at least five company officials, including their lawyer.

Mr. Small broke the silence and asked: "We are quite baffled as to why we are here. There have been no formal charges against Captain Power-Waters."

The other team all looked very sheepishly at each other and then the "king pin," Sessa, stated: "I have a piece of paper here that I want Captain Power-Waters to sign."

My lawyer remarked: "What happens if the captain signs it?"

Sessa's reply: "If he signs it he will be put back on the line with full pay. If he doesn't, he will not be allowed to fly until he does."

Well, this must indeed be a very important piece of paper. It was passed over to us and we read it together. In essence it stated that "I acknowledge and believe the ATC System to be safe." Well, that's all I had to see. I told my lawyer that the meeting was over and I was going to leave, which I did.

This situation reminded me of being in a German prisoner-of-war camp when the commandant confronts a prisoner and says: "You will sign the paper or else."

The next letter from Mr. Sessa related that I was now off the payroll and that my initial grievance was denied. Each time we met with Mr. Sessa he let you know that he was indeed the vice president of flight, and he acted as though he had the situation "wired." After six months of no pay and a lot of frustration, my day in court finally arrived. I decided to seek outside council because I didn't think that ALPA would really press for a favorable decision for a pilot who didn't agree with them about the ATC system. I retained the services of Mr. Don Katz of Washington, D.C.

Incidentally, immediately after my removal from service, Mr. Henry Nash, my chief pilot from Washington, had an extensive phone conversation with my co-pilot. He spoke to him at length, trying his darndest to pressure him into saying that my P.A. announcement contained remarks that it didn't. My co-pilot was a good fellow. He stuck to his guns and told Nash that the announcement I made wasn't that bad at all. It was a nice try on Mr. Nash's part. I have a complete transcript of the proceedings, the following are pertinent excerpts from the document.

On February 3, 1982, in Washington, D.C., my case was heard by the Supreme Court of ALPA, the System Board of Adjustments. In attendance were two company employees, two USAir pilots, and two management officials. I had the pleasure of sitting across the table from Mr. Sessa. His mood was quite different now that he wasn't in his familiar office with his surrounding subordinates. Now he had very little to say. When Mr. Sessa was asked why I was removed from the line, he said it was because of the announcement I made and that I was trying to promote my book on his airplane.

This was the first time in these many months that finally I was told why I was suspended. The next question the board asked was why I was removed from schedule without being given a specific reason. This was contrary to our union contract and the whole case was really resting on this salient point.

Under oath, Mr. Sessa then stated that he had instructed his subordinate, Mr. Sullivan, to tell me why I was being removed. The board had a short recess when, I imagine, they contacted Mr. Sullivan to check out Mr. Sessa's statement (a direct lie).

When the board resumed, Mr. Sessa was asked the same question again. The ALPA lawyer and mine both stated that never, at any of the numerous meetings with the company, did Mr. Sessa make a specified charge against me.

Well, it was a good battle while it lasted, but the company, even with their devious means, couldn't make my reprimand stick. I was returned to flight status with full back pay. I had won the battle, but lost the war, the war being that I must return to the uncertainties of the ATC system.

While lifting weights in my gym, I reinjured an old back muscle. I don't believe I was ever so happy at being all bent over. My back problem was so severe I knew I would never again fly as an airline pilot. I felt no remorse and I was glad to leave the unfriendly skies.

Now let's get back to the ATC.

At San Jose, California, August 17, 1981, at 12:49 PDT, a Piper Arrow collided with a Cessna 172 about two miles east of the Municipal Airport. The weather at the time allowed visual flight rules (VFR). The pilots did have the responsibility of avoiding each other. However, neither pilot was advised of the whereabouts of other aircraft as required by regulations 711065B.

The mid-air collision occurred at 1600 feet as both aircraft were maneuvering for landing on Runway 30R. The pilot of the Cessna was killed, and the pilot and passenger of the Piper were injured.

Because President Reagan fired the striking controllers, the tower personnel were reduced from 19 FPLs to 16. At the time of the accident, there were only two qualified supervisors working the traffic when normally there were five FPL controllers. The supervisor, who was responsible for proper separation, had been working nine-hour shifts for the last 12 days.

At 08:47 EDT on September 23, 1981, a Bell helicopter and a Seminole air charter aircraft collided two miles south of Teterboro Airport in New Jersey. The helicopter fell into the Meadowlands Sports Complex parking lot and both occupants were killed. The aircraft was skillfully belly-landed in a marsh, despite the loss of the right engine and eight feet of the wing. Both occupants got out alive.

Prior to the strike, Teterboro Tower was authorized to have 17 FPLs. However, the highest compliment reached before August 3 was only 12 FPLs. At the time of the accident, the total work force included 11 controllers, 5 trainees, 6 military, and 3 fully qualified. In January of 1985, they were authorized 19 FPL's; they had only 11.

Prior to the strike, Teterboro Tower was short five FPL controllers. In 1986, they were short eight. I guess that's the FAA's idea of progress. It has taken five years to rebuild the system so that today they have three fewer journeymen than they did in 1980.

Once again, the man in charge of separating these aircraft was a supervisor who had been working 10 hours a day, 6 days a week, for over a month.

The tower tapes clearly show that when both of the aircraft checked in with the local controller, neither gave its position. The controller should have requested this in order to keep proper separation, but because of the high workload, he neglected to ask. To add to the scenario, the supervisor answered a telephone call and became engrossed in an administrative matter that required his attention as a supervisor.

For over a year prior to the strike, Teterboro Tower was equipped with a radar monitor BRITE display. This repeater radar screen was an excellent tool that enabled tower personnel to identify the whereabouts of traffic and to aid them in visual separation. This unit was on and operating at the time of the accident. Why wasn't it used? That's easy. The FAA had never trained any of the tower personnel in its operation.

The NTSB gave the air traffic control system a clean bill of health. The conclusion of their past strike investigation, report #SIR-81-7, contained this statement: "The ATC system was operated safely in the two months following the strike." That sounds like something the NTSB might say.

On September 27, 1981, there were 1,585 developmental controllers (trainees) assigned to various facilities. Some of these men and women came from the FAA's training facilities in Oklahoma City. Since the FAA needed people to fill the vacant slots left by the strikers, various devious means were implemented to fill the ranks.

The NTSB-SIR-81-7 report states the following:

"There were 93 trainees in the FAA's Mike Monroney Training Center on August 3, 1981. Of these 93 trainees, 29 failed."

This was certainly a poor showing for the academy and certainly not a positive means to rebuild the system. What's to be done? The FAA decided that they would change some of the failed grades and upgrade them to passing.

On December 22, 1981, House investigator Ed Hugler submitted the following report to Representative William D. Ford, Chairman of the Committee on Post Office and Civil Service:

"The grades of 26 students were changed at one time or another. Records of 14 students who originally failed by less than two points were altered so those students would pass."

Only 49.3 percent of the first three post-strike classes made it to graduation. Nearly all facilities cut their training time in half. Now, controllers were checking out at a radar position (the most difficult) in 52 weeks instead of the usual 126 weeks. Could it be that the FAA decided that all the training times previously used were in error? Or perhaps it's because the system had to be rebuilt as rapidly as possible.

The Reagan Administration was not satisfied by simply firing the controllers; the wrath of the commander in chief was to be echoed in a long line of vengeful deeds.

Leaders of the various PATCO locals were arrested by U.S. Marshals, chained hand and foot, and led off to jail. Numerous fines were imposed, and some of the controllers were incarcerated and fined. Attempts were made by Housing and Urban Development to foreclose on PATCO members' delinquent home mortgages. The Department of Defense denied overseas employment to them, the Department of Labor denied them unemployment benefits, and the Department of Agriculture denied them food stamps.

With the firing of the controllers, came a tremendous tax burden but very few gave it much thought. Although you may believe that President Reagan did the proper thing, you might change your mind after reading the following.

DOT Secretary Drew Lewis estimated that the taxpayers would have to pay $100 million to train 8,000 new controllers. Wrong! The cost to train one controller is $175,000. To train the additional 8,000 controllers now on board has already cost taxpayers $1.4 billion. Although more than one-third of these controllers will never make it to journeymen, the cost per man is still the same.

Airlines were losing $5 million each day and we had to chip in our tax dollars because Reagan wanted to show America who was boss. The strike affected many of the airline employees, since over 10,000 workers were laid off. This, added to the 11,400 controllers, totaled a tidy tax package that the government never received.

It had to stand ready to refund approximately $250 million in pension payments to the fired controllers. State-owned airport landing fees were down $600,000 to $800,000 per day because of reduced traffic. The American Hotel & Motel Association estimated losses of over $25 million daily for the first few months of the strike, with a total loss for 1981 of $2.2 billion.

On January 13, 1982, the snowbound Washington National Airport had all the ingredients for a tragedy of errors. The Deregulation Act of 1978 allowed numerous "fly-by-night" airlines to compete with the scheduled carriers. Air Florida was one of them. Palm 90 was a Boeing 737 scheduled to Fort Lauderdale. There were five crewmembers and a total of 74 passengers on-board. Weather and ATC had caused one-hour 45 minutes delay before these final words from the tower crackled over the cockpit speakers: "Palm 90 cleared for takeoff." Two seconds later, the local controller spoke again. "No delay on departure if you will, traffic's two and a-half out for the runway."

The Palm co-pilot replied: "Okay."

The throttles were advanced, and slowly, very slowly 102,000 pounds of fuel, metal, and human cargo started down short, slippery Runway No. 36.

Eleven seconds after brake release, the power was set. The first officer stated: "God, look at that thing, that don't seem right! Ah! That's not right."

The captain replied: "Yes, it is there 80."

"No, I don't think that's right," exclaimed the co-pilot.

By now the aircraft was nearly out of runway. The captain who was acting as co-pilot on this leg exclaimed:

"Vee one, Vee two" (at this speed, it meant the aircraft was committed to flight).

As backpressure was applied to the yoke, the snow covered aircraft reluctantly inched into the gray skies. With insufficient thrust and a blanket of snow covering the aircraft, there was little chance that it would remain safely in the air. Three seconds after liftoff, the stick shaker (a device on the control column that vibrates when a stall is approaching) started its death rattle. At an altitude of 350 feet over the Potomac River, with the air speed down to 140, she started her descent for the icy river. Knowing only too clearly that they were headed for disaster, the first officer made his final statement: "Larry, we're going down, Larry."

The captain must have recounted the number of unforgivable mistakes he made as he said these final words: "I know it."

At 1601, 36 seconds after leaving the runway, Palm 90's landing lights pierced through the snow and its engines screamed at maximum power, but disaster was only seconds away. Traffic on the 14th Street Bridge was snarled and the motorists gazed in fright as over 100,000 pounds of metal tore through six of the parked cars, killing four of the motorists. The north side of the bridge railing was next to break the impact as 97 feet of it fell over the side. It was only a few more feet to the river where Palm 90 plunged through the ice and sank in 30 feet of water. The tail section was all that could be seen sticking out of the ice-encrusted water.

Seventy-eight lives snuffed out. Why? The captain made some unforgivable mistakes but we are concerned here with ATC's "no-no's."

Washington's flow control should have curtailed the number of inbound to the airport.

President Reagan's firing of the 11,000 controllers made a solid impact on the traffic that could be handled and the lengthy ground delays caused the aircraft to ice up. I have flown out of National for over 10 years and I have never had a delay there of such magnitude.

Because of the heavy snow showers at the airport, the tower personnel could not see the runway, so the local controller (person in charge of air traffic that is in the process of taking off or landing) was entirely dependent on radio conversations with the pilots.

ATP 7710.65B requires controllers to issue runway visual range (RVR) and runway visibility value (RVV) whenever visibility is less than one mile. The night of the crash, visibility was one-half mile and varying. None of these prescribed calls were made to Palm 90. Nor was the ATIS report updated or given to them.

At most air carrier airports there is a continuous taped report concerning the operation of the airport; it's called the ATIS (Automatic Terminal Information Service). This broadcast is usually transmitted from a navigation facility on or near the airport. As weather or runway conditions change the tape must be updated. This update was not performed.

When clearance delivery issued Palm 90 its airways and route, they neglected to ask if Palm 90 had the latest ATIS. This is an ATC requirement.

The night of the crash, the tower was manned almost exclusively by developmental controllers in the following positions:

Local Control (in charge of takeoffs and landings)

Ground control (in charge of all aircraft and vehicles on the ground).

Clearance delivery (in charge of issuing airway clearance, route of flight).

Departure control (in charge of aircraft on takeoff after leaving the airport boundary).

The man on local control was qualified but he was a supervisor. The regular local controller who was working the flights was not spacing the traffic tight enough to satisfy the team supervisor, so he took over the position eight minutes before the crash. He wanted to show the FPL how to speed things up. With slippery runways and taxiways, traffic must be kept at a slow pace. This was not the appropriate time to accelerate the movement of traffic.

The sequencing of traffic on final approach is handled by the radar final approach man. He then hands them over to the local controller in the tower. From this time on it's up to the local controller to apply speed reductions or turns to keep the proper spacing. On the night of the crash this was not done.

Air Traffic Control Handbook 7110.65B, paragraph 743, Traffic Training Program Lesson Plan, stresses "NOT TO CLEAR A DEPARTURE FOR TAKE-OFF WHEN THE ARRIVAL IS 2 MILES FROM THE RUNWAY; IT'S TOO LATE THEN. NORMALLY, DEPARTURE ACTION MUST BE TAKEN AT 3 MILES TO REALIZE A 2 MILE MINIMUM."

By the local controllers taped transmission to Palm 90, it was clearly evident that he did not have the prescribed two-mile separation.

Well, the traffic may have been two and one-half miles from the airport at the time Palm 90 got spooled up and started to push the deep snow out of the way with his wheels, but that separation disappeared immediately. In fact, an Eastern 727 was actually on the same runway touching down as Palm 90 was on the departure end, trying to get airborne. Since Runway 36 is only 6,869 feet long, the two aircraft were barely a mile apart.

The local controller knew that he had a problem when he told Eastern: "Keep it at reduced speed."

It is not only potentially dangerous to slow an aircraft down, but it is against the FAA handbook to request the speed reduction inside the final approach fix. Eastern had already passed this fix.

The captain of Palm 90 was under tremendous pressure. He had his aircraft deiced several times. This service was performed by American Airlines, and it was not done properly. It also was costing his company money. And this deicing was an annoyance to the passengers who were irritable because of the delay. If he didn't takeoff and cancelled the flight, it would not sit well with his company because they would have to bear the expenses of meals and lodging for all on-board.

The captain lacked any real experience in winter weather flying since in Florida, cold weather was hard to come by. And if he delayed the flight again to go back to be deiced he would lose his slot for takeoff.

After the strike, when you were given a takeoff time, you had to make it good, or you could be delayed for hours until ATC could fit you into the sequence again. This was not the way ATC ran before the PATCO job action. When he was cleared for takeoff he knew that Eastern would soon be on his tail; he was using a runway that was short and slippery, and there were no over-runs that could be saving graces, should an aborted takeoff become necessary. As he pushed those throttles for takeoff, he had all these deterrents to ponder. He forgot to turn on the engine anti-ice, thereby giving him false power readings. He was actually using only two-thirds of his available and computed power.

Things weren't going well on the takeoff roll and the crew knew it. Halfway down the runway, he was committed. If he didn't pull it off he would soon be in the river at the end of the minimal length strip and if he stayed on the runway, he would surely have Eastern ramming into his back end.

In spite of the numerous ATC discrepancies, the NTSB had no mention in their final report of controller errors in their probable cause. As usual, the crew received all the blame. It is true that the captain had the last word on all decisions, but you will never convince me that the way he was handled by the air traffic controllers did not have a great influence on his bad judgment.

On November 20, 1982, a North American Rockwell Aero Commander and a Cessna 182 collided in mid-air at 2,000 feet over Livingston, New Jersey. Once again, it was the pilot's responsibility to avoid collisions, but the controller who was working the flights failed to point out the conflicting traffic to the Commander pilot. The Commander pilot was on his way to Teterboro Airport to practice approaches. All persons aboard both aircraft perished in the fiery crash.

The year 1982 proved to be the second worst since 1957 with 36 mid-airs killing 59 people. Of the 36 accidents, 33 of them were between the little guys (general aviation). These figures are quite significant when you take into consideration the fact that the number of aircraft in the skies had been cut by over one-third.

Fifteen weary controllers at the Hartsfield International Airport in Atlanta signed a petition calling for a return of the fired PATCO controllers. Arthur Barrett, an aggressive air traffic controller, was the man who circulated the petition.

Mr. Barrett was contacted by NBC for an appearance on the "Today" show. After airing his legitimate gripes on the show, Mr. Barrett was contacted by his supervisor,. Michael Powderly, the chief of Hartsfield tower. He was relieved of all control duties and was ordered to take medical and psychiatric exams. This tactic has frequently been used to harass boat-rockers. Controller Barrett passed all the tests with flying colors and was recertified for duty, but not without a letter of reprimand.

In 1982, the FAA administrator was J. Lynn Helms. I couldn't find any statements from him concerning disciplinary action from workers who spoke out, but there is an interesting statement about coercion that was made by one administrator, Donald Engen, when he appeared on "Face The Nation" on August 11, 1985.

There were several controllers who appeared, but only behind a shaded screen. CBS moderator Lesley Stahl asked Engen: "But you know most controllers are afraid to talk. We couldn't get a controller to come on who wouldn't insist on being in shadows and having his voice altered."

Mr. Engen replied: "Well, I think every air traffic controller, and I hope everyone in the FAA, understands that I believe in saying the truth and telling it like it is. And I would never penalize anybody for coming and saying what they individually believe."

In 1982, the FAA air traffic control director said that by 1984 the system would be "fully recovered," with no supervisor working in control positions. It is now 2001 and the shortages still exist.

"I assure you we aren't making the headway the FAA tells you; we're not going to rebuild the system by 1983 or 1984 or 1986," says Allen Depoc, an Atlanta tower controller. He must certainly have known what he was talking about.

Prior to the strike, controller instructors had many years of experience. They also were instructed in various teaching techniques. Because it was necessary for supervisors to work control positions, no one monitored controllers' workload, training, proficiency, or detection of fatigue and stress. A group of controllers at the Washington Center in Leesburg, Virginia, were tired of dealing with supervisors who only offered lip service. They were at the end of their rope. A letter was written to the FAA boss, (at that time) J. Lynn Helms.

> "You have stated that the system is back to near normal. While this may appear to be true for the traveling public and the airlines, it is not true for controllers. What is so discouraging is that we can only see our situation at best remaining in the present unacceptable condition. Most of us love our job and have a sincere sense of pride in how we perform our duties, but we are becoming increasingly fatigued and morale is steadily following. As taxpayers, we appreciate the need for government to operate as efficiently as possible. However, there comes a point which we have clearly reached where safety is being sacrificed for false economy."

> 135 Controllers
> Washington Center
> Leesburg, Virginia

On September 27, 1983, at Los Angeles International Airport, a trainee had a small problem. She was working the local position in the tower and was doing fine until she had to handle two DC-10s. One was a Western airline and the other an Air Force aircraft that was going to make a low pass as part of a military celebration that was in progress. The following is her conversation with the pilots and her departure controller:

"Western 270 heavy cleared for takeoff 24 left."

The pilot replied: "Western 270 heavy."

Soon after the departure release of Western, the Air Force DC-10 was nearly above the active runway starting his low pass. If these two aircraft were allowed to continue, the one on takeoff would enter the flight path of the Air Force transport. After getting into trouble, she contacted her departure man and excitedly said: "Augh shit, it's not working out at all. No, he's not. Wait, he's going 250 (pause) 310, this is not going to work. Can you turn the DC-10?"

"No, I can't, not right now" said departure control.

"Okay, she said, I can't abort him either (meaning the airliner). You gotta do something now."

"Okay, I'll climb Salve to 3,000, you maintain—maintain 1,500 feet with—with the other guy."

She replied, "Okay, Western 270 heavy maintain 1,500." Western replied, "Have a good day."

This was another deal that was never investigated by the FAA.

The FAA center in Aurora, Illinois, is perhaps the busiest facility of its kind. The PATCO strike cost them over two-thirds of their journeymen controllers.

On October 3, 1983, an incident involving a young trainee and a supervisor standing behind her watched two radar blips representing aircraft at 7,000 feet over Pontiac. She watched the targets converge until the collision alert system sounded (an oral warning in the center when two aircraft get too close). She gave them a quick turn while the supervisor sauntered away for a coffee break. Veteran controllers who witnessed the incident said the supervisor never reported the "deal." He said he "didn't see a thing." A senior controller said, "It happens all the time. Someone makes a mistake and they don't report it because they don't want the place to look bad."

The annual overtime worked by Aurora controllers in the year 1983 was 96.6 hours. That was more than double the 47-hour average that helped cause the PATCO strike in 1981.

In June of 1983, at a congressional subcommittee hearing, FAA boss Mr. Helms made the following statement regarding overtime: "No one is scheduled for and must work a 48-hour week today."

Under questioning from Ranking Minority Member Molinaro, Helms' position underwent a perceptual change.

Mr. Helms, you mentioned that there was no controller today that, if I understand you correctly, that is working a 48-hour week?"

Mr. Helms replied: "Under normal conditions none of them work more than 48 hours a week."

Overtime and management are two of the main causes of controller unrest. At facilities in Atlanta, Illinois, Virginia, and New York, the men and women were trying to get another union started.

In the spring of 1983, the FAA installed the first piece of new equipment in over six years. The initial implementation would begin at the 20 Air Route Traffic Control Center, and later at the terminal facilities. Since there was so much criticism by the media and the NTSB concerning the inadequacy of the ATC system, this would give the FAA something to brag about.

The new piece of equipment was affectionately known by pilots and ATC as the "Snitch" system because that is exactly what it does. Whenever two aircraft get closer together than 1,000 feet vertically and five miles in trail, or three miles in terminal areas, this electronic marvel sounds an alarm at the ATC supervisor's desk. It also prints pertinent data such as aircraft identification, airspace sector, and closet separation distance.

Prior to "Snitch," pilots and controllers worked out discrepancies among themselves. As long as there was no flagrant or dangerous proximity, no report was filed. Now, if two aircraft get as much as 4.9 miles apart instead of 5 miles, off goes the alarm and the printer starts spinning its yarn.

The supervisor immediately informs the controller that he has just had a "deal" (operational error) and depending on the severity of it, may or may not be pulled off the position. In typical FAA fashion, the punishment for these "deals" varies from one facility to the next. However, it is usually understood that controllers are allowed two errors before they are put on the carpet. Pilots don't have this luxury. Most of the time, pilots receive a letter in the mail, perhaps months after the conflict in question. Then they have to check their logbooks to see if they were even flying on the day in question. They then have to try to remember what the situation was all about, a nearly impossible task, especially after months have elapsed.

The "Snitch" is really a detriment to the system. Big Brother is now continually watching over the shoulders of pilots and controllers. It's like being on a continual check ride. With this in mind, what effect does it have on the traffic? That's an easy one. Controllers have no interest in going to hearings for minute infractions, so they do the only logical thing: spread out the traffic. The FAA management continually prods controllers to work more traffic and do it faster. The "Snitch" will set aviation back years because many pilots don't realize that the "Snitch" machine does it's deed automatically; they think that the controllers have it in for them. This produces even more animosity in a system that needs all the help it can get. If the FAA wants to show congress what they are doing to improve safety, they should hire back the PATCO people who were fired.

A few years ago in the vicinity of the Phillipsburg, Pennsylvania navigational aids, four air carriers and one corporation jet were all involved in a conflict. KLM Flight 621, a Boeing 747 operating from the Netherlands to Atlanta, Georgia, was heading southwest toward Phillipsburg at 31,000 feet. The flight was in New York Center air space and rapidly approaching the East Texas high altitude sector controlled by the Washington Center. USAir Flight 2, a Boeing 737, was flying northeast toward Phillipsburg, in Cleveland Center air space. He was climbing to 33,000 feet on a route that would place him in Washington East Texas sector about four miles west of Phillipsburg.

Three other aircraft, Northwest 157, a Boeing 727; United 1009, a Boeing 727; and a corporate Cessna Citation, were all close to the boundary of the East Texas sector, and all were at 31,000 feet. To say that the three controllers of the East Texas sector were busy would be putting it mildly. Their intermediate task was to fit KLM and USAir into the proper sequence of traffic conveying at 31,000 feet near Phillipsburg. This would not have been much of a task were it not for the fact that they were busy talking to 18 other aircraft in their sector. Forty miles north of Washington's boundary, New York Center initiated an automated interfacility hand-off (when one facility automates a hand-off, the data block adjacent to the target starts to flash, alerting the receiving controller). Cleveland also initiated the hand-off for USAir. The Washington controller could see a conflict brewing on his scope so he told his hand-off man to call Cleveland and put USAir on another heading. At this time, the Washington Center controller directed VAL 1009 to turn 20 degrees to the right. These steps increased the separation but he already had a "deal." Vertically, the traffic was good, but horizontally they were only 1.2 miles apart when they passed.

While Washington was busy with this conflict, they neglected to see the flashing target of KLM who was rapidly entering their air space. The controller who was working the KLM flight was a trainee being watched by an FPL. Now KLM was nearly up on the control boundary and still had no response from the receiving center.

"Why doesn't he answer the flash?"

"Question the controller," he said to his hand-off man.

"Call New York and tell them KLM is not going to get, tell them to spin him."

The hand-off man never did make the call; he was snowed under. The radar controller saw that KLM was still barreling along with no place to go. The controller attempted contact with New York to turn KLM 360 degrees to the right. However, the hand-off man mistakenly activated the circuit to Cleveland who had no control over KLM whatsoever. A supervisor who was plugged in to observe the trainee in New York took the potentially grave situation into his own hands and ordered KLM to turn left. This order was followed but too late. KLM was already into the Washington air space without permission. I'm sure if the crew on KLM were cognizant of the danger they were in, their hearts would have all been beating a lot faster. The supervisor issued another clearance. "KLM 621 immediate descent to FL300."

The Washington controller observed KLM 621 had started a left turn towards VAL 1009. He rapidly told the crew: "United 1009 climb immediately to FL 320."

Too late. Another "deal." VAL and KLM came within 750 feet vertically, and one mile horizontally of each other.

It was definitely not a good night to be flying in this sector. As KLM turned, it was heading directly toward NW157, and if he missed NW, the corporate jet was next, both of them at FL310.

The New York Center controller saw the potential conflict that KLM was causing so he issued the following clearance. "KLM 621 nearly hit two aircraft. He passed within 580 feet vertically and 1.8 miles horizontally of NW 157, and within 1,400 vertically and 3.4 miles horizontally of the Citation. Another "deal."

This will give you a brief glimpse at the unbelievable pressure that a controller is constantly subjected to. With ancient equipment and understaffing, it's a wonder we don't have more "deals."

The radar controller who originally ran the East Texas sector was all alone. He had the task of both separating and handing-off. His supervisor, who could have jumped in to give him a hand, was at a meeting with the facility manager. Another supervisor, who was not as familiar with the sector, was put in charge of the East Texas sector. He could see the controller was "going down the tubes" so he managed to find two men to give him assistance.

On May 18, 1984, the NTSB noted that there were 23 air carrier airplanes in this sector within a 15-minute period. Management erred by allowing a single controller to man this busy sector alone. At the time of this incident, the Washington Center was short 71 controllers and 13 data men. Between April 28 and May 12, 1984, Washington Center scheduled 1,772 hours of overtime. This means the taxpayers are stuck for the time-and-a-half pay simply because the FAA would not rehire the PATCO people.

Prior to the strike in August of 1981, the average daily traffic count at Washington Center was 4,400. In spite of the restrictive flow control, the count rose to 5,700 in 1982. On May 9th, the day of the "deal," the count was as high as 6,900. During the one-hour period of time encompassing the incidents, 53 aircraft transited the East Texas sector.

In a 1984 interview with pilot Jim Good of the AirLine Pilots Association, Administrator Engen stated: "I'm sure some people are overworked in very exclusive segments probably for 15 minutes. But those 15 minutes are pretty doggone fast and heavy, and we are trying to look at ways that supervisors can see them coming up ahead of time and get their people on the scopes." More FAA lip service.

Prior to the PATCO strike in July of 1981, the New York Airports had a total yearly traffic count of 1,013,000 operations. In 1983, it increased to 1,340,000; that's a 35 percent rise. The facility that controls all approaches and departures at La Guardian, Kennedy, Newark, and untold satellite airports is called New York Tracon. It is located on Long Island adjacent to the town of Hempsted. This complex is the busiest in the country, so naturally the FAA maintains adequate personnel.

Prior to 1981, a shift consisted of 14 FPLs; now they had five. This is less than half the number before the job action and there are very few in training. Evidently, FAA Chief Engen did not believe that the terminals were short of men.

"I have a few more controllers in the terminal option at the tower than I really need. And I'm in the act of moving those to the en route option." August 1985, Meet The Press.

When overtime is scheduled, it must be worked. The break period from a busy position is not as it was in the PATCO days. Then, a break was a period free of all duties; now, they simply take you off the scope and let you work the hand-off position. Supervisors are important to the system. They can oversee the scopes, check on training, check for signs of fatigue in the workers, and assign personnel to a busy sector. That is they could do this if most of them didn't work control positions at least 40 percent of the time.

Working a hot position by yourself is dangerous. With at least one person to help you it's much safer. When you are concentrating on a busy part of the scope, it is easy to loose your scan for the satellite airport traffic. A hand-off person takes this burden off your back and coordinates traffic flow with adjacent sectors.

I have asked numerous controllers how they feel about training on the job. They all stated that they would rather not. When a trainee is allowed to sit in the controller position, the training controller should give his complete attention to his student. This can't be done unless a third controller is there to assist. When traffic starts to increase, the instructor is compelled to act as his student's hand-off man. Working the scope is a full-time job and it's hard for a student not to help him out. What happens when the instructor gets on the landline to talk to another sector? Well he can't be watching two places at once. He can either watch the student or be a good guy, hand-off, and have a "deal." No matter what the student does, it's the instructing controller who is responsible. I could fill a book with all the errors that this kind of training has caused.

Since bodies are needed to fill the positions, training time has been vastly accelerated. Today, a trainee off the streets can qualify in two years. It used to take three to five years. Yes, the FAA is pumping out FPLs faster today, but they are paying a dear price for it. Safety is being jeopardized because of the rapid checkouts.

In 1980, the Newark, New Jersey, sector used to handle 800 aircraft per day. Today it's up to 2,600, and this with half of the FPLs of the old days.

Just a few miles east of the New York Tracon sits New York Center. Here traffic is controlled as far as four adjacent states. Before 1981, the center had 337 FPLs and 97 developmentals; today there are only 129 FPLs and 109 trainees. "We have every controller that we need at this time; I couldn't hire." So said Mr. Engen on "Meet The Press," August 1985.

In February of 1981, the traffic count was 129,000; in February of 1984 the count was up to 147,000 with a daily record of 7,000 set on the 17th day of February, 1984. Before 1981, there were 11 FPLs on a crew with perhaps a trainee. Today, there are only 3 or 4 FPLs to a crew, with continuous training in progress. In the old days before a man became qualified in a sector, he had to pass a checkout with an FPL and under the eyes of a supervisor. If he failed to pass, he could be eliminated from ATC. Today, the only requirement is that a supervisor signs one off. This he can do at will, without an official checkout.

Various high officials of the FAA have stated that no controller is ever required to work overtime. Let's examine that statement and see if it's valid. At New York Center, controllers are required to work overtime. If you're scheduled for it, you do it. But supposing you were dead against it and you were willing to put it in writing. What would your fate be then?

One controller told me what happens to those who defy the FAA. He was a senior FPL who had a shift with Sundays off. He was geared to this working schedule and so was his family. After writing the note declining overtime, he was called in to talk to his supervisor. His boss said that since he didn't want any overtime, he would have to take him off his regular shift and instead work a crazy schedule. The controller said he didn't want to have to work that way. The boss then said: "The only way you can work a normal schedule is if you accept the overtime. Are you willing to do that?" The controller answered: "Okay, but I don't like it."

Centers

When an airliner takes off, it is guided by the airport radar departure controller. He guides the flight until it reaches a given geographical limit. Here, it is passed on to a center controller who watches it until it leaves his sector (geographic area). It is then handed off to another sector, and finally to another center where this process through sectors continues until he is passed on to the destination airport approach controller.

There are twenty of these centers in the continental United States and each is responsible for over 100,000 square miles of air space. In 1990, these centers controlled over 38,000,000 flights, a figure the "feds" projected would increase to better than 50,000,000 flights by the 2000s. The FAA has continually wasted billions of dollars to update the equipment in these centers. They award contracts to manufacturers who promise to deliver in a specified time, but it is always years late and always over budget. Recently I spoke to some controllers and asked about their new equipment since the PATCO strike. One fellow summed it up nicely: "The only new equipment that works since 1981 are some new binoculars in some of the towers."

Instead of completely updating the equipment, the "feds" continue to patch up the 30-year-old military junk and wonder why it is prone to break down. Computer hardware tends to deteriorate with age. As a result, if a system is over seven years old, there is a high probability that it is outdated. Most of the hardware at centers was originally purchased more than 30 years ago. New Host hardware did improve the reliability of the en route system, but problems continue. From 1987 to June of 1991, over 3,991 software problems were reported. Some of these problems were related in a 1991 GAO report that stated: "1,661 reported problems were not resolved. Seventy-four percent of these unresolved problems were considered by FAA to have the potential to adversely affect the air traffic system by causing system interruptions or otherwise disrupting the flow of information to air traffic controllers."

It should be understood that controllers are dealing with aircraft flying at over 400 miles per hour. When two are headed toward each other, they close at a combined speed of over 800 miles per hour. It only takes a very few seconds for targets to merge. Radar scopes must be functional at all times.

There is another new radar system the FAA was thinking about; the Initial Sector Suit System (ISSS). This system was supposedly better than what is presently used, but here are some of its shortcomings. On today's hardware, the controller only has to turn a knob to project a sector line on his scope. This line is a valuable tool because it enables the controller to see a target for as long as eight minutes. And all he or she has to do is turn a knob. But with the new system, in order for an ATC to achieve the same function as turning a knob, it now requires sixteen keystrokes. This is not only more work but also causes the controller to remove his or her focus from the radar screen to punch sixteen buttons.

There are other features, bad features that require the controller to completely disregard the screen while their attention is directed to typing in new commands. This takes precious time away from the all-important traffic watch.

Software problems can lead to temporary system interruptions that usually last only a few seconds, but some may last for minutes or more. The GAO reports: "During the 27 month period from October 1988 to December 1990, the 20 centers reported 863 system interruptions caused by software problems, including 81 that FAA classified as system outages because they lasted more than 1 minute."

A series of high-priority outages at the Salt Lake City, Los Angeles, and Houston centers between September 1989 and April 1990 were caused by software defects. These outages ranged from 13 to 24 minutes. In June of 1990, during the morning rush at LA. Center, a 77 minute outage of the primary system resulted in 57 aircraft being delayed an average of 22 minutes. As of June 1991, nine centers reported 310 patches consisting of 172 new patches and 138 carried-over from previous software versions.

Center radar controllers work with computer generated targets whereas the terminal controller (at airports) depends on straight radar hits. Let's look into the ASR-9 which is the latest state-of-the-art radar. This relatively new unit has cost us over $1 billion.

Did we get a good deal for all that money? Not on your life. It never ceases to amaze me how the "feds" spend years checking out various radar manufacturers, installing the equipment around the country, and then find it does not live up to the advertisement that came with the unit. Many times, they spend millions on a project, only to find that the equipment fails to work as expected, and the whole program is dropped, along with the money. Kenneth M. Mead of the GAO had this to say in this 1991 statement before a subcommittee on transportation: "Another cost associated with modernization delay is incurred when equipment is stored because of delays in developing system software. Two years ago we testified that of 24 modernization systems we received, 14 had equipment stored. The value of the stored equipment was about $59 million. FAA continues to store equipment. We recently obtained information on three modernization projects with equipment that FAA is currently paying to store at either the Logistics Center or contractors. The stored equipment is worth approximately $39 million with a total storage cost to FAA of $312,000 per year. For example, one system designed to provide data on equipment performance to maintenance technicians involves equipment worth $15 million that must be stored because it does not meet performance specifications or the needs of system users. FAA HAS NOT DETERMINED HOW TO USE EQUIPMENT FOR THESE THREE SYSTEMS OR HOW LONG IT WILL HAVE TO BE STORED" (capitals mine).

It should be understood that all air carrier turbojet aircraft must file an instrument flight rules (IFR) flight plan. Even if there isn't a cloud in the sky, they must fly by these rules. If the weather at the airport is bad, radar is a must. However, if the weather is good, the crew has a chance to see outside and keep themselves clear of other traffic. Radar controllers are completely engrossed in that green arc that lights up the target on their screen.

They usually are situated at the base of the control tower in a dark room with no windows. They really don't even know if it is raining or not. Their only concern is that their scope continues to display the traffic they are controlling.

Some of the airports around the country are finally getting some new equipment but most of the controllers say that although their old equipment was not as precise as these new ASR-9s, it was a damned-sight more reliable. This new radar system was designed to safely guide jets into and out of the nation's busiest airports well into the twenty-first century. But some of its shortcomings are targets that disappear, phantom targets that appear on radar screens, and frequent outages. The FAA claims that this system was operational 99.9 percent of the time. But FAA employees show that the ASR-9 is only operational 99.4 percent of the time.

That .5 percent difference may seem insignificant but in reality, it amounts to thousands of hours of down time. The "feds" do not include in the outage figures scheduled repair time, only unscheduled. This can make a world of difference to some FAA bosses. The Cleveland Plain Dealer newspaper did a fine piece concerning the ASR-9 radar outages. Mawa McGrath, Safety Director for the Professional Airways System Specialists, the union representing FAA technicians says: "When I worked in the field, I saw it myself. I would work on an outage and I'd come back the next day and the coding and figures would all be changed."

McGrath speculated that one reason for figure juggling was that October raises for managers reporting outages were linked to equipment failures. The less recorded outages, the better the chance for a raise.

FAA Technicians

Geoff Tinelli was making his daily checks on the navigation aids for Runway 10 at New Orleans International Airport. As he cautiously worked his way along the narrow 3,000-foot catwalk over the swampy shores of Lake Pontchartrain, he suddenly stopped. The stick he always carried with him would come in mighty handy.

Loosely coiled around the handrails not 10 feet ahead of him were two deadly cottonmouth snakes. Geoff dislodged them with his stick, and as he moved further along, there were more of them on various levels of the bridge lying peacefully in the hot sun.

Steve Bollinger had just completed half of his 100-mile trip to check on a power generator at Needles near the Colorado River. When he climbed to the site, he was tired and hot. He removed his jacket and laid it on the ground. The generator was mounted on four, 8-inch legs. In order to check the cause of the generator malfunction, Steve would have to reach under the base of the unit to make any adjustments. As he slid his arm under the stand, he heard an ominous rattle just before the snake's fangs sank into the flesh of his hand. He quickly withdrew his arm and cut open the bite in order to suck out the deadly venom. Steve managed to stagger to a telephone before he collapsed. He was rescued and made a complete recovery.

Larry Brosan has to be a man of many talents. His territory is atop Squaw Mountain's 8,819-foot peak. It's bad to get to in the summer, but in the winter it's hell. The snow runs 14 feet deep and the winds have been clocked at over 100 mph. In order to reach the navigation site, numerous means of transportation must be utilized. Snow cats take you up to the ski-lift area; here, you ride the lift to the top of Squaw; and now you must head out on skis. When a storm hits, the temperature may drop well below zero. At least once each season, the workers become snowbound at the site for as long as a week at a time. Many workers have been injured and last year, a man fell to this death.

What do all these gallant men and women have in common? They are members of an elite and skilled group known as FAA technicians. The union that represents these workers is known as Professional Airways System Specialists (PASS).

Since September of 1994, there have been six major outages at the Chicago Air Route Traffic Control Center. The majority of these outages occurred because of a breakdown in the IBM 9020E display primary computers. Although this equipment was made using 1960s technology, it is still in use—40 years later.

Wanda Geist had this to say concerning their equipment: "The problem is not that our technicians cannot fix the 9020. They can. The problem is that IBM no longer manufactures or repairs the parts needed to fix the equipment. Because there are no available parts, we are currently using parts cannibalized from another DCC system, the 9020, located in a warehouse at the FAA Depot in Oklahoma City. As you might expect, there are a limited number of 9020 parts remaining, and those parts are also 40 years old."

Outages cannot be tolerated. They cost vast amounts of money and while the system is down, safety is jeopardized. Busy facilities such as Chicago Center is designated as "4Z" by the FAA, meaning "immediate restoration is required," and technicians should be on-site 24-hours a day, seven days a week, in order to carry out such restoration. There are many units in the Chicago Center that are only covered 16 hours a day, and elsewhere, units are never maintained on the night shift.

When a system goes down and there is no one there to repair it, the traveling public is not living in a completely safe environment. Sure, there are usually backups (that may or may not function), but what about power outages that can affect all equipment? The FAA continues to break its own rules. They state that a technician must be on site to repair any faults, and in the same breath they fail to supply these important PASS technicians.

We have discussed the normal ATC system that is the 40-year-old IBM 9020 computer that accepts targets from the host computer where it is processed for displays. When this beauty fails, it's a scramble to get the backup Direct Access Radar Channel (DARC) system on line. After a computer failure and extensive traffic delays, the FAA management can always be seen on local TV stations stating that "safety was never compromised." Well, let's see about that.

When the backup is used, some safety features are immediately lost. There is no conflict alert system that sounds a warning when two targets get closer than they should, and there is no minimum safe altitude warning system to alert targets that are getting too close to mother earth. And when the host computer goes off line, other automated features that controllers have become accustomed to such as automatic target identification, automated hand-off to or from adjacent sectors, and automatic flight-plan processing are also lost. The only time controllers get to practice with the DARC stand-alone system is during the low-traffic midnight shift. If a technician hasn't worked this system recently, he could really be in a dilemma when it comes time for him to use it.

The ancient equipment is not only unreliable, but also is time-consuming when training technicians to care for it. Mark Scholl, the local president for the National Air Traffic Controllers Association (NATCA) at Chicago Center, made the following statement at a Congressional Subcommittee on Aviation: "A reduction of FAA personnel trained to repair equipment that is no longer manufactured or supported by IBM, and a lack of spare parts for the aging system—it is very time-consuming to train new technicians to trouble-shoot and repair this old equipment. For example, the original training course for the 9020 was over one year. The course has been reduced to four months of training, followed by on-the-job training. It is obvious that FAA must rely heavily on the currently qualified staff to maintain this equipment during the remainder of its projected life."

Most of the following quotes came from a very fine article in the August 7, 1995, Newsweek Magazine, written by Beck, Hosenball and Chinni. "The evening rush was just ending at Chicago O'Hare Airport on July 17 when David Cottingham's radar screen blinked an ominous message: Not updating time and display. Cottingham, a veteran controller, knew what that meant: the 40-year-old computer system was crashing again."

The main computer came back to life after 55 tense minutes—only to fail again the following week. The PASS workers were probing for system faults for over 28 hours. The FAA made their usual statement, "Safety was never compromised," but Cottingham isn't so sure.

"People who do this job day in and day out say IT'S NOT SAFE ANY MORE. I CAN CERTAINLY SEE DISASTER OCCURRING" (capitals mine).

Even when the system is functioning normally, controllers are not happy with what they see on their scopes. Washington Center controller David Carmichael says planes sometimes vanish temporarily from the radar screens. And sometimes the radar sees planes that aren't there.

On July 1, six phantom "blips" suddenly appeared on Carmichael's screen, all moving eastbound at different altitudes and speeds. "I was absolutely sure they were aircraft heading straight into oncoming traffic. Pilots in the area were notified, and some quickly veered from their flight plans to avoid possible collisions. Then the phantom squadron just disappeared."

Controllers watched in house, on one still functioning screen, as two planes headed for each other at 33,000 feet. They frantically called another FAA facility, which alerted one pilot to descend.

"The equipment needs to be replaced from top to bottom," says longtime Chicago controller Lauren McCormack, who's quitting his $85,000-a-year job because he feels he can't guarantee safety. "The FAA," he says, "is playing Russian roulette."

In the Oakland California Center on August 9, 1995, the critical power was lost and all computers, radar displays and air/ground communications failed. At 7:30 a.m. PDT, the FAA technicians located the problem and manually restored critical power. As a result of the power failure, the DARC backup system suffered damage. At 7:55 a.m. PDT, controllers began accepting limited traffic from adjacent FAA facilities. Fifty-nine minutes after the initial failure, the PASS people restored the main computer. The original system was down for nearly an hour. If you had the misfortune to be flying in the vicinity of one of these outages, your captain would have had no idea of the dangerous conditions through which he was flying. If the weather was good, he could keep himself clear of other targets, but if the weather was bad, he was probably better off not knowing what trouble he was in.

There were 344 air traffic delays reported, and one near-collision—all caused by the faulty equipment.

A PASS member at Syracuse Airways Facilities Sector Field Office stated: "Presently at our Level III facility, we have no fully-certified technicians."

A Virginia field office said that his facility was grossly understaffed. "These technicians can no longer carry the workload of six technicians, and still provide adequate maintenance and service to ATC."

Pittsburgh Sector staffing shortages are critical. They are authorized 80 PASS people but only have 66 on board. This facility also has 10 employees that are past retirement eligibility.

Within the Shenandoah Sector, in Roanoke, Virginia, they are authorized 12 electronic technicians. There are currently eight on board. Also in this sector, there are only two PASS members, where as the FAA has authorized eight. These people are required to support new equipment that is scheduled for installation.

The Hopkins radar system was blind for five hours. Controllers drove half an hour to Oberline and, using telephones, helped their colleagues back at Hopkins land four planes that were in a holding pattern above the field and rerouted other traffic to other airports. In all, airline officials postponed 19 flights and 15 jets were diverted to land at other airports.

At the Naval Air Station in Moffett, California, their ASR-9 was down for 83.1 hours in 1991.

And at Boston's Logan Airport on February 18, 1991, the system was shut down for maintenance. When it was restored, it failed and was out for 16 minutes more.

Since 1990, Tri-Cities Airport in Pasco, Washington, is the record-holder for outages. It has been down for 3,545 hours. That's 49 days in one year.

In July 1995, the old IBM 9020 computers at the Air Route Traffic Control Center at Aurora, Illinois, caused traffic delays to at least 24 flights. The problem was attributed to a faulty computer element in the 40-year-old equipment. The backup system was in use for over a day. This system is not as safe as the main system, and the main system isn't as good as it could be. The 9020 is now being used as a processor something it was not designed for. The system overloads easily and can fail. Other critical safety features that do not function in the backup mode include lack of histories, target trails, map data, weather data, and, most importantly, conflict alerts.

Many times after the media catches a failure in the system, there's an FAA official who will state "There was absolutely no compromise of safety in the system." If you believe that, you probably still believe in the tooth fairy.

Air Transport Association (ATA) president Carol Willett stated in a letter to former FAA Administrator David R. Hinson: "The 20-year-old technology is subject to more frequent and longer-lasting equipment failures. The systems are operating without full redundancy on an average of 50 percent of the time. Restoration times are becoming longer due to parts shortages. Failures are becoming more complex."

The Aurora ARTCC covers an area of much of Iowa, Wisconsin, Indiana and Illinois. Through this system, there were over 400 flight delays.

On August 9, 1995 in the Oakland California Center, a defective circuit board caused a power outage to computers used for ATC. One power center was down for maintenance and the two remaining experienced circuit board failure; the third could not handle the power surge, resulting in a shutdown.

Not only did the radar fail, but also radio communications to aircraft was nonexistent. During the outage, there was a near mid-air collision, but because the skies were clear, the pilots were able to avoid a mishap.

On September 9, the Aurora ATC shut down again, causing a slowdown of all Chicago O'Hare bound aircraft for about 40 minutes. The backup system was in use for over 28 hours.

On October 17, 1995 in Fort Worth, Texas, the ATC scopes went down for three hours, delaying over 300 flights for up to 90 minutes.

And on November 17, 1995 in New York Center, computer software problems at Ronkonkomo caused numerous delays at the New York airports. The equipment was down for 48 minutes. "Air traffic safety was maintained at all times," said FAA's John Walker.

While the radar scopes are necessary items for the control of air traffic, radio communication is just as important. If a controller loses radio contact with a pilot, there is very little that can be done. Sure, you can watch two aircraft on the scope that are getting a little too close, but if you can't talk to them and warn them, you will have to sit there and watch the targets hit. Of course, you can contact another facility that has working radios, but this takes time, which you may not have. Radios have failed nearly as much as the radar scopes, but that's to be expected with the ancient junk that controllers are forced to work with.

Mr. Ludwig, the BWI controllers Association president, sums it up nicely: "We have 1960 equipment, 1970 staffing, and 1990s traffic; and the federal management says to make do with what we have."

In 1995, Mr. Jack Johnson, former President of the Professional Airway System Specialists, appeared before Congress to try to get some satisfaction for his 10,000 FAA employees. "Since 1977, PASS has served as the exclusive representative for Technical and Aviation Systems Specialists employed by the FAA. Presently, PASS proudly represents more than 10,000 FAA employers, including the Airways Facilities (AF) employees who install, repair, maintain, and certify the entire realm of electronic, electromechanical, and environmental systems used in air traffic control and national defense. Significant staffing shortfalls exist which result in eight of the nine FAA regions being dangerously understaffed."

In 1980, there were over 11,000 System Specialists who maintained 19,000 FAA facilities through our nation. Today, the number of complex electronic systems has increased to 31,000, whereas the ranks of the specialists have been reduced to under 6,000 trained, partially trained, or completely untrained technicians.

The FAA has already projected that employment in Systems Maintenance is being reduced by 156 technicians. The GAO recommended that by 1995, a field work force of over 11,900 would be needed. This will make the all-important technician position understaffed by 3,700 because over 50 percent of today's system specialists are eligible to retire.

In testimony before a congressional subcommittee recently, James Landy, President of the Air Transport Association of America, stated: "The FAA's air traffic control system has operated in a manner that has resulted in an average of between 700 and 1,100 flight delays of 15 minutes or more each and every day." The former DOT Secretary Pena says, "These delays cost the airlines and their passengers in excess of $3.6 billion a year."

So it seems that the controllers today are not the only ones who are understaffed. There are about 3,000 new technicians urgently needed to keep the system at a minimum standard of safety. Most of the systems used by ATC are understaffed by 30 percent. Does this sound like a system you feel safe to fly in?

The FAA shows no mercy when it comes to eliminating positions. The lower-level towers are now being manned by private sector controllers. The "feds" are doing the same with Airways Facilities workers. They are being replaced with technicians off the street who don't know the equipment and many times have to ask the senior FAA technicians to explain the intricacies of the system they are responsible for.

It takes between three to five years before technicians are fully certified and there are very few new ones that are being hired. A quote from the GAO: "While system specialists have chosen this business as a career, contract workers have chosen it for profit.' Also, the GAO questioned why the FAA "did not consider using in-house staff which the agency estimates would save about $45,000 per staff year compared to using contract staff."

The FAA's own projections show that nearly 60 percent of the men servicing the latest automation equipment will retire before 1999. In September of 1995, Wanda Geist, President of Chapter 101 and an active airways specialist (PASS), appeared before Congress to explain the problems of her people. She aptly stated that there were "three problem areas that hinder our work force: antiquated equipment, understaffing, and lack of training."

The current president of PASS, Mr. Michael D. Tanfalone, had this to say at a 1999 congressional hearing: "The FAA Airway Facilities Service workforce is staffed at only 66 percent of the agency's own standard, despite the fact that antiquated air traffic control systems are breaking down in record numbers, with as many as 4,000 pieces of equipment out of service every day."

Delays

If there is a word that airlines hate it is "delays." I can see their point, and it makes a big difference to a passenger who is making a connection at another airport. A delay can ruin a perfectly good day but we also have seen that the government works in very strange ways.

The Official Airline Guide is a book printed twice each month. In it are all the airline flights and times of departure and arrivals. Each airline decides how long it will take to go from A to B, including a built-in delay. With the faulty ATC equipment, inefficient airway technicians, the lack of sufficient airports, and the scarcity of journeymen controllers, it's no wonder there are delays.

At any rate, the "feds," in order to look good, pressured the airlines to lengthen their theoretical time en route. This would give them a better chance to look good. And another government brainwave; when the delay time is supposed to start.

You and I, being mere mortals, would say that if a plane is supposed to depart on the hour and it fails, it is delayed. Wrong. The "feds" say that a delay does not start until the airliner leaves the gate; if the plane has an ATC delay at the gate for, say, 30 minutes, and this causes you to miss your connecting flight, it's not a "delay" in the eyes of the FAA.

The feds state that the majority of airline delays are caused by weather. This is most definitely incorrect but it gets them off the "delay" hook. In reality, delays are really caused by the ATC system. There aren't enough runways, and the system is about 1,200 controllers short. The DOT says that the annual cost of delays for airlines is $5 billion. It costs major carriers $90.03 per aircraft per minute of delays.

According to the FAA, June of 2000 was the worst month for delays in U.S. airline history: a 20 percent increase over June of 1999 to a record 50,000 flights. It is estimated that by 2012, over 8 million landings and takeoffs will be added to the twenty-six million in the year 2000. And the number of passengers will increase from 680 million to one billion in 2012.

The big problem today is the fact that on a clear day, with all the radar working perfectly, many of our airports already exceed their traffic capacity. When radar goes down or weather moves in, delays are inevitable.

Poor planning also can be blamed for delays. By that I mean when airports are constructed, they are built far enough from a city to allow expansion. The surrounding barren land is soon diminished by real estate sales that causes people to complain about jet noise. People who buy property adjacent to an airport must realize that jets make noise and the flight paths might be directly over their homes. Unfortunately, disgruntled neighbors can block the expansion of an existing airport or halt the building of a new runway.

The government is way behind the power curve when it comes to thinking ahead. Overworked airports have only one way to eliminate their delays; build more airports.

It takes at least ten years from the time a new airport is started until planes start landing. What does that mean to you, the traveling public? It means that you can expect increasing delays every year until the new concrete is added.

There are hundreds of new aircraft being added to the airline fleets. The air space remains the same, so it behooves air traffic planners to pack more aircraft into the existing air space. One possible solution is to build larger aircraft that can hold more passengers. The size of an aircraft has little bearing on how it is handled by air traffic control. A small general aviation aircraft uses up the same air space as a 747. When it comes to the number of landings per hour, a small plane will land and discharge two passengers whereas a large one might deplane hundreds. They both use up the same precious air space.

While I hate to suggest it, it might be prudent to limit small aircraft from the larger terminals. There are numerous satellite airports that a small plane could utilize. Large airports for the large planes; small airports for the small aircraft. I can hear the general aviation pilots screaming at this suggestion, but it might work.

If you think that the airport delays today are way out of line, you ain't seen nothin' yet!

Air Traffic Controllers

As of today, the ATC system is about 1,200 controllers short. If you ask the "feds" about this shortage, you will hear that the system has all the ATCs that it needs. When the "feds" decided to shrink the number of controllers to conform to their newly devised scheme, various unsavory tactics were inaugurated.

One of the key ways to make the numbers look good was to combine sectors. The "feds" have used this unsafe tactic for years but now they are running it into the ground. While it is true that if a controller is given more air space to control it will decrease the number of controllers needed, it will decidedly increase the controller's workload. In some sectors, there is little traffic. Others have far too much, even before their limits were increased. In 1994, there were 80 less sectors than before the 1981 strike. This is not a safe practice.

Prior to the PATCO strike, it took about five years for a person to go from a developmental (trainee) to an FPL (full performance level). If a controller were assigned to a tower cab, radar room, or a center, he or she would have to qualify in all the positions in that facility. This training gave them a great feel for all the positions so that they would instinctively know when someone was going "down the tubes," and perhaps he or she could send help. Today, the FPL is still in the system but there have been modifications. Some controllers have reached this status in as little time as two years. In order to confuse Congress, the "feds" came up with a new title for the development controller. They called him an "operational controller." It may sound like a slick name but he or she is still a low-time trainee.

To be a good controller, you must be able to make split-second decisions. You must be able to look at a scope and see your traffic in three dimensions, not just left and right but vertically. When I was flying for USAir, I was responsible for only 100 lives. When a controller keys his mike, thousands of lives are dependent on him to give the proper instructions.

Visualize working 18 aircraft, each one averaging 200 passengers. That is 3,600 people whose lives are in your hands. The system is "cooking," and all targets are showing their proper data blocks. You have just issued a climb to American and a descent to USAir. Without a warning, the computer goes down and the screen goes completely blank. Now all you have to do is remember, in three dimensions, the heading altitude, speed, and destination of 18 aircraft. The 3,600 people still are hurtling head-on at over 900 miles per hour. As you activate the backup system and hope that it will function, precious minutes are wasted, minutes that could spell disaster.

In 1993, the FAA published its yearly budget, calling for an additional 150 air traffic controllers and pushing the FAA's count to 17,871. The agency's use of "controller workforce" numbers makes it appear there are more controllers today than in 1981. If you discount clerical workers, supervisors, and maintenance workers, there are really fewer than 15,000 full-time controllers as compared to 16,200 before the strike.

Recently, President Clinton lifted the ban on hiring the striking PATCO controllers; however, the "feds" are only planning on hiring approximately 150 new controllers per year. It would only take them a year to train the old PATCO people because the equipment they used 30 years ago is still in service.

Since the 1981 PATCO strike, there has been a decrease in the number of controllers by about 1,500. This does not fare well with the traffic increase of about 30 percent. Now we have fewer controllers working more traffic than we did 20 years ago. According to John Thornton, Director of Legislative Affairs for NATCA, approximately one-third of the total work force, or 50 percent of the full-performance controllers, would be eligible for retirement in 1999. For example, at the Washington Tower, there are approximately 270 FPLs, of which 135 were eligible for retirement in 1999. Since the "feds" claim to have all the controllers they need, why is it that each year the FAA requires that thousands of hours of overtime be utilized? This overtime is a deterrent to safety. When an ATC has put in a grueling day, he does not want to have his time on the "boards" extended.

The following is a list of controller staffing at en route centers.

FACILITY	AUTHORIZED WORK FORCE	ON BOARD WORK FORCE	FPLS	% FPLS
Albuquerque	339	327	209	64
Anchorage	177	169	92	54
Atlanta	525	518	317	61
Boston	49	335	188	56
Central Flow	44	28	28	100
Chicago	488	490	233	48
Cleveland	465	458	300	66
Dallas/Ft. Worth	417	401	248	62

Denver	386	382	219	57
Guam	19	12	9	75
Honolulu	68	58	32	55
Houston	383	373	223	60
Indianapolis	368	354	222	63
Jacksonville	32	354	214	60
Kansas City	408	414	242	58
Los Angeles	353	385	198	51
Memphis	378	341	210	67
Miami	331	325	197	61
Minneapolis	287	314	210	67
New York	370	347	190	55
Oakland	345	322	170	53
Salt Lake City	238	239	140	59
San Juan	64	57	33	58
Seattle	294	284	169	60
Washington	513	464	291	63
Total	7,971	7,751	4,584	59

The following is a most informative list compiled by the NTSB depicting the numbers of controllers in various countries.

	NUMBER OF AIR TRAFFIC CONTROLLERS	NUMBER OF AIRCRAFT MOVEMENTS	NUMBER OF COMMERCIAL AIRCRAFT	WEEKLY DOMESTIC DEPARTURES
United States	17,300	38 Million	18,440	142,930
Canada	2,050	7.4 Million	5,680	16,950
Australia	1,140	3.6 Million	260	5,500
Germany	2,000	2 Million	680	15,000
United Kingdom	1,630	1.5 Million	3,120	4,840
Switzerland	300	1.5 Million	N/A	N/A
New Zealand	300	1.2 Million	130	3,670

It is estimated that the FAA will go through at least $35 billion to update the ATC system. Much of the equipment, if they can get it to work, will be outmoded years before it is ever installed.

The Cleveland Hopkins radar has failed 58 times for a total of 213 hours since its installation in 1991. From Michael Sangiacomo and Dave Davis' report in the Plain Dealer: "The radar screens at Hopkins went blank. Not only did the airport's radar system fail, but when FAA officials tried to switch to the backup system at Oberlin, that system also failed.

On March 28, 1996, the radar at Pittsburgh International Airport went down for five hours, causing hundreds of flights to divert. There were over 12 airlines that were flying with closer than minimum separation and there was a near-head-on collision.

What went wrong was nothing new for this facility. In the six months prior to March 1996, there were nine radar failures although not as devastating as this one. The radar, radios, telephones and electricity all were inoperative. Traffic was building and there was no control at all. An alert controller kept his fingers crossed as he headed for a pay phone in the terminal and managed to contact Cleveland Center to warn them of the outage and to shut down all in-bounds to Pittsburgh. All of the controllers on this watch were under extreme stress and seven of them requested some time off to deal with their jangled nerves.

I feel ashamed to tell you that out of the hundreds of terminal facilities in the United States, only 30 have a bona fide backup system. The ATC system is in shambles. The FAA is so far behind the power curve in equipment, controllers and technicians, they will never catch-up.

The former FAA Administrator made the following statement at a 1996 press club luncheon:

"But I can tell you with certainty that the air traffic control system today is 99.4 percent reliable. It runs 365 days a year, day in and day out, weather good, bad, and otherwise. And it is the most reliable it has been in the history of the FAA."

So help us all.

CHAPTER 9

▼

THE INTRUDER

"Aircraft collision avoidance systems cause mid-air collision. No survivors."

This could easily be a headline in your local newspaper unless changes are made to the present Traffic Alert and Collision Avoidance System (TCAS). The vast majority of airliners were equipped with this system, and by the end of 1994, all large commercial carriers should have had these units installed.

Before we get into the workings of this system, I would like to acquaint you with a little background of how the ATC system operates.

Whenever there is more than one aircraft in close proximity to another, the potential for a mid-air collision always exists. When the weather is clear, the "see and be seen" rules are in effect. You still must keep a constant visual outside the cockpit and avoid bumping into other aircraft. When the visibility is poor, this responsibility is squarely on the shoulders of the ATC and that is where it definitely belongs.

During WW II, a device was invented that shows a positive identification of aircraft flying in the vicinity of a radar antenna and was called Identification Friend or Foe (IFF). It worked, was carried over into the civilian ATC system, and is used today. After WW II, IFF beacons were called transponders, and with years of refinement, they work very well.

It was not until the mid-1970s with the advent of the Mode "C" Air Traffic Control Radar Beacon System (automatically reports aircraft altitudes) that a newly refined system emerged. Prior to this innovation, the ATC had no idea of an aircraft's altitude unless they were told. So this new transponder cuts down on the workload of the pilot and controller.

It should be understood that a controller's main mission in the ATC system is to separate aircraft. They do a superior job with the ancient equipment they have to use. As usual, improvements to ATC are triggered by crashes. In 1956, a TWA Super Constellation and a United DC-7 collided over the Grand Canyon. This tragedy led to greater radar coverage throughout the United States. A series of more mid-air collisions brought new and better equipment. On the morning of September 25, 1978, Pacific Southwest Airlines Flight 182, a Boeing 727, was on descent for a landing at San Diego's Lindbergh Field. It collided with a small Cessna 172 that was practicing simulated instrument approaches. All souls on board both aircraft were killed, as well as seven people on the ground.

In August of 1986, California saw another mid-air collision, this time in a suburb of Los Angeles known as Cerritos, just 100 miles from the PSA San Diego tragedy. An Aeromexico DC-9 was inbound for a landing at Los Angeles International Airport when it struck a Piper PA 28-181. Both aircraft were on the scope of the controller. In fact, the airliner was told of the presence of potential traffic. The Piper had a transponder but not one that reported altitude, nor was one required. The DC-9's tail sheared off the top of the small plane, decapitating the pilot, his wife, and his daughter. The jet slammed into a house, killing all on board and fifteen people on the ground.

To say that the area surrounding Los Angeles Airport was up in arms was putting it mildly. Congress held fact-finding sessions and directed the FAA to put a foolproof collision avoidance system on board all airliners.

Congressman Henry Gonzalez stated the following on the floor of the House of Representatives: "The FAA's hands are not as clean as he would like them to be, and they will, in my judgment, get dirtier with the blood of countless victims of air tragedies if its policies are allowed to continue."

Well said, Congressman, I couldn't agree with you more. The policy-makers of the FAA are guided by the following policy ... Don't make waves, we will be retiring soon.

The first effort pushed by the "feds" was called the Beacon Collision Avoidance System (BCAS). The government was appraised of better systems that were being developed but they insisted on doing their own in-house, thing. Nine years passed while the FAA continued to play. Many millions of the taxpayers' money went down the drain before the BCAS was finally abandoned.

In 1981, it was recognized that a viable system was possible, and input from the ATA, private research organizations, electronic equipment manufacturers, the FAA, and others developed the Minimum Operation Performance Specifications (MOPS) for TCAS.

The FAA continually backpedals when it comes to new equipment. The first units were installed in 1990 and half the airliners were to be TCAS equipped by 1991. The remainder of the fleet was to have been outfitted by December of 1993. The target date was not realistic as only about 80 percent of the fleet had TCAS aboard in 1994. Some of the first airlines to install TCAS were United, Northwest, and USAirways. USAirways was the first airline to obtain TCAS certification.

Well, enough history. Let's get into the workings of a TCAS unit. In the United States, three companies (Collins, Honeywell, and Bendix/King) all produce TCAS units at a price of $150,000 each. The basics for TCAS II are a computer, some form of a cockpit display, and a transponder. You might be wondering what ever happened to TCAS I? Well, it is being developed for use on smaller aircraft. It is not as sophisticated as TCAS II, but then what can you expect for a mere $150,000? The functions of all these systems are similar in one respect. They all help to keep aircraft clear of conflicting traffic. And now there is TCAS III?

- TCAS I only gives a warning of intruder traffic, no escape information.

- TCAS II gives a warning of intruder traffic and issues escape information to climb, descend, or maintain present altitude.

- TCAS 111 by far is the best of the lot. It issues a warning of an intruder and shows escape routes for both climbs and descents, as well as turns to the left or right.

The manufacturers are having enough trouble trying to perfect the existing TCAS II. TCAS I is next to be produced for smaller aircraft. TCAS III is just a dream in the eyes of the manufacturers and may never come to pass.

Before we venture too far into tomorrow, let's examine today's TCAS II system and how it works. A typical system includes a Mode S transponder, a signal processor, and two antennas, one on top of the fuselage and one on the bottom. The pilot will be looking at either his vertical speed indicator, modified to include a small airplane symbol at the bottom, and a ring around the outside that shows the rate of climb or descent necessary to escape. The trick is to keep the vertical speed indicator (VSI) needle always in the green arc. This ensures the proper vertical rate to escape. The other instrument that can be used is the airborne radar that will display a similar symbol as does the VSI. There are a few more interesting things to discuss before we get into the meat of this unit.

The first signs of a conflict are known as Traffic Advisories (TA). The signs of potential trouble are depicted by a hollow white diamond at the outer reaches of the display. It shows up when the intruder comes within six miles and 1200 feet of an aircraft. Adjoining this diamond symbol is an arrow that points up or down for the vertical direction of traffic, and it also displays a number signifying it's altitude. If the traffic continues toward you, the diamond turns to a solid white. When the intruder poses a continued threat (35 to 45 seconds away), the white diamond becomes a solid yellow circle; at the same time, an audio advisory is issued in a nice female voice (the FAA is smart about some things)—"TRAFFIC, TRAFFIC". Now is the time for the pilot to check the yellow circle and look out the window for the intruder. At this juncture, no evasive action should be taken. If the TCAS determines that the two aircraft will collide (20 to 30 seconds away), the yellow circle turns into a red square and an Resolution Advisory or a command to escape is given. Now the female voice really gets excited and yells out "CLIMB, CLIMB," "INCREASE CLIMB," "REDUCE

CLIMB," "DESCEND, DESCEND, DESCEND," or any of the eight other advisories.

Simultaneously, the outer arc of the VSI will show green- or red-colored areas. The pilot must climb or descend, and keep the vertical speed needle in the green area. The initial rate of descent or climb calls for 1,500 feet per minute up or down. After the intruder is clear, the display will revert to a nonthreatening target and that nice girl will be saying, "CLEAR OF TRAFFIC, CLEAR OF TRAFFIC."

That's a thumbnail sketch of how the system works. It looks good and it sounds great, but is it? If this unit functioned perfectly in the ATC system, there would be no complaints from pilots or controllers; but it does not always live up to the advertisement on the box it came in. First, let me reiterate the assigned job of the ATC and the pilot. The ATC is trained to properly control traffic under his jurisdiction to be sure that aircraft do not bump into each other. That's the job, and he or she does it well considering the ancient equipment they have to work with. The pilot, on the other hand, is well-versed in the manipulation of controls and making the proper decisions. He is not trained in controlling traffic, and with the workload in a modern jet's cockpit, being burdened with trying to sharpshoot the controller it is not a good idea. I have been kept alive for 30,000 hours because of three distinct facts: one, my personal skills; two, large quotas of luck; and three, because of the controllers who gave me the right information at the correct time.

I'm sure you have heard the old adage, a little knowledge is a dangerous thing. Well, that applies to pilots who are in the cockpit training to be controllers. If all the bugs were eliminated from the TCAS system, I would be more than happy to take full advantage of it, but as it stands now, it is a "crap shoot."

Following are a few of the discrepancies concerning TCAS II.

Shouting

The volume of that nice girl who issues the warnings is so loud that you cannot hear any transmissions from ATC, and that is a must.

Parallel Runways

The only time a pilot has to earn his salary is during landing and take-off. This is the very time that TCAS does most of its chattering. Pilots shooting a landing at a field where there are dual approaches in progress (aircraft landing on parallel runways) have been issued advisories by TCAS to "CLIMB, CLIMB NOW." The unit was receiving a warning from the parallel aircraft. Below 1,000 feet, it would seem provident to switch the TCAS to TA mode and just hear Susie saying, "TRAFFIC, TRAFFIC." In this mode, she is not as excitable and will help to keep a serene cockpit. Most airlines have what they call "sterile time" in the cockpit when operating below 10,000 feet. This means it is all business up front. The flight attendant is not supposed to come up and no paperwork is to be done. Just drive the airplane. All you have heard about so far is Susie who yells out commands. She's not alone in the modern cockpit that is like a flying video game. There are at least two more audio voices and they come on loud enough to wake the dead. One is the Ground Proximity Warning System (GPWS) that has an exceedingly loud male voice that activates whenever the aircraft is descending at a rapid rate near to the ground. It starts chanting with a loud "WHOOP, WHOOP, PULL UP." This racket continues until the unit is satisfied by a decreased descent rate.

The wind shear detector is supposed to yell out "WIND SHEAR" whenever a severe wind shift is in progress near the ground. On November 15, 1993, the veteran crew of a Continental 727 nearly made a wheels-up landing. They were on a long, final approach at Chicago's O'Hare. The TCAS was busily issuing false warnings. At 500 feet, the GPWS did its thing. At 50 feet the GPWS finally stopped yelling and Susie stopped giving advice, but by now a small item had been forgotten. The landing gear was not down. The aircraft scraped the rear of the belly on the runway. At this time, the alert tower operator yelled into his mike "Continental go around (do not land)." Needless to say, after one of the noisiest cockpits in history, the crew was delighted to "pour the coals" to it and try again without warnings. I am not making excuses for this crew; they should have completed their checklist and made a normal landing. But this time the warning devices nearly caused an accident.

The Holding Pattern

There are three aircraft in a holding pattern: one is at 10,000, one below at 9,000, and one below that at 8,000. Now, along comes a new customer heading "down the chute" at 2,000 feet per minute. He is going to stop at 11,000 feet and join the aircraft below who are awaiting clearance to land. Since TCAS on the aircraft at the top of the pattern, at 10,000 feet, has no idea that the new aircraft above him is going to level out, off goes Suzie again, concerned about the one at 10,000 saying "DESCEND, DESCEND." If the pilot obeys this false command, it will trigger the TCAS in the aircraft at 9,000 and so on down the stack.

TCAS cannot think. It only operates when there is a potential conflict. Since it has no idea that the newcomer to the stack is going to stop at 11,000 feet, it does its thing.

Look Out Below

Terrain features have no effect on TCAS. By that I mean if two aircraft are heading toward each other, things will happen. Say the aircraft at the lower level is at 5,000 feet over a 4,000-foot mountain. Along comes another airplane descending to his assigned altitude of 6,000 feet. Suzie starts to prick up her ears as this descending aircraft barrels down to 6,000 feet. She suspects trouble and yells, "DESCEND NOW, DESCEND NOW." If the pilot of the lower aircraft takes Suzie's advice and descends at 1,500 per minute, in a little over 30 seconds he could barrel into the mountain below.

A Case of the Dog Chasing His Tail

On November 21, 1993, two passengers and two crewmembers were injured on Northwest Flight 90, high over the Pacific Ocean. Flight 90 was cruising at 37,000 feet when Suzie called out, "CLIMB, CLIMB, CLIMB" and the 747 climbed abruptly. There was no conflicting traffic for Northwest 90; it was picking up its own transponder. The crew did not want to argue with Suzie so up they went. FAA official Tom Williamson said, "It left them trying to outrun their own shadow."

Ghosts

On December 8, 1993, Continental Flight 291 was on approach to Cleveland Hopkins Airport when Suzie yelled, "TRAFFIC, TRAFFIC, TRAFFIC." The pilot quickly pulled up, passing over the landing runway. After the go-around, a successful landing was accomplished. There was no reported traffic in the vicinity, just a faulty warning.

Turn It Off

Earlier this year, Greensboro's radar and beacon were not functioning normally. Controllers were getting false mode C readings. This disruption cannot be taken lightly; it plays havoc on the controller scopes. Targets appear to merge when in fact they are thousands of feet apart, or worse, they can be closer than depicted. FAA management refused to deal with the problem. Luckily nearly all controllers are members of the National Air Traffic Controllers Association (NATCA). The Greensboro local filed an Unsafe Condition Report. This brought the FAA to their senses. It turned out that a TCAS-equipped airplane was parked on the apron and the TCAS' interrogator had been left on. Once the TCAS was turned off, the false readings on the controller scopes ceased.

Radar Problems

When a TCAS-equipped aircraft comes in contact with more than fifteen similarly equipped planes, the system will decrease its own signal as well as reducing the signals of others. The ATC radar also could be affected and this would cause a dangerous situation. This could be a major problem as we move toward the 100 percent TCAS requirement.

It's Too Hot to Work

The following is a quote from the August issue of FAA Aviation News:

"RA's will not be reliable between sea level and 5,300 feet mean sea level when the outside air temperature exceeds standard temperature by more or less than 50°F. This normally occurs when the aircraft is at a low speed in specified limiting configurations during takeoff or landing at "hot day" high altitude airports (such as Mexico City or La Paz), or where temperatures are extremely cold. Under these circumstances, TCAS should be operated in the "traffic advisors" mode.

Too Many Parrots

Airports equipped with radar have an aircraft-type transponder fixed on top of a pole or atop a tall building. This parrot, as it is called, is utilized by FAA technicians to properly align their radar system. Too many times, this transponder is not set to a below sea level altitude, or 99,000 feet. These parrots are not always set correctly and the net result is that an airliner is sent on a wild goose chase. Not only do parrots on poles spell trouble; we also have to contend with transponders on ships. More than once, ships maneuvering near airports or even out at sea have caused unwanted RAs in the aircraft instrument.

It Takes Two to Tango

Without a mode C or S transponder, TCAS will not operate and issue escape routes, which means it takes at least two aircraft with functioning transponders before an RA will be issued by the TCAS unit.

You might think that a valuable piece of equipment such as a transponder would be mandatory in today's aircraft. Not so. While it is true that all military aircraft and airliners, large and small, must have a functional transponder, there is a vast general aviation (all aircraft other than airliners and military) fleet out there that not only lacks a transponder but also a two-way radio.

All foreign airliners must be TCAS equipped or they will not be allowed to land in the United States. That sounds like a really safe idea and the FAA should be commended. But what do you think of large fleets of U.S. jet transports that are busy flying freight into most of our busy airports? Surely they must be TCAS equipped. Not so. The FAA, in their infinite wisdom, treats all the U.S. air cargo carriers as though they were small general aviation aircraft.

Some freight carriers such as UPS have more 747 aircraft in their fleet than many large commercial passenger carriers. The FAA feels that there are usually only two or three crewmen on the freighters, not enough to get excited about. But let one of these freighters bump into a passenger airliner and watch how fast TCAS is required.

It is interesting to note that the United States is the only country in the world that requires its airliners, other than freight carriers, to have TCAS on board. Are we the leaders of the industry? It looks as though the rest of the world is waiting to see if the U.S. ever perfects this faulty system.

The FAA has much experience in partially developing new gadgets and expecting controllers and pilots to get the bugs out of them. The only problem with this bad concept is the fact that you and I have to fly with unproven equipment. There are 184,000 GA aircraft in the U.S. Here is a breakdown of how they are equipped:

12,173 or 6.6 percent have made a mode A transponder

51,604 or 82.2 percent have a mode C transponder

1,107 or .6 percent have a mode S transponder.

That leaves a grand total of 19,116 aircraft without transponders, and 27,600 without two-way radio communications. What does all this mean to you, the airline passenger?

Since TCAS must have a functioning transponder to operate, there are a lot of planes below 18,000 that are nontransponder, nonradio equipped. ATC radar is not as particular as the TCAS system. They can see aircraft with no transponders, which means the 19,000 GA aircraft may show as targets on ATC radar, but NOT on the airliners TCAS system. Does this sound safe to you?

While it is true that all en route airliners are protected by a 1,000-foot vertical block of airspace, there could very easily be numerous GA aircraft in between that vertical piece of air. Airliners usually fly at one thousand-foot levels up to 29,000 feet. Above 29,000, the spacing is 2,000 feet. But what about the "little guy?" At all altitudes above 3,000 feet, all GA aircraft are supposed to maintain even +500 feet or odd +500 feet (3,500 feet to 4,500 feet depending on whether the flight is east to west or west to east). At what altitude will you find a GA aircraft below 3,000 feet? The FAA doesn't care. Any safe altitude will do. All this is just to clarify that airliners are spaced 1,000 feet vertically from each other, but not from visual flight rules (VFR) planes that are out there only 500 feet vertically from commercial airliners.

Well, now that I have made my point, so what? With the advent of TCAS, there is now a greater chance for a mid-air with a general aviation aircraft than there used to be.

Picture, if you will, two airliners, both separated vertically by 1,000 feet of altitude. One is at 8,000 feet and another is at 9,000 feet; the weather is hazy and bumpy. At 8,500 feet sits a light plane with no radio, no transponder, no nothing. ATC clears another airliner to descend and maintain 10,000 feet. As the descending airliner starts to descend, TCAS senses a problem and issues an RA for the aircraft at 9,000 to "DESCEND, DESCEND." This is because of the many TCAS bugs. It does not know that the descending aircraft is going to level at 10,000 feet. The pilot at 9,000 starts his descent at 1,500 feet per minute. In 20 seconds, he will be head on with the light traffic at 8,500 feet. This is a hypothetical scenario, but one that could easily happen. When large chunks of altitude are used by TCAS RAs, frightening things can happen.

When some aircraft are flying over the Atlantic Ocean, their vertical separation is recently reduced to 1,000 feet. There is no radar guidance over the ocean because as radar cannot extend much further than a hundred miles from the antenna site. In order to sandwich in more aircraft, the close proximity has caused numerous aircraft to dive or climb simply because of the idiosyncrasies of TCAS.

In 1997, the FAA started Phase II of a program requiring pilots to rely on TCAS traffic displays to maintain proper separation. Let's not forget that there are hundreds of aircraft over the ocean and many of them are not TCAS-equipped. That means they will not send or receive any traffic advisory signals. In 1999, the FAA has allotted zero funds for any oceanic updating programs.

As I stated at the beginning of this chapter, it shouldn't be too long before you see a headline similar to mine. "Aircraft collision system causes mid-air collision. No survivors."

In October of 1999, the Wall Street Journal had an excellent report on TCAS. Here is their headline: "Flawed Safety Device in Jets Gets Blamed for a Near Catastrophe."

In this incident, no one was killed, but that is only a matter of time.

On June 28, 1999, a British Airways jumbo jet was flying east toward Hong Kong. A Korean Air jet was on the same route flying in the opposite direction. They had a 2,000 separation but that was being reduced slowly. An automatic warning in the Korean cockpit exclaimed CLIMB, CLIMB, aiming the jet directly into the path of the British Airways B-747. The two jets missed each other by a mere 600 feet. What went wrong? The TCAS system or the Korean jet was at fault. It should have exclaimed DESEND, not CLIMB, CLIMB. The engineers from the manufacturers of the TCAS components are still searching for clues.

It appears that the fault stems from an electronic component on board 3,000 airliners worldwide including Airbus A-300s, Boeing 747s, B-727s, and B-737s. The British Civil Aviation Authority issued a rapid airworthiness directive asking all their airlines to check out this system. In the U.S., the FAA officials state that the fault is so rare they are going to study more options. Where have we heard this reasoning before?

The British report states "there are potentially thousands of aircraft operating with such an equipment configuration and hence the possibility for their hidden failures to occur posing a very high risk of the loss of the aircraft involved and all those on board."

As I have stated before, the TCAS is supposed to be a safety device, not a potential killer.

Airborne Controllers

I am sorry to say that pilots and controllers live in different worlds. By that I mean the name controller does not sit well with most pilots. Let's face it, the controller, while he is not manipulating the controls of your airliner, is telling the pilot what altitude to climb to, what airways to fly, whether to speed up or slow down, what taxi routes to take, when to push back from the gate, when to start engines, and on and on it goes. Pilots, as a group, dislike being told by controllers where to put their aircraft. Since the present system is designed the way it is, pilots will have to bear with it until something better shows up. Is TCAS the answer? Now a pilot can legally control traffic. If a pilot deviates from his assigned clearance because of an RA, no disciplinary action will be taken by the FAA.

When a pilot responds to an RA, it might be to save your life or it might be to end it. A controller is primarily interested in separating traffic, and I might add, the controller is the only one who has the COMPLETE PICTURE. The pilot has a small traffic display with only a very few targets as compared to the large picture and the myriad of targets the controller is watching. It is a very disturbing thing for a controller to sit there and say nothing while his traffic is going "down the tubes."

Here is a quote from the January 6, 1994, ATP 7110.65 (air traffic procedures) which is the controller bible: "New TCAS Resolution Advisories (C.) Once the subject aircraft has begun a maneuver in response to an RA, the controller is not responsible for providing standard separation between the aircraft that is responding to an RA and any other aircraft, airspace terrain, or obstruction when one of the following is met:"

I would like to quote Mr. Barry Krasner, the former president of NATCA, when he appeared before a congressional subcommittee to debate about TCAS. "TCAS causes pilots to second guess directions given by controllers. When TCAS sounds, which is far too often in normal traffic sequencing situations, the pilot probably thinks the controller "missed one," and he takes evasive action. Such evasive actions not only wreak havoc on the system, but the pilot's false perception of controller error disintegrates the critical working relationship between controllers and pilots. For the system to work well, controllers must have nothing but the fullest confidence that pilots will do their jobs properly, and pilots must expect the same from controllers."

An analysis of almost 1,300 RAs reported during a seventeen-month period pointed up the fact that almost two-thirds of them occurred when the TCAS aircraft was below an altitude of 10,000 feet and nearly 27 percent lower than 2,500 feet. Nearly 90 percent of all conflicts could be resolved by the pilot making a 300-foot change of altitude. This, however, is not the case. In 23 percent of incidents, the escape maneuver covered more than 700 feet. It is unfortunate that the majority of the RAs occur in the vicinity of the airport. This is the busiest time for both the controller and the pilot.

In August of 1993, newly refined software for the TCAS system, which should greatly reduce the number of nuisance alerts, was introduced into the Delta fleet. This software is known as 6.04. Prior to this new software, Delta was experiencing an RA every 20 flight hours. With this new equipment, flights are averaging over 100 hours per RA. After analyzing 4,000 pilot reports and 6,000 controller reports concerning TCAS incidents, it was learned that 60 percent of the time pilots complied with RAs. It is interesting to note that any changes in the TCAS software were initiated without controller input. What else is new?

On February 5,1997, a pair of F-16 fighter jets were ordered to intercept an aircraft not identified in their military airspace. They were off the coast of New Jersey and were seeking a target that proved to be a National Air 727 airliner. As they closed in for a visual check, their vast speed set off the TCAS in the airliner. The captain dove steeply, as he was commanded by the airliner's TCAS. This abrupt move caused injury to three passengers. There was no danger of collision, but the TCAS did not know that.

It seems to me that the TCAS system would be much more efficient and safer if the powers to be designed the system so that pilots could escape by turning left or right. In most cases, to descend or climb nearly always impinges on another's assigned altitude whereas a turn would do little harm unless near the terminal area. Pilots dislike going up or down because they know there may be another target to hit. It would also be less disruptive to passenger comfort because no one likes being pushed down in the seat when a simple turn can do the trick. If TCAS III ever gets off the drawing board, escaping turns will be commanded. But if it takes as long to debug it as it has for TCAS II, don't look for it until the next century.

The following statistics were compiled by NATCA through the thousands of reports received from ATC that were submitted to the FAA TCAS II transition program.

CONTROLLER REPORTS FILED	NUMBER	PERCENT
Total Number of Reports	5,244	100
Reports from Terminals	3,601	69
Reports from En route	1,643	31

ALTITUDE AT WHICH RA OCCURRED	NUMBER	PERCENT
Surface to 2,500	719	14
2,500 to 10,000	1,106	21
18,000 to 29,000	658	12
29,000 and above	518	6

ALTITUDE DEVIATION AMOUNT	NUMBER	PERCENT
0 Feet	338	6
Less than 300	426	8
300 to 500	933	18
500 to 700	1,002	19
700 to 1,000	550	10
More than 1,000 feet	394	8
No Altitude Deviation Reported	1,601	31

	NUMBER	PERCENT
Individual TCAS RA Occurrences	3,892	74
Approved Separation Existed Before RA	325	6.2
Unnecessary Missed Approaches	233	7.3
Ghost of Phantom Targets	517	16.3

ATC Clearance Deviations		
Yes	3,420	65
No	1,609	31

Controllers had to contend with 3,420 TCAS deviations from assigned ATC clearances. That is a large amount of "puckering" for the controllers. How would you feel if you were controlling the lives of thousands of people and all of a sudden, your smooth flowing sequence was suddenly disrupted by an unnecessary RA?

Now a final word concerning TCAS pilot and controller training. You are not going to believe the following. Controllers may get to watch a videotape and read a few pamphlets, but that's it. It fares worse for the pilots; they don't even get to watch a tape. At American, they have used video training and testing of all pilots during recurrent training since TCAS was implemented.

The following is a quote from Captain Terry Hanson, (Delta) chairman of ALPA's ATC Committee: "TCAS still is not available in the overwhelming majority of flight simulators, and most airlines are not using effective training. Only the minimum TCAS information is covered in recurrent training." Captain Hanson continued. "Some improvements must be made to the system."

The next time you are sitting in the first class section and you hear "Susie" screaming, "CLIMB NOW, CLIMB NOW" you will have a little better insight as to just what is going on in the cockpit.

Special thanks to two good friends, William A Faville, NATCA former director of safety and technology, and to Chuck Finfrock, FAA Avionics technician, for the generous amount of time they spent with me concerning the inner workings of the TCAS system.

CHAPTER 10

▼

Is Your Airport Safe?

Since the advent of deregulation in 1978, aviation has expanded enormously: up 65 percent from 278 million passengers in 1978 to an estimated 800 million this year. This increase places a tremendous burden on many of our larger metropolitan airports. As usual, the government has done nothing to give the flight crews more concrete to land on. Shocking but true, the last major airport, Dallas/Fort Worth, was built 14 years ago. Denver's new airport was operational in 1994 and the old Stapleton Field closed.

In 1939, New York's LaGuardia Airport was completed. At the time, it was one of the finest air carrier fields in the country. At peak capacity, it could handle a maximum of 10 million passengers. Today, LaGuardia serves over 22 million per year. There has been a lot done to enhance the terminal buildings and parking facilities, but little to lengthen the DC-3 runways that are handling large jets.

Only one runway at LaGuardia has any overrun area to allow for error. Most of the airport is submerged when a heavy rain hits it. In fact, there are permanent pumps in place to try to eliminate flooding conditions. A dike was built around the perimeter of the airport to keep the bay from submerging the pitifully short runways. If a pilot comes in a little too low, he could shear his wheels off on the dike at the end of one of the runways.

In fact, an airliner did just that and flipped over on its back. Luckily, only a few people were injured.

LaGuardia, Newark, and John F. Kennedy are all in such close proximity to each other that if landing flow at one airport is shifted to another runway, the tower chiefs must coordinate this change with the other two adjacent airports. There are only two minimal runways at LaGuardia and they cross each other.

Crossing runways put an added burden on the controller. He must make sure that when an aircraft lands, he waits until it has cleared the intersection of the takeoff runway before he rolls his traffic. This does not happen at airports such as Dulles, Dallas/Fort Worth, Los Angeles, JFK, and Detroit. All those airports have parallel runways that are much safer for all concerned.

Reagan International Airport is the granddaddy of dangerous airports. It is similar to LaGuardia with respect to its proximity to water and crossing runways. Situated in the nation's capital, the airport is one we can well be ashamed of. Its longest runway is only 6,870 feet long as compared to Dulles: its shortest strip is 10,000 feet.

Reagan is the 14th busiest airport in the world, ranking ahead of the major airports in Rome, Paris, and Boston. As we have previously discussed, the ILS is the safest and best approach. Reagan Airport has only one on the North runway. The reason there isn't another on the other end of the strip is because it would create traffic over the capital and come dangerously close to the Washington Monument. In fact, the Washington Monument spears into the existing final approach altitude by 100 feet over minimum terrain regulations. Aircraft landing south of the airport continually triggered an alarm in the approach controller's room. As they head toward the Monument, the radar computer picks up potential ground conflict and sounds the alarm. The Monument was taken off the controller's video screen to eliminate this problem and so far, no one has hit it. But don't hold your breath.

This writer is not the only one concerned with the dangers associated with Reagan International Airport. Steve Gendel of WDVM-TV in Washington, D.C., conducted a poll by sending surveys to 500 airline pilots who fly out of the airport. Steve received replies from 215 who agreed that Reagan was well below standards for the industry. "Eighty-seven percent said an accident was more likely at [Reagan]; 73 percent said landings are poor; and less than 10 percent said takeoffs and landings are good. Eighty-nine percent rated the south river approach below average, and of those, 68 percent said the instrument approach used in bad weather is one of the worst of all the airports they use."

There's an airport on the west coast that has a reputation nearly as bad as Washington's Reagan International: Lindbergh Field in San Diego, California.

It only has one runway and it is only 9,400 feet long, but the runway is displaced 1,810 feet because of a six-story parking garage at the runway edge. They do not want airplanes hitting it so they have moved the displaced threshold down to 7,590 feet. The majority of flights landing at Lindbergh do so to the west, but this direction has no ILS (precision approach). As a result, pilots have to fly visual glide slope well below skyscrapers on both sides of the final approach.

I think it is disgraceful that an airport that serves a city as large as San Diego lacks the luxury of a first-rate ILS approach. Sure, it has one to the east, but 90 percent of all trips land to the west. It is a lucky thing that the weather in San Diego is nearly perfect or there would be problems with a west wind and bad weather.

In 1982, Reagan International was host to the crash of an Air Florida B-737 that took off on runway 36 and slammed into the 14th Street bridge. If the runways at the airport were longer, this crash might not have happened.

It is interesting to note that numerous airports that don't have scheduled airline service have runways that are longer than LaGuardia or Washington's Reagan. A few of these include Lake City, Florida, Kalispell, Montana, West Hampton Beach, New York, Eugene Oregon, and Champaign, Illinois.

The past president of the Airline Pilots Association Captain Randolph Babbett, said the association is "looking for solutions to Lindbergh Field because it can no longer be upgraded to meet current or future air traffic demands." He continues, "However, we believe that the concept of using

Miramar Naval Air Station as a civil or joint-use facility as local San Diego groups have advocated has much merit and should be explored fully."

The International Federation of Air Line Pilots Association (IFALPA) is an organization consisting of various pilot associations. It represents nearly all of the airline pilots in the world. Deficient airports are rated by a "star" system with the black star being the worst. It was quite a shock to some airport managers to find that their multimillion dollar airport was so far below standards that IFALPA branded it with a black star. Nah, Okinawa; Osaka, Japan; Hong Kong; Teheran, Iran; Rhodes, Greece; Bimini; Bari; Anchorage; Los Angeles are all black star airports.

In 1972, Resolution #7467 was instituted by the Board of Airport Commissioners, City of Los Angeles, California. Because of the numerous noise complaints, all traffic landing between the hours of 11:00 P.M. and 6:00 A.M. had to approach the airport over the ocean, providing the wind did not exceed 10 knots on the tail of the aircraft. Takeoffs would be to the west in the opposite direction over the water. Now there was conflicting traffic: takeoffs pass landing traffic in the opposite direction. The two parallel runways at Los Angeles are separated by less than a mile, making this operation questionable.

Aviation Week had this to say concerning an FAA survey. "Unless steps are taken to improve air traffic control's ability to handle increased flights, the report forecasts that by 2003 major airports at Boston, New York, Atlanta, Washington, Miami, Los Angeles, and Houston, to name a few, will experience annual delays well in excess of 20,000 hours. Other airports listed include San Diego, Honolulu, St. Louis, Minneapolis, St. Paul, Phoenix, Charlotte, Pittsburgh, and Nashville. By 2005, U.S. air carriers will conduct more than 80 million flights annually, an increase of almost 38 percent as compared to the 1992 levels."

Most people in the industry agree that air travel cannot continue to expand at the present rate without positive action being taken to increase the capacity of the airports. When demand exceeds capacity, there is an accumulation of airliners waiting for service that is directly proportionate to the excess demand over capacity.

For example, if the capacity of an airport is 60 flights per hour and the demand rate is running at 70 flights per hour, each hour will add an additional 10 aircraft to the string of planes awaiting the runway and 10 minutes to the delay for subsequent flights. Even if the demand for operations drops to 40 per hour, delays still will persist for quite some time because the long lines of airliners can only diminish at the rate of 40 trips per hour.

Railroads may be experiencing a tough survival but their planning is far superior to the aviation community. There are a myriad of airways between terminals, but when the airplane reaches the destination airport, there may be only one runway on which hundreds of flights can land. Railroads have very few tracks between towns, but when it comes to the end of the line, there are many platforms for the numerous trains to use.

Delays at airports are caused by two main factors: weather and insufficient runways. If you are in a holding pattern and you can see your destination airport clearly, there's only one reason why you aren't landing: too much traffic for the amount of runways and poor scheduling.

Unfortunately, the decision to build new airports is left to the discretion of the state and local authorities, not to the federal government. People do not want an airport near their home, and they raise such a fuss about the noise, it's nearly impossible to get authorization for a new facility. If more airports were constructed in rural areas, there would be no noise problems and if the old airports were closed, airlines would have to move out into the country where they rightly belong.

When Dallas/Fort Worth was constructed, the powers that be were worried about getting airlines to move from Love Field. They certainly had no problem since Dallas/Fort Worth is one of the finest airports in the world. Washington Reagan International should follow the fate of Love Field. Airlines should be told to go to Dulles, also on a par with Dallas/Fort Worth. Then it could revert back to a general aviation field or, better yet, closed down and made into a park.

A federal master plan "similar to the plan that led to the construction of our interstate highways during the 1950s should be put in effect so that we would have a chance to build new airports, which is what is mainly needed to cope with the vast expansion of air traffic."

The Air Line Pilots Association states that 60 percent of air carrier airports in the U.S. are substandard. They also have a number of guidelines to aid the FAA in the proper construction and maintenance of an air carrier airport. Some of their minimum standard requirements are as follows:

- Runways should be at least 6,500 feet in length.
- There should be ample underrun and overshoot extensions at both ends of the runways.
- The strip should be grooved.
- All runways should be equipped with approach lights, centerline lights, high intensity runway lights, runway-end identification lights (REIL), and visual-approach slope indicators (VASI).
- Runways should not cross each other (parallel strips are most desirable).
- ASDE should be installed at all major terminals.
- A control tower should be equipped with radar monitoring of all approaches
- Sufficient fire-fighting equipment to handle the largest aircraft that frequents the field should be available.
- There should be back-up power for all navigation aids, communications, and lights.
- There should be an ILS on at least one of the runway ends and preferably all of them.

If your airport has the previously mentioned equipment, consider yourself extremely lucky. I doubt very much if you would find all of the minimal equipment even at the busiest of metropolitan terminals.

February of 1987 saw Congress rattling the cage of the FAA when they held hearings concerning appropriations for fiscal year 1988. Admiral Engen, the past administrator, made this statement, and for a change he was right on track: "Traffic is compounding at about 3 to 7 percent per year and is going to continue. We have the NAS Plan coming along which will provide that equipment to grease the skids, if you will, in the air-navigation facility's radars, computers, and that is going to increase the throughput, but that doesn't change what is at the bottom, and that is the airport. That is our problem ..."

Control Towers

On October 14, 1984, a USAir DC-9, a charter flight for State University football team, was holding over Erie, Pennsylvania, awaiting improvement in the below-limits weather. The latest weather report for Erie was obtained from the flight dispatcher in Pittsburgh. At this stage in the game, the crew is usually in contact with the tower at the landing sight. Not so here.

The weather limits at Erie for an ILS on runway 24 are one-half mile visibility with a decision height (to land or not to) of 200 feet. These limits are based on the premise that all components of the ILS are fully operational. The tower controllers at Erie are the people that give the pertinent field conditions, operate the intensity of the runway and approach lights, issue current weather information, and maintain proper spacing between aircraft on and around the airport. The captain on USAir flight #4381 knew that he was getting down to a minimum fuel condition. He would have to land at Erie or divert to Harrisburg where the weather was good. The decision was made to land at Erie. The crew was fully aware that they could vary the intensity of the airport approach lights by clicking their mike button a prescribed number of times. However, they were so intent on landing that they forgot to even turn the lights up, making their approach far more hazardous.

At 200 feet, the first officer called out "Decision height."

The Captain replied, "I don't have it." (runway not in sight)

The crew pressed on and faintly picked up the low intensity runway lights that were at their bottom setting, Step #1. He had used up a good part of the runway, and when ground contact was made, it was anything but smooth. The aircraft veered off the end of the strip and came to rest over a highway. Luckily, this time none of the 77 passengers was injured.

What had gone wrong with this approach? To begin with, construction on the airport had damaged the runway lights so that they would illuminate only at their lowest setting. Step 5 is the brightest and best for a low-ceiling and low-visibility approach. The crew was not aware of this, and the tower didn't tell them. The approach lights, a vital component of the ILS and the first visual clue that a pilot sees as he scans for a look of the runway, were not operating. The tower never even put these lights on, even though it was the middle of the night. Why didn't the tower people do any of the things they were supposed to? That's an easy one. They had all gone home hours before USAir 4381 left the ground at Nashville, Tennessee. Erie tower's hours of operation are from 7:00 a.m. to midnight. After that time, the airliners have to fend for themselves. There is no law that requires there be an operable control tower at an air carrier field. While it is a shame to jeopardize the lives of innocent people, the "feds" say it's perfectly legal.

There is a grand total of 3,699 airports that are non-towered. However, only 500 of these airports that are used by large scheduled airlines. Out of this number, 300 of them are minus the luxury of a control tower. While it is true that the vast majority of these non-towered fields cater mostly to commuter flights, is there any reason why a passenger on a small commercial carrier should be less safe than a passenger on a larger one?

Pierre Huggins of the ALPA safety department was kind enough to give me the following computer printouts. Here are a list of just a few of the non-towered airports that are handling aircraft that hold more than 100 passengers such as Boeing 727s, 737s, 767s, Douglas DC-9s, and smaller commuters:

Alaska—Nome, Skagway

Arizona—Kingman

California—Bishop

Colorado—Montrose, Telluride, Vail Eagle Co.

Hawaii—Laenoi

Maine—Presque Isle

Montana—Butte, Kalispell, Glacier Park National

New York—Watertown, Massena, Saranac Lake

Pennsylvania—Bradford

South Carolina—Hilton Head

Texas—Paris

Utah—Cedar City

Puerto Rico—Ponce

Wisconsin—Eauclair Co.

Wyoming—Bellingham, Jackson Hole

In addition there are hundreds of airports equipped with towers that sanction flights to operate after the tower is officially closed for the night.

The benefits derived from a functional control tower are many. The primary responsibility of a tower controller is to provide traffic separation on the ground and in the air. The alert tower operator could prevent many potential accidents by alerting the aircraft crew. A pilot could be advised of obstructions on the ramp or that a certain taxiway was very slippery. More than once, a controller has warned a pilot that he is lined up with the wrong runway, perhaps one that is closed. Who will alert the crash and rescue crews to be in position to handle an aircraft that is having an emergency, or one that blows a tire or slides off the runway? Many times, the man in the tower is also an experienced pilot. His knowledge could avert an accident by guiding a lost pilot to the field or he could convince a pilot to cancel a takeoff that might otherwise have crashed. Controllers have warned pilots that their gear pins (devices that keep the wheels from retracting while parked) are still in place, or worse, that their exterior control locks were never removed or that their landing gear was not down.

The proper setting of the altimeter is a most important item. If it is not set to the pressure of the intended landing airport, the potential for a serious accident is greatly increased, especially during instrument weather conditions. When a pilot lands at a field without a tower, he gets the altimeter setting from the nearest FAA facility that could be 50 miles away. This setting could easily be erroneous by as much as 100 feet or more. Airlines usually have a company altimeter at their outlying stations, but many times these instruments are not checked on schedule, leaving more of a potential error.

Do you know who replaces the control tower operator at a non-towered airline airport? He's the fellow who checks your bags in at the airline counter. When your flight calls in on the company radios for landing information, your friendly ticket agent goes out of the building, scans the sky, and informs the company pilot. "Looks okay, flight so-and-so. I don't see any traffic in the pattern, although a cub did taxi by the window a few minutes ago. You should be able to land before he takes off." After this transmission, the agent goes about his business of checking his passenger's tickets and luggage.

I would like you to see what the "feds" have to say about control towers as reflected in their manual 83-2, "Establishment and Discontinuance Criteria For Airport Traffic Control Towers," dated August 1983, page 22. Regarding the merits of having a control tower as a hedge against collisions, "The resultant mean values 9.704 accidents per million operations on non-towered airports vs. 4.538 accidents per million at towered airports." In other words, the accident rate is nearly doubled at non-towered fields.

"Air carrier pilots are required to have a radio communication with ground personnel who are able to observe some of the conditions which lead to these accidents. But such personnel would not normally have as good a view of the airport environment as a tower controller would, and after providing an initial traffic advisory, there is little further contact."

Page C-1 of the manual relates an accident period that encompassed 15 years of compilation by the NTSB. "These data files were queried to obtain information on the six categories of accidents judged to be TOWER PREVENTABLE (emphasis mine) (section IV.B). There were 144 air carrier, 654 air taxi, and 14,434 general aviation accidents in these six categories during these 15 years which occurred within 5 miles of an airport during taxi, take-off, climb to cruise, descending, holding, or landing phase of operation."

What do the "feds" use for criteria for the installation of a control tower? Well, it certainly isn't safety. We have already gone through the unquestionable safety features that are found at a controlled airport. Now we are confronted with the irrational criteria that are really used.

The number of flights in or out of an airport is all the FAA understands. The minimum criteria for a tower to be installed is as follows:

General Aviation	160,000 operations per year
Air Taxi	90,000 operations per year
Air Carrier	38,000 operations per year

We are obviously talking money here and not safety. Page 6 of the manual shows exactly how safety is comprised: "On the other hand, 38,000 air carrier operations per year—about 100 per day—generate enough benefits to offset establishment costs."

On October 23, 1995, the first snow to hit Denver's new $5 billion airport caused quite a commotion, both on the ground and in the air. The crew on United's Boeing-727 Flight 367 had just completed its landing checklist, and were about 11 miles from touchdown. An early snowstorm had cut the visibility considerably. The F/O keyed his mike. "Denver Tower. United 367. We're 11 miles out for 35 left."

The tower replied, "Braking action reported fair to poor, runway 35 left … cleared to land."

Two minutes later, an airport operations truck was in the process of checking the runway breaking action. "Ops 13 is at the south end of 35L." He erroneously reported his location to the tower and was cleared on to the wrong runway. The driver of the operations truck transmitted, "Ops 13, approaching end of 35 right, requesting the runway for inspection."

The tower's reply was, "Ops 13, Denver Tower proceed northbound on runway 35 right."

Ninety seconds later, United was now less than a mile from the touchdown and was in visual contact with the runway. As the United plane broke out of the clouds, the captain saw a rotating beacon on the approach end of the runway. There was no time to ask questions about the light as the jet leveled out momentarily while power was applied and the landing gear was commanded to the up position.

The startled crew got a glimpse of what was obstructing their landing path. A truck was right where they would have landed. The F/O transmitted to the tower, "United 367 going around, there's somebody on the runway."

"United 367, roger, fly runway landing, maintain one zero thousand."

Because of the alert United crew, a disaster was averted. If the crew had not picked up the truck, Denver's new masterpiece would have had its first major catastrophe.

Why would the tower clear an aircraft to land on top of a truck? That's an easy one to answer. Since the storm was so intense, the tower controllers could not see the runways that they were responsible for. The driver of the vehicle thought he was on a different runway. He was probably as shocked as the crew when United Flight 367 flew a few hundred feet over his vehicle on their way to safety and another try for the runway.

Denver International Airport is equipped with two ASDEIII (airport surface detection equipment) radars. One is located on top of the control tower and another northeast of the terminal. Most airports are extremely lucky to have one of these, but because of the size of this airport, it takes two of these units to properly cover the airport surface.

When I spoke with Michael Coulter, President of NATCA Local at Denver, he told me that two radar units are not sufficient to cover the entire runway complex. Why didn't the ASDE radar show the truck parked in the center of the active runway? It seems that these two ASDEs have been plagued with problems, the main one that there are numerous positions on the field where the units go blind. By that I mean, there are known areas where you could park a 747 and it would not be painted on the radar screen. Mind you, these units are the latest state-of-the-art masterpieces that have taken decades to develop, and they don't do the job.

The Denver ASDE units have frequently broken down, and only last summer, one of these units was replaced. The ASDE radar is not the only radar problem. The terminal weather Doppler radar has a bad habit of painting thunderstorms in areas where the weather is clear. Hours after the aborted landing, a power failure knocked out power to the same ASDE radar from 7:42 a.m. to 9:25 a.m. Now for the crowning blow as told by controller Mike Coulter: "Problems multiplied with the bad weather Sunday night. After midnight, when flights usually shut down, delays piled up 160 operations onto two remaining controllers. At the same time, the FAA tower itself began leaking, and snow fell directly into the control area. Mike Coulter had arrived at work the day before to find plastic protecting some of the consoles from falling water.

Denver Airport had problems from the beginning. It cost many millions more than originally planned to build, and opened nearly a year late because of faults in the baggage conveyor system. The ASDE radar had numerous blind spots, the Doppler weather radar showed thunderstorms when there weren't any, the tower roof leaked allowing the delicate inside equipment to become covered with snow, and the power supply to some of the radar units were known to kick off the line.

What does the FAA have to say about the world's most technologically advanced all-weather airport? Fred Isaac, administrator of the FAA's northwest mountain region stated that during the snowstorm at Denver, the $4.9 billion airport operated "extremely well; we are extremely pleased with Denver International's performance under extremely harsh weather conditions earlier this week. The snowstorm proved that DIA is head and shoulders above every other airport in terms of efficiency in severe weather." In 1996, the administrator of the FAA made the following statement at a National Press Club luncheon concerning Denver's newest airport: "So I will tell you without reservation, from the FAA's standpoint, it is the finest operational airport in the world."

Do you agree with him?

Level One Towers

The "feds" provide air traffic control services through a network of 460 control towers ranging from levels one to five. Level one has the least activity and caters mostly to general aviation aircraft. Charlottesville, Virginia, airport tower controls approximately 63,000 operations a year. At the higher end of the spectrum, Chicago O'Hare International Airport controls over 840,000 operations each year. This makes it a level five tower, one that works about 14 times more aircraft a year than a level one tower. Level five towers are not only confronted with more aircraft but also their whole system of operation is much more complicated than the folks who operate a level one tower. As a general rule, new controllers are assigned to low level towers where they can learn and progress up through the ranks until they qualify for a level five tower. This is not to say that level one controllers have an easy time of it. In fact, some level one tower controllers have a more difficult task than their counterparts at the larger airports. This author flew fighters at Westfield, Massachusetts, for about seven years. Westfield has a level one tower, but the controllers there have the difficult task of sequencing high-speed fighters and very slow light planes, something the controllers at O'Hare rarely have to worry about.

It takes a lot of money to build, maintain, and operate a control tower. Since the FAA is penny-wise and pound-foolish, many of the existing towers will be closed, and very few new ones will be constructed. The cost to erect a level one tower is approximately $2 million, quite a large sum. But compared to what the FAA wastes (over $1.5 billion on a bug-ridden Advanced Automation System that is, new computers), it is really just a drop in the government's wasteful bucket. How many people would buy a house if they were told that it would require extensive refurbishing at the end of 20 years? Well, that's the way the FAA does business. A control tower has a designed life of 20 years.

The "feds" waste far more money on pet projects that never materialize than would ever be needed to keep the level one towers going as safely as they used to be. For purely monetary reasons, the wasteful FAA is planning on contracting out all of their level one towers. You might ask, so what? Won't their new civilian workers be as qualified as the old FAA people?

You can decide that for yourself.

The following is a press release from NATCA (National Air Traffic Controllers Association): "Washington, D.C., November 30, 1994— While the Federal Aviation Administration (FAA) begins to take much-needed steps toward improving commuter air safety, its plan to contract out smaller air traffic control towers will effectively lower safety margins, according to the union representing this nation's 15,000 air traffic controllers."

In a process already underway, rigorously trained FAA controllers are being replaced by less qualified contract employees at all U.S. level one airport towers, used largely by commuter and general aviation traffic. Furthermore, the FAA is currently reducing the level of safety oversight for air traffic control at these towers that serve airports providing vital links for small and mid-sized cities to the rest of the country and the world. As a result, the National Air Traffic Controllers Association (NATCA) has asked the FAA to place the safety interests of the flying public above all other considerations by eliminating the short-sighted contracting out plan. "FAA controllers are better prepared to serve the safety interests of the flying public." FAA controllers are required to go through exhaustive training at the "Academy" in Oklahoma City and receive over six months on-the-job training at their control facility. Contract controllers only receive between one and three weeks of training.

On October 16, 1994, the tower at Hagerstown, Maryland, went under this new contract. The tower cab was manned by four controllers with a total facility experience of eight days. They took the place of nine controllers, each with an average of over four years experience.

FAA controllers are subject to stringent drug and alcohol testing on a continuing basis. Contract controllers are only required to be tested for drugs when hired. From then on, the tests are only randomly given. FAA controllers will not be hired after age 30 and are subject to mandatory retirement at age 55. Contract controllers are hired well into their 50s and some into the 60s. FAA controllers are limited to two hours on position as a safety precaution. Contract workers may be required to work as long as eight hours alone without a break. FAA controllers are not required to work a split shift. Contractor workers do not have this luxury. A split shift would consist of getting paid for the same number of hours a day, but it might require being on duty for a much longer period of time.

Many facilities get their traffic rush between 7:00 to 10:00 a.m., then from 6:00 to 9:00 p.m. To have the most people on position at rush hour, you are told to get lost between busy periods. If you live nearby, it might be all right, but if you live an hour away, that would mean four hours driving each day, not a pleasant thought but it could be mandatory at some contract facilities.

FAA controllers receive monthly refresher and proficiency training; contract workers receive none. Level one FAA staffing requires that a minimum of seven controllers be available to safely work traffic and allow for rest periods, vacations, and sick leave. Contract controllers work with only four people that puts an undue strain on the working controllers. FAA towers are evaluated on over 240 safety-related factors on a yearly basis, and daily by an in-house manager. They are checked twice a year by FAA Headquarters. Contract controllers are evaluated on 100 factors and then only once every two years. Whereas contract controllers' pay is less than FAA controllers', staffing levels are tighter and work shifts are reduced. At a typical contract tower, four workers average 37 hours a week. In contrast, a 14-hour-a-day FAA tower has seven controllers and one supervisor, all of whom are guaranteed 40 hours per week.

According to a September 1994 GAO report, the FAA claims they will save as much as $120 million if it contracts out the operation of all level one towers. The FAA claims their present cost of operating FAA towers is about $450,000, whereas the cost to operate contract towers would be $250,000.

Bear in mind that if most FAA facilities are already understaffed and are operating on a "bare bones" level, there is no reason to believe a contract-operated facility could safely operate with even fewer controllers. When the FAA was operating the tower at Bellingham, Washington, it was staffed by 13 controllers and one manager who would not normally work traffic. With the tower contracted out, the staff has now shrunk to six controllers and a manager who does work traffic. Unfortunately, tower managers are there for a purpose: managing, not controlling. If the FAA thought a tower manager was not needed, they would have done away with the position. Sure, it's fine for a manager to jump in and help a person when he's "going down the tubes," but not as a steady diet.

It's interesting to note that the criteria to erect a control tower are based on the number of aircraft that frequent the airport. If the number is sufficient, a tower is erected. If the number goes down, the tower could be decommissioned. What has traffic count got to do with safety? The answer is nothing. As long as there are two aircraft in the same air space, there is always a potential for collision. If there are many aircraft, it is obvious there is more chance for a disaster. But why should the two aircraft not be monitored by a tower controller?

Don't get me wrong; I don't believe there should be a tower at every grass strip in the country, but at all airports where there are commuters, a tower is a must.

Actual Staffing Compared with FAA-Estimated Staffing for All Contractor-Operator Towers

FACILITY LOCATION	CONTRACT CONTROLLERS	FAA CONTROLLERS
Ardmore, Oklahoma	3	6
Bellingham, Washington	8	14
Cape Giradau, Missouri	4	5
Cleveland (Cuyahoga Co), Ohio	6	8
Enid, Oklahoma	4	7
Farmington, New Mexico	4	9
Flagstaff, New Mexico	4	6
Hailey, Idaho	4	7
Hobbs (Lea Co.) New Mexico	3	7
Lakeland, Florida	7	9
Laredo, Texas	5	7
Lewisburg/Greenbrier, W. Va.	3	6
Nashua, New Hampshire	5	8
New Iberia, Louisiana	4	8
North Myrtle Beach, SC	7	8
Owensboro (Davies Co.) KY	5	7
Pacoima/Whiteman, California	5	8
Paducah (Barkely) KY	5	8
Pendelton, Oregon	4	7
Smyrna, Tennessee	4	8

Topeka (Phillip Ballard), KS	3	7
Valdosta, GA	6	6
Waukegan, ILL	6	9

As you can see, every contract tower lost at least one controller, and in the case of Lewisburgh, West Virginia, their compliment was cut in half. Of the remaining 151 level one towers, 36 failed to meet FAA's benefit cost criteria for them to continue in operation.

In order for a tower to continue to function, the tower must have a benefit/cost ratio greater than one—the point where benefits are equal to costs. If the benefit/cost ratio drops below one, it should be closed. Nowhere in the decisive ratio can we find any mention of safety. Let's not forget that the penny-wise, but pound-foolish FAA has already squandered $1.5 billion on a faulty computer program (AAS); now they are worried about "peanuts."

Eleven of the 36 towers have already been temporarily closed since the PATCO strike in 1981. Where else but in the FAA would you consider anything to be temporary for as long as 14 years?

There are many controllers who could not hack the fierce workload at a level five tower, so they transferred to a level one where things were more tolerable. What happened to those workers at a level one tower when the contractors take over? The likelihood is there would be many controllers sent back to a busy facility to which they were previously unable to handle the workload. Union officials estimate that approximately 60 percent of the 1,000 level one controllers who failed to perform at high-level facilities will be subjected to another go-around with the hope they will try harder this time. The FAA says they will relocate these workers again if sufficient funding is available. Again, don't hold your breath.

The GAO report of September 1994, pg. 11 states: "Of the 13 controllers at two Level One towers that we visited, 10 had transferred there because they could not perform the required duties at higher-level towers."

I believe a fellow named Peter had this principle all figured out.

Just a word before we finish up on this level one business. The level one tower has the least amount of traffic to control out of the five FAA classes of towers. Can there be a level lower than one? The answer is a most decided yes. There are thousands of small airports throughout the United States that have no tower at all, yet jets as large as Boeing 757s are landing there daily. In the case of air carriers, there must be someone to talk to them before they land, usually a ticket agent or baggage handler.

But what about private aircraft such as Lear Jets and other private aircraft? Who do they talk to? There is a party line radio called a "unicom" found inside a fixed-base operator's office. When a plane calls in for the active runway, he may get an answer from the operator's office. And then again, he may not. If the people in the office are not too busy drinking coffee, or trying to get a prospective pilot to sign up for a flight course, or if they are not out pumping fuel, he may get an answer. But it will be short and to the point. You will be told the number of the active runway, and that's it: no wind information, altimeter setting, or traffic information. He is now in the danger zone flying in and around a non-controlled (no tower) airport.

We have been discussing the various towers and unicom radios, but what if your aircraft is not even radio-equipped? Yes, it is quite legal to fly an aircraft from coast to coast without the benefit of any radio communications.

Since accidents double at or near an uncontrolled airport, I believe this is a good benchmark for having and keeping a working control tower. According to the FAA's Minimal Establishment and Discontinuance Criteria for Airport Traffic Control Towers, page 22, regarding accidents: "The resultant mean values are 9.704 accidents per million operations at a non-towered airport vs. 4.538 accidents per million at towered airports, a difference of 5.166 per million operations."

Later on in this chapter, you will see how 14 people burned to death in a runway collision in Quincy, Illinois, at an airport without a tower.

The September 1994 GAO report, concerning level one towers, makes the following statements: "Page 1, FAA does not believe that safety will be jeopardized by closing or contracting out Level One towers. Page 16, FAA assesses both the safety and efficiency benefits of towers. However, the primary emphasis is on safety; that is, preventing or reducing (1) collisions between aircraft (such as midair or air-to-ground collisions), and (2) other such accidents as wheels-up landings or collisions with field obstructions. Under this scenario, lives are saved and few aircraft become damaged."

It would seem that the above FAA statement was so much "hog wash." The "feds" are busy closing the following towers:

Ponce, Puerto Rico—airliners use it.

Plainview, Texas

Pine Bluff, Arkansas—airliners use it.

Merced, California

Mayaguez, Puerto Rico—airliners use it.

Akron, Ohio

Spartanburg, South Carolina—airliners use it.

Hickory, North Carolina

Benton Harbor, Michigan

New Bern, NC—Commuter lines.

Hot Springs, Arkansas

This is only a partial list. There are many more control towers that are scheduled to close.

GAO September report, page 4: "The Vice President's National Performance Review also commented that FAA contracts out Level One tower operations because the Review believed that contractors can provide the same level of service at less cost to the government."

The statement from Vice President Gore's Performance Review does not always ring true, at least not in the case where he or President Clinton are concerned. In 1994, when President Clinton took his vacation at Martha's Vineyard, a very strange chain of events took place. We have been hearing how the contract controllers are every bit as good as the FAA people whom they replaced. Well, that may hold true for you and me, but when the President flies into Martha's Vineyard, those good old contract boys in the tower were only bystanders when Clinton's plane landed. The landing and takeoff clearance for Clinton's plane were handled by substitute FAA

controllers who were specially requested to man the con\
Martha's Vineyard. I wonder why?

It seems that the FAA wants the safety of FAA controllers whe ꜰer the President's plane is concerned, but they don't care about the little people.

Safety on the Runway

Los Rhodes Tenerife Airport was in the grip of some of the worst imaginable weather. Low clouds drifted over the airport causing the visibility to fluctuate between zero and less than one-quarter of a mile. Because of the fog, the tower controllers were unable to see the runway and there was no airport mapping radar. A bomb scare at Las Palmos, Canary Islands, caused numerous diversions to Tenerife that saturated the airport with aircraft, making normal taxi routes impossible. The only route to the active runway was by taxiing down it into takeoff position. To add to this dilemma, the runway center line lighting was inoperative, making even the slowest taxiing extremely hazardous. The control tower was short one operator, which increased the workload of the other controllers.

KLM 4805, a Boeing 747, had just completed fueling and was ready to start taxiing. The first officer keyed his mike: "Approach KLM 4805 on the ground at Tenerife."

Tower: "KLM 4805, Roger."

KLM: "We require backtrack on 12 for takeoff runway 30."

Tower: "Okay, 4805, taxi to holding position runway 30, taxi into runway and leave runway third to your left."

KLM: "Roger, sir. Entering runway at this time, and the first taxiway we go off the runway again for the beginning of runway 30."

Tower: "Okay, KLM 80. Correction, 4805 taxi straight ahead for the runway and make a backtrack."

KLM: "Roger. Make a back track. KLM 4805 is now on the runway."

Tower: "4805, Roger."

KLM: "Approach, you want us to turn left at Charlie one, taxiway Charlie one?"

Tower: "Negative, negative. Taxi straight ahead up to the end of the runway and make a backtrack."

KLM: "Okay, sir."

The tower controller was issuing instructions for the aircraft to follow, but he could not see any of his traffic. The fog was still too dense, and he hoped that the pilots under his control would follow his directions to the letter because his view of the runway was nil.

PAA Flight 1736, also a 747, was unable to taxi to the runway because he was blocked by KLM. Now that the path was clear, they called the tower for clearance.

PAA: "Tenerife the Clipper, 1736."

Tower: "Clipper 1736, Tenerife."

PAA: "We were instructed to contact you and also to taxi down the runway; is that correct?"

Tower: "Affirmative. Taxi into the runway, and leave the runway third, third to your left."

PAA: "Third to the left, okay."

The stage is set. We have three different nationalities talking to each other—American, Spanish, and Dutch. The crews are at a strange airport taxiing on the same runway with no center line lighting to guide them, visibility less than one-quarter of a mile, and no surface radar to enable the tower controllers to see the traffic they're directing. As Pan Am taxied down the active runway, there was a discussion in the cockpit concerning the controller's instructions. With a foreign accent, "third" sounded very similar to "first." In any case, the co-pilot asked again, and his doubts were dispelled as the controller told him "The third, sir—one, two, three. The third."

The KLM aircraft had reached the end of the runway and was gingerly making a 180-degree turn to be in position for takeoff. Pan Am was slowly edging its way towards KLM, straining to see their third turnoff.

Most countries have strict flight time limitations, but none as stringent as the Dutch. If a crewmember is caught breaking this regulation, he could be fired or jailed. The crew of KLM was delayed in their fueling and loading, so now they were crowding their legal duty time. The captain on

KLM nervously advanced the throttles and the aircraft began to roll. The co-pilot exclaimed, "Wait a minute, we don't have ATC clearance." The captain replied, "No, I know that. Go ahead, ask."

KLM: "The KLM 4805 is now ready for takeoff and we're waiting for our ATC clearance."

Tower: "KLM 8705 (wrong number mine), you are cleared to the papa beacon; climb to and maintain flight level nine zero. Right turn after take-off, proceed with heading zero four zero until intercepting the 325 radial from Las Palmos VOR."

KLM: "Roger, sir. We've cleared to the papa beacon flight level nine zero, right turn zero four zero until intercepting the 325, and we're now at takeoff." (There is no such altitude as 90. It is either 9,000 feet or 90,000 feet.)

I have never heard the phrase "we are at takeoff" used before. As it stands now, this statement meant nothing except they were in takeoff position or ready for takeoff, but by no means could it have meant they were rolling. And they were. The tower, thinking they were going to hold their position, replied: "Okay."

Pan Am was still on the active runway and had not as yet cleared onto their assigned taxiway. While the KLM co-pilot was still reading back his clearance to the tower, the captain, who was eager to get going, was already starting his takeoff roll.

The tower controller could see nothing from his cab as he keyed his mike, and said, "Okay." Two seconds later, he added, "Stand by for takeoff. I will call you."

The 229 passengers on the KLM were gently being forced back in their seats as the four giant turbines started that eerie scream.

The PAA captain, hearing the KLM transmission, grabbed his mike. "No. We are still taxiing down the runway, the Clipper 1736."

Tower: "Papa Alpha (the phonetic alphabet for PA) 1736, report runway clear."

PAA: "Okay, will report when we're clear."

This transmission was audible to the crew of KLM. Inside the KLM cockpit, the flight engineer questioned the captain. "Is he not clear then?

Is he not clear, Pan American?" The captain's answer to this question was a most emphatic, "Oh, yes."

Nine seconds before impact, the Pan American crew saw a most bizarre sight. Bearing down on them were the powerful lights of the 747 getting brighter and brighter as the KLM loomed at them through the dense fog. The Pam Am captain shouted in desperation, "What's he doing? He'll kill us all. Get off! Get!"

He quickly applied power and swerved to the left trying desperately to cheat death. By now, the KLM crew was near enough to see Pan Am directly in front of them. At this point, there was only one alternative left. The captain horsed back on the yoke and 700,000 pounds of man's genius clawed for the sky. The aircraft pitched up so violently that the tail left a 65-foot impression on the runway. The trail of sparks ended as the aircraft started to slowly climb. He was now directly over Pan Am. Unfortunately, only a few more feet were needed to avert what was the world's worst aviation tragedy.

KLM's No. 3 engine and its massive landing gear ripped through the top of the Clipper's fuselage with such a tremendous force that it sliced it as though it were cutting through tinfoil. The KLM fuselage, already a fiery tomb for its occupants, continued down the runway for 1,500 feet, leaving in its wake a trail of bodies and debris.

This needless accident took the lives of 583 persons. Airports throughout the world, especially those that take some of the larger transports, should be properly equipped: 583 people would be alive today if Tenerife Airport had been equipped with ASDE.

At Atlanta Hartsfield International Airport, 1990, an Epps Air Service plane had just landed on runway 26. An Eastern 727 also was landing on the same runway. The 727 hit the Epps aircraft and killed the pilot. The weather was such that neither the tower nor the 727 crew could see the plane on the runway. This accident is similar to a February 1991 accident in California.

At Detroit Metropolitan Airport on December 9, 1990, the visibility was varying between one-quarter and one-eighth of a mile in fog. Northwest Airlines Boeing DC-9 and another Northwest Boeing 727 were both taxiing out for takeoff. The DC-9 crew got lost in the fog and taxied onto the active runway. The 727 was on takeoff roll when its right wing sliced the DC-9 fuselage from behind its cockpit to the tail where it knocked off an engine. The impact damage and resulting fire claimed eight lives on the DC-9. There were no injuries on the 727.

At Los Angeles International Airport on February 1, 1991, a USAir 737 was cleared to land on top of another airliner that was parked on the same runway. The resulting collision took the lives of 34 people. This time the weather was clear, but some lights obscured the vision of the control tower operator. And in November 1994 at Lambert-St. Louis International Airport, it was evening, and Cessna 441 was taxiing out to what he thought was runway 31. This would be his first flight at night. The Cessna pilot was instructed by the tower to "Back taxi on runway 31 and position and hold on that runway." The pilot became confused as to his exact position. In reality, he was holding on runway 30R. An airport at night can be a real problem, even for experienced pilots who are not familiar with the full layout. TWA Flight 427 was assigned Runway 30R for departure. The airline crew did not observe any exterior lights on the Cessna. TWA started his takeoff roll and saw no other aircraft until three seconds before impact. The airline's wing sliced the top off the twin Cessna, along with the heads of the two occupants. Out of the 132 passengers on TWA, eight sustained minor injuries during evacuation.

In an effort to save expenses at night, many towers may have one operator to work three positions. This was the case on the night of the accident. The tower controller was giving instructions on three separate frequencies. As you can see, this is not a very safe procedure.

Lambert Field did have ASDE.3 ground radar, but a computer hard drive failed on the day of the accident. This unit easily could have prevented the accident by enabling the controller to spot the Cessna that was sitting on the active runway. This accident was very similar to the previous mishap at Los Angeles. In both accidents, there was an unseen aircraft on the active runway. At least in St. Louis, there was a ground radar, but what good is it if it's not functioning?

In this day and age, why are such accidents happening at all? Let's examine the impossible duties of the control tower personnel. They are responsible for separating traffic in the air and on the ground. The FAA has no visibility limits for any movement on the ground, only in the air.

You might be wondering why is it that airplanes can taxi in dense fog? Surely they cannot expect to fly if they can barely see the ground. Weather does strange things. Many times I have taxied out in "pea soup" only to find the runway visibility good enough for takeoff. But if you are the crew of an airliner taxiing through the fog on the way to the runway, it's very easy to become lost, especially at a strange airport.

What about the poor controller who has the impossible task of controlling traffic that he or she cannot see? Now we have a situation of the blind leading the blind. At times, the tower cab may be in the clouds and the ground might be in the clear. The ATC is governed by radio transmissions from the aircraft under his control stating his position. Sometimes they are accurate, and sometimes they are not. Does this sound like a safe practice? I think not.

In 1977, the worst air disaster of all time took place in Tenerife on the Canary Islands, Spain. Two jumbo jets were on the same runway heading toward each other. They hit, killing 583 people. Have we learned anything from this? Obviously not. There is still no ground radar at Tenerife, and hundreds of other airports also lack the life-saving aid. Let's see what we have learned since 1977.

It was October 31, 2000. The main airport at Taipei was soon to be hit with a 90-mph typhoon. The winds at the airport were already up to 40 mph, and the driving rain had cut visibility down to a point where the tower controller could not see the threshold of the main takeoff runway, 5Left. When there are parallel runways, they are lettered from left to right. Runway 5Left (5L) is adjacent to, but past, runway 5Right (5R).

Captain C. K. Foong, a 10,000-hour pilot, was cautiously taxing his Singapore Airlines 747-400 out to the takeoff runway. On board were 179 people and 20 crewmembers, 47 of whom were Americans. Singapore Airlines flight SQ006 was a scheduled, nonstop service to Los Angeles.

It was a black night, and the fierce wind and rain made taxing a hazardous situation. As Captain Foong approached his takeoff runway, the tower stated: "Singapore 6, Runway 5L cleared for takeoff."

Eight seconds later, the pilot read back "Cleared for takeoff runway 5L Singapore 6."

The before-takeoff checklist was completed. Captain Foong stated "We can see the runway; not so bad. OK. I'm going to put it on high (referring to the speed of the windshield wipers). He advanced the throttles and the world's largest airliner started down the rain-swept runway.

At about 150 mph, Captain Foong exclaimed, "There's something there!"

Indeed, there was. A concrete barrier and numerous pieces of heavy excavating machinery blocked his path. The airliner hit the equipment and burst into flames, finally coming to rest in three giant sections and killing 81 people. You might ask, what in the world are cranes and bulldozers doing on an active runway? That's an easy one. The airliner tried to take off on 5R instead of the parallel 5L. The runway used (5R) was closed from August 31 to the present, and all crews were warned about it.

Let's review some of the pertinent information.

1. The flight dispatchers were supposed to warn all pilots that 5R was closed. Was this done?

2. The tower was supposed to issue warnings to all crews concerning the status of 5R. This was not done.

3. It is against regulation to take off from a runway that is not properly lit. The airport authority claims that there were no lights on the closed runway. I find it hard to believe that an experienced crew would attempt a takeoff with the runway lights not activated.

4. The international marking for a closed runway is a large X painted or displayed on boards. Was there an X, as required?

5. All runways have extremely large numbers painted on their surfaces. If the crew saw a 5R painted on the runway, they would not have taken off on the closed runway. Were these numbers painted on the runways?

6. The tower controller could not see the threshold of either 5L or 5R. How are they expected to control traffic that they cannot see?

7. There was no ground radar. The tower could have warned the crew that they were lined up with the wrong runway had they had the proper equipment.

8. There is also a large sign at the end of each runway stating the runway number. The signs are lighted at night. Were the lights on this sign the evening of the crash?

Reuters News Service reported that Singapore Airlines chief executive Cheong Choong Kong said, "The airline accepts full responsibility for the crash. It was obviously a pilot error. We should also look at safety features at airports."

That last statement concerning equipment at airports is the key to the 81 needless deaths. I will be willing to bet you that they still will not install ground radar. It is a mystery to me how airports around the world can operate without this life-saving equipment.

We have just discussed five aircraft accidents that should never have happened if our airports were properly equipped. In 1950, ASDI-2 was installed at a handful of U.S. airports. It is a tool that can increase significantly the efficiency and safety of an airport, and make the controllers' job a bit easier. In 1950, 12 airports in the states had the benefit of this system. When it worked, it was fairly useful, but it failed when needed the most: in bad weather.

The FAA contracted with Norden Systems, Inc., and Cardin Electronics for a new and better ASDE-3. The first testing of these units was set for March 1988. From 1950 to the present, out of 12 ASDEs in service, only a few are operational. So for 30 years, the FAA has not kept their in-house ASDEs in proper repair.

From 1976 to 1982, the FAA slowly organized the criteria necessary for their ASDE-3 by writing operational requirements, technical specifications, and testing an engineering model. Since there are very few days in the year when the weather is so bad that the controllers cannot see the runways, the FAA let the old ASDE-2s slide by choosing instead to absorb themselves in compiling statistics weighing the advantages of a new system against the cost of installation. Since the FAA has two primary missions, one to promote aviation and the other to regulate it, it's a wonder we ever get any safety devices.

ASDE-3 is an updated, ground-based radar designed to provide surveillance of all ground-based vehicles under all weather conditions, including fog and rain. In 1992, Congress provided funding to procure 11 additional ASDE-3s. Each unit costs over $4 million, and the warranty for each unit was not as long as the one for your personal TV set: only 30 days. After that, the feds have to pay for repairs.

You would think that after 30 years of research and a $4 million price tag, the darned thing would work. Well, it doesn't. My good friend Richard Sullivan, President of ATCA Local Union and a working FPL in Boston's Logan Tower, has this to say about ASDI-3: "The unit was installed about a year and a half ago, and it is not commissioned yet. The bearings were lubricated with a cadmium material that filtered down into the tower cab. This material is carcinogenic, and the whole cab had to be cleaned. The unit presents multipath targets. The beam hits a target and returns to the antenna after displaying two targets. The display screen in the tower cab is much too small, 13" diagonal. There have been numerous requests for a larger screen, but they fall on deaf ears. The main use for this unit is to display targets when the weather is down—fog, rain, etc. When the precipitation is anything but light, the radar picks up the rain drops and blanks out any existing targets on the airport surface.

"When the unit was turned on, the mapping display of the runways and taxiway was not exact. So a Norden representative attempted to realign some of the taxiways strictly by eyeballing. Needless to say, it did not display an accurate map of the airport. High-tailed aircraft such as DC-9s, 727s, MD80s, etc., all return to the screen as split targets. Instead of one airplane, it cuts it in half and shows two.

"There are very few spare parts for these units, and when something blows, it takes months to get a replacement part. Not that it really makes much difference since the unit has only worked for a very few days since it was installed nearly two years ago."

The GAO reported in April 1993 that, "The FAA has begun exploring solutions to the target-splitting problem and plans to correct it soon at a cost of about $7.7 million."

What is the FAA doing to rectify these "low bid" units from the Norden Company? They managed to find a cheaper unit produced by Raytheon, one used by ships. This unit is less than one-quarter the cost of an ASDE-3 and it works very well most of the time.

It is interesting to note that at Boston's airport, the landing limits go up when the tall ships are in the channel near the end of the instrument runway. These ships do not have to contact the tower people, and if the weather is down they can't be seen. How then can a tower controller warn a pilot if he can't see the ship himself? If the ground-based radar is working, the ship will be displayed on the screen. If not, there might be a slight jolt before the airliner lands.

Pittsburgh Airport has one of the ASDE-3 units installed. It works about as well as the Boston unit, which isn't saying much. There is a key pack associated with each display. These buttons must be depressed to make the screen presentation larger or smaller, or vary the intensity. Since the unit was installed, they have gone through five or six new key packs. That's not the way it's supposed to be.

As of January 1994, the "feds" have targeted 30 airports that are going to have to struggle with the Norton ASDE-3. The following is a list of airports that are now "lucky" enough to have this state-of-the-art toy: Pittsburgh, Philadelphia, Portland, Denver, Houston, Los Angeles, Cleveland, Detroit, Dallas, Atlanta, San Francisco, New York JFK, and Seattle. The only one that is presently commissioned is the unit in Seattle. The "feds" are also toying with new devices to be used in conjunction with the ASDE-3 called ASTA (Airport Surface Traffic Automation) and AMASS (Airport Movement Area Safety System). When these three systems are combined, they should perform the following functions:

1. Enable controllers and pilots to identify aircraft and vehicles.

2. Alert pilots when a runway is in use for takeoff or landing.

3. Provide taxi route clearances between aircraft and the tower through aeronautical data link.

Of the seven ASDE-3s purchased, the "feds" are planning to install two systems. The other five installations will be cancelled. The FAA will purchase the remaining units and put them in storage. They expect to have all units in place by November 1999. In the meantime, let's all pray for good weather!

Airports that don't have a functional ASDE-3 are indeed unsafe. Richard Sullivan from Boston Tower estimates that at least 60 days a year the weather is so bad he cannot see the airport from the tower. How then can he be expected to do the impossible like control traffic in a dense fog?

Over $8 billion sits in the Airport and Airways Trust Fund just waiting to be used by FAA to make aviation safer. But it is like pulling teeth to get them to ask Congress for proper appropriations. For example, for $120 million, 30 airports could have the benefit of the advanced ASDE-3 radar. The FAA is very big on cost analysis and very shy when it comes to safety. They actually consider the cost justification of the ASDI-3 system to be correlated with three basic concepts. The 1986 GAO report shows FAA's methodology for determining if the ASDR-3 program is cost-justified.

1. Efficiency from reduced aircraft operating time.

2. Savings to passengers from reduced travel time.

3. Enhanced safety to aircraft from fewer accidents on the airport surface. (Passenger safety is not a quantifiable benefit in FAA's methodology.) You will notice that passenger safety is last on the FAA's list.

The Department of Transportation had this to say concerning the new ASDE-3 that was recently installed for testing in Alaska: "ASDE is an effective tool for minimum runway incursions and potentially dangerous situations during reduced visibility conditions. An ASDE that was placed in Anchorage, Alaska—the forerunner of the ASDE-3—prevented a potential accident between a Boeing 727 and a YS-11 aircraft within 90 days of installation. The two aircraft operating from different runways, but with intersecting flight paths, had started their departure roll at the same time. This human error was picked up from the ASDE, and the YS-11 was ordered to abort its takeoff.

The 583 people who met a fiery death at Tenerife didn't even have a chance. A rational person would consider safety as being paramount; not so with the feds. Here is a quote from the FAA airport planning book 7031.2C dated 2/10/86. "An airport is a candidate for ASDE, provided the: (1) Airport has a Category Three runway, or (2) Tower reaches 180,000 or more annual itinerant operations, of which 100,000 or more are annual certified route air carrier operations."

If the tower should record less than 150,000 annual itinerant or less than 80,000 air carrier operations, the equipment will be removed. The "feds" are far more interested in what a safety item might cost than they are with saving lives. How soon will it be before another Tenerife will take place at one of our own numerous substandard airports?

Runway Incursions

On November 22, 1999, at Los Angeles, the crew of an MD-80 landed on runway 25L and failed to hold short of 25R as instructed by the tower. A Boeing 757 was on takeoff roll and flew directly over the MD-80, missing it by an estimated 60 feet. Among the passengers on board were Senator Dole and his wife Elizabeth. During a twenty-one day period from November 22 through December 12, eight additional runway incursions were reported at United States' airports. The following airports were the scenes of the near accidents on the ground: Los Angeles, Richmond, Fort Lauderdale, Fresno, LaGuardia, Chicago's Midway, and Dulles in D.C.

A runway incursion occurs when two aircraft, or a vehicle and an aircraft, nearly collide on an airport ramp, taxiway, or runway.

From November 1988 to December 1999, there were twenty near tragedies at various airports. Two were at O'Hare and three at Los Angeles. In 1999, there were 326 runway incursions reported, an increase of four more than in 1998. These incursions nearly always occur at fogged-in airports or at night. It is difficult for a crew, in good weather, to negotiate the maze of runways and taxiways, but during poor visibility it becomes a terror.

As you can see, ASDI radar, which can pick up objects on the ground, is a must, but most airports do not have this life-saving equipment.

Bad Weather Landing Aids

There are many different ways to get down to a runway when the weather is so bad that the airport is completely obscured.

There are two broad approach categories. The more dangerous are called "non-precision." That is, they lack the vertical guidance of a glide path and only tell direction laterally. Some examples of this type are VOR, Localizer, NDB, Back Course, ASR, and Circling. We will only discuss the main approaches. None of the landing aids are subjected to various operating limitations as much as the ADF, or non-directional beacon approach. Let's take a look at what these various approach aids have to offer, starting with the best and working our way down to the worst.

The Instrument Landing System (ILS) Precision Approach

The ILS is comprised of electronic guidance both left and right as well as a normal three° glide slope. There are outer and middle markers that emit an oral and visual signal when they are traversed on final approach. There is usually a compass locator or beacon (NDB) associated with the outer marker situated about five miles from the runway. As you can see, the beacon is only a very small part of the ILS system. But at substandard airports, that's the only approach aid to be found.

In 1954, when I was flying DC-3s into Newark Airport, the approach system was far safer than it is today. From the initial approach fix all the way to a landing, you were radar monitored. There was a controller who operated a precision radar device that was linked with the ILS localizer by a controller's voice. If you were off course or heading he would tell you: "You are 10 feet below the glide slope. Please bring it up." Today, once you pass the five-mile marker on the way to the runway, you are on your own. The GCA (ground control approach) radar system is history except at military airports. Today, tower controllers might get a low altitude alert display on their radar if the aircraft should stray below the 3 degrees glide path. But the fine precision, both in direction and altitude, is long gone.

Non-precision Approach

The next best approach is the VOR (VHF omnidirectional range). This aid emits 360 different courses that can be flown and they are relatively unaffected by weather. When you pass over the station, a needle on the panel goes from "to" to "from." There is no glide slope associated with this let-down, hence the name "non-precision approach." Believe it or not, the Morse code is used to identify most of these approach aids. Many of these VORs have a voice identifier. That is to say, the name of the navigation aid can be heard in the pilot's headset, but most of these aids have Morse code identifiers which are much more difficult to tune in and identify.

The Non-directional Beacon (NDB)

This approach is the worst of all the various ways to descent through the clouds to the runway. I would like to quote from the pilots' bible, the AIM (Airman's Information Manual). This book is published by the FAA. Page 1-1: "Radio beacons are subjected to disturbances that may result in erroneous bearing information. Such disturbances result from such factors as lightning, precipitation, static, etc." Factors that can effect the reception of the NDC receiver include:

Night Effect—Radio waves are reflected by the ionosphere returning to earth some 30 to 60 miles from the beacon.

Mountain Effect—Bearings taken in the vicinity of mountains may be erroneous.

Shoreline Effect—As radio waves travel from land to water, their direction of travel changes.

Precipitation Static—Found in moist precipitation, it can easily deflect the guidance needle.

Thunderstorm Effect—the trusty NDB needle will always point to a source of more power such as a thunderstorm. Before the days of airborne radar, I used my NDB radio to point to thunderstorms so that I could steer around them.

The ILS (the best approach) has a number of components: localizer, glide path, outer marker, middle marker, and approach lights. None of thee high-precision aids are found in a lowly NDB, only the beacon itself. So there are five basic components to an ILS and only one to the NDB. Not a very safe way to get to a runway, but at some airports, that's all there is.

The NDB has no warning flag in the cockpit panel to alert the pilot when erroneous bearings are being displayed. The previous approach aids both have warning flags to tell the pilot if all is not well. The NDB is at least half a century old and has never been updated. Many of the third-world countries use these potentially dangerous aids because they lack the funds to purchase and install a VOR or an ILS.

The Flight Safety Foundation statistics show conclusively that aircraft flying a non-precision approach are five times more likely to crash as compared with pilots who utilize a precision ILS letdown.

Let's examine one of the most recent non-precision beacon approach disasters.

In 1996, a crash in Croatia took the lives of Commerce Secretary Ron Brown and 34 others. Their USAF B-737 aircraft was penetrating a storm-ridden airport surrounded by mountains with nothing but a low-powered NDB (non-directional beacon) for an approach aid.

1. The Air Force crew was never properly trained to fly a beacon approach.

2. The crew was making an approach to an airport that was not considered safe by top Air Force authorities.

3. The various altitudes depicted on the approach chart did not meet USAF standards.

4. The weather was gusty with accompanying heavy rain.

5. Last but not least, the ancient NDB beacon was probably giving false readings as it was busily guiding the crew into a storm-swept area instead of to the runway.

I firmly believe that all NDB approaches in mountainous areas should be eliminated. Why should passengers be subjected to the dangers associated with this type of approach simply because the FAA considers it a safe, inexpensive landing aid? If the only approach aid at your airport is an NDB, good luck.

The "feds" go to great detail and have written many manuals concerning the cost-effectiveness of an ILS. They depict the inconvenience that a passenger might experience because his flight might have to divert to another airport. What costs would be incurred to the airline if a flight should crash because of the lack of an ILS, and what would it cost the carrier to replace a smashed aircraft and the court costs to pay for the injured and dead?

There are 12 thousand airports in the United States, but only a scant 500 are utilized by large, scheduled air carriers. There are a total of 1,174 runway ends. By that, I mean each runway really has two ends. Each end could be utilized by an aircraft making an instrument approach, providing there was an approach let down at both ends. Combining all the airline runway ends, we have a grand total of 2,348 touch down areas. Each end has the potential for an ILS. That leaves us with 1,743 airline runways without a first class aid.

The FAA APO83-10 manual makes a most revealing statement (on page 11) concerning the merits of an ILS: "The lateral, vertical and distance guidance information that aircraft equipped with the proper avionics receiver improves the level of safety during landing procedures above the safety level associated with non-precision approach procedures."

Wind Shear Detectors

On August 2, 1985, 57-year-old Captain Edward N. Connors was executing an ILS into the rain-swept runway at Dallas/Fort Worth Airport. There were a few scattered thunderstorms in the area. When they were only a few miles from the runway, the crew of Delta flight 191 was discussing the final phase of their approach.

Captain: "Watch your speed." He detected that his first officer, Rudolph Price, was letting the giant 1011's air speed get dangerously low. "Push it up. Push it way up!" "Way up!"

Power was applied by the first officer in an effort to arrest the horrendous sink rate that was forcing them earthward. The three Rolls Royce turbines started screaming as their 41,030 pounds of thrust were ordered to increase.

Captain: "Hang on!"

First Officer: "What's Vref?"

"WHOOP! WHOOP! PULL UP!" summoned the automatic ground proximity warning system.

"Push it way up."

About a mile from the safety of the 11,388-foot runway, Delta Airlines Flight 191 was about to make its final landing. The undercarriage dug into the ground 240 feet short of the runway. The crew was trying desperately to nurse the giant back into the air. They succeeded for a very short distance before colliding with an automobile on State Highway 114 that borders the airport. The aircraft began disintegrating after crossing the highway. They continued forward to the airport property until reaching their final resting place between two giant water tanks. The fuselage broke in half and some of the passengers were ejected from the plane. The rear of the fuselage and tail section had the least damage. The remainder of the 324,800-pound giant exploded and burned fiercely, killing 163 people.

As usual, the crew was blamed. The NTSB stated in part: "The lack of specific guidelines, procedures, and training for avoiding and escaping from low-altitude wind shear, and the lack of definitive, real-time wind shear hazard information resulted in the aircraft's encounter at low altitude with a microburst-induced, severe wind shear from a rapidly developing thunderstorm located on the final approach course."

At the time of the accident, the Low Level wind shear Alert System (LLWAS) at the airport was functioning but it failed to trigger an alert in the tower cab until 10 minutes after the airliner had crashed.

Wind shear is an abrupt change in direction and/or velocity of the wind. The most dangerous type of wind shear, the microburst, creates highly divergent wind outflows covering a very short distance (one-quarter to two and one-half miles). They can have disastrous impact on aircraft taking off or landing. This phenomenon was the downfall of Delta Flight 191.

In 1976, a LLWAS was developed and is presently installed at 87 of our major air terminals. Each LLWAS consists of six ground-based wind direction sensors and a computer. Whenever a peripheral sensor's average wind reading for 30 seconds shows a difference between speed and direction of 15 knots or more from that of the sensor at mid-field, an audible alarm will be triggered in the control tower.

This system is better than nothing, but should not be compared with Doppler radar. It has proven to give false warnings. It is unreliable for detecting microbursts, and the wind shear alert must be monitored by the tower controller and transmitted to the pilot via radio. A controller's primary function is to keep traffic separated. At times, he becomes so busy he just doesn't have time to discuss anything except orders to the aircraft under his control. A wind shear warning may well go unheeded.

The wind shear alert, as we have seen in the Delta crash, can only give a reading between the airport sensors. They are ground-based towers and can give no alarms to any weather beyond the boundary of the airport or at altitude. A pilot needs to know about wind shear while he is in the air. Sure, an alert to an aircraft about to take off could change the captain's mind, but any aircraft above 50 feet will never receive a warning for his altitude.

The "feds" are toying with a few new ways to keep us all alive. The enhanced LLWAS was to be installed at 110 airports by August of 1992. They intended to increase the number of ground-wind sensors from 6 to 11 and to improve the computer processor. It really wouldn't matter if they increased the sensors to 50; they still wouldn't give you any warning in the air.

Terminal Doppler Weather Radar is the FAA's finest state-of-the-art, ground-based, wind shear detection system. These units can scan the final approach area and give the pilot a clear picture of what he may encounter traveling down final approach. Not only will this system save lives, but it also will decrease the time consumed in changing runways. Aircraft usually land as nearly into the wind as possible, so any instrument that would enable tower personnel to foresee a wind shift coming would save the airlines thousands of dollars in fuel costs. Doppler can predict wind shift alerts for as long as 20 minutes before they hit the airport.

These units were scheduled to be installed at 100 airports before 1995. There are 500 large airline airports, and as of 1996, there were only six units installed and they are not all fully certified.

Unfortunately, there are still a few weak captains out there and help is needed to enable them to make the correct decisions. Nearly every major carrier has a statement in their operating manuals forbidding their pilots to fly near thunderstorms. Experienced pilots need no warnings when it comes to the terrible dangers associated with these storms. I believe that all major air carrier terminals should have an in-house meteorologist able to tell the tower personnel when to expect a thunderstorm at the field. This person should have the power to close an airport during inclement weather.

As it stands now, the only person who can close an airport is the airport manager, and he is the one person who is most reluctant to curtail all that good revenue. His aeronautical expertise is usually far less than that of the tower operator but the man in the tower has no authority to close an airport except after a crash. Pilots hate to have their authority questioned, but there are far too many weather-related accidents that could have been prevented by simply closing the airport until the storm had passed.

Safety Zones

The crash of a Southwest 737 at Burbank, California, shows the dire need for 1,000-foot safety zones at the end of each runway. As the name implies, a safety zone is a one thousand-foot extension of the existing runway. In the case of the Southwest airliner, it looks as though it was pilot error. He was on a steep approach and landed at a good 50 knots over the appropriate speed. He could not stop the aircraft in the confines of the short runway, only 6,032 feet long. Larger airports have longer runways. Eighteen miles away, Los Angeles (LAX) has dual runways that are over 10,000 feet long.

If Southwest had made the same approach at LAX, he would have stopped at least three thousand feet short of the runway's end.

Now we have seen the differences between an airport with safe runways as compared to a substandard field. The problem with most airports is the fact that they were built decades ago and there was, at the time, ample room for runway expansion. The valuable real estate was sold off and the towns began expanding right up to the airport boundaries. There was a time when safety zones would have been feasible, but not in this day and age unless the airport is out in the sticks. Airports such as LaGuardia, Midway, Washington's Reagan International, and Lindbergh Field have nowhere to expand.

Since 1988, the FAA has required a 1,000-foot overrun at all major airports. Unfortunately, nearly all major airports were constructed prior to that date. What can the "good old boys" do to soften the blow to airports that were built prior to 1988? Well, they want to borrow from Peter to pay Paul. They authorized a foam substance at the end of certain runways. It has proven to stop aircraft before the end of the runway, but they may be sacrificing good concrete and shortening the useable runways.

Last May, an American eagle landed long at Kennedy and became stuck in the foam at the end. I guess it does work, but there is no substitute for a long runway with a safety zone.

Foreign Object Damage (FOD)

Concord—the word means harmony—has made civil aircraft capable of flying at over mach two (1,450 mph). The first concord flew on March 2, 1969, and the first supersonic passenger service was inaugurated on January 21, 1976. The Boeing Aircraft Company also was toying with the idea of building a supersonic transport (Boeing 2707) but the project proved to be uneconomical and was cancelled.

The concord airframe was built by British Aircraft Corporation (BAC) and Aerospatiale of France. The four powerful turbojets, developing 38,050 pounds of thrust, were designed jointly by Rolls-Royce and Snecoma Corporations. The concord is a slim, delta-winged aircraft powered by four turbojets under the wings. The aircraft is 202 feet long with a wing-span of 83 feet. The plane carries 24,000 gallons of fuel and consumes approximately 5000 gallons an hour. Since there is a limited tail section, fuel management is critical to maintaining balance. She cruises at 60,000 feet, about 20,000 feet higher than subsonic airliners. At this altitude, there are few storms and turbulence to affect the flight.

Flying faster than a bullet generates a lot of heat. The airframe temperature reaches as high as 239 degrees F. On the leading edge, nose, and tail, the temperature goes as high at 266 degrees F.

Because of the slim fuselage and pointed nose, the three-man cockpit is far smaller than that of a 747. From the cockpit windscrews to the tip of the nose is a long 24 feet. Because the forward visibility is so poor, the nose is rotated down for all takeoffs and landings.

There are only two carriers that operate concords: Air France has five, and British Airways has seven.

The particular concord model 100 in the following account was the exact aircraft used in the film "Airport 79." It was also one ton heavier than the other concords in service. It had made 3,978 landings and completed 11,989 flight hours. The concord lifts off at about 50 mph faster than a 747, or at about 250 mph. At this speed, the tire friction is so great that many tires have ruptured. Up until now, however, all made it back for a safe landing.

On July 25, 2000, Air France concord flight #4590 departed the gate at Charles de Gaulle airport with a total of 109 passengers and crew. The travelers included 96 Germans, two Danes, an Austrian, and one American. Most of the passengers were bound for New York to start a two-week, luxury Caribbean cruise. The passengers were in high spirits because of the thrill of flying at over mach 2, to see New York, and then take a leisurely cruise.

The graceful jet was taxing out to runway 26R. The flight attendants had already given their passengers the takeoff briefing and were securely strapped into their seats. As the concord neared runway 26R, it was cleared into position for takeoff.

Controller: "Air France 4590, runway 26R, authorized takeoff."

Co-pilot: "4590 taking off 26R."

Captain Christian Marty (to his crew): "Is everyone ready?"

Co-pilot: "Yes."

Flight Engineer: "Yes."

Captain Marty eased the power levers forward and the four turbojet engines increased their thrust and noise level to an ear-shattering roar as 408,000 pounds of magnificent aircraft started its journey down the runway.

Co-pilot: "100 knots."

Captain Marty: "Confirmed."

Flight Engineer: "Four green." The vast array of instruments on the engineer's panel showed all was well.

Co-pilot: "V one." (At this speed, a takeoff becomes mandatory because there is not enough runway left for a stop.)

Co-pilot: "Watch out."

From the control tower, the local controller exclaimed in alarm: "Concord 4590, you have flames, you have flames behind you."

The flight engineer's panel was now flashing numerous warning signs as he yelled "Break down engine, break down engine two!"

Switching sounds were heard, along with a fire alarm.

Captain Marty and the crew had no idea of the severity of the fire. It was happening too far to the rear for them to see.

Captain Marty: "Engine fire procedure."

Air traffic controller: "It's burning badly and I'm not sure it's coming from the engines."

The concord was now only a few hundred feet above the ground. Fire in the air is one of a pilot's worst nightmares, especially when combined with failed engines and stuck landing gear.

Captain Marty: "Gear on the way up." (The landing gear retraction had started.)

Control tower: "4590, you have strong flames behind you. At your convenience, you have priority to land."

Cars on a nearby highway were stopping to observe the fate on one of man's greatest achievements. There was a 100-foot stream of flames coming from the left wing.

Captain Marty was using every piece of knowledge he had ever learned. He knew there was big trouble and he was doing his best to keep a stricken aircraft from hitting the ground. He said to his co-pilot, "Are you cutting engine two?"

Engineer: "I've cut it."

Co-pilot: "The gear won't come up."

The ground proximity warning system started bellowing WHOOP, WHOOP! Pull up.

Co-pilot (shouting): "The airspeed indicator."

Captain Marty was dealing with numerous emergencies at once: No. 2 engine was out, No. 1 had little power, the landing gear would not retract, and he was flying a fiery inferno with the controls probably burned through.

The cabin was filled with smoke and one of the passengers on the left side could clearly see the sheet of flame coming from the left wing. Passengers were in a panic and screams were heard over the roar of the engines. The cockpit crew knew this was their last flight. They could not turn to land at Charles de Gaulle so they planned on landing at Le Bourget that was close. The aircraft was becoming more uncontrollable and dipping lower to the ground.

Captain Marty: "Too late." "No time, no …"

At 1644:31, less than two minutes after takeoff, concord flight 4590 crashed into a small hotel, killing all on board and four people on the ground. The fire that ensued nearly burned all of what was left of a great aircraft.

Was it pilot error? Definitely not. Was it a fault of maintenance? No evidence to date. The concord had been in service without an accident for over twenty-five years. So what could have caused such a tragic accident? An 18x3 inch piece of aluminum from a Continental DC-10's gear just prior to the concord's departure. This caused a tire on the concord to blow and damage the fuel tanks in the left wing.

The official accident report might take six months, but the facts the governments are presently aware of are:

1. Front right tire of left landing gear burst during the takeoff run, probably because it ran over a piece of metal.

2. At least one fuel tank was punctured, maybe more than once, leading to a major fuel leak.

3. The leading fuel ignited, leading to an intense fire within a few seconds of the tire bursting.

4. One, then two engines lost thrust.

5. The crew was not aware of where the fire was or how it started.

6. The crew could not contain the fire.

The preceding accident is probably the most impressive to show what debris on a runway can do. An 18-inch piece of metal killed 113 people.

It is interesting to note how different countries regard the safety of the flying public. After the concord crash, British Airways grounded their concords for 24 hours, then resumed service. Mike Street, British Airways operations director, stated "We would not have resumed concord services unless we were completely satisfied that we had taken every conceivable step to assure the safety of our concord operations."

The French seemed to care more for human life than they do for generating revenue. As of this writing, Air France continues to keep their fleet of concords grounded. A government spokesman said this: "We will wait until we learn more about the chain of events that caused the accident."

The French airline pilot union rectified the government's "wait-and-see" attitude.

There is an area on the airport that should be kept as clean as possible. No, it isn't the rest rooms or the restaurant; it's the runway. Foreign Object Damage is a constant source of worry to pilots and airport operators.

During the propeller era, FOD was not as important as it is now in the jet age. It doesn't take a large object to damage a propeller or the blades on a turbine engine. A small bolt or a screwdriver could easily ruin a multimillion dollar jet engine.

At many of the larger airports, there are crews that operate giant vacuum cleaner-type machines that suck up any loose debris. Speaking of vacuum cleaners, a jet engine is one of the greatest suction devices around. Even when the engine is idling, it has sufficient force to pick up a man and send him into the engine's turbine blades. More than one careless mechanic has met his death by walking too near the intake of a jet engine.

I flew a jet with tail-mounted engines that were attached high above the ground. We used to like taking off behind an aircraft with low-mounted engines such as the Boeing 737 because they would tend to clear the runway of any FOD before we would start our takeoff roll.

Some of the debris that has been cleared from runways and aprons include blowing trash, misplaced tools, luggage tags, sticks, stones, birds, and ice. One airline maintenance record covering a period of three years showed that 60 percent of engines requiring repair from FOD were the engines mounted on the right side of the aircraft, the side where the baggage is loaded. The reason for this is carelessness on the part of the baggage handlers. Consequently, it is people who contribute to the lion's share of all foreign object damage.

According to Mr. Robert Taylor, FOD prevention director at American Airlines, his company changes more than 10 tires daily because of damage sustained from striking foreign objects. An engineer with the Northrup B-2 project stated that on a test run for the B2 bomber, an engine sustained FOD that halted the project for weeks and cost over $10 million. A paper written by Professor Wilfred A. Jackson had an interesting twist concerning FOD: "During certain off-shore wind conditions near Groton, Connecticut, sea gulls gather oysters and drop them on the nearby airport runway in an effort to break them open and expose their contents. The birds and oysters are obvious hazards, but so are shell fragments which are left behind."

While throwing debris from your automobile is detrimental to the environment and might cost you a fine, it is not a potential danger to other motorists. Foreign object damage can cause death and destruction to the flying public. It is estimated that the total cost of FOD to all air carriers each year is over $100 million. That's a tidy sum caused mostly by people who really don't care where they discard their garbage.

Rescue and Firefighting

A review of aircraft accident statistics relates that the vast majority of crashes occur on or near airports instead of en route. This fact is illustrated by the following statistics: 90 percent of aircraft accidents are on or in the departure/approach zones of airports; 70 percent of deaths are caused by fire and associated toxic by-products of combustion; 35 percent of the deaths caused by fire occur in underrun/overrun zones; and 45 percent of all underrun/overrun zone deaths were caused by fire. These figures vividly illustrate the critical nature of fire response capabilities of the airport fire department. Since the modern aircraft lacks the means of preventing post-crash fires, it is essential that each air carrier airport be equipped with a rescue and firefighting unit capable of timely response. Unlike building or structural fires, aircraft fires have the potential to develop into lethal proportions within seconds that eliminate any possibility of occupant escape. Without the rapid deployment of trained rescue and firefighting RFF units who arrive at the crash site in minimum time and apply massive amounts of extinguishing agents, a post-crash fire could not be extinguished and cabin evacuation would be nearly impossible.

You would imagine that all airports that have air carriers the size of DC-9s and 737s would be equipped with appropriate RFF equipment, regardless of the number of operations per day. The FAA would rather overlook terminals that have fewer than five of these flights per day. In the "fed's" regulations Part 139, Certification and Operations: Land Airports Serving Certain Air Carriers, in which all the requirements for certifying an airport are explained, there is one paragraph, no. 139.19, "Exceptions," that allows the airport management far too much leeway. "In addition, the applicant for an airport operating certificate for an air carrier airport enplaning annually less than one-quarter of one percent of the total number of passengers enplaned at all air carrier airports, may petition the Administrator under 11.25 of this chapter (general rule-making procedures) for an exemption from the firefighting and rescue equipment requirements of 139.49 on grounds that compliance with these requirements is, or would be, unreasonably costly, burdensome or impractical."

The "feds" go into great detail as to what type of equipment is mandatory, and then they explain how to shoot holes in their own regulations. The Federal Register periodically publishes an Advisory Circular pertaining to airports. The Part 139 regulations are loose enough, but when the government publishes requirements to make an airport safer, it would be beneficial to all if the rules were at least binding. The Advisory Circular, as the name plainly states, are only advisory in nature. Even though they are the only federal documents to cover airport "standards," they are not mandatory.

Over the years, instead of the airport safety standards becoming more stringent, they have gradually eroded to the farce they are today. The extinguishing agent requirements have been reduced by over one-third. For example, the lone fire truck necessary for a DC-9 operation of under five departures a day contains a scant 500 pounds of chemical and 300 gallons of water compared to the acknowledged standards of 3,000 gallons of water and 500 pounds of chemicals.

The "feds" are not only concerned with keeping the airport operators' expenses to a minimum but also are laboring under the assumption that if an airport has five airliners a day, there should be ample equipment. If, however, the airport schedule reduces to under five a day, these passengers are not nearly as well protected.

Two In, Two Out

The sun was slowly setting, and the weather and winds were perfect for flying. There was a chill in the air and people were watching as a twin-engine airliner started to approach the airport. It was November 19, 1996, a day that will long be remembered by the onlookers in the terminal area. Baldwin Field had no control tower and very rudimentary firefighting equipment.

United Express Flight 5925 was making a scheduled stop to pick up passengers for Chicago's O'Hare Airport. A private twin-engine King Air was in the process of taxing out to runway 4 for a takeoff on an intersecting runway. The United Express touched down on runway 13, and was in the landing rollout and approaching the intersecting runway 4. The King Air started its takeoff roll and headed toward the path of the United Express. The two aircraft collided and rapidly burst into flames. The two occupants of the King Air were burned to death immediately in spite of the fact that both aircraft remained relatively intact.

Witnesses who ran to the crash scene said that they heard sounds of life coming from the United Express cabin and they were even talking to the airliner's Captain in the cockpit. The crew of the airliner tried desperately to open the cabin door but it was jammed. People from the outside also tried in vain to get the door open. Adjacent to the door was a door operating sign with letters two-tenths of an inch in size that was very difficult to read. Without proper instructions, the people had no way of knowing exactly how to get the door open. Three months after the crash, the FAA put out a directive that said clear and larger operating instructions must be installed by the doors. In the meantime, 12 people were near death from carbon monoxide poisoning. You might be wondering why the airport firefighters and rescue unit did nothing to aid the crash victims. That's an easy one. The FAA has ruled that no firefighters are needed at an airport unless an aircraft has a seating capacity of 30 or more passengers. All large aircraft must go through extensive evacuation testing before they are certified by the FAA. That is the way is should be for all passenger aircraft, but the FAA does not treat all crashes the same. The NTSB draws attention to the fact that the FAA "does not evaluate the emergency evacuation capabilities of transport category airplanes with fewer than 44 passenger seats. So next time you are on a small commuter, count the seats and figure out your chances.

The autopsies performed on the ten passengers and two crewmembers proved that all survived the crash, only to die from toxic fumes and FAA negligence.

The nearest Fire Department to the airport was located about 10 miles away. It was summoned to the crash site two minutes after the crash. It took them 14 minutes to arrive at the airport, and 11 minutes longer than recommended to get to the aircraft. It has been determined that crash crews should be located adjacent to the runway because time is imperative. The aircraft skin may burn through in 60 seconds, and in another three minutes, the inside temperatures can reach a lethal 1,800 degrees F. Rescue crews must be at the crash site within three minutes or there is little chance that lives will be saved.

In case you think the FAA has learned a lesson from the previous crash, read on.

June 1, 1999, is a night that will never be forgotten by the passengers and crew of American Airlines flight 1420. The MD-82 was being violently buffeted by an intense thunderstorm located directly over the airport at Little Rock, Arkansas. The crew was diligently trying to get the rain-soaked runway in sight. Numerous mistakes were made by the Captain. His decision to land with a crosswind that far exceeded the aircraft's limitation was inexcusable. Flight 1420 touched down at a speed far in excess of normal landing speed. They skidded 5,000 feet down the rain-swept runway and slammed into approach light structures, breaking the aircraft into three sections. Fire ravaged the ruptured cabin as nine of the 145 passengers burned to death. Five minutes had elapsed since the crash and there was no sign of a crash rescue crew. One survivor dialed 911 on his personal cell phone. "There are a whole bunch of us hurt," he related to the local emergency operator.

Another five minutes passed. The hail, wind, and rain grew more intense as the survivors tried to aid the other trapped passengers. Finally, 15 minutes after the crash, survivors saw the lights of a rescue truck as it tried to maneuver toward the blazing airliner. The truck had to backtrack because of a rocky berm that had to be circumnavigated and a locked gate had to be opened. In the meantime, trapped passengers were burning to death in the remains of the gutted cabin. It took a total of nineteen minutes for the first airport fire truck to reach the crash scene because the tower told them to proceed to the wrong end of the runway.

That length of time is inexcusable. The FAA estimates that if passengers are not out of a burning plane in under ninety seconds, there is little chance for survival.

At the time of this crash, there were two firefighters on duty to man their fleet of two fire trucks. Other units from nearby fire stations responded but all were too late to save lives. Greg Feith of the NTSB stated that a review of airports' certification documents showed a lack of a required grid map and any plan for locating an aircraft crash site on the airport. Little Rock Airport had crash crews based at the airport, and it still took 19 minutes to get to the airliner. What would be your guess as to the amount of time it would take for off-field units to get to the disaster site?

Much of the following is taken from Hank Kims' excellent paper on Surviving The Crash. Jeffrey A. Marcus, Civil Aeromechanical Institute of the FAA had this to say: "Take a few hundred people, put them in a long, narrow aluminum tube, seat them closely together, surround them with thousands of gallons of jet fuel, give them only a few exits to use, and you have what may be a fire safety official's worst nightmare."

What I am about to tell you will shock you. It did me, as I had no idea that I was not only a pilot but also a well-trained firefighter. If there is a fire in the cabin after a crash, pilots are expected to exit their cockpit through the side windows and lower themselves by a rope that is stored over the windows, and assist passengers out safely. Now the only people left on the aircraft are the flight attendants who are expected to fight fires and evacuate passengers while the rest of the rescuers remain outside.

I can remember the only in-flight fire that I ever experienced. I asked my co-pilot, Thomas Block, now a Captain on B-757s, to go to the rear of the aircraft and try to extinguish the blaze. He aimed the tiny extinguisher at the fire and squeezed the trigger. Nothing happened. It took Carolyn Baker, flight attendant, to tell him to pull the pin to release the trigger. In 28 years of commercial flying, I attended dozens of crew training classes; only once did I ever actually fire an extinguisher.

You have all seen movies where there are numerous pieces of firefighting equipment stationed at the active runway in preparation to aid a stricken airliner. Don't you believe it. Sure, there are large airports with state-of-the-art firefighting equipment, but they are very few and far between.

The FAA requirements for firefighters and equipment are at the very bottom of the list of the various firefighting organizations. The National

Fire Protection Association, Department of Defense, and the ICAO (International Civil Aviation Organization) all have more stringent fire-fighting rules than the Federal Aviation Administration.

If you should be caught in a crashed airliner, the fire has started to emit toxic fumes, and you can see the numerous trucks and men outside standing and waiting for you to emerge on your own, you are probably wondering why these men in the fire-resistant rubber suits with the built-in breathing apparatus are not trying to knock down the door to get you out. There is a reason. Current Federal Aviation Administration regulations do not provide for firefighters to enter the aircraft, rescue passengers, or extinguish fires inside the aircraft. The principal function of airport firefighters is to follow federal air regulations part 139 which states that firefighters provide only enough fire protection to ensure a single path through burning jet fuel for those fortunate passengers who can escape on their own. FAA regulations also state that it is the aircrew's responsibility to ensure that all passengers are evacuated, and that all fires inside the aircraft are dealt with by crewmembers.

Well, I thought I had heard it all, but that takes the cake. I am trained to fly an aircraft, not how to cope with cabins ravaged with fire and passengers that are incapacitated. How would you feel if your car caught on fire and the rescue team waited until you got out? What are your thoughts about rescue teams at the site of a high-rise, or your own home, when all the rescuers are waiting for you to emerge under your own power?

Part 139 of the FAA relates the number of pieces of firefighting equipment that are necessary at an airport, not the number of firefighters needed to operate the equipment. In essence, if your airport has the proper equipment and only one firefighter to operate it, that is sufficient.

In 1997, a Fin Airlines DC-8 cashed after takeoff from Miami Airport. Within minutes, nineteen rescue units were on the scene along with 100 emergency personnel. This was a cargo flight and no passengers were involved. It took 100 firefighters to put out a fuel fire of some 5,700 gallons. What would the chances be at a lesser airport with a burning plane and only one firefighter who is responsible for 280 passengers? The FAA sees fit to have one flight attendant for every fifty passengers. Yet they assign one firefighter to rescue as many as 280 passengers.

All the large firefighting organizations require that there be at least 4 firemen to do the job properly. The two in, two out requirement is only a minimal concept. It allows two rescuers to enter the aircraft, with two firefighters for assistance to the ones who have entered the aircraft. This is a minimal number of men, but the FAA requires no specific personnel requirements, only equipment. Military airports are the best equipped, so if you have a choice of using an airport that is joint military and civil, you will be much better protected than utilizing a civil field. There are over 100 joint use civil/military airports in this country.

Cheer up. We are not as bad as Canada when it comes to airport rescue and firefighting. Our neighbors to the north have two hundred airports with commercial airline servers, yet only 28 are required to provide firefighting services.

FAA airport firefighting requirements are the worst in the nation. They demand less equipment, fewer firefighters, and trucks with less water and foam than any of the other recognized agencies. In 1996, a FedEx DC-10 freighter caught fire in flight and landed at Stewart Field in New York. The FAA requirements stated that 4,000 gallons of water should be sufficient to fight the fire. In fact, over 30,000 gallons were needed and the aircraft still burned to the ground.

If you are wondering why the FAA is so lenient with airport authorities, it is because they not only sleep with the airlines but also bed down with the airport managers.

What happens when the weather is down and the visibility is so poor that the rescue team cannot even locate the downed airliner? Well, they just try their best and hope that they can get there before too many people are burned to death. A crashed aircraft with thousands of gallons of fuel on board is the perfect vehicle for a fire or explosion. Since the speed of the rescue team is paramount, there should be a device on all airliners that emits a signal so that the exact whereabouts of the crash can be pinpointed. Such a unit is mandatory on nearly all planes except turbojets, scheduled airliners, or single-seat aircraft. The Emergency Locator Transmitter (ELT) has been around for many years and costs under $200. The ELT automatic signal is initiated automatically as soon as the prescribed number of "G' forces" are applied to it as experienced in a crash. The ELT has saved hundreds of downed light plane pilots. Why the "feds" are more concerned with locating two pilots in a crashed piper cub than 400 people in a downed 747 is more than I can fathom.

There are numerous air carrier airports that have no rescue or firefighting capabilities whatsoever. Most of the terminals have an average of 200 flights per year, some as high as 6,000. Many of these airports not only lack firefighters but also towers and the people who alert the crash crews. If you should ever be unfortunate enough to be trapped in a burning airliner at one of these airports, don't look for foam trucks and men dressed in silver suits operating a vehicle with powerful extinguishing nozzles. The best you will get is someone wielding a bucket of sand.

The following is a government list of fire-related crashes.

Civil Transport Aircraft Accidents (1987–1996) with Fire-related Deaths and Destruction of the Aircraft by Fire

Date	Carrier	Accident Location	Aircraft Type	Occupants	Fatalities
Apr 4, 1987	Garuda	Medan	DC-9	45	28
Aug 5, 1987	Lan Chile	Santiago	B-737	33	2
Aug 16, 1987	Northwest	Detroit	DC-9	155	154
Nov 15, 1987	Continental	Denver	DC-9	82	28
Nov 28, 1987	South African	Indian Ocean	B-747	161	161
Jun 26, 1988	Air France	Habsheim	A-320	136	3
Aug 31, 1988	Delat	Dallas	B-727	108	14
Sep 15, 1988	Ethiopian	Bahr, Dar	B-737	104	35
Oct 17, 1988	Ugandan	Rome	B-707	57	32
Oct 25, 1988	Aero Peru	Juliaca	F-28	89	12
Feb 3, 1989	Burma	Rangoon	F-27	28	26
Mar 10, 1989	Air Ontario	Dryden	F-28	86	24
Jul 19, 1989	United	Sioux City	DC-10	286	111
Feb 14, 1990	Indian	Bangalore	A-320	146	92

May 11, 1990	Philippines	Manilla	B-737	119	8
Dec 3, 1990	Northwest	Detroit	DC-9	44	8
Deb 1, 1991	USAir	Los Angeles	B-737	89	22
Jul 11, 1991	Nationair	Jeddah	DC-8	261	261
Jul 30, 1992	TWA	New York	L-1011	292	0
Dec 21, 1992	Martinair	Faro, Portugal	DC-10	340	56
Jul 2, 1994	USAir	Charlotte	DC-9-31	57	37
Jun 8, 1995	Valujet	Atlanta	DC-9-32	62	0
May 11, 1996	Valujet	Miami	DC-9	109	109
	TWA	New York	B-747	230	230
Jun 1, 1999	American	Little Rock	MD-80	145	9

Balloons and Lasers

As if we don't have enough worry concerning bird strikes (more on this in a later chapter) and the potential danger that exists when we encounter them, now the FAA is allowing tethered balloons to float unannounced near busy airports. The Delaware Department of Transportation is using tethered observation balloons with TV cameras to oversee traffic jams and special events. These balloons are often above the maximum altitude of 200 feet but the "feds" waiver this to allow the pencil-thin tethers to altitudes above 1,500 feet. It is nearly impossible to forewarn pilots that a balloon is going to be launched.

On the first day of operation in Delaware, a light twin aircraft struck and severed the cable. The aircraft managed a safe landing. If the FAA continues to grant waivers to the balloon companies, I feel sure it will spread to other states and the potential for more collisions will become a reality.

Throughout the U.S., there are numerous custom-service radar balloons that reach a height of 15,000 feet. Unfortunately for us, the balloons are launched before they're depicted on the flight charts. In poor weather, it is difficult to spot the thin cable; at night it is impossible because the cable is unlit. These balloons are used to interdict dope smugglers and I guess they are quite efficient. So far, they haven't caused a collision, but it's only a matter of time.

On October 30, 1995, at McCarran International Airport in Las Vegas. Southwest Airlines Flight No. 1367 departed Runway 25 for its trip to San Antonio, Texas. The first officer was flying, and moments after takeoff, he executed a steep right turn over the Las Vegas strip. He wasn't giving his passengers a view of the brightly lit hotels and casinos; he was trying desperately to escape the tremendously bright laser beam from one of the new hotels on the strip. The light flashed through the cockpit and caused him intense pain and temporary blindness. He told his captain to take control because he could barely interpret the instruments. A few minutes later, his sight became clearer and he was able to continue the flight. He was later examined by doctors at Brooks Air Force Base. They determined that there was no permanent eye damage, but follow-up checks would continue.

Laser technology is a relatively new way of flashy advertising. Its impact is not widely understood concerning the safety of crews and their passengers. Since November 19, 1993, there have been over 50 laser-related encounters reported to the control tower at McCarran Airport but none as devastating as the Southwest incident.

Some of the following is taken from NASA's Aviation Safety Repertory System "Callback."

"LasersLight Amplification by Stimulated Emission of Radiation"—are light beams powerful enough to cut through metal or delicate enough to perform microscopic surgery. The most explicit restrictions define a horizontal and vertical eye-safe distance for each display, depending on the type and intensity of lasers used. Exposure to laser beams closer than this distance is potentially injurious to pilots' or passengers' eyes.

A first officer flying near Miami at night reported the following: At 10,000 feet, approximately eight miles from downtown, a green laser was being used for a laser light show. "The laser flashed directly into my eyes. I was blinded for about two seconds. I had trouble with near focus for 15 seconds. My eyes hurt for about two minutes." Loss of night vision can be particularly dangerous for a single pilot who has no one else in the cockpit to provide assistance while initial recovery of night vision begins.

Another pilot, 90 miles south of Las Vegas, reported: "I was flying at 31,000 feet." The captain saw a bright flash and said, "Look at the laser show in Las Vegas." I looked at Las Vegas and we both got hit in the eyes with a green laser. After we turned our eyes forward again, we both noticed a green glow around the periphery of our vision. This was a momentary condition lasting no more than 10 minutes." The F-16 fighter jocks based at Nellis AFB near Las Vegas now have more than mountains to contend with. If a rock pile doesn't get them, perhaps a laser will.

Airplane Scrapers

Here is a story that I can personally relate to because it directly concerns the airport behind my home. In March of 1992, a cellular telephone company received authorization from the FAA, Eastern Region, to construct a 500-foot tower close to the approach end of my hard-surface runway. How close, you may ask? Well, it was directly in line with my runway and one mile from the approach end. My airport was not the only airport involved. My neighbor also has an airport, and the tower sight was less than half a mile from his strip. There were three other airports involved, all under three miles from the proposed tower sight. My strip has been displayed on the Washington Sectional Chart (aerial navigation chart) for over 40 years, so it wasn't as though the "feds" could not find it. Yet their sight approval form, AA7460-1, (8-85), had this interesting statement: "C. Name of nearest airport, heliport, flight park, or seaplane base. Easton airport. Distance from structure to nearest point of nearest runway 20 nautical miles."

Most of the people who live near the proposed sight got a petition going, along with a town meeting, and it did the trick. Their tower was never constructed. It really makes you wonder.

Federal regulations require that anyone planning to construct a tower or building that is taller than 200 feet must notify the "feds" so that they can determine if it will present a hazard to flight. They are supposed to send a notification to the nearest airport requesting that their announcement be posted. This was not done. Even if the "feds" believe the proposed structure is a danger to aerial navigation, the building still can be erected, and then it might take years in the courts for a final disposition.

Not only is the height of a structure important but also the radio signals that it transmits can even be more of a danger to a low-flying aircraft.
There are numerous radio towers throughout the U.S. that transmit radio
signals that can adversely affect airborne electronic equipment.

For over a year, Swissair has been complaining about difficulties with an
Anchorage, Alaska, instrument approach caused by local FM radio broadcasting stations. At times, the autopilot received spurious signals from the
11 FM stations and promptly went to the off mode. These radio stations
also have interfered with important navigation equipment. Radio towers
are definitely a danger to any aircraft flying in low visibility. You would
think that if a pilot has a new flight chart, he would have little problem
trying to spot a tower. Some towers go as high as 2,000 feet above the
ground. Sure, they have flashing strobe lights, and they often are painted
orange and white, but you can't find it if it's not on the chart. You would
think that the FAA would prohibit the construction of a tower until it is
depicted on the latest charts. This is the safe way of doing business, but
not the FAA way. New charts go to the printers approximately every six
months. There is a 500-foot tower near my home that was erected over
three years ago, and it is still not shown on the latest sectional charts.

The following is taken from the AOPA Air Safety Foundation booklet
entitled "A Pilot's Guide to Avoiding Wire Strikes."

It's been a long flight, but the prospect of a hot shower and a comfortable
mattress allow tedium to fade into relaxed anticipation. Thirty miles from
the airport you begin a descent, and now, with the setting sun squarely
on the nose of your aircraft, you decide to make a detour over a lakefront
community close to your airport. Squinting through your sunglasses, you
realize the picture isn't quite right. On your letdown through the haze you
spot a pole about 50 feet inland. It stands about 100 feet tall; you are
descending just below its height. A bolt of terror sweeps through your body
like an electric current. Your hand is on the throttle, and just as you start
to apply backpressure, you feel a jolt. You slam forward into the shoulder harness and feel a sharp blow to your forehead. You hear the contents
of the baggage compartment glancing off the windscreen. The commo-
tion stops momentarily—rather, suddenly—and you have a sensation of

weightlessness. Again, the jolt against the seatbelt, this time accompanied by the excruciating noise of metal being crushed. That's all you remember until you awaken in the ambulance.

If this is an "average" year statistically, you have just been involved in one of 115 wire strike accidents nationwide. Hundreds more wire strikes will occur without being reported. During a 10-year period, 216 strikes were reported. During the same period, two large utility companies recorded 1,232 wire strikes. Between 1986 and 1990, more than 120 persons lost their lives in fixed-wing wire strikes with over 41 fatalities in rotary wing aircraft. Aeronautical charts do not depict lines constructed below 200 feet above ground level. Be careful out there.

New Airports are Needed Now

Massachusetts, Illinois, Texas, and Georgia are all looking for new ways to expand their existing facilities or look for an entirely new sight. Their airports are all at or near capacity whereas Colorado's new airport was finally opened in 1995 after nearly a year was spent perfecting their baggage conveyor.

Every time a 747 lands at JFK, it costs the airline about $2,000. A B737 might get by with as little as $200. The United Kingdom will charge a 747 $3,685 and can range from $2,686 in Madrid to as high as $5,620 in Frankfort. A B737 airliner would have to pay $866 to land in Madrid, approximately $1,480 at Charles de Gaulle and $2,566 at London's Heathrow. That will give you some idea why airline tickets are so high. And this is just one of the many costs of operating an airline.

Airports International shows the following lists of the 1994 top ten busiest airports in America and around the world.

	U.S.	Worldwide
1.	Chicago O'Hare	Chicago O'Hare
2.	Atlanta	Atlanta
3.	Dallas/Ft. Worth	Dallas/Fort Worth
4.	Los Angeles	London Heathrow

5.	San Francisco	Los Angeles
6.	Denver	Tokyo Haneda
7.	Miami	Frankfort
8.	Newark	Denver
9.	Las Vegas	Miami

The FAA reports that by the year 2001 U.S. airports will handle over 800 million passengers annually, with estimates greater than one billion per year by 2005.

During the past 30 years only three new U.S. airports have been built. Dulles International, Dallas/Ft. Worth and Denver. It might take as long as 10 years to plan and build a new airport, and the longer we wait the more it will cost. A new runway at Dallas cost $420 million, approximately $35 million more to build than the original JFK airport.

At a recent meeting in New York, the former FAA administrator David R. Hinson, made some positive statements concerning new airports. "The threat posed by inadequate airport capacity strikes to the heart of our system. Solving ATC problems only requires money, new technology and good management," but, "airports are different."

CHAPTER II

▼

A RIDE IN THE BOX

At the age of eight, I knew that flying was all I wanted to do. Nothing has changed. I was lucky enough to have been chosen for pilot training in the USAF. After winning my wings in 1950, I was sent to Germany to serve in the occupation forces. I got a lot of great flying in, but I could see the inevitable handwriting on the wall. The Air Force wanted officers first and pilots second, the reverse of how I felt. I could envision myself counting liquor bottles as a club officer, or perhaps being assigned to a supply depot where I would be allowed to fly for five hours a month. While there is no flying that can compare to military, especially fighters, any job that would keep me in the air was what I needed. While I was still in the service, I got all the flying ratings I could. I also queried numerous airlines concerning a pilot's position. In 1954, my last year of active duty, I received a favorable telegram from American Airlines. They said that they would be conducting a new-hire pilots class in a few months, and asked would I be interested?

At this time, I only had a few months left on my tour and a 30-day leave accrued. Not realizing the importance of the airline seniority system, I elected to take my leave in Germany. When I finally returned to the States, I donned my military uniform, and drove to the American Airlines executive office at LaGuardia Airport in New York. My appointment time with Chief Pilot McCabe was at hand, and I marched in, all but saluting. I thought I had it made but little did I know. We shook hands and the interview began. He studied my application and spoke: "I am impressed with your flying experience and I believe you are what we are looking for, but there is a problem here."

Until this time my thoughts were all positive. Now came the blockbuster.

"You are 32 years old, is that correct?"

"Yes sir," I said.

"Well I hate to tell you this, but you have missed our last pilot class of the year, and when we conduct our next class you will be over our age limit."

I was stunned. I had second thoughts about being separated from the military. Captain McCabe suggested that I try Eastern because their age limit was a little higher. I visited Eastern's executive offices at Rockefeller Center in the heart of Manhattan. I passed their physical and aptitude tests, and was sent to Miami to visit their main base. I felt confident because I was under their age limit and the scores on my tests were all good.

After waiting two hours at the chief pilots office, the moment of truth was finally at hand. I was ushered into Captain Kurns office and he told me to have a seat. Once again, the man behind the desk had my future in his hands. Surely there would not be a hitch this time.

"Brian," he said, "I like what I see here on your score sheets, but there is a problem."

My pulse quickened. What can it be this time? They had a minimum of 5'10." I believe they didn't want the passengers to think they were being flown by a midget.

"I see you are five feet nine inches. I don't know why they sent you down from New York. They should have caught it there." As the chief pilot stood up I could see that he certainly was not anywhere near the required height. The top of his head was level with my chin. I guess he got in when they were hiring midgets. Well, you can't fight it.

The flight home was smooth but I was in a turmoil. I began to think that leaving the service was probably the biggest mistake of my life. I queried nearly every airline in the states and a few overseas. It was the same sad story. Too old!

I did have a trade I could fall back on. I was an experienced mason. I went back to construction but every time a plane would pass overhead, I nearly fell off the scaffold, watching it and picturing myself in the cockpit. A terrible frustrating year went by and then a pilot friend of mine said that he heard Mohawk Airlines was hiring. The only Mohawk I had ever heard of was the rug company. However, I contacted them in Ithaca, New York, and was issued a pass on one of their DC-3s. Once again I found myself patiently waiting to be interviewed by their chief pilot, Captain Joseph Lewis. To say I was nervous would be putting it mildly. I wasn't getting any younger and this might be my last chance. Captain Lewis examined my logbook and licenses, and said, "Let's go out to a DC-3 and take a little ride."

Gone are the days when a new-hire pilot would get to show his skills in a real live aircraft. Today it's all done in the "idiot box" (simulator). But let's get back to my first airline check ride.

Perhaps the third time I wouldn't strike out; I would be accompanied by a furloughed Pan American pilot. I was in the co-pilot's seat first and Garry Falck from Pan Am would be second. I was a little rusty, but managed to call the proper dead engine and move the knobs and buttons appropriately. When Garry's turn came, he failed to recognize a dead engine and I guess that gave me the job.

I still had to pass the physical and an all-day stanine exam at Cornell University, but at least I was still in the running. The examination at Cornell was the usual "shrink's delight." The first part was to do with aviation; the rest was psychological. They wanted to know if I liked girls? What is a pongee? Who painted blue boy? And where are Harley Davidson Motorcycles manufactured? I must have checked the proper boxes. I got the job.

To show the validity of these stanine tests, the following excerpt should provide some thought on their continued use.

A pilot who took these tests with me got a top score of nine in all sections. This would ensure that the airline was getting an exceptional pilot, at least on paper. When this pilot checked out as Captain, he landed with the wheels up, he simply forgot to put them down. A short time later, on a different aircraft type, he took off in a thunderstorm, which slammed him back onto the runway. He managed to kill himself and numerous passengers, but he did have a perfect score on the stanine exam.

Another case in point; two brothers both flew for Mohawk Airlines. One was a captain, the other a new-hire first officer. The captain previously was fired by Eastern for incompetence but checked out as a Captain on Mohawk. His brother could not "hack the program" at Mohawk and was terminated. He became a Senior Captain on Eastern.

There are some Chief Pilots who are down on military flyers because they were rejected by the military. They have a grudge to bear toward hiring well-trained Air Force men and instead may hire a low time "putt putt" pilot.

Airline requirements have varied throughout the years, but it's the old story of supply and demand. When there are an abundance of qualified pilots, hiring becomes more stringent and vice versa. In 1954, two thousand hours was a bare minimum and pilot logbooks often are tailored to meet the demands of a perspective employer. Pilots record their flying time in their own personal logbooks. Many times, the book will be bulging with "bogus" time. This falsification usually shows up on the first simulator training session.

A person who has to pay for all his flying time would soon go broke. A single-engine plane today costs about $60 per hour and a multi-engine over twice that. The way to circumvent these high prices is to get a job instructing, to be a co-pilot on a non-schedule, or fly for an air taxi. When you build your time with a charter line, you may reach your goal, but there is a chance you may end up dead.

Unscrupulous operators push their pilots to the limit. They realize that the only reason that they can get pilots to do their dirty work is because the pilots desperately need the experience, and could not afford to pay for it themselves. That is to say, most pilots could not afford to pay for the training. Some have gone into hock by taking out large loans or mortgaging their homes. There are airlines out there that will sell you a seat in their cockpits for a price, somewhere around $10,000. This only goes to show you that once the flying bug has bitten you, it's very hard to work in some other field. Today, flying jobs are so scarce, and there are so many pilots out there, that there are now many companies who will give you a job in their cockpit if you are willing to pay "big bucks."

Check Pilots

Who trains the new hires, checks the line pilots, and upgrades first officers to captains? Check pilots are the ones entrusted to this very important position. There are some very fine check airmen, but unfortunately not enough.

Super being, fearless, unrivaled, arrogant, haughty, pompous and second to none, those are just a few of the words that describe some of the airline check pilots. The majority of these pilots come directly from the "line" (a pilot who flies and does nothing else). The airline runs them through a quick course in how to deal with people, how to instruct, and what discrepancies to look for in their students. If a particular pilot is known for flying by the book, and turning down airplanes that are marginal—maintenance-wise—and refuses to bend when it comes to fuel loads, this person must be taught a lesson. This is done during routine checks (check pilots observe on a scheduled flight) or during six-month checks (every six months a Captain has to show his flying skills). If one of these problem pilots is due for a check, the Director of Flight will instruct his Check Airmen to really "lay it on." He will see to it that old Captain so and so knows he has been put through the wringer. This is the company's best method of getting the attention of some of their nonconformists. I have seen pilots taxing out with so much snow on their wings they look like a moving snow bank. Well almost, I have held my ground on never flying with any form of ice, snow, or frost adhered to the plane. I also have been badgered by dispatch as to why I have remained at the gate while other flights were departing. My answer was usually the same: "If you want this flight to leave, you'd better get another Captain."

Years ago, I remember a problem I had with the prop reverse light coming on in flight. When I landed at Plattsburgh, New York, I told Bill

Dollar, the mechanic, my problem. A short time later he returned and said, "Captain, it's all set."

I replied, "How could you fix it so quickly?"

"Well, I just wired the reverse handles so they can't be used."

"What the hell is that? I am not using the reverse in flight, but I am getting a light."

"Well, I checked the manual and that's the fix." He said.

I said the trip was canceled until the real problem was found. I got the usual response from a Mohawk dispatcher. "Captain, we have done the fix just the way the book says."

I replied, "Since you have such faith in the book, send it over and let it fly the trip because I'm not."

Then they saw the light go on, and tore into the engine and found a dangerous situation.

After the United Airlines strike, there was an abundance of scabs (workers who cross picket lines) in the training department. You can imagine what havoc these people were causing. It's one of management's way of taming the mavericks.

I have spoken to pilots who have been yelled at by the instructors during a training session in the box. One pilot was really disturbed when his instructor bellowed, "And you call yourself an airline captain? I have never seen such stupidity!"

Other pilots have put a stop to such behavior by threatening the instructor with a knuckle sandwich. These cases are few and far between, but there is one salient point to be made. I believe Captain H. T. Nunn from Northwest Airlines hits the nail on the head: "He enters the simulator, whether he likes to admit it or not, whether the company likes to admit it or not, whether the FAA likes to admit it or not, with the feeling in the back of his head that somebody is trying to take his certificate away from him ... to remove his livelihood. I submit that can only lead to a basically negative training program."

I heartily agree with that statement. The ride in the box should be training to meet a standard, not one of 'do it right the first time,' or you could be required to take more training. Some airlines allow you to practice procedures and letdowns until you feel confident. Then when you say you are ready for the ride, the check begins. This is the way it should be instead of coming aboard the "box" cold and be expected to perform maneuvers that you have not done for the last six months.

Just to dispel a myth, the vice president of flight, the chief pilots, and the check pilots all do very little flying. In the airline business, it is experience in flying the line that is paramount, not the hours you have spent watching some poor fellow sweating in the simulator (a machine in a building that simulates a real airplane cockpit). It is not uncommon for a check pilot to have a small fraction of the experience of the man he is testing. These chair-born "jockeys" very seldom fly the line after they have tasted the good pay and relative safety of the simulator. Here there are no icy crosswind runways, no decisions to be made, and you can't get killed. The actual experience of line flying can never be equaled, so when you see that a certain airline is on strike and that they are operating a small percentage of their flights, beware. It's the desk jockeys that are out there slithering off icy runways in a real live airplane.

Many years ago, a check pilot for North East Airlines put one airliner in the bay, smashed another on the airport, and his third, and last, ended up crashing onto Rikers Island moments after takeoff. He ended up as a chief pilot where he did little flying of aircraft and a lot of deskwork.

At USAir, the captain responsible for all training on their newly acquired 727 airplanes was taxing away from the gate at Pittsburgh. Up front were a qualified co-pilot and a check pilot engineer. They managed to drive the wing tip of the 727 into the nose of another aircraft, causing thousands of dollars in damages.

Years ago when I flew for Mohawk, I was on approach at Albany, New York, in a Convair 440. Flight Attendant Carol Baker entered the cockpit and said, "Brian, we have a fire in the back." I thought it was probably a cigarette in the carpet. I had flown with Carol for many years so I felt free to tell her "Piss on it." She opened the cockpit door and the whole rear bulkhead was blazing. I sent my co-pilot, Thomas H. Block, back to extinguish the blaze. He tried to fire the extinguisher but failed to pull the pin. Carol Baker, had to show him how to remove the pin on the fire extinguisher. Tom Block was one of the worst co-pilots I have ever flown with. He was arrogant, self-assured, and always right. This co-pilot was later elevated to the ranks of check captain. Now he would be instructing other pilots at USAir.

The fire was caused by a mechanic who replaced the baggage compartment light bulb with one that was too powerful. The heat from the bulb set a mailbag on fire and eventually burned a hole in the roof of the plane about the size of a dinner plate. Incidentally, the flight crew was questioned about the fire by management. No thanks for a good job was ever received, but the mechanic who extinguished the fire after landing was rewarded with an all expenses paid trip for his family to Los Angeles for three days. Mohawk Airlines really hated flight crews. At the time, most of the pilots disliked Bob Peach, the President, but he was really a "pussy cat" compared to the then top officials at Continental Airlines, Frank Lorenzo, or People Express President, Donald Burr.

On March 27, 1977, at Los Rodeos Airport in Tenerife, Canary Islands, two 747 aircraft collided on the runway. So far, this is the worst accident in aviation history. Why were the lives of 583 people snuffed out? The major cause of the accident was the Captain of the KLM Airliner. He was not a line pilot. In fact, he was the head of the flight-training department at KLM. He averaged only twenty-one hours a month as commander of a 747 aircraft. He had not flown the line for twelve weeks prior to the accident. What did he do wrong? He elected to take off in a fog without clearance from the tower and crashed head on into a PAA 747. The following quote from the Air Line Pilots Association, says it all: "Pilots involved in training often lose proficiency in the real world situations: and the instructor does not always get as much line flying as desired and is not exposed to the everyday flexible decision making process that is so much a part of line flying."

Approximately forty years ago, the flight simulator was first used in the industry. Since that time, major improvements have taken place concerning the various modes of flight simulation. Prior to the widespread use of simulated flight in a ground-based electronic marvel, pilots took their training in the air in the actual aircraft. Here is a story about one training flight.

Every pilot has a burning desire to upgrade into bigger, faster, and more productive equipment. Many wait years for their chance because of the democratic seniority system.

Captain James W. Morton, forty-eight, was originally hired by Chicago and Southern Airlines (C&S merged with Delta in March, 1959). In July 1959, after eight years as a co-pilot, he finally got his chance to upgrade on a four-engine jet. Jim was a highly skilled pilot with over 16,000 hours in the air. His license proudly displayed the fact that he was captain-qualified in the DC-3, DC-6, DC-7, CV-240/340/440, and the DC-9. His latest proficiency check was conducted in the DC-9 in September 1966.

The DC-8 was the next plane he had to master. Jim already had completed successfully all phases of ground school and simulator training, and was presently undergoing his final grooming at New Orleans, Louisiana, before he would take his FAA rating ride. Captain Morton was an exceptionally apt student, but because of the voluminous amount of knowledge that must be absorbed during flight and briefing periods, he decided to take a room at a motel near the airport where he could devote all his time to this latest challenge.

With fourteen hours of intensive flight training under his belt, he felt he was ready to tackle the FAA oral exam. On March 28, after attending eight hours of final ground school briefing, he took the equipment exam. He was asked a multitude of questions, most of which had little bearing on actual day-to-day operation of the DC-8. He had memorized what he thought would be on the quiz because to understand the intricacies of complicated circuitous diagrams completely would be possible only for a skilled aeronautical engineer. Jim was asked: What is the total weight of the aircraft? How high is the tail? How long are the wings? What is the tire pressure? (Mechanics take care of this item.) How many vortex generators on each wing? (This is of little concern to a pilot since the only check he has to make is to be sure that none are broken.) What is the RPM of the APU? (There is no RPM indicator in the cockpit.) At what temperature do the various over-temperature lights come on? (The fact that they light up is sufficient. It tells you that it is time to do something.) On and on, the irrelevant questions continued. But Jim had all the answers. To fail this exam would mean a trip back to ground school and the possible termination of flight training until a later date.

After eight hours of ground school, and a few more absorbed in FAA trivia, Jim was ready for a good night's sleep. He was not to get it. After going to his room and studying until about 9 P.M., he turned in, his brain a mass of temperatures, pressures, and procedures. After a two-hour nap the alarm rang. It was time for flight training which would begin at 11 P.M. Almost all of Captain Morton's flight training was conducted at night because that was when a spare aircraft was available.

After a two-hour flight, he returned to his motel, dog tired, and slept for five hours. He attended another full day of ground school, and at 6 P.M., went to his room for a rest. He was beginning to wonder if he would ever get a full night's sleep. At 11 P.M. he was once again preparing to strap the DC-8 to his backside and continue flight training.

On March 29, Jim reported to the field for his fifth training hop with Captain Maurice Watson, the company check pilot.

"Hi, Maurie," Jim said, "How's everything going?"

"Well, I had a pretty good day today. Played golf most of the morning. Shot an eighty-five."

"Say, you're really getting down there. Well, my day consisted of another filled with mock-up, pressures, and temperatures."

"You're a glutton for punishment, Jim. We'll take it easy tonight. Just a few emergency procedures and then we'll spend the rest of the training period shooting ILSs. The FAA will be with us tonight."

The preflight check was completed and a clearance to runway one was received and acknowledged. This runway has no ILS for the direction in use and is marginal in length, only 7,000 feet.

The first simulated engine failure occurred at V1. As the plane was now committed for takeoff, Jim kept it headed down the runway and waited for the next call from the check pilot. "Rotate," said the instructor. Captain Morton skillfully applied backpressure to the stick and 180,000 pounds of dead weight reached for the evening sky. One minute later, check pilot Watson chopped a second engine. The craft had now lost the numbers one and two engines that meant it would have to be nursed along with only fifty percent of its total power. The altitude was 1,200 feet and the air speed 200 knots. At a critical time such as this, any airspeed lost can be recovered only by pushing the nose down. This would sacrifice precious altitude that could not be regained.

Jim called for the appropriate emergency checklist and the engineer started to clean up the two dead engines (perform the necessary check items). The check pilot signified to Jim that he had just lost his rudder boost. This was simulated by pressing the warning light. One more emergency to contend with. As the flight turned left, the altitude was down to 900 feet. Jim called "Flaps 25." As the flaps were sliding down their tracts, a feeling of being thrust forward in the seat signified that they were indeed doing their job.

The check pilot began to prompt his student, "Don't get below 160 … Ball in the middle whatever it takes to put her in there now …" On most airplanes the needle and ball instrument is nearly hidden behind the yoke. So far everything was going as advertised. The landing checklist was called for and the check pilot elected to dump full flaps. Shortly thereafter, the air speed bled off to 165 knots. They were now 2.5 miles away from the runway, and without the benefit of any glide slope—either visual or electronic—it would be a game of chance to judge the proper approach profile.

Check pilot Watson finished the last item on the checklist and stated, "Before landing complete. 129 knots is approach, 24 is threshold … Okay, looks good. How "bout that now, we've straightened out."

The lights of the runway were now only a mile away and closing rapidly.

"Call my air speed for me," Jim said with authority.

"140," the instructor replied.

From this point, the need for immediate corrective action became apparent. The air speed was dwindling to an unsafe condition. At 136 knots and half a mile from the strip, the need for more thrust was readily recognized. Power was applied to numbers three and four and the plane made an immediate turn to the left coincident with a drop in airspeed and altitude.

"135 is your airspeed," shouted the check pilot. "See you're getting her ... put the rudder in there ... you're getting your speed down now ... you're now going to be able to get it."

The ground was now only seconds away.

"I can't hold it, Bud," exclaimed Jim.

Captain Watson shouted, "NAW, DON'T. LET IT UP ... LET IT UP ... LET IT UP!"

The cockpit voice recorder ended at 12:50 p.m. One of man's most significant achievements fell to earth, instantly killing the five men in the cockpit. As it knifed through two forty-foot trees it continued its destructive journey, clipping a corner off a house. It lost some of its deadly momentum as it plowed through another house. A third dwelling was demolished, and as the fiery missile's speed diminished, it skidded over a railroad embankment and came to rest against the Hilton Inn Motel. Here the remainder of the hulk was demolished by explosion. In its 700-foot wake, thirteen people lay dead.

This training catastrophe is only one of a long line of needless deaths. The following list compiled by the Flight Safety Foundation deals exclusively with engine-out maneuvers. If a worldwide list were included, it would fill many more pages.

2/25/59 B-707	Pilot failed to maintain flying speed during two-engine minimum-control speed.
1/26/61 B-707	Due to loss of control A/C dove into the ocean.
9/13/65 CV-880	Loss of control during simulated engine-out takeoff.
9/26/66 B-720	During a simulated engine flameout, student misjudged distance and undershot runway.
2/20/67 DC-8	Aircraft crashed during simulated engine-out.
3/30/67 DC-8	During two engine-out landings, aircraft crashed.
12/30/68 DC-8	Loss of control during simulated engine-out.
7/26/69 B-707	Aircraft went below minimum control speed during a two engine-out maneuver.
6/24/69 CV-880	During critical engine chop on takeoff, aircraft was destroyed.
3/31/71 B707-720	Aircraft crashed during three-engine abort.

Flight Simulators

Statistics prove conclusively that of all the fatal flight training accidents occurring in this country, over 70 percent are caused by engine-out maneuvers, 17 percent in simulated hydraulic emergencies, and the remaining 13 percent under flight control conditions. All the major carriers utilize the simulator that has greatly reduced the numerous training accidents but the smaller carriers still train in the air because simulators cost many millions of dollars.

There are three types of simulators:

—Phase I allows proficiency checks and night landings.

—Phase II allows transition from one aircraft to another similar one, and upgrade from first officer to captain on the same type.

—Phase III is the most sophisticated of all the boxes. You can do just about any training in this model. Pilots can transition from engineer to captain.

The simulator is an exact replica of the aircraft cockpit. If you were to slice off the front section of a 747 at the cockpit door, mount it on various hydraulic jacks, and place a large screen in front of the aircraft, you would have a fair idea of the size of the simulator. Its functions are similar to what you would encounter in a real aircraft cockpit. The simulator can be made to simulate rough air, the bumps in the runway expansion strips can be felt as you taxi, engine noise is similar (but not as loud), various airports can be displayed, different cloud formations are available, and wind can be simulated from any direction. When you touch down, you hear the wheels squeak. You actually pass other aircraft on the ground and in the air as the aircraft approaches the terminal. Details such as airline signs and the parking man are there waving you in; even his footprints in the snow can be seen. They have a radar set that will display storms. At times, it is hard to believe that you are not in a real aircraft.

These machines do have drawbacks. The feel of the actual aircraft controls is not there and switches that activate various systems take longer to function in the simulator. I can remember the BAC 111 box at USAir.

When you approached the ground for a landing, you wouldn't dare round out as you would in a real plane because if you did the simulator would start to climb. It was much more sensitive than a live aircraft so it just doesn't feel the same.

In spite of these faults, captains are being checked out completely in the box. The next time you see your captain coming aboard the aircraft, there is a chance that this will be his first time to set foot in the real thing. The simulator is an exact replica of the aircraft that it represents but it is only the size of the cockpit. It lacks wings, tail, and fuselage. To taxi a real aircraft with immense wings that barely can be seen from the cockpit is quite another story.

Northwest Orient Airlines petitioned the FAA for a one-year test and evaluation of a new training concept. Up until now, the airlines were teaching how to manipulate the controls but not how to command the aircraft. There is still a lot more to this concept but at least it is a start. Northwest wanted to test a total crew concept called Line-Oriented Flight Training (LOFT): A flight scenario of a typical flight is fed into the computer. A full crew is aboard the simulator, and will take off from Washington and land in New York. Prior to the exercise, the crew is briefed on the weather. The flight plan, weights, and fuel are all checked, similar to the real world. During this exercise, the crew is handled by ATC, who, in reality, is the simulator instructor. It is difficult for a check airman to witness mistakes building, but in order to be authentic, he must not show himself or offer suggestions until the training session is complete. A thorough debriefing is a must because this is where problems are threshed out. Some airlines videotape the flight, then play it back after the session.

Prior to the LOFT experience, twice a year, pilots would have to shoot (execute) approaches of all kinds at various airports on their system. There are various types of instrument approaches into airports. ILS is the best because you have vertical guidance and azimuth. It's also known as a precision approach. There is a back course approach that usually only emits azimuth signals and no glide path. This is second best and it's known as a non-precision approach. Next in descending order are VOR, NDB, and the most rudimentary approach, circling, which is a maneuver using visual reference to the ground. Most all of the large carriers do not allow their pilots to make a circling approach in bad weather.

Preferably, aircraft still are landed into the wind but at some airports there is only one instrument runway. If the wind is blowing in the same direction as the approach, and it is of sufficient velocity, you will have to circle to land. This is accomplished by descending on the regular instrument approach until reaching a specified altitude, usually 500 feet above the ground. Here, you must have the field visually when you turn to enter a downwind leg. FAA is most specific about keeping the field in sight. If, for any reason, you lose contact with the runway, you must pull up and execute a missed approach. It is easy to fly in and out of low clouds while executing this "Mickey Mouse" letdown. In mountainous terrain, you could be in deep trouble. Most airlines do not shoot circling approaches.

The FAA Principal Operating Inspector (POI) is the boss of the FAA for each airline. He is assigned to their main base and it is he who must be "buttered up" before any regulations are changed. There is a master set of Part 121 regulations, but individual POIs can do as they will for their particular airline. For example, United Airlines has a deal with their POI whereby their captains only have one simulator check a year. The other check is an open book written exam. I think this is far better than the usual ride in the "box" every six months. Since the advent of these realistic simulators, vast amounts of money have been saved. The weather, in the old days, was a controlling factor in giving a check ride in the aircraft. This could cost the company a bundle for hotel rooms and meals for crew awaiting good weather for a real plane check. There is no longer any need to pull a plane from the normal passenger schedule and there is no fuel involved in a simulator ride. It is estimated that over 200 million gallons of fuel are saved each year.

Many airlines are reaping good profits by selling time on their simulators to other carriers. A real live 727 aircraft costs about $3,000 per hour for a training flight compared with a few hundred dollars an hour in the simulator. United, American, and USAir all sell simulator time at a huge profit. The box at USAir never stops, it's used 24 hours a day, seven days a week.

A Pilot's Life

The training of an airline captain usually takes three times longer than it does for a doctor to finally hang out his shingle. When a pilot signs on with an airline, he or she is married to the company forever. If a doctor dislikes the way his hospital is doing business, he can move on to another one. Sure, pilots can change airlines, but if a captain decides to leave his company, he will immediately revert back to a low-echelon co-pilot or flight engineer. Your airline seniority is lost as soon as you change companies. Once a doctor gets his degree, he is seldom required to take any further tests. A pilot's actions are constantly under scrutiny from the government, fellow pilots, and the airline's training department. When a pilot errs, he is in big trouble. All control movement and conversation are recorded compared to a doctor who botches an operation and gets off scot-free.

If the airline has aircraft requiring three crewmembers, the normal time for a pilot to check out as captain could be as long as twenty years. He can expect to be an engineer for at least five years, then into the right seat (co-pilot) for another fourteen years. Pilots who sign on with a carrier that has only two pilots up front could have considerably less waiting time.

During this waiting period, the pilots' pay is steadily climbing. A co-pilot on a large scheduled carrier will start out at about $36,000 a year. If he makes it through all the checks, he should be looking at the captain's chair in ten years at a salary of $200,000 a year. As I said before, it's not the easiest job in the world with regards to checks. A pilot puts his job on the line at least six times a year. He must pass two proficiency checks a year (proficiency training and proficiency check), in addition to a route check yearly. He also must pass two FAA and one company physical every year of his career. An FAA inspector or a company check airman can board your flight and scrutinize you at any time. The FAA people are extremely jealous of the crews they check. Our salary is easily three times more than theirs and airline captains have a profession admired by many as compared to those of the FAA people who are usually not that popular. There is an unwritten law that most of the airlines subscribe to that consists of not training a captain on a new airplane if he only has a few years before reaching the mandatory retirement age of 60. This is purely for economics.

It costs many thousands to transition to new equipment and the airline is only too glad to pay the pilot for the new equipment while he continues to fly his present aircraft.

I am sure that it is just a coincidence, but USAir was paying a captain who was one number senior to me for the more productive equipment. When they got my number, they decided that I would have to fly the 727 or not be paid for it. When the company wants to waste money just to show who is boss, that's their business. The answer is don't write books exposing their secrets and don't make waves while flying the line.

After appearing on many TV shows concerning air safety, and especially air traffic control, I was held out of service for a number of months. I won my case with full back pay but Mr. Ron Sessa who was the VP of flight at USAir, decided to withhold my salary for months, just to prove in a juvenile fashion who was boss.

When airline management has it in for a pilot, they really know how to play dirty. The USAir pilot group can be thankful that Mr. Sessa is now retired, and a likable, understanding captain has taken over the reins.

The whole airline pilot system is based on seniority. The all-important date of hire can make or break your flying career. It completely controls the equipment you fly, where you are based, what trips you can bid on, and vacation preference.

At times of furlough, if your number is high enough, you can maintain your position while the junior man may be put out to pasture.

Airline pilots are continually shifting from the right to the left seat. If the company expands a route out of your base, you may check out as captain. Then when the time is shifted to another base and you don't want to chase it, you will find yourself back in the co-pilot's seat again. On USAirways, it is not uncommon to have two captains up front. There is only one in charge but there may be two up there.

At age 60, all 121 carrier pilots must retire. It sort of gets to you: the day before your 60th birthday, you're qualified; the next day you're a bum. Pilots must retire at 60. Flight engineers can fly past age 60. Some captains retire at 60, then start riding sidesaddle (flight engineer) until who knows when. It certainly seems unconstitutional to demand retirement at 60 when you aren't allowed to collect Social Security until reaching age 62.

The airline privileges are great: paid hospital plans, nearly free insurance, free rides on your airline and other carriers for you and your family, and hefty retirement consisting of a lump sum between $1 and $2 million.

It's interesting to note some of the distances pilots and flight attendants have to travel to report for work. There are numerous pilots who live in Florida but are based in Washington, D.C. There are many who commute from coast to coast. I had a flight attendant who lived in Germany but was based in the District of Columbia.

Let's examine the Federal Air Regulations (FAR) to which pilots must adhere. The maximum hours of flying time are as follows:

—1,000 hours in any calendar year,

—100 hours in any calendar month.

—ALPA only allows a maximum of 85 hours a month, 30 hours in any seven consecutive days, and on-duty/time of 14 hours (FAA says 16 is legal). We can all thank God for airline unions.

Before you can start thinking, as most people do, about 85 hours a month, I must emphasize that in order to reach this plateau it is usually required that a pilot be on duty for over 200 hours. That is more working time per month than is required of any average person. "No domestic air carrier may schedule a flight crewmember for duty aloft for more than eight hours during any twenty-four consecutive hours." Now that doesn't sound bad on the surface, but when you take into consideration some variables, the whole complexion changes. The key word in the above regulation is SCHEDULE. No pilot can be scheduled over eight hours, but when the crew experiences holding delays, circuit routing caused by circumventing questionable weather, mechanical problems in flight, and the necessity to reduce thrust for extended turbulent penetration, that eight hours scheduled can easily be extended to ten. Would you like to be sitting behind a crew who has been confined to the cockpit for ten hours? It's perfectly legal.

A domestic pilot usually performs over 75 landings each month, whereas a long-haul pilot may only land ten times in thirty days. While it is true that the landings and takeoffs require the lion's share of concentration, the overseas pilot must live with boredom and fatigue. The FAA believes that the long-haul job is so easy they allow their crews to be SCHEDULED for twelve hours. Now how do you feel about being propelled through space by a crew that may have been locked in their cage for thirteen or fourteen hours? Probably not much. The jet lag, experienced by some of the long-haul crews, can and has made some trips risky.

There are a few airlines that reward a crew for beating the scheduled time. This makes speedsters out of a person who wouldn't normally consider such an operation. I am sure you have ridden behind a "cowboy" who cuts the other airline off at the pass, sinks his spurs on the brakes after landing in order to make the first taxi way, and slams on the reverse thrust as though he were reining in a wild bronco. Airlines that foster this "go fast" pay, are in, reality causing rapid deterioration of their valuable equipment. Brakes and tires cost money, not to mention passenger comfort.

In the year 2000, "airline pilot bashing" by the media became a stark reality. Headlines proclaimed "American Airlines pilots stage a sick out." "United's pilots refuse to fly overtime." There is one thing I think the public ought to know. Each month, pilots bid a "line of time" that states the trips he or she will fly for the month. It is the pilot's responsibility to fly the trips bid, but that is where it ends. He or she is not required to fly other flights, only the ones that are in his or her block. Overtime complaints are something used by airline management and the media. There is no requirement to exceed the flight time the pilot has bid. Under certain circumstances, pilots will elect to fly extra trips, but they are not required to do so by their union.

Let's get down to the nitty-gritty. Management has always expected crews to fly extra trips. This way, they can reduce expensive training costs to check out new crewmembers. This is the crux of the dilemma. Airline management fails to anticipate the fact that they may have added new aircraft to their fleet, increased the frequency of flights, and inaugurated new routes, all with little thought as to who is going to fly these planes.

The pilots at United warned their company over a year before of the pilot shortage and United's management did nothing. I am sure in the back of their minds they believed that their crews would fly overtime.

A new pilot contract with ALPA was months overdue and the pilots were worried about a merger with USAirways. There is no reason why a pilot group should keep working without a current contract.

There are many desk jockeys in the airlines who would love to be airline captains. I say to them, do what airline pilots do. Fly for the military or pay a great sum of money to learn to fly at a flight school. Pilots have a great life and the ground pounders are often jealous. When management makes a mistake by not hiring enough pilots, they shouldn't say, "Our pilots refuse to fly overtime."

Many times, pilots fly for years past their contract expiration date to keep management happy. How do the desk jockeys repay their pilots for flying without a current contract? They fail to negotiate a new contract and don't want to hear any mention of higher pay, better retirement, better working conditions, or the like. Is it any wonder that pilots are fed up with their treatment and threaten to strike? The longer a carrier can postpone a new contract, the more money they can put into their coffers, and the pilots will take years to recover what they have missed by not striking earlier. Long live ALPA.

Resource Management

Some airlines are offering courses on Resource Management Training. This course teaches the captain how best to utilize his crew. They are all skilled people or they wouldn't be there. It is true that the captain is the supreme commander of the flight. By federal law, he is responsible for the aircraft, the passengers, the crew, fuel loads, and decisions concerning the operation of the aircraft. He has the first and last word, but he shouldn't allow this power to compromise safety. The captain's decision is final, in more ways than one.

On June 7, 1971, 39-year-old Captain David Eastridge was in command of an Allegheny jet prop Convair. Tweeds New Haven Airport in

Connecticut was fog-bound with visibility of just over one mile. Captain Eastridge's adrenaline must have been boiling because of the problem he had on the last three approaches at Groton, Connecticut. He descended to approximately 175 feet on the first two tries, and on the third attempt, went down to 125 feet. The descent limit at Groton Connecticut Airport was 610 feet. Now it was time to try his luck again. Here is some of the cockpit conversation with his first officer, 34-year-old James Alfred Walker. The minimum descent altitude on this approach was 380 feet.

First Officer: "You got a hundred and five, sinking five."

Captain: "All right." "Keep a real sharp eye out there."

First Officer: "Okay." "Oh, this is low."

Captain: "I can see the water, I got straight down."

First Officer: "Man we ain't 20 feet off the water. Hold it."

A few seconds later the aircraft struck some brick houses and burst into flame. Thirty people died, including the captain. First Officer Walker suffered severe burns and amputation of both legs.

On December 18, 1977, a United Airlines DC-8 was experiencing electrical problems in the vicinity of Salt Lake City. The weather was overcast and the flight was encountering intermittent snow showers as it circled over mountainous terrain. Forty-nine-year-old, Captain John R. Fender, along with his two crewmembers, were trying to rectify a radio and landing gear problem caused by an inoperative generator. Captain Fender apparently had devised his own holding pattern plan that he failed to share with the rest of his crew.

First Officer: "Are you planning to make a procedure turn?"

Captain: "No, I … I wasn't going to."

This left the rest of the crew in a quandary as the Captain kept his plan to himself. The First Officer queried the Captain about the terrain and the Captain replied, "Mountains everywhere."

The co-pilot checked his charts and suggested to the Captain, "We should be a little higher, shouldn't we?"

Moments later the sky lit up over Kaysville as the DC-8 slammed into a 7,000-foot mountain. All on board perished. The Captain was warned by his co-pilot moments before the crash.

On December 28, 1978, a United DC-8 was having a problem with it's landing gear. The crew circled the Portland Airport for nearly one hour. By this time, their fuel was seriously low. At 1750:34, the flight engineer spoke to the captain concerning their low fuel state: "Fifteen minutes is gonna ... really run us low on fuel here." This warning came 23.04 minutes before the flame out. At 1802:22 the engineer announced, "We got about three on the fuel and that's it." This warning came about five minutes before the first engine died. The flight crashed six miles short of the runway. Ten people died and many more were injured. Once again, the captain was warned by a crewmember twice before the accident happened.

On January 13, 1982, the granddaddy of a "tragedy of errors" was unfolding at Washington's National Airport. An inexperienced crew was being guided by an overzealous supervisory controller. A violent snowstorm was blanketing National airport and in fact it was so bad, they had to close the airport for snow removal.

Thirty-four-year-old Captain Michael Wheaton was in the left seat of the Boeing 737. The right seat was occupied by 31-year-old First Officer Allen Pettit. The aircraft was deiced before the final flight but it was not done properly. The FAR (Federal air regulations) states that aircraft will not be flown with any ice, snow, or frost adhering to its vital parts. The Air Florida plane had ice on its wings as it taxied onto the active runway. The crew also had failed to activate the engine anti-icing switches. This caused the engine recordings to be erroneous. During the takeoff roll, the co-pilot stated, "God, look at that thing (referring to a faulty reading on the engines). That doesn't seem right, does it?"

Three seconds later,

Co-pilot: "Ah, that's not right."

Captain: "Yes it is, there's eighty."

Co-pilot: "No, I don't think that's right."

By now, the end of the critically short runway was in sight and the aircraft was hauled into the air.

Co-pilot: "Larry, we're going down, Larry."

Captain: "I know it."

Barely a half-mile past the runway's end, Air Florida's Flight 90 crashed into the frozen Potomac River, instantly killing 78 people.

On August 10, 1994, a Korean Airlines A-300 airliner was on an instrument approach at the rain-slick Cheju Island Airport. The Korean co-pilot asked Canadian Captain Woods several times, "Go around, go around." He was concerned the aircraft lacked enough runway for a safe landing. Woods answered, "No, no" and repeatedly told Chung to "Get off" in reference to him trying to adjust the thrust levers.

The aircraft tore through a runway perimeter fence and came to rest in a rice field. The six cabin crewmembers succeeded in evacuating all 152 passengers. The Captain and First Officer exited through their cockpit windows but the aircraft was a total loss.

Why did all these needless accidents happen? In all of the cases mentioned, the captain was the culprit. Simulators are unable to produce snow on aircraft wings. In spite of all the sophisticated electronic marvels that man has produced, it's still up to the captain to decide what should be done. What happens in the "box" is not the real world, though. There are entirely too many grizzled captains causing havoc on the flight deck and not enough crewmembers who question a captain when he is "off base." Many of them would rather die than face the potential of loosing their job by infuriating their boss. The aircraft commander should tap all the resources at hand and make good use of his crewmembers. Think of the lives that could have been saved in just the slim smattering of examples cited so far. If crewmembers would question the Captain when they believe he may be in error and follow it up with some positive actions, things would be a lot safer. I certainly don't condone taking the controls away, but a direct threat of this, perhaps, would shake some sense into the old boy in the captain's seat.

Most crewmembers are well trained and know their duties. It's a much safer operation when all members of the crew can contribute to flight safety without being ignored by the superman in the left seat.

Today's jets are nearly completely automated. The flight guidance system (FGS) can be programmed to do practically all the work of the captain. The course, altitude, speed, and destination runway can all be brought up on the cockpit computer. The pilots of the Boeing 767 must taxi manually from the gate, line up on the runway, put the power to it, and take off. At 1000 feet, the autopilot can be engaged and the aircraft will climb to the proper cruising altitude. At level off, the throttles will automatically return to cruise and the crew has little to do until after the aircraft lands on its assigned runway. Airliners today automatically capture the glide path and the throttles will continually adjust to maintain the desired speed. Only thrust reverse, wheels, and flaps must be manually controlled. The aircraft will sense when it nears the runway and the throttles will automatically adjust. In fact, the state of the art is so good that during really bad weather, the only way the crew knows they're on the runway is when they feel the bump and the tires squeal. Now the captain releases the automatic pilot and taxis to the gate.

Flying has gotten so automated that it is quite easy to get rusty. New captains receive intense ground school concerning all the aircraft systems, but when it comes to the actual flying of the aircraft, he or she takes a back seat to pushing those buttons on the computer. They are told that the auto-pilot can fly the plane better than a human pilot can and that they should utilize it as much as possible. When it comes time to enter a holding pattern, the FGS is programmed and the aircraft will hit the fix, throttles will retard, and it will enter the holding pattern at the proper altitude and speed. This is great. The computer does all the thinking for you, but what happens when the computer and the backup systems fail?

Let's stop here for a moment and examine the ramifications of what happened to a crew who believed that the computer knew best.

It was a moonless night in December 1995, as American Airlines Flight 965, a Boeing 757, was descending in mountainous terrain for a landing at Cali airport in Columbia. The airline was being flown by the onboard computer that inputs to the autopilot. Captain Nick Tafuri was in command and his first officer, Ron Williams, was flying the aircraft. Captain Tafuri was an experienced pilot and had flown this route many times. Williams' experience on this route was limited. The crew was requested by ATC to report when it passed the Tulua non-directional radar beacon. We have already learned that these aids are not to be trusted.

It was now just five minutes before 159 people would meet their death by slamming into a mountain a scant 300 feet below its peak. There was confusion in the cockpit as Captain Tafuri, his head down, began typing new information into the computer. His new commands had suddenly cleared a map of their route from the screen.

First Officer Williams asks his captain, "Where are we headed?"

This is certainly not the time to be punching new commands into an electronic marvel. Instead, it was time to punch two all-important buttons: the autopilot on the yoke and on the side of the throttle handle. This operation takes a maximum of three seconds. Then the crew would be able to control the aircraft as it was originally designed for: manual control.

Here is the rundown of necessary buttons to push in order to feed the computer.

Press 1. Quiet intercept

Press 2. Identifier of radio fix. A variety of various fixes will be shown. You must select the proper one. This was not done. The Captain selected the wrong one.

Press 3. Verify new route with the crewmember to see if they concur.

Press 4. Press execute button and the dashes change to a solid purple line.

The only problem was it took over 90 seconds to push these buttons whereas it would take only three seconds to fly it manually.

The aircraft was now thirteen seconds from disaster and the Ground Proximity Warning system was screeching, "Terrain, terrain: Whoop, Whoop"

Captain Tafuri excitedly says, "Pull up baby!"

Again, "Whoop, Whoop, Pull Up"

Williams: "It's OK."

Tafuri: "OK. Easy does it."

Sound of autopilot disconnecting.

Williams: "Nope!"

Tafuri: "Up, baby!"

Stick shaker starts its rattle (warning of potential stall). The speed boards were never retracted (devices on top of the wings to spoil lift). The crew realized they were in big trouble now, but far too late. A final warning from the GPWS and the aircraft's crew were history.

The captain had set up the wrong fix and the aircraft did exactly as it was told to do. The only problem was that there was a mountain between the aircraft and that incorrect destination fix.

The crash in 1998, of a Swissair MD-11 near Nova Scotia, Canada, shows that crews were not coordinated in the cockpit. Two hundred twenty-nine people died as the aircraft dove into the ocean. A fire broke out in the aircraft and a rapid descent and landing became imminent. The First Officer was flying the plane and he asked the captain whether he wanted to descend over the water and dump some fuel. The captain was busy running through the checklist. He told his First Officer he didn't want to be interrupted and that he should do whatever was appropriate.

Any captain worth his salt would have taken command of his machine, headed for shore, and landed, overweight or not. When you are on fire, the only place to be is on the ground, ASAP.

Airlines today teach the crews to use the computer and trust it. Well, in the heat of battle, it only takes one bad input to ruin your day and life.

Here is what a few experts think about automated flight.

Earl Wiener of the University of Miami has to say: "He has warned for years that excessive reliance on cockpit automation dulls the reactions and thought processes of pilots."

David D. Woods of Ohio State University says "Cockpit automation creates new demands on the pilot that can create opportunities for new kinds of human error and new paths to system breakdown that did not exist in simpler systems."

This crash is only one concerning automated flight. There were several Airbus aircraft that crashed while the crew was bumbling around computer inputs. Airlines are now instructing their crews to disconnect the autopilot whenever there are discrepancies in its operation.

The president of American Airlines Union, Jim Sovich, said that the "feds" made the following statement concerning training: "The FAA said it was more important that they could type on a computer rather than fly an airplane."

Because aircraft has gotten so sophisticated over the years, the third man in the cockpit has been eliminated. I don't care what size the new airliners are. There will only be a crew of two. Why do you suppose airliners are built to be flown by two pilots? The answer is money. To save money on safety is very foolish. Many emergencies have been handled successfully and accidents averted by the third man, the engineer. He monitors all systems of the aircraft allowing the pilots to concentrate on flying.

Pressure + Fatigue = Disaster

It's nearly midnight and you are completely exhausted. You have flown almost eight hours in some of the worst frontal weather imaginable from Chicago to Salt Lake City to Dallas. Your next leg will be on a storm-doted course to Little Rock, Arkansas.

Captain Richard Buschman was in command of American Airlines MD-82 trip #1420. Buschman, age 47, was married and the father of two. He graduated from the Air Force Academy and entered the Air Fiore pilot training at Laughlin Air Force Base. I can tell you this. Graduating from the Air Force Academy is a great feat in itself. Many are called but few are chosen. Buschman was a good Air Force pilot and an experienced American check pilot with 5,500 flight hours in the MD-82. He had served American Airlines for over 20 years.

I have very little history concerning First Officer Michael Origel. He was hired a few months before the accident and had a scant 200 hours in the MD-82, but he would play a leading roll in trying to prevent a tragedy.

The crew had spent most of the past seven and a half hours in the cramped cockpit of the MD-82. They had eaten on the run and the food wasn't very good. After dodging storms most of the day, along with crew and equipment changes, they were eager to get on the ground and get a decent night's sleep. It should be understood that the captain is completely in charge; the first officer simply carries out his orders. That's the way it usually is, but on this trip, you can catch numerous glimpses of roll reversals.

The crew was told by ATC that there were level 6 (the highest rating for a storm) thunderstorms approaching Little Rock with associated high winds, hail, lightning, and intense rain. None of this is what a crew wants to hear after being on duty for 13 and a half hours, only 30 minutes shy of the maximum allowed by the Airline Pilot's Union (the FAA allows crews to be on duty for 16 hours).

Let's look back in on the cockpit 16 minutes before their landing at Little Rock.

Little Rock Approach control radios the crew: "American fourteen twenty, Little Rock approach, roger. Ah, we have a thunderstorm just northwest of the airport moving, ah, through the area now. Wind is two eight zero at two eight, gusts four four and, ah, I'll have new weather for you in just a moment I'm sure."

First officer Origel: "Yeah, we can see lightning."

Section 12 of American Airlines Flight Manual has this to say about thunderstorms and airports: "Do not enter or depart terminal area when such areas are blanketed by thunderstorms except when known thunderstorms are clear of turbulence.

Little Rock Approach: "Right now, the wind is 290 degrees at 28, guests to 44."

The captain was worried about the direction and velocity of the crosswind as he spoke to his first officer: "Thirty knots is the crosswind limits but is thirty knots the wet [limit]?"

Co-pilot: That's the dry. What about wet?'

Captain: "Because Little Rock Approach did not issue any visibility [report], we don't know if this quote from the American Airlines Manual has any bearing: "Max crosswind for visibility from three-quarters of a mile to one-half mile is 15 knots. Less than one-half mile, it's 10 knots."

Little Rock Approach: "American 1420, ah, your equipment's a lot better than, ah, what I have. How's the final for 22 left looking?"

Now we have a controller who is using ancient equipment asking a crew what their airborne radar shows for a landing on 22L. Believe me, this crew had much more important things to do than to scan their radar. When near the ground, the aircraft's radar is usually filled with unwanted ground clutter. The controller was trying to do the best he could with old equipment. Doppler radar, which is the best, could easily have picked out the best and worst parts of the storm, but it was not installed at Little Rock.

After circling around in the turbulence and rain, and trying to shoot a visual approach (one that requires visual reference to the ground), another misery rose its ugly head. Approach announced that there was a wind shear alert on the field. This phenomenon have killed more people than any other weather disturbance.

Captain: "I hate driving around visual at night in weather without having some clue where I am."

First Officer: "See how we're going right into this crap?" He had the situation pegged: "See, we're right on the base of these clouds."

Captain: "Yeah."

Michael Origel summed up a dramatic situation: "It's not worth it."

How right he was.

Approach: "American 1420. Right now we have, ah, heavy rain on the airport. The, uh, current weather on the ATIS is not correct. I don't have new weather for you, but the, uh, visibility is, uh, less than a mile. Runway four right RVR (runway visible range) is 3,000."

Now we have a small part of the weather situation to go on.

The American Airline Manual states that three-mile visibility equals a maximum crosswind of 15 knots. The present crosswind far exceeded that.

Approach: "American 1420, that's correct sir. And runway 4R cleared to land. The wind is 350 degrees at 30, gusts to 45."

The crosswind was way over the maximum allowed to land.

The ATC called and warned of another wind shear alert, and stated that the RVR had dropped to 1,600 feet. This was below landing limits.

RVR is an instrument on the runway that tells a pilot the distance, horizontally, that he or she can expect to see from the approach end of the runway. The limits on runway 4R were 2,400 feet; 1,600 feet is 800 feet shy of being legal. But because of a technical loophole, the airplane still could shoot the approach.

Approach control called and again warned the crew of another wind shear alert. This was the third such warning. A few miles from the runway, the captain made this statement: "This is … this is a can of worms."

Three minutes earlier, the first officer stated, "It's not worth it." Both crewmembers knew that they were in a potentially dangerous situation. Still, they pressed on.

There was plenty of fuel to go out and hold clear of the storm, or cancel the landing and go to an alternate airport, but this was never mentioned. For some reason, perhaps because of their preoccupation with getting to the runway, the landing checklist was never completed. Because of this, the ground spoilers were never activated. More about this later. While I should not jump inside the captain's head, I feel reasonably sure that he was mulling over the following:

1. I am really tired and I would like to land and get some sleep.
2. If I don't land here tonight, American will have to ferry in another aircraft to make up a morning flight.
3. It will cost the company to house and feed my passengers if I don't land here.

A line pilot who flies 85 hours a month might have had a different slant on landing at Little Rock. They are pilots, not management.

The aircraft was being buffeted by the winds and the hail was beating a tattoo on the cabin roof. Flaps were still at the approach setting as they slid down the glide slope.

First officer: "Do you want 40 flaps?"

Captain: "Oh yeah, thought I called it."

Flight 1420 touched down about 2,000 feet beyond the beginning of the runway at a speed of 164 knots. The wing spoiler never extended (pieces of metal that extend on top of the wings when the wheels spool up. These spoilers put most of the weight on the wheels so that brakes can be more effective).

First Officer: "We're down. We're sliding."

A wind gauge at the airport recorded a peak gust of 87 mph.

American Airlines Flight Manual clearly states that any wind over 51 knots closes the field for takeoffs or landings.

Wind was hitting flight 1420 from the side and rear. The captain was desperately trying to keep her straight, but with the tremendous crosswinds, it was impossible. No sooner had they touched down than the intense rain caused them to lose sight of the end of the runway. The captain was in and out of engine reverse thrust in an effort to stay on the runway. The aircraft slid 5,000 feet and turned 60 degrees. It became airborne again just before slamming into a series of steel towers at the end of the runway. At a speed of 90 knots, the plane broke into three sections, rupturing the fuel tanks and causing fire and smoke to rush through the cockpit and first class section. Parts of the steel structure struck the aircraft like spears. One such spike protruded under the co-pilot's seat, barely missing him. The captain died instantly. So did a first class passenger who was thrown from the aircraft. Within minutes, six people in rows 17 to 19 burned to death. Flight Officer Origel was lucky to be alive with just a broken leg.

The crash and fire killed nine of the 139 people on board. It took the rescue crews nine minutes to reach the site because the tower inadvertently directed the crash team to the wrong end of the runway. I firmly believe the death toll could have been much smaller if the approach light tower at the far end of the runway had been frangible (breakable), as they are supposed to be. The rigid tower is what cut the aircraft into pieces, not the landing.

This accident happened because the crew was fatigued after a long day at the controls. Flying a complex machine in terrible weather is much more tiring than sitting at a desk all day. Those who sit at desks work eight hours a day, the same as airline pilots, only with much less stress as a rule. Pilots not only have to put up with as much as 16 hours on duty, but also have to deal with dangerous rules and situations.

See if you agree with me regarding the maximum time a person should be on duty.

According to Federal Air Regulation 65.47A, a control tower operator cannot be on duty longer than 10 hours. In accordance with their union (NATCA) rules, a controller should be given a rest after working traffic for two or more hours.

Until a few months ago, there was no maximum on-duty time for an airline pilot. Now the FAA says 16 hours is the longest a person can be on duty. It should be noted that pilots cannot park their aircraft in the sky, and may be stuck in the cockpit for eight hours or more. There is no way a pilot can take a break. He is stuck in the beast until the final landing. I have personally been at the controls for over nine hours, with no breaks.

Allied Pilot Association, the union that represents American Airlines Pilots, states that pilots will not be scheduled for an on-duty period to exceed 12 hours. The crew can go as long as 14 hours if they choose to, but that is a maximum. The latest FAA regulation states that 16 hours on duty is perfectly legal for an airline captain, but an air traffic controller's maximum time on duty is 10 hours (during which time there will be at least four breaks). Both jobs are highly stressful, but a tired-out controller's life is not in danger. A fatigued pilot might make a mistake and die. You can plainly see the power of a good union, and how they are more interested in your safety than is the mighty Federal Aviation Administration.

By the way, there is no limit to the time a mechanic can be on duty. That is obviously another potentially dangerous situation.

The complete story of the number of crashes and the potentially dangerous rule that the FAA mandates would fill a book, and that is why I have only touched lightly on this subject. The more people up front, the safer the operation. But then airlines are not that interested in safety.

Before we leave the realm of pilot training, I would like to discuss with you a very important issue.

Upset Training

Unusual attitudes, Advanced Maneuvers Package (AMP), Upset training or Aerobatics … call it what you will, they all spell safety.

When you board an airliner, you probably are under the impression that the crew up front is perfectly capable of controlling the aircraft in any position of flight. Wrong. If your captain was trained by the military and he or she engages in sport aerobatics, you probably have a good chance of surviving a sudden upset. Only these pilots are familiar with spins and rolls, and how to control such maneuvers using the least amount of altitude.

Airline pilots are thoroughly trained to deal with a bad engine on the ground, but in the air it's another story. Airliners are thought to handle the controls smoothly so as not to spill any of the passengers drinks. They are not taught full-throw or violent control movements, that when used properly, could avert a potential crash.

During the past few years, there have been numerous high altitude upsets involving MD-11, an updated version of the DC-10: two China airliners, a Korean, an Alitalia, and the certification flight of the original MD-11. There have been numerous autopilot glitches that have caused airliners to be upset, causing a loss of thousands of feet of altitude. There have also been various theories concerning the crash in 1994 of a USAir near Pittsburgh, Pennsylvania. The NTSB has blamed a hard-over rudder for causing the problem. Perhaps the crew did not apply the proper control inputs, providing the flight controls were operating normally. I am in no way faulting the crew but instead the lack of compulsory upset training.

By far, the most important part of any aircraft is the flight controls. Sure, engines are needed, but if you have normal power and you don't have control, what have you got? Little or nothing.

In March of 1995, United Airlines was the first carrier to inaugurate AMP on their B-757/767 aircraft. Eventually, all United pilots will go through the AMP training and the skies will be a much safer place. While the United training is a great improvement, it is not the last word. Most simulators used by the airlines cannot be flown inverted. Steep turns and high angles of dive or climb can be simulated, but what happens when you end up on your back? That remains to be seen.

I believe that all airline pilots should be subjected to some flight training that they would thoroughly enjoy, in aerobatics in a light aircraft. Here, the experienced airline pilots could be introduced to something they probably have never had before: spin and roll recovery. If each pilot were allowed the opportunity to learn these aerobatic skills, it would be training that he could look forward to instead of the miseries of a ground-based simulator.

The pull of excessive Gs cannot be felt in the modern simulator, only in a live aircraft.

Aircraft have been upset by wake turbulence, autopilot malfunctions, wind shears, clear air turbulence, and full stalls. There is no question that all airline pilots should be capable of correcting an upset aircraft in all modes of flight. We will never know the number of crashes that could have been prevented by this all-important upset training. Airline pilots who are not trained by the military, or don't have civil aerobatic experience, have no idea what to do if their aircraft suddenly gets thrust upside down. I am not advocating that aerobatic training is all that is needed to save an aircraft. It also is necessary to have sufficient altitude to complete any upsetting maneuver. Even though a light plane has a vastly different feel than a large airliner, corrective control inputs remain relatively the same.

When an airline crew is suddenly thrust on their backs, the unskilled pilot most likely would try to fly it out by exerting backpressure on the wheel. This is not the way to get the aircraft back to normal flight. A great amount of altitude will be lost, not to mention an excess of speed while completing the split "S" maneuver. What should be accomplished is a roll to the lowest wing while exerting forward pressure on the yoke. This enables the aircraft to make the shortest roll to level flight and will avert a screaming dive at high "G" forces, possibly directly into the ground.

When members of an inexperienced crew become disoriented, they are thinking to themselves, "What the hell do we do now?" The FAA once again is "asleep at the switch." United took the initiative concerning this training, and USAir is following suit. However, there is no mandatory upset training required by the FAA. I guess there are not enough confirmed upset crashes for the government to make this vital training mandatory.

CHAPTER 12

▼

THE CREW

Dennis Callaghan, a bright young controller at Washington National Airport, is typical of the men at this facility. He was bitten by the flying bug at an early age, soloing at 16 and completing his commercial license at 18. He yearned for the life of an airline pilot and applied to United for a job. His experience was too low to be accepted so he tried to fly for the Army. At that time, there was no training for fixed-wing, so he elected to go to Officer Candidate School (OCS). After separation from the military, he once again pursued a flying job, but none were available. He decided if he couldn't fly aircraft, then the next best thing was to control them.

Dennis came through controller school in the top of his class and was assigned to Washington Center. Dennis has completed his checkout at Washington National and enjoys the rapidity at which the traffic is moved there. Dennis has flown with me many times, both on my airline, and in the cramped cockpit of my aerobatic biplane. I spent hours with him on the job and met many of his ATC friends whom you will meet shortly.

Washington National Airport is a DC-3 Airport in the jet age. It has three intersecting runways. Two of them are approximately one mile long while the main runway extends for 6,869 feet. After the crash of an Air Florida 737 in 1982, a 750-foot overrun was constructed at the end of RW36. This proved a godsend to an Eastern pilot who had to abort his takeoff to avoid a collision with a helicopter. No telling what this extra bit of concrete would have done for the captain of the ill-fated Air Florida jetliner. There is only one ILS (Instrument Landing System) and that is to the north. If the weather and winds are not favorable to a north approach, the airport would close and divert flights over to Dulles or Baltimore, two good airports, both of which have three ILS and runways that can handle jumbos. With what the controllers have to work with at National, they do a superior job handling over 360,000 movements a year, and when Congress is in session, the daily count gets as high as 1,200 landings a day or over 100 an hour. That is "moving tin."

I would like to take you on a typical airline flight from Washington to Bradley Field in Connecticut. This time, instead of sitting in the passenger compartment, come along with me up front. This trip will be as authentic as I can make it. You will spend part of it with me in the cockpit and the rest of the time with the controllers as they "work their magic."

The crew for this trip will consist of myself as Captain and First Officer, Chris Ganas, a great fellow to fly with. He is normally most cheerful, but today even more so, because he has just completed his one-year probation period. In the cabin, Flight Attendant A is Laurette Bollinger, a great looking gal with a wonderful personality. She will be assisted by Kay Lawrence, a tiny package of femininity who is married to one of our captains. The plane is a BAC 1-11 (British Aircraft Corporation), the first twin-engine jet to be put in service and I might say the greatest. She's built like a tank and flies like a fighter. The DC-9 is a copy of this machine, but a poor one. The JT8 engines on the 9 can't compare with the Rolls on the BAC.

While you're on your way to the airport, the crew has already checked in and is scanning the weather, the fuel loads, and alternates. We must be there an hour before takeoff. The flight attendant must be on board thirty minutes before departure to check the galley and emergency equipment. After completing our paperwork we head for the aircraft.

It is the first officer's job to completely circle the aircraft and check for any discrepancies. While he is doing this, I go to the cockpit and scan through the logbook to be certain the plane is airworthy. About this time,

I hear Chris in the cabin trying to get a cup of coffee from one of the flight attendants. He finally tears himself away and settles down in the right seat. He opens the checklist and starts to recite while I answer his commands.

"Logbooks"

"Checked"

"Gear Pins"

"Stowed"

"Battery"

"Checked"

I will cut these checklists short as I don't want to bore you with a lengthy question-and-answer session. After completing the intermediate list, Chris dials in the ATIS. This station transmits a continuous updated information broadcast that tells us the weather, wind, runway in use, and any other pertinent data. Each broadcast begins and ends with a specific letter such as A for Alice, or B for Betty. This call sign must be transmitted to clearance delivery when we ask for our route of flight.

Chris selects 128.25 on the radio and when the frequency is clear, calls "Washington clearance delivery USAir #452 with Alice." Keith Donaldson, an ex-Navy man, checks his roster for the proper flight strip and answers. "USAir 452 depart south on the 183 degree radial for vectors to the Washington 072 radial maintain 5,000 expect 250, ten minutes after department, frequency 126.55 squawk 7044."

This clearance is copied down in pilots' shorthand and is read back in its entirety by the co-pilot (most of the later jets have a computer readout in the cockpit).

It is now about ten minutes before we are due to start engines and the passengers are filing on. The flight attendants are checking their tickets and seat assignments, and are having their usual problems with a passenger who doesn't want to take his heavy briefcase from the overhead rack and place it under the seat in front of him.

The airplane pushback tug is attached to the nose gear to await the push back signal from the pilot. I say to my co-pilot, "Say Chris, How's your kangaroo?" Chris actually has a kangaroo for a pet.

"Well, he's fine, but the neighbors are starting to complain about the thumping around. I think I'll have to get rid of him."

"Well, not before you bring him out to show my kids."

"I'll be over, never fear."

"Hey Chris, take a look at this. A real knockout blonde was just coming down the jetway."

"Hey, that's something. Maybe I should go in the back and see if I can give her a hand with her packages."

"Can't say I blame you for that."

It's now about two minutes before we're due for our pushback. The gate agent enters the cockpit and says. "You have 72 on board, the count is okay. Do you have 14,000 (pounds of fuel)?

"Yes, she's showing 14."

Here's your weight slip, have a good trip."

"Thanks"

The next visitor to the cockpit is "Screamer," my nickname for the captain of the cabin or flight attendant, Laurette Bollinger. "I will bring your usual apple juice up in a minute."

"Brian power for the steps please."

"You have it."

It takes hydraulic pressure to raise the stairs since the engines are not yet running the auxiliary system.

"Say, Chris, if you can get your mind off that beauty in the back, how's about calling for a push" (permission to push back).

"Washington ground USAir 452 push gate 17."

"Cleared for a pushback, there is a Delta behind you shortly."

The permission to push was issued by Pat Walsh who not only knows the business of ATC, but also is a decorated helicopter pilot from the Vietnam War.

When they are in a south operation at Washington Tower, the controllers are stationed so that the man on the far right is the clearance delivery man and next to him is the ground controller, and so on until reaching the local controller (man in charge of takeoffs and landings). He is the last to talk to the pilot. Here he commands the best view of the all-important airplane touchdown zone.

Our flight strip (airline name, number, route of flight, and squawk) has now changed hands from the man who issued the route clearance over to the ground control man. This strip will pass through two more controllers before we get takeoff clearance. As the pushback tug strains under the weight of the plane we find ourselves moving slowly backward to the start area.

"Okay, Chris, before start check."

"Okay, Sir." (He calls everyone sir or ma'am, even his cat.)

"Your year is in, now can't you try calling me Brian or anything other than sir?"

With a chuckle, "Okay Sir Brian."

"Engine generators"

"Trip"

"Boost pumps"

"On"

"MAC valves"

"Closed"

"Mains"

"Checked"

"Seat belt—no smoking"

"On"

We have now been pushed back to the start area. The mechanic who has been walking alongside my window raises his hands and clenches his fist. That is the signal to set the parking brake. Next, I see his hand going around in circles, signifying that its clear to wind them up. As I reach one hand to select the start master and igniters, the beautiful Rolls Royce engines groan to life. The mechanic gives me the wave-off and now its time to taxi. Chris calls ground control: "USAir 452 taxi."

"Clear to 18 hold short of 15."

With the parking brakes released and a nudge on the power levers, we slowly move out toward the active runway.

Chris knows the checks to be read and proceeds with them after start.

"Electrical"

"Reset and checked"

"Hydraulic panel"

"Air system/air conditioning"

"Set for takeoff"

"Door lights and lock"

We are now approaching 15, an active runway, and must wait to be cleared across.

Meanwhile, in the tower, Dave Robertson, the man who assists the local controller, has passed our flight strip to him where it is positioned as he likes it. Each tower controller has his own way of keeping tabs on traffic and the strip is placed where he can't miss it.

Chris picks up the checklist again and starts the never-ending list.

"Shoulder harness"

"Fastened"

"Takeoff data"

"BUG set at 140 knots"

"TP1, trim tabs"

"Set for takeoff"

"Master warning"

"Lights in/armed/checked"

"Speed brake"

"In collar up"

"Safety valve"

"Closed"

"Standby valve"

"Closed"

"Standby horizon"

"Checked"

"Flight controls"

"Free/PWR/Field light out"

"Brake temperature"

"Checked"

"Flaps"

"Set for T.O."

"Flight Recorder"

"On"

"No1AC pump"

"On"

By now, you are probably feeling sorry for poor, overworked Chris. Looks like he is the only one doing things up there. Well, you are right. The co-pilot does the lion's share of the work. His chance is coming though on the next leg when we switch jobs and I do all the work while he flies.

Pat Welsh, the ground controller comes over the radio for the last time. "USAir 452 contact tower on 119.1"

"452"

We are now in the block adjacent to our takeoff runway 18 and Chris switches over to the tower on 119.1. "Washington Tower USAir 452 ready."

Over the radio comes the rapid clear voice of my good friend Dennis, the fellow who you met at the beginning of this chapter.

"USAir 452 taxi into position and hold on 18, traffic will depart on 15."

"452"

No sooner are the brakes set than a beautiful Lear Jet races past our runway and climbs out like a rocket.

I pick up the PA mike and tell the cabin crew "Cabin attendants, please take your seats; we are number one for departure."

The local controller speaks "USAir 452 cleared for takeoff."

"452 rolling."

Brakes are released and the throttles are advanced. Before we reach 60 knots, the power is set and the high crackling roar of two mighty Rolls Royce turbines strains as over 20,000 pounds of thrust are unleashed.

"Chris calls 80 knots both sides" (a check on both our air speed indicators).

I take my left hand from the nose steering wheel and place it on the yoke. As we gather speed she starts to get lighter and the runway bumps are not as noticeable. I have started to take some weight off the nose wheel by a slight backpressure on the yoke. Chris calls "V1 rotate V2". As the air speed climbs past 140 knots, I apply more backpressure to the yoke and my command is felt at the tail, 97 feet away. As the speed increases, 79,000 pounds of sheer delight reaches for the sky.

Most people believe that the takeoff is the "hairiest" part of the trip. Not so. Now we are attacking the "Indian Territory" (Piper Cherokees) and won't reach the relative safety of 18,000 feet for quite sometime. Reaching 1,500 feet, we start the noise abatement nonsense to pacify those people who move near an airport after it's built. It would really be more beneficial if we kept our normal power on and disturbed a few people for a short time rather than a lot for a long time. Airplanes don't climb very well on a hot day with a full load and the air conditioning power packs on.

Now we are climbing out over the Woodrow Wilson Bridge about five miles south of the airport following the Washington OMNI 183° radial that is keeping us over the Potomac River. The after-takeoff check is completed (bet your glad I didn't write this one out)

Let's go back to the tower and see what Dennis is doing. From the time we changed to the tower frequency, I have been listening to Dennis' rapid instructions to planes in his assigned block of air. He's running them on runways 15 and 18, constantly calculating how he can get the arrivals in between the departures. Quite a feat at DCA with intersecting runways. Complete cooperation is required of all the pilots in order for Dennis to keep his rhythm and have adequate spacing.

Now we are two miles south and Dennis has not forgotten us. "USAir 452 contact departure. See you, Brian."

"So long and thanks."

Now the tower man has relinquished control of my flight. He punches a button on a panel in front of him marked East Boundary and speaks to a controller on a lower floor. "USAir boundary" (leaving his jurisdiction).

Below the tower ca sits the radar room. Here in a dimly lit chamber, sit controllers skillfully manipulating departures and arrivals. Gone is the visual contact of the glass house atop the tower. Now when the ATC talks to the pilots, all they see are numerous small green targets on their individual radar scopes.

Jack Ludlam has worked traffic for nine years at this facility, and he has over 15 years with the FAA. His hobby is throwing darts and he is good, he will soon be a national champion. He says that throwing darts in a tavern is very much like his job: both places can be noisy at times, but you must keep your concentration. Chris calls, "Washington departure USAir 452 out of 1.8" (1,800 feet).

"Roger USAir 452 expedite climb to 170" (17,000 feet).

Now Jack has thrown us an unfamiliar bone. He is requesting that we get up to 17,000 rapidly. This is one legal way to break the slow noise abatement climb. He must have traffic coming up our tailpipe, hence the request for an expeditious climb. "USAir 452 turn left heading 050 for the Washington 072. This is repeated back to him verbatim. We will now head northeast to intercept a new course from the VOR (Navigation Radio Aid).

Chris dials in 131.1 the company frequency and tells USAir the time we left the gate, the time off the ground, and when we will arrive in Hartford.

"Hello Washington USAir 452 out on schedule, off at 32 Bradley schedule."

"Roger, 32 scheduled."

The after-takeoff check has been completed. This is one of two checks that doesn't require command and response. We seem to have a moment of silence so I pick up the phone to the cabin and do a little public relations work. "Sorry we couldn't take you by all those important buildings, but because of our south takeoff, there isn't going to be much to show you.

In another few minutes we will be over the Chesapeake Bay. The weather today is good, so later on you will be able to see Philadelphia and New York City. We'll be cruising at 25,000 feet and the weather at Bradley is much the same as Washington's. We should be there on schedule, and thanks for flying with USAir."

ATC calls. "USAir 452 turn left 030 degrees for the 072 radial."

"Rog USAir 452 left 030 degree for 072."

We are now passing 10,000 feet and we are allowed to increase our speed to 300 knots. As I decrease the altitude, the air speed starts to climb. When it reaches 300, it's time to take a rest. On goes the autopilot and now I can fly her with hands and feet off the controls. With the simple movement of a few fingers on my right hand, she does just what she is told.

The flight attendants in the cabin are busy arranging their beverage cart for their trip down the aisle. Soft drinks and coffee are free; cocktails are $4.00.

Jack Ludlam, our Washington Departure man, is closely checking his scope to see the status of our flight. The radar handoff system is completely automatic when it is working properly, and the change of control from one facility to another is self-contained. He notices our target is displaying a letter "C." This tells him that we are now entering a "handoff" mode where our control will be shifted to Washington Center some 20 miles from National Airport. When Jack observes the letter "C", he knows that the whole data block (a tag that follows our target which tells the controller the airline, the trip number, the altitude, and the speed over the ground) at the center is flashing, alerting the controller from our next sector that he should be ready to accept another aircraft in his allotted air space. If he has no conflicting traffic, he allows the computer to continue its function. As soon as the block stops flashing, it simultaneously starts the flash on Jack's scope at National. He gets about three flashes and then it stops. This whole automatic procedure has taken place in just a few seconds. When our target ceases to flash, the handoff is completed. "USAir 452, your 15 miles NE of Washington. Contact the Washington Center on 127.2."

"Rog 452, 127.2. Good day."

After turning the radio to the prescribed channel, we now talk to another facility.

Our next ATC has charge of all aircraft from our present position up to 20 miles west of Woodstown, New Jersey. In the Aberdeen Proving Grounds area, he controls from 10,000 feet up to 23,000 feet. Baltimore approach owns the lower altitudes.

Lew McClanahan has worked this sector for a number of years and he feels right at home doing his thing. Now it's time to talk to him. "Hello. Washington's finest USAir 452 is out of 13.4 for 17,000."

"Good afternoon 452, climb to and maintain 230 clear direct to Woodstown. Traffic for you opposite direction four miles."

"Direct Woodstown up to 230 no "joy" on the traffic" (not in sight).

Now Chris and I both scan the area in front of us. We have been told that there is a plane headed directly toward us, and the controller has no idea of his altitude. We continue to scan up and down but still see nothing. This sort of thing goes on continually.

"Say, where's the traffic now?"

"Two miles still 12 o'clock."

If the weather wasn't as clear as it was, I would have asked for a turn away from the target. We feel that we should see it before it hits us.

Lew calls again. "USAir 452, that traffic has passed you, he's six o'clock, one mile."

"Thanks 452, never saw a thing."

He was probably down low and we just couldn't pick him out. We are now approaching the airline pilots' haven, 18,000 feet. Sure, there have been near misses up here, but the potential is less than it is in the "Indian Territory".

Philadelphia is passing our left side, and because of our direct course to the Robinsville VOR, we will save some time and fuel. We both reach over and set our altimeter on 29.92 which is the number used by all airplanes about 18,000. This keeps us all on equal vertical separation.

Lew McClanahan at Washington keys his mike. "USAir 452 contact New York Center on 127.4 and have a good trip."

"452 thank you sir."

The exact same automatic handoff has been made again, this time to New York Center at Islip, Long Island.

"Hello New York's finest USAir 452, 19.4 for 230."

"Good afternoon USAir 230; radar contact; proceed direct to Robinsville; climb to 250."

"Direct to Robinsville 250."

We only traverse a small section of this man's air space so we don't stay with him very long. It's a cardinal sin, in fact, on a par with not spacing aircraft, to allow a target to penetrate another man's air space. The various air space borders are a veritable "no mans" land and you don't enter without permission. "USAir 452 contact New York on 133.05."

"Rog 133.05. See ya."

We have now traveled about 150 miles, some of it circuitous, some direct. Unfortunately, due to the complexities of controlled air space, the days of taking off and flying direct to a destination have long since gone. Direct courses may, however, be in the near future.

We have safely traversed the "Indian Territory," and have reached the safety of the high altitude sector, (above 18,000 feet). Mr. Ciro Assante will be guiding us through his sector. He is in charge of a strip of territory approximately 40 miles wide and 75 miles long, and all traffic at or above 18,000 feet. We have just been handed off from our last sector man and its time to converse with Ciro. "Hello New York's finest USAir 452 flight level 250."

"452 radar contact descend to 180."

"452 to 180."

The altitude hold on the autopilot is released and a few turns forward on the vertical control wheel starts us down at 1,000 feet per minute. As the air speed increases, the throttles are retarded until the fuel flow stops at about 2,000 pounds per hour.

The cockpit door opens and there stands Screamer in all her glory.

"Nothing for me thanks." Chris says.

"Likewise." I answer.

"Well, Brian, are you going to go into your act? It really is clear over Manhattan."

I like to play to a full house so here goes. I flip the public address system switch.

"Off to our left is an exceptional view of Manhattan. That bridge is the Verrazano and it connects Brooklyn and Staten Island. Off to the right is Long Island, and we will be over the bay in a few moments. As you can see, we have started our decent and should be landing in about 12 minutes."

"USAir 452 contact New York on 128.1. Have a good one."

"128.1 good day."

"Good afternoon New York USAir 452 passing 21.8 for 180."

A voice with a decidedly British accent flows smoothly over our speakers. "Roger USAir 452 New York ident." (Depressing a button on the console puts a double slash on the controller's radar screen that is now filled in for a positive ident).

One minute passes.

"USAir maintain 15,000 altimeter 30.07."

"Okay, maintain 15 altimeter 30.07."

"Descend to 11,000 turn right to 070. What's your rate of decent?"

"One thousand feet per minute."

"Can you increase that?"

"Sure can."

"You will be crossing traffic at 13,000. I'll be turning you back when you're out of 12,000."

"452"

"452 turn left heading 340."

"452 to 340."

"Call me out of 13 and 12, that traffic at 13 is presently at 11 o'clock when you complete your turn he'll be at 1 o'clock about 12 miles."

"USAir 452 level at 11."

"Roger contact New York on 134.0. Thank you for your help."

"452 anytime."

The next sector is traversed in a matter of minutes, nevertheless, radio contact is still the only sure means of getting the instructions across. Hopefully, that will be changed soon.

"Hello New York USAir 452 level 11,000."

"USAir at 11 ident understand 340 heading maintain it for the Bridgeport 014 radial."

"Okay will do."

"USAir 452 contact New York on 132.3."

"Roger 132.3."

"New York Center USAir 452 level 11."

"Roger USAir maintain 11 Bradley altimeter 30.02."

"30.02."

"USAir 452 heading 050 descend to 9, contact Bradley Approach Control 125.8."

"Down to 9 and 125.8."

While monitoring both ATC radio, and company, we now have a third one to listen to, the ATIS landing information at Bradley.

"Information Romeo 2000 Greenwich, 9,000 scattered, visibility 15 miles, temp 44, wind 310/8, altimeter 30.03, expect ILS or visual to runway 24 and 33, advise on contact you have message Romeo."

John Sweichek has been in the agency for 20 years, indeed one of the few to last this long, and at Bradley for the last ten. His territory extends on a radius of about 40 miles around the airport and up to 7,000 feet. He has accepted the handoff from New York and now it's time to add one more pilot for him to talk to. Chris keys the mike. "Hello Bradley Approach USAir 452 at 9 with Racquell." Somehow Racquell sounds more appealing than Romeo. Makes no difference, just as long as you tell them you have received the message that starts with an "R".

John replies, "Roger USAir 452 descend to five vectors (guidance) to runway 33 traffic pattern for the visual approach."

"USAir 452."

Time now to inform the flight attendants that we are almost there.

"Cabin attendants, please prepare the cabin for landing."

Chris is reaching for the checklist and starts to recite the Preliminary Landing.

"Altimeters"

"Set"

"Hydraulic Pressure and Quantity"

"Checked"

"Landing DATA (taking into consideration the fact that we have burned about 5,000 pounds of fuel, we will be that much lighter on landing our speed will be 124 knots).

"Checked"

"Shoulder harness"

"Fastened"

By now the cabin is secure and the flight attendants are making their final check of the passengers, ensuring that all seat belts are fastened and that all trays are up and locked.

Both Chris and I are scanning the ground at our 11 o'clock position. In times gone by airports were easy to spot because they were always in sparsely populated areas. Since people just love to move nearer to airports and complain about the noise, it has made airports blend in with many of the towns.

I finally sighted it and called Jack. "Approach USAir 452 "tally-ho" (an old British saying held over from the fox hunts and the RAF) your place."

"Cleared for the visual approach runway 33 if you think you can make it, or you can set up a downwind for 24 if you prefer."

"Yeah, we'll go for 24."

"USAir there's a flight of two A-10s on about a two-mile final. Should be well ahead of you cleared for the visual approach runway 25 contact tower 120.3."

Before changing over, Chris makes a call to our company and tells them that we are going to be at the gate in five minutes.

The approach controller now has relinquished control of our trip and handed us over to the local tower controller. His world is on top of the fine restaurant at Bradley, and it is here he issues all takeoff and landing clearances.

John Vacon has been a controller for seven years and at Bradley for two. Off duty, he is a volunteer fireman and a sports car buff.

"Good afternoon Bradley tower USAir 452 downwind for 24." (This leg of the landing pattern is parallel to the runway.)

"USAir 452 you're cleared to land."

"452 thank you sir."

We are now slowed to 160 knots and the first quarter of the flaps have been extended. I reach over across the cockpit and place the landing gear handle in the down position. This hydraulically releases the gear doors and one by one, the wheels drop in place. On the panel we can trace the position of the wheels by three lights. When they are all green, it signifies that all wheels are down and locked. The two mains glow green first and the lighter nose wheel is usually the last to signify and okay condition.

Chris reads the Final Landing checklist.

"Speed Brake." In/Collar up"

"Seat Belt—No Smoking"

"As required"

"Anti-ice"

"Off"

"TTC"

"Only"

"Gear"

"Three green handle in pressure up"

"Auto pilot"

"Released"

All prescribed checks have been fulfilled. All that is left is for me to set up the correct power and rate of descent. We are now turning final approach and it looks like we are in just about the right place at the right time. The ideal situation for a good approach is to leave the power set and control the descent with the flaps. Sounds better for you because there is less of that whining noise as the turbines are increased and decreased. It is also the mark of a good airplane driver. Unfortunately, this ideal approach is not always possible due to changes in wind velocity and direction.

We are now about three miles from the runway. Our speed is 140 and sink rate 800 feet. Chris is busy, as always, calling our air speed, sink rate, and anything else of interest.

Over the threshold power is reduced to idle and we literally glide to a landing. All I have to do is try and figure out when the wheels are about three inches above the runway. I believe she's ready to quit flying now. The nose is slowly raised until she hits. Speed boards are extended fully. There are four boards that extend on the top of the wings. These little devils kill the lift on the upper surface of the wing and create drag. Squeak, squeak as the mains hit the runway. Lucked out on this one, everything was okay. I hold the nose off by entering backpressure on the yoke. As the nose starts to drop I keep holding it off with backpressure while, at the same time, selecting reverse thrust so that my engines can now be used to slow us down.

We are nearly stopped in less than one-third of the runway. Bradley is an excellent field with three long runways. The main one is 2,633 feet longer than the longest in Washington. They also have three ILS here compared to National where there is only one.

I promise I'll not bore you with anymore checklists, although we do have eleven more items to check before we park at the terminal.

Bradley tower calls. "USAir 452 crosses runway 33 turn left Sierra contact ground control point nine when clear of the runway."

"Roger ground on Suzy."

We are now clear of John Vacon's domain that consists of all the active runways. He has handed control of our flights to a most cheerful Robert Pierce. He has been in the FAA longer than he cares to mention. He is the team supervisor in the tower (boss of the tower cab on this watch). Chris keys the mike; "Bradley ground USAir 452 is clear of the active."

"USAir 452 is cleared to the ramp."

"452 thank you."

Here are a few interesting points concerning this trip:

1. We talked to 15 different controllers and traversed an equal number of control sectors.

2. We were assigned 11 different altitudes.

3. We were issued over 15 heading changes.

4. We used 800 gallons of fuel.

5. We took 55 minutes from gate to gate.

6. We arrived six minutes ahead of schedule. (This is the one that concerns the passengers and the company the most.)

I hope that you have enjoyed the previous trip. The primary purpose was to show the great need for cooperation between the pilots and controllers. Unfortunately, through the years for one reason or another, there has been far too much turmoil between the two groups. Pilots have the mistaken idea that since they are, by law, responsible for the crew, cargo, passengers, and aircraft, they don't like being told where and when to go. A senior captain who has been driving airplanes for 20 or 30 years dislikes a 25-year-old controller guiding his plane. A few years ago when pilots were really "bugging" controllers, the ATC group came out with a license plate frame for their cars. It read:

Air Traffic Controllers Tell Pilots Where to Go

You can take that statement anyway you like, but the fact of the matter is, its true. Pilots that don't like being separated from other airplanes should seek other employment. Time and again I have heard my fellow pilots say that they don't like some guy on the ground flying their plane. Yet that is precisely the controller's job. No, not to manipulate the controls or work the throttles; that's where we come in. But all the dimension of flight are directed by ATC; we simply move the controls. Every time we change from one control facility to another, a new man or woman has control of our plane. From the time we get the clear-to-start-signal from the ground controller until we stop at our destination, we are under direct control at all times. We must get permission at some airports to start our engines, authorization to taxi, we're told when to take off, how high to climb, when to level off, what direction to fly, when to descend, when to reduce power or speed up, what runway to use, and how to taxi to the terminal. The company tells us the gate to use. If that's not being in the cockpit, I don't know what is.

What's good for the goose is good for the gander but pilots don't see it that way. When pilots are looking for a new contract or the company is harassing them, they go on a "Safety Campaign," or by the book operation. This means we don't cut any corners, use the runways into the wind instead of those on course, never ask for a visual approach even with the field in sight, taxi slowly, and on and on. Pilots believe that this operation will bring the company around and that it certainly does not affect ATC at all. Wrong. A plane that is taxiing so slowly that it barely moves can put an added burden on the ATC. Now all the other carriers also must slow down because it's a follow the leader affair out to the runway. When a pilot on a slowdown is told to increase descent, he doesn't; when told to keep speed up, he doesn't. All these actions play havoc with the controller, and he has enough work as it is.

Now if the controllers are on a slowdown, the pilots scream bloody murder. Pilots have a right to strike; controllers do not. The only way ATC can get their point across is to slow the traffic. This gets noticed rapidly.

You often hear the pilots bemoaning the fact that they are forced to waste fuel. That is a legitimate complaint. Funny, you never hear a controller say, "Those guys on a certain airline could have been on the ground by now if they weren't dragging their feet; they're really wasting fuel."

Some pilots take the controllers slowdowns as a personal thing. ATC does not feel that way towards pilots when they are playing their little games. Over 40 years ago familiarization flight in aircraft cockpit (FAM) trips were inaugurated, and they are still in effect today. According to FAA Facility Management Book, the reason for these trips is: "It is desirable for ATC specialists to become acquainted with the in-flight problems affecting ATC and communications by observing the operations from the "jump seat" of the aircraft" (seat between pilots).

This is a sterling idea. Something of this nature should be added to our regulations whereby we are required to sit at a control center and observe. Each controller is allowed eight trips a year, not more than four allowed during duty time. That regulation most certainly should be changed. If the facility is adequately staffed, controllers should be encouraged to take FAMs. The red tape should be eliminated. Any time a controller wants to ride in my cockpit and there is space for him, he should be welcomed there. They certainly have a carte blanche invitation to ride on my plane anytime.

If the ATA would get off its high horse and allow controllers to ride in the cockpit of its member airlines, their profits would improve. Because flying is foreign to many controllers, they just don't know what it's like. When they ride with us and watch us work, the other side of the coin gets clearer. They see what we do in order to change altitude, they can watch us look for traffic out of a small cluttered cockpit window, they learn that it is not possible to descend at a good rate and slow down as well, they see the many other duties that we have to perform, and they see the complexities of a modern jet cockpit. Operational techniques would improve. For instance, we might learn that on a certain departure, if we climb as rapidly as possible we will be sent on course sooner. We would learn the altitudes of the "dump zone" (a specified location and altitude for descent). We would learn the reason why we are kept at a low altitude for so long because of arrivals or departures that would be in conflict. In short, we both would benefit greatly.

In order for an ATC to get a request for a jump seat (SF-160), he must traverse a mountain of red tape. First, he must complete two forms, a 1500-7 that is a request for SF-160. This form must be in the hands of the airline at least ten days before he wishes to travel. The airline must send this form back to the ATC supervisor with a notation that he has not flown on the carrier during the past year. Then, if he speaks politely to his supervisor, he may get the pass. However, this is not the end of the red tape. The day of the trip he must report to the airline operations and check with a dispatcher to see if he can still get the seat in the cockpit. Now comes the toughest part of all; the airline captain who has the last word on whether or not the controller gets on board. The power of a captain is supposedly great. This is dead wrong, he only has the power to deny the jump seat; he cannot authorize that someone use it. The only way we are ever going to smooth out our operation is by controllers observing us in flight, and by us observing of the controllers at their facility. There are a very small percentage of ATC who utilize the jump seat. One reason is the red tape involved; another is that he has to confront the supervisor of the sky, the captain.

Here is a true story that was told to me by the controller involved. The airline and the captain shall remain nameless because salt in the wound won't heal it.

A controller and his family were off on a trip down south. His wife and children had full-fare tickets and were on board. The captain for this trip was late reporting so the controller thought it best to leave the airline operations and wait to meet the captain on board. As the pilot reached the cockpit door, the controller approached him and said: "Captain, I would like permission to ride the jump seat." He showed him the authorization as well as his ID card. The captain examined both and spoke with great authority. "I see you are an air traffic controller"

"Yes sir"

"I'll tell you one thing. You'll never ride in my cockpit. Get off." With these kind words the controller deplaned and hurriedly bought a full-fare ticket, boarded the flight, and took a seat with his wife and children.

Meanwhile, back in the cockpit, the captain had seen the controller getting on board. The cockpit door flew open, propelled by the captain. He stormed down the aisle and homed in on the controller and his family. In front of a plane full of passengers, he pointed his finger at the controller and bellowed. "I told you before that you were never going to ride my plane." The controller, in an obviously nervous state, exclaimed, "When you said I couldn't ride up front, I bought a ticket for the cabin."

"I'm not going to tell you again. You and your family get off my plane, or it will sit here until you do."

Not wishing to delay the other passengers, the controller and his family gathered their belongings and left the plane.

The ATC reported the incident to his supervisor and also to the captain's chief pilot. He is still waiting the outcome of this conflict.

Rest assured that the airline in question was not handled by ATC in an expeditious fashion and the company will pay heavily in the months to come. I certainly can't blame the controllers for being up in arms about such disgraceful treatment. Now you can see the team at work. I'm sorry to say the above case is only one of many. A senior pilot on a large carrier earns approximately $170,000 a year and only works two weeks out of every month.

A senior co-pilot earns approximately $80,000 a year and also only works two weeks a month. Both have a company paid retirement far in excess of controllers.

A controller earns between $60,000 and $100,000 a year and works six days a week. And they must contribute to their retirement.

Airline pilots usually don't have to operate faulty equipment but controllers do. Due to the complexities of the ATC, they usually burn out approximately ten years quicker than pilots. Probably the most dramatic differences between the two professions is the fact that controllers have the awesome task of separating as many as 25 airplanes at one time; pilots are only responsible for one. It is true that they don't run the risk of being killed, but when they run two aircraft together, they are as good as dead.

Captains partially trained in other crewmembers positions can perform their job better. The ATC is as much a part of my crew as my co-pilot is.

He may not be working in my cockpit, but he is there. The backbone of commercial aviation is the pilot, the controller, and the mechanic. Without these vital crewmembers there would be no airline industry.

CHAPTER 13

▼

THE GIMLI GLIDER

On July 5, 1983, Mr. Conrad Yaremko, a certified aircraft technician (first class mechanic) was having a time of it checking out the fuel gauges on Air Canada's latest jet, the Boeing 767. This new wide-bodied craft belonged to a new generation of aircraft. Because of advanced technology and sophisticated instrumentation, this plane was designed for the pilot to make the takeoff. From this point on, the plane can fly to the destination, make the approach, and land without the pilots having to handle the controls. Airlines are continually striving to reduce the cockpit crew. The 767 requires only two pilots; in this machine, the flight engineer is gone. One down, two to go.

Technician Yaremko had experienced the problem of inoperable fuel gauges before on this same craft. He found that by deactivating the channel two circuit breaker (similar to electric circuit breakers in your house), he could obtain a fuel indication. In accordance with standard procedures, Yaremko marked the pulled circuit breaker with a yellow tape that was labeled, "inoperative." He placed another tape above the fuel gauges marked "see logbook." Aircraft maintenance discrepancies in Canada are commonly referred to as "snags." The aircraft was dispatched per minimum equipment list (MEL) with one of the processor channels inoperative. Now, the fuel must be manually checked at each stop by the drip-stick check. At various positions under the wings, sticks are pulled down. When the level of fuel is reached, they begin to drip.

July 23 saw the same jet back at the maintenance base in Edmonton. Mr. Yaremko briefed Captain John Weir concerning the faulty gauges. However, Weir believed that the mechanic was referring to a recent "snag" and not one that originated on the 5th of the month. The flight from Edmonton to Montreal was uneventful. All three fuel gauges checked out normally. Before the flight left Montreal, avionics technician, Mr. Ouellet entered the cockpit and saw that the breaker was pulled. He reset it and the fuel gauges all went blank. He proceeded to try and isolate the fault but was unable to pin it down. Mr. Ouellet was distracted from his work by a fueler and he forgot to reposition the number two circuit breaker. When Captain Robert Pearson entered the cockpit, he noticed all three fuel gauges were blank. He knew he couldn't fly it in this condition and was about to check it out when another technician assured him that the aircraft was cleared for flight by their highest maintenance authority, Maintenance Central.

For quite some time, all of Air Canada's aircraft have been fueled in liters. However, pilots calculate their fuel in pounds. Air Canada decided that their new 767 aircraft would have the fuel gauges reading in kilograms, a metric measurement. Takeoff weight would now have to be computed in kilograms. With all the new computations, no one got the fuel loads correct. Each time the trip was fueled, it ended up with about half of what the load called for. Lack of standardization is usually a catalyst for a potential disaster. This will give you some insight as to the difference in Air Canada's fueling criteria. On the Boeing 767, the drip sticks are calibrated in centimeters, and this is converted to liters to kilograms; on the Lockheed 1011, Boeing 747 and Douglas DC-9-32, the drip sticks are calibrated in imperial gallons and the conversion goes from gallons to pounds; on the Douglas DC-8 and the Boeing 727, drip sticks are calibrated in inches and the conversion is from inches to imperial gallons to pounds. If you can figure all that out, you are way ahead of me.

Captain Pearson decided in Montreal that he would board sufficient fuel to take him through his first stops at Ottawa and on to Edmonton. As the maintenance people were filing down the steps, Robert Desjardins, the senior flight attendant, was anxious about the unusual fueling procedure. "We better have enough," he exclaimed as the maintenance people were closing the door. "You've got enough to go all the way to Vancouver," replied the mechanic. The trip from Montreal to Ottawa was routine. The fuel sticks were checked again, and the same erroneous calculations were recorded. Once again, Air Canada Flight 143 was winging westward. It was a smooth, clear, night. As they leveled out at 41,000 feet over Red Lake, Ontario, Captain Pearson, an avid fisherman, spoke to his First Officer, Maurice Quintal. "I'm going to sit here and watch the trout swimming in the lake."

The autopilot altitude hold was snapped on and First Officer Quintal picked up the public address phone, pressed the button, and said, "Good evening ladies and gentlemen, this is your First Officer. We're presently coming up over Red Lake, presently 800 miles from Edmonton cruising at 41,000 feet, the temperature in Edmonton is beautiful, the day is clear, temperature of 24 degrees Celsius. Thank you."

"Temperature in Edmonton is beautiful."

The cockpit door opened and Mr. Richard Dion, a mechanic from Montreal, entered the flight deck. Captain Bob turned and said "Come right in." Apologetically, Mr. Dion replied "Don't want to disturb you, if you want me to get out."

"No problem. Glad to have you visit with us."

Captain Bob had a great time talking over maintenance problems with the mechanic who was on holiday with his wife and children back in the cabin. The cockpit crew was enjoying the ride while the cabin attendants were busily catering to the passengers. At 8:10 P.M. the serenity was broken.

BEEP, BEEP, BEEP, BEEP came the low fuel pressure warning signal along with its associated flashing red lights. Captain Pearson exclaimed "Holy fuck."

Co-pilot: "Something wrong with the fuel pump."

Captain: "Left forward fuel pump, okay what have we got here? I hope its just the fucking fuel pump failing, I'll tell you that." First Officer Quintal was already studying the emergency procedure and associated diagrams.

Co-pilot: "Why do we get ..."

Captain: "You know, I would not take this air ..." The captain never got to finish his sentence.

BEEP, BEEP, BEEP, BEEP ...

"Oh fuck, we've got to go to Winnipeg," exclaimed Captain Pearson in a disgusted tone. He questioned the mechanic. "What would you, what would your assessment of that be?"

"I would say if both your lights are on the left, you've got no fuel pressure going to the engine other than what its sucking now. You got that light out cause you got cross-feed on."

Captain Pearson was using all the resources on hand. He knew that Mechanic Dion could offer expert advice concerning a maintenance problem and he felt no qualms about asking. A lesser commander would probably have told the mechanic to return to his seat in the cabin. This is the very time the expertise of the flight engineer would be advantageous. But airlines want that engineer out of the cockpit to save money.

Captain Pearson spoke to the mechanic. "Well, what does that mean about fuel?"

"Ah—you could—my own personal thoughts, you might be low on the left tank."

Captain Bob was contemplating the possibility of fuel exhaustion and Richard Dion's statement confirmed his thoughts. "Let's head for Winnipeg, NOW!"

Co-pilot Quintal keyed his mike: "Winnipeg Center Air Canada 143."

"Air Canada 143, go ahead"

"Yes sir, we have a problem, we're going to uh ... requesting direct Winnipeg."

"Air Canada 143 you're cleared present position direct Winnipeg, we're landing on runway 31, you're cleared to maintain 6,000 feet."

Mechanic Dion could see that things were getting sticky and asked,

"Would you rather I go back in the cabin?"

Captain Bob replied "Oh no. Why don't you stay up here and see if you can be of any assistance."

That kind of thinking can only come from a pilot who is a true captain in every sense of the word.

"God damn they're all going out, ay? … how about uh …

Again, Captain Bob didn't finish his sentence. He was distracted by BEEP, BEEP, BEEP, BEEP. Captain Bob exclaimed, "All the lights are on now."

The fuel problem with the left engine was getting critical. Captain Pearson decided perhaps the attitude of the aircraft would enable the boost pumps to better feed the fuel.

"It's in the pump, I would think level would be to your advantage" exclaimed the mechanic.

BEEP, BEEP, BEEP, BEEP, the warning signal again for low fuel pressure accompanied by two red lights. The beep warning was now drowned out by a loud bong. This is probably the most dreaded sound on a 767; it signifies an engine is in the process of stopping.

Captain Pearson would, in the next 20 minutes, earn all the pay he would normally receive from a lifetime of boring flying. The engine shutdown checklist was performed and Captain Bob requested Maurice to advise Winnipeg "we want the crash trucks out."

Within a few minutes, Captain Pearson would be confronted with a real dilemma. The other engine started to display fuel problems and shut itself down. They were just descending through 26,000 feet and the chance of stretching the glide to Winnipeg was looking mighty grim. First Officer Quintal was doing all the computing and checks while Captain Pearson flew the aircraft and handled the radios.

Captain: "What's the best speed here for descent?"

Co-pilot: "Make it 230."

The center radio gave the crew a progress report. "143 we show 65 miles from Winnipeg and approximately 45 miles from Gimli."

This emergency situation was almost too much to cope with. Here was a giant wide-bodied airliner passing through 26,000 feet with both engines dead. The instrument panel was blank and the only instruments available were an altimeter, air speed, stand by horizon, and a compass that was of little use. The crew had very limited experience in the 767. Captain Pearson had just over 100 hours and First Officer Quintal just under 100 hours. To add to the problem, they were on top of a cloud deck and could not see the ground. If that wasn't more than enough to turn the average pilot white with fear, they would not be able to use flaps and the gear would have to be lowered by emergency means. I think you get the picture.

There was a ram air turbine that extended just aft of the main landing gear. This device consists of a small propeller that operates a hydraulic pump that enables the use of the three primary flight controls. With the two engines gone, the normal cockpit lights extinguished, and as Pearson tells it later, "That cockpit became the darkest place in the world."

Flight 143 was descending as slowly as possible, without sacrificing any of its precious air speed. Captain Pearson keyed his mike and almost as calmly as if he were making a routine report said, "Center, this is a MAYDAY, and we require a vector (steer) onto the closest available runway. We are down to 22,000 feet. Both engines have failed due to, looks like fuel starvation, and we are on emergency instruments. "… Now please give us a vector to the nearest runway."

Talk about cool, this crew certainly had it.

Back in the cabin, the flight attendants were preparing the 61 passengers for a crash landing. There were teenagers on board, businessmen, some elderly folks, and young mothers with their infant babies. The most able-bodied people were positioned by the emergency escape windows and were instructed on their operation. The air noise was all that was audible in the cabin as the silent giant descended steadily toward near certain destruction. The passengers were in good hands and remained relatively calm.

"People were very afraid and some were crying silently, but there was no panic." That was the statement by Flight Attendant Anne Swift as she told the accident investigation board.

Captain Pearson was having difficulty trying to follow the tiny magnetic compass (similar to the ones you find in automobiles). By using the cloud deck below him as a reference, he was able to follow the controller instructions. The cockpit of a 767 is quite wide and the standby compass is situated right in the middle. It was nearly impossible to see the tiny instrument while sitting in a normal position.

As he stated later in an interview: "I steered by the clouds underneath us. I would ask Winnipeg Center for a heading and they would say left to 220 degrees, and I would turn left about that much, judging by the clouds, and then I'd ask Winnipeg how my heading was using the clouds. I kept eyeballing it."

Co-pilot Quintal was making some rapid calculations. He estimated that in the last 10 miles they had descended 10,000 feet. Quntal exclaimed, "Bob, we'll never make Winnipeg."

A quick call to the center prompted the alert controller to suggest a landing at Gimli, an abandoned training field formerly used by the Royal Canadian Air Force. Co-pilot Quintal, at one time, was based at this strip so he was able to recall the adjacent terrain. They were now 12 miles out from Gimli and just overheading the western shore of Lake Winnipeg. Captain Pearson queried the controller concerning the airport at Gimli. His reply was "Use the right-hand runway, 6,800 feet long."

After crossing the south end of Lake Winnipeg, they broke clear of the clouds and began searching for an unfamiliar, abandoned airport.

"There it is!" exclaimed Maurice.

Captain Pearson would now put to use his extensive gliding experience. At least on a glider, you always have spoilers (a lift-killing device) and the glide ratio is fantastic. The 767 has a sink rate similar to a bucket of cement. Captain Pearson knew that he would have only one chance at the field and it had better be right the first time. Bob was about six miles out and the beautiful concrete strip at Gimli was right where it should be. He called: "Maurice, drop the gear, and call out the air speed. I can't take my eyes off the strip so you take care of all the checks in here."

"You got it Bob."

Now they were a scant four miles away from the runway and Bob stated, "It looks like we're a little high. Do you think we could make a 360?"

Maurice answered, "It looks like we may be a little low for that."

Captain Pearson answered, "I'm going to slip this beauty in. I'm sure the passengers won't appreciate it, but it's the only safe thing to do."

Bob had many hours of "slipping" to his credit when he flew a Super Cub as a glider-towing plane. A slip consists of banking in one direction and applying rudder in the opposite. This sends the airplane sideways through the air, accompanied by a rapid descent.

Captain Pearson was using the runway for a reference and manipulating the controls in such a fashion that he was able to establish a slipping final approach. The runway was looking good, and all the rubber tire marks on it made Bob think that they were caused by landing aircraft.

Maurice remarked, "Looking good, speed 180, five hundred feet above." Bob had never landed a 767 without engines or flaps, but in a few seconds he would be trying it.

As the end of the beautiful strip passed under the aircraft, Bob started to break the glide. Only a few more feet and it would be over. With the wheel nearly all the way back, he heard the familiar squeals as the tires contacted the runway. Bob hit the brakes, and for the first time, he saw a frightening sight. At the far end of the runway he saw people and cars scurrying to safety. Now he knew that the rubber marks on the runway were caused by dragsters. He had landed on their strip. As the breaks took hold, the nose slammed to the runway, making a loud bang and producing a vivid shower of sparks. The nose wheel was never fully down and with the application of brakes, it retracted back to where it came from.

Captain Pearson had done it! He had made a perfect landing in the normal spot, about 800 feet down from the approach end of the runway. Now all that remained was a safe evacuation. When the aircraft stopped, there was still 3,000 feet of unused runway left. A grateful planeload of passengers showed their appreciation by applauding loudly. The emergency chutes were deployed and the cabin crew, consisting of three female flight attendants and one male, supervised a near-perfect evacuation. I say near-perfect because I must be honest. One elderly lady sprained her ankle going down a near-vertical rear chute. When the passengers and crew were all clear of the aircraft, Captain Pearson and chief Flight Attendant Robert Desjardins went back into the cabin to be certain that everyone was out. By now, the cockpit was filling with dense smoke caused by the friction of the nose scraping the concrete. The two men left the aircraft, and as soon as they reached the ground, some of the auto racers were gathering around the giant, wounded bird. "Can we be of any assistance, the leader asked?"

Captain Bob replied, "Do you have any fire extinguishers?"

"We'll bring them over and we'll get this fire in the nose squelched."

Here's an amusing story. The Air Canada maintenance crew from Winnipeg who were driving down to Gimli to repair their damaged aircraft, had a small problem with their truck: it ran out of gas. Not a good day for the airline.

Let's review some of Air Canada's operating discrepancies.

A few months prior to this incident, Air Canada was not faring too well, safety wise, to their normal public image. There were two DC-9s that ran off runways, and there was a terrible fire on board a DC-9 that landed in Cincinnati. The airline was only too willing to tell the public that the company was not at fault in any of the accidents. I'll let you be the judge.

When Captain Pearson was trained by Air Canada on the 767, he was one of the first crews to go through their simulator program. Unlike United Airlines, who also flies the 767, Air Canada decided not to wait until they received their two-seat trainer, and they continued to train a two-man crew in a simulator that was made for three. Nearly all of the instruments and switches were not where they would normally be on a real airplane. How could they be, with a complete engineer's panel in the simulator and no engineer on the real aircraft? The ground school training was not the best. It was a case of a new instructor teaching new students and there was never any discussion on lowering the landing gear by emergency means.

The following are just a few of the operational discrepancies discovered by the Canadian Board of Inquiry concerning their final report on the Gimli incident.

"The inquiry received documents from Air Canada on March 20, 1985, now marked as Exhibit 261, which reveal that the two newest 767s aircraft 611 and 612 have both experienced many snags in the fuel system including, on some 21 occasions, blank fuel gauges. From October 1, 1984 to March 4, 1985, there were 48 snags recorded in relation to the fuel system on these two aircraft."

They were still having fuel problems two years after the incident. Here are a few of the airlines that have trained fuelers to service their aircraft: United, British Airways, TWA, Lufthansa, Swissair, Delta, and American all have fuel personnel that are responsible to the captain for accurate fueling. Air Canada had no such trained people.

At the time of the incident, Air Canada had a large supply of "one" fuel processor (unit that was inoperative on the Gimli aircraft) to supply a fleet of 12 airplanes. The MEL at Air Canada was most misleading. Nearly all airlines list the exact number of components that are required for dispatch. Air Canada's MEL has the majority of the precise numbers missing. This is the way they get to bend the rules.

The cabin crew's training on the 767 consisted of a movie that was displayed concerning the emergency equipment on board. This was shown to cabin crews who were qualified on the Boeing 747. There was no hands-on training.

It is clear that management, in their quest to save money by eliminating the second officer (engineer), had failed to adequately train the crew of two on just how to accomplish the work of the missing engineer.

On the older aircraft, there were very few working parts to the vertical speed indicator. It worked strictly by differential air pressure. Now the same instrument on the 767 takes the input of 38 different computers. In the electronics bay of the 767, there are over 100 computers. They are all down there chattering away to each other, and as Captain Pearson says jokingly, "I doubt if even Boeing knows who is supposed to be talking to whom."

Captain Pearson and his crew were put through the ringer by management and the Board of Inquiry. He was on the stand for five days straight, and he said, "It was easy to see that Air Canada wanted to use me as a scapegoat."

The crew was held out of service for three months while the powers to be decided the fate of a most heroic crew. It was leaked to the press that Captain Pearson would have to go back to flying as a First Officer for six months, and his co-pilot, Maurice, would be suspended for two weeks. Bob heard this news in his car while he was driving home. He said, "I nearly drove off the road when I heard the news over my car radio." He had a talk with his boss and told him, "You will have to fire me, because I won't go back to co-pilot."

Captain Pearson was assured that it was all a big mistake. He would have to take a few check rides in the "box" and he would be back on the line.

The people that count in this business are your peers. Captain Pearson was awarded a trophy by the Canadian Airline Pilots Association for a job well done. His fellow pilots, mechanics, and cabin attendants all hold Pearson in high esteem. He has received hundreds of congratulatory letters from all over the world, and on February 20, 1995, an excellent television documentary was shown depicting the whole Gimli incident.

Each year on the 23rd of July, the date of the mishap, the employees all throw a big bash for the crew of the "Gimli Glider."

By now you are probably wondering what makes Captain Bob tick. He is a friendly chap and looks like a pilot should. He is a rugged individual who stands 5 feet 10 inches and weighs about 170 pounds. He is a great outdoorsman and is on the first string of the Air Canada hockey team. He is presently in Switzerland where he will represent Air Canada in competition with the Swissair hockey team.

I have been around aviation for 50 years and I have never in my life heard of any pilot who could even come close to matching the airmanship of Captain Robert Pearson, a pilot's pilot.

CHAPTER 14

▼

HOLDOVER TIME

On March 22, 1992, the weather throughout the northeast United States was terrible. Blowing snow and poor visibility conditions were prevalent and LaGuardia Airport in New York City was having long traffic delays caused by icing.

USAir's Flight 405 was under the command of 44-year-old Captain Wallace J. Majure. His logbook showed a total of over 9,000 hours, 2,200 of which was in the F-28. He was accompanied by 30-year-old First Officer John J. Rachuba, who had a total of 4,507 hours in the air. This crew was on the last day of a four-day trip and had just departed Jacksonville, Florida, with LaGuardia as their destination. Because of ATC delays, they arrived at LaGuardia one hour and six minutes behind schedule.

The aircraft was de-iced with type I fluid (a mixture of 50/50 water/glycol). Because of a breakdown on one of the de-icing trucks, the aircraft was unable to push back from the gate for twenty minutes. Captain Majure wisely requested that the aircraft be de-iced again. This action was completed at 2100.

First Officer Rachuba keyed his mike. "Ground USAir four oh five's ready to taxi."

The sequence controller replied: "USAir four oh five turn left on the inner and hold short of echo."

"Left inner hold short of echo USAir four oh five".

As the captain advanced the thrust lever, 66,295 pounds of cargo fuel and 51 passengers started out on a night they will never forget. The crew was in good spirits and conversing about how some of the better airports conduct their de-icing nearer to the takeoff runway.

First Officer Rachuba: "You see that car wash (aircraft wash) they have at Denver? They like mount it to the hard stands. That's the ideal way of doing it."

Captain: "Yup".

First Officer: "They oughta have somethin' like that—this is New York you know. They oughta have that out there."

Captain: "Yup."

First Officer: Zip, Zip, Zip man just you know. Put it on the tab. Just cruise on out and take off.

Captain: "That's really the only sure fire safe way to do it."

The crew was discussing the fact that LaGuardia should have a de-icing facility near the end of the runway. This would eliminate having to sit on the taxiway in the snow and hope that your wings were clean enough for a safe takeoff. The FAA should have initiated such a facility years ago. Just one more crash and it might bring them to their senses.

At 2133:55 the tower called. "USAir four oh five taxi into position and hold one three."

First Officer: "Position and hold one three USAir four oh five."

He then transmitted to the cabin through the public address (PA): "Ladies and gentleman, from the flight deck we're now number one for departure and we would like our flight attendants to please be seated. Thank you."

Tower: "USAir four oh five runway one three cleared for takeoff."

First Officer: "Cleared for takeoff USAir four oh five."

This transmission came through at 2134. Over thirty minutes had elapsed from de-icing to takeoff. That's eighteen minutes past the safe holdover time for the de-icing fluid to "do its thing." As the power levers were pushed forward, a total of 19,000 pounds of thrust came to life as 405 started its final journey down the 7,000-foot slush-covered runway (this runway is barely long enough when it's dry).

I would like First Officer Rachuba to relate to you what went on in the cockpit. The following is taken from the June 29, 1992, issue of Aviation Week, and was written by James T. McKenna:

"The takeoff began smoothly, Rachuba said, with a few minor errors on his part. He failed, as the nonflying pilot, to call out when the aircraft reached 80KT. After Majure called it, Rachuba repeated it. After he called V1 at 110KT, Rachuba said, "being a creature of habit, I made a mistake. I called VR." V1 and VR normally are equal for F-28 takeoffs.

"There was a notably smoother transition from roll to flight," Rachuba said. "Just as I was about to call V2 and the aircraft was about to climb out of ground effect, there was a single, pronounced buffet, and I felt separation of lift and cessation of climb and a dramatic roll to the left."

He next felt a "sinking sensation through the seat of my pants," apparently at the moment the left wingtip struck the runway. He said Majure's thought was to find a safe place to crash.

"With the aircraft still rolling left, Rachuba said, he spotted a clear area to his right that he did not believe Majure could see. He inputted right rudder and felt Majure do the same. He said they succeeded in turning the aircraft away from the water and touched down flat." Then he spotted the orange-and-white checkered pump house directly in front of the aircraft.

"I remember thinking after the first impact, that wasn't so bad," he said. That impact likely was the left wing being sheared as it plowed down 18 steel I-beams supporting the instrument landing system localizer platform. The aircraft then struck the pump house. "Then I saw a fireball on the right side of the aircraft. I felt a freak sensation of weightlessness."

The next thing he remembers is struggling to free himself in the overturned, flooded cockpit.

Twenty-five passengers died, as well as the captain and one of the flight attendants. A $13 million aircraft was totally destroyed.

I am pleased to report that the probable cause of this accident was not the usual pilot error. This time it was the FAA. Here's a partial quote from the NTSB Probable Cause: "The National Transportation Board determines

that the probable cause of this accident was the failure of the airline industry and the Federal Aviation Administration to provide flight crews with
procedures, requirements, and criteria compatible with departure delays in
conditions conducive to airframe icing."

This chapter deals with all kinds of icing, but before we get into that
subject, I would like to discuss the various objects that USAir 405 hit while
breaking up.

To begin with, LaGuardia Airport has always been one of the worst
airports around. It was built on a garbage dump in Flushing Bay and all
its runways are minimal. Around the perimeter of the airport, adjacent to
the bay, sits a tall dike. It was built to keep the water from the bay from
flooding the airport. When there is a steady rain, the runways would be
submerged if it were not for the pump house adjacent to runway 13. It is
highly advisable to have a clear area on each side of the runway so that a
bad landing or takeoff need not end in disaster.

The FAA has proclaimed that a clear area of 250 feet on either side of
the runway is quite sufficient. Well, this minimal safety zone is nothing
short of a farce. Aircraft that land and take off at speeds well over 100 miles
an hour can eat up a lot of real estate before coming to rest. ICAO Annex
14 Aerodromes Vol 1. states that there should be a minimum of a 400-foot
clear zone on each side of the runway. In other words, you are nearly twice
as safe in Europe or Canada should your aircraft veer off the runway. Let's
review the objects that Flight 405 traversed on its way into the bay.

The first collision was with the VASI lights. Next, it hit the localizer
platform which was atop 18 steel I beams. Then came the pump house,
and last but not least, the dike before the bay. These objects all should have
been frangible (breakable on contact) but none were. We will never know
how many lives these nonfrangible obstructions may have taken.

Now that these objects have all been replaced, how many were updated
to nonfrangible? The localizer ground plane was replaced with the same
steel nonfrangible I beams. The VASI lights are the same and the dike is
still there. The pump house is the only killer that was placed underground.
Talk about not learning by experience. The NTSB did not like the nonfrangible replacements but they had a soft spot for the "feds." In their

report regarding the crash on page 71, I found the following: "Although the localized ground plain antenna, pump house, and dike did not meet the criteria of AC 150/5300-13, Appendix 8 of the ICAO 8.6.1, the Safety Board understands the difficulties that LaGuardia faces in that regard, SINCE THE AIRPORT IS PHYSICALLY RESTRAINED BY SIZE, LOCATION, AND WATER BOUNDARIES" (capitals mine). What they are politely saying is, it was built in the DC-3 era and never has or never will be a safe jet port. At least three other crashes come to mind concerning nonfrangible objects that managed to dig holes into aircraft before their final stop.

On June 2, 1999, an American Airlines MD-82 was landing on a rainswept runway in Little Rock, Arkansas. The Captain, who was also a chief pilot, broke many rules by making this landing. It is against company regulations to land at an airport with thunderstorms present. Landing on a wet runway with a crosswind of over 20 knots is not allowed. The winds at the airport were reported to be as high as 87 mph and a crosswind of 50 mph. The aircraft skidded and turned the length of the runway, coming to rest at the far end where it crashed into runway approach lights that tore the aircraft into three sections. Nine people died mainly because the FAA still allows nonfrangible structures at or near airport runways.

Now, to get back to all types of icing and their effects on aircraft. Some of you may not have the slightest idea of why frost and ice must be removed from an aircraft before flight. If you will bear with me, I will try to explain why it is vitally important to take off with the "clean aircraft" concept.

Most aircraft are certified without any tests to determine what effects a thin coating of frost might do to a wing. So, with that in mind, it behooves pilots to be sure that their wings are "squeaky clean." It is a fact that snow, ice, or frost forming on the upper surface of a wing can reduce the lift by as much as 30 percent and increase the drag by 40 percent. The most minute traces of frost on the upper surface of a wing may keep it from ever leaving the ground.

A wing gets its lift because the upper surface has more of a camber than the lower part. As the wing speeds through the air, on takeoff, the air going over the upper surface is forced to speed up and this causes the pressure above it to decrease. When this happens, along with the downwash off the trailing edge, the giant beast leaves the ground. Any, and I mean any, surface contaminates can decrease the lifting force. This includes a thin layer of frost, de-icing fluid, and even rain. It is not the added weight of the contaminant, although it does have some effect; instead, it is the rough surface that spoils the lift of a wing. When you take off in an aircraft with a contaminated wing, you become a test pilot, flying in an aircraft with a new wing shape that has never before been tested.

There are some airliners that have what is known as a "hard-wing," one that has no leading edge high lift devices such as slats. I am sure you have noticed these devices, just ahead of the leading edge of the wings that protrude on landing and takeoff. These wings ahead of the main wing are used to aid the airflow over the wings at slow speeds. Ninety-seven percent of all the major airlines use aircraft with these lift devices. That leaves three percent that have aircraft with "hard wings" such as the F-28, early DC-9s, and BAC 1-11s. The only reason I mention the difference in design of a "hard-wing" or one with lifting devices is because the FAA claims the "hard-wing" is more adversely affected by any ice contamination and must be checked more carefully. I flew the BAC 1-11 "hard-wing" for over 10,000 hours and found it to be a gem in all conditions.

Another important item is the location of the engines. Jets have engines all over the place: under the wings, in the center of the tail, and on either side of the fuselage near the tail. The aircraft with tail-mounted engines can cause quite a problem if ice breaks off the wings and gets ingested in the rear engine. On these types of jets, it is doubly important to have clean wings and a clean fuselage.

While we are on the subject of keeping things clean, who do you suppose is responsible to ensure that the wings are clear? The fellows who man the de-icing equipment are the most likely candidates because they are the nearest to the wings. But they are not the ones responsible. The captain, even though he is stuck in the cockpit well forward of the wings, is the one held responsible.

The FAA regulation pertinent to icing conditions is as follows: "121.629 Operation in icing conditions. (b) No person may take off an aircraft when frost, snow, or ice is adhering to the wings, control surfaces, or propellers of the aircraft." I believe that the FAA forgot to mention a very important part of the aircraft: the tail, which is nearly as important as the wings.

That puts it plainly enough. Yet I have seen airliners taxiing out with a good coating of snow that may not blow off. If the "feds" would spend more of their time saving lives instead of shuffling paper in their nice warm offices, we would all be better off. They should get in their cars and go out to the airliners waiting in line for takeoff. Once the word got out that the "feds" are checking the aircraft for ice, there would be a lot more vigilant crews commanding our airliners. Some captains will do anything to keep the flight on schedule and help to secure their position in the company. I am not suggesting that this was the case with the LaGuardia crash. That crew was doing what the letter of the law required, but the law was faulty.

Snow and sleet are not the only causes of ice developing on aircraft wings. It can be caused from inside the wings. A few years ago, a Scandinavian Airliner MD-80 lost both engines after takeoff but managed a successful crash landing in an open field. Ice had formed on the upper wing surface before takeoff. During the liftoff, the flexing of the wings caused the ice to break up and it was ingested in both the rear mounted engines. The fuel in the wings comes in close proximity to the aircraft skin. Flight at altitude causes the fuel to become cooled. When the aircraft lands with the cold-soaked fuel inside the wings, it acts like a refrigerator and cools the outside air sufficiently to cause frost or ice to form. This ice could develop when there is no visible moisture present.

Turbine anti-icing systems use hot bled air from the turbines to heat the leading edge of the wings, tail, and cowling. Smaller surfaces such as windshields and static sources are heated electrically. The problem with all these heaters is that the majority of them is not designed to be used on the ground.

During the past fifteen years, there have been eight major takeoff accidents/incidents involving commercial aviation. According to NTSB, over the past ten years, ice has been a factor in twenty-four crashes causing the deaths of 138 people.

After each crash, the "feds" tried to substantiate their existence by offering a few safety-related suggestions. In 1982, after ice contributed to the crash of an Air Florida Boeing 737 at Washington National Airport, the "feds" drafted an advisory circular (AC) concerning icing hazards. In case you are wondering what an advisory circular is, it is a paper with ADVICE (capitals mine) from the FAA on how to perform a certain task. There are thousands of these circulars in existence covering subjects on how to build a runway or how to safely evacuate an aircraft. As the name implies, they are advisory in nature, and have no hard or fast rules. Having the FAA put out advisory circulars so that pilots will be cognizant of their information is really next to useless. The only way to get a copy of one of these gems is to write or call the Department of Transportation in Washington, D.C. And believe me, there are only a small number of pilots who have ever seen or heard of these publications.

Here is a quote from an AC (advisory circular): "The FAA issues advisory circulars to inform the aviation public in a systematic way of NONREGULATORY (capitals mine) material of interest. Unless incorporated into a regulation by reference, the contents of an advisory circular are not binding on the public."

So you can see, for the FAA to say that they issued an AC after a crash is pretty near saying they did nothing.

In 1988, after a Continental DC-10 crashed on takeoff because of ice, an icing hazard conference convened to discuss what to do about aircraft ice. Little or nothing came from this meeting other than to reissue the 1982 AC as "Must Read" material. Since then, five airline crashes have been caused by ice but the USAir LaGuardia crash finally got their attention.

In May of 1992, the FAA sponsored an international conference on ground icing held in Reston, Virginia. It drew over 800 interested parties from all corners of the world. What prompted this meeting? The crash of USAir Flight 405 at LaGuardia, two months prior to this assembly. Finally, after over fifty years of commercial aviation, a few good proposed rules were developed.

Each airline must have a properly trained de-icing crew; during the time that a given de-icing operation will keep the aircraft protected, there must be a radio frequency for use between the de-icing crew and the captain; and if the holdover time expires before takeoff, a hands-on wing check must be made. The only aircraft that always must have a hands-on check are those with "hard-wings." The other aircraft, which comprise 97 percent of the entire airline fleet, will not require this close, highly important check.

Well, this is a definite step in the right direction but it comes after too many ice-attributed crashes. It is interesting to note that none of these proposed regulations apply to smaller aircraft, those with fewer than thirty seats.

If any pilots need a helping hand, it is the part 135 operators (small airliners). They are up and down far more than the big boys, so they are subjected to many more takeoffs than the part 121 (larger airliners). They usually have less experience than the larger carriers, and they come under many of the same flight regulations as the trunk carriers. The FAA says that there has only been one ice-attributed crash on a smaller airline so these de-icing regulations are not as important for them. It took fifteen weather-related crashes for the larger carriers before something concrete was done about de-icing. After fourteen more crashes, perhaps the 135 carriers will be treated like the rest of the world.

Let's discuss the feasibility of a captain being responsible for decision-making as to whether his wings are fit to fly. The de-icing operation usually takes place at the gate or at a specified taxiway. The aircraft door must, obviously, be closed or the de-icing fluid would enter the cabin. Since de-icing is accomplished as close as possible to pushback, there isn't time to get out and check the wings. If you are out on a taxiway being de-iced, there is no way that you could exit the aircraft as the jetway is a long way off. It is interesting to note that Orly Airport in France has been de-icing airplanes near the end of the runway for many years. The United States should learn a good lesson from this.

I was extremely lucky to have flown the BAC 1-11. It was a gem to fly and more than once, I have extended the steps just prior to takeoff in order to give the wings one last hands-on check. Most larger jets have no way to the ground except at the gate. When I flew fighters for the USAF, there was ALWAYS a mechanic at the end of the runway to check over my aircraft.

It was called the "last chance" check. All commercial airports should have personnel in the takeoff area to check the aircraft, not just for ice but for any other discrepancies that might have developed since startup. Of course, the ATA would throw a fit because this operation might cause the most hated word in their vocabulary: DELAY.

The majority of today's larger jets has swept-back wings that make the likelihood of checking them from the cockpit next to impossible. Picture, if you will, the task of today's cockpit crews. They have de-iced at the gate and have gotten the word from the de-icing crew that the wings are clean. They have to take the crew's word for it because the snowfall makes the wings difficult to see. They taxi to the takeoff runway. Because of traffic, it has taken ten minutes. The aircraft has been sprayed with the cheaper fluid, type I, and now there is only five more minutes' holdover time left. The trip is already late departing, and there are a good number of close connecting passengers at the next landing. As captain of the airplane, you turn on your wing inspection lights, but through the moisture-covered cockpit window, you see very little. So you open it and stick your head out. Now you see more of the wing, but not clearly enough to see if you have a thin layer of ice or not. Remember, the book says no ice is allowed and you still haven't received takeoff clearance. Now you are down to three minutes for the clear-wing regulation. You are number two to take the active and you feel that you really should go back in the cabin and get a closer look at those all-important wings. Sure as hell, if you leave your seat to go back, you'll miss the takeoff clearance. The intensity of the snow is increasing and now you are beginning to really worry about those wings. The aircraft ahead of you departed and the tower tells you: "Taxi into position and hold."

The monkey is squarely on your back. Going through your mind are the following problems:

1. I am already late

2. About those wings

3. The runway is short, no chance for a rejected takeoff

4. Holdover time has expired

5. If I don't leave soon I'll never make my daughter's graduation party

6. I am already late

7. About those wings

8. If I taxi back, I'll lose my place in line

9. About those wings

All these thoughts, and more, are decisions that the captain must make. I can tell you personally about how I coped with it. If I had ANY doubts at all about making a safe takeoff, I did not go. Of course, I would have to put up with harassment from my company but that was a small price to pay for not becoming a statistic.

It is very difficult to check the condition of the wings, but for the crew of a high-wing aircraft, it is impossible. All the talk so far is about clean wings. No thought has been given to clean tails that are nearly as important as the wings. What about the snow on the roof? It, too, can blow back and cause havoc with your rear-mounted engines.

De-icing Fluids

There are two types of fluids that are used on moisture-contaminated air-craft: type I and type II. Type I, which is widely used in the United States and is known in the trade as "glycol," is usually mixed with water and sprayed from a truck that heats it to about 140 degrees F. This type of fluid is known as a de-icing agent. It does little to prevent new ice from forming but it disperses what is already built up. The cost to spray a small jet averages well over six hundred dollars, and the expense of de-icing a 747 costs over three times as much as the little fellow. To purchase a single spray truck is in the neighborhood of $150,000. This gives you a small idea of why flying is not a cheap way to go.

Mixture type II is by far the best. It is composed of a much more viscose fluid. After de-icing the aircraft with type I, type II should be applied. This fluid is three times as costly as type I; it is also many times more effective.

It is used mostly in Europe and Canada. US airlines that use it are Delta and Federal Express. The following are the numbers of gallons of de-icing fluids used annually at various airports in North America: Chicago O'Hare International Airport, 2 million; Detroit Wayne County Airport, 1.5 million; Pittsburgh International Airport, 900,000; Denver International Airport, 500,000; Buffalo International Airport, 200,000; and Winnipeg International Airport, 150,000.

Blue Ice

The following is a quote from a 1990 NTSB News Digest: The NTSB reported an American Airlines Boeing 727 flying over Las Cruces, New Mexico, on April 16, 1985, and a Northwest Airlines B-727 flying over Madison, Florida, on January 4, 1990. Both had engines separate from the fuselage when blue ice struck the No. 3 engine.

In each instance, the engine fell to the ground but the flight landed safely. An Eastern Airlines B-727 was forced to shut down its No. 3 engine on a flight from Atlanta to Sarasota, Florida, on February 12, 1990, after blue ice struck the engine.

The NTSB said the FAA also addressed the problem for B-737 series 300 and 400 aircraft after a Continental Airlines B-737 shut down an engine that had ingested blue ice during a flight on January 16, 1989.

A quote from a February, 1992 Boeing Flight Operations Review has this to say about blue ice: "There have been 33 in-flight "blue ice" incidents involving Boeing commercial air carrier aircraft: 21 on B-727s and 12 on 737s."

What is blue ice? Next time you use the restroom on an airliner, you might be contributing to the loss of an engine. Far too often, the "O" ring that seals the toilet leaks, and the blue liquid in the bowl seeps out onto the lower fuselage. At altitudes where the temperature is always many degrees below zero, these leaks can continue to build and make a giant ice ball. Some of these chunks have weighed as much as 35 pounds. When a piece this heavy dislodges and is propelled backward by the 550-mile-per-hour slipstream and enters the engine, it will tear the engine from its mount.

Look out below. You know that old saying "When the s_ _ _ hits the fan." Well, this is about as realistic as it gets.

Most of these leaks are noticeable and should be picked up on the walk around (crew must make a visual inspection of the aircraft before boarding) because the traces of the blue can be seen streaking down the belly of the aircraft.

By now you are probably tired of hearing about ice so we will get on with the next subject. But before we do that, I would like to leave you with a most important thought. If you are sitting in a seat over the wing, and you see any ice on it, fluid leaking from it, or panels that are loose, PLEASE tell the flight attendant who will relay your message to the flight deck. You are in the best position to view the wings. Don't be bashful. The life you save might be your own.

CHAPTER 15

▼

HOSTILE ENVIRONMENT

The mysteries of the sky, the Northern Lights, meteor trails, lightning, as well as the beautiful cloud galleons drifting peacefully across a clear blue sky, long have intrigued man.

True to nature, the loveliest of the species is usually the most treacherous. On a clear summer day when the sun heats the earth, it produces updrafts of varying intensity. At a given point, the rising column of air is cooled and condensation can be seen in the form of a cloud. If the air continues to rise, the water vapor will continue to pump out fleecy white clouds. Vertical growth will continue until the updraft can no longer support the water droplets, and they fall to earth as rain.

Not all vertically developed clouds mature into full-blown thunderstorms, but on a hot, humid, summer day. These graceful clouds stand an excellent chance of expanding as high as 60,000 feet and can cover an area of 50 miles or more.

As the water droplets fall to the earth, they drag air along with them that causes downdrafts. When this downward rush of air hits the ground, it spreads out horizontally, producing strong and gusty winds. The energy released in a full-fledged thunderstorm has the potential destructive force of an atomic bomb.

Hail is formed by water droplets that have been propelled upward in the cloud until their weight increases sufficiently to overcome the upward current of air, and they start their downward journey. Many times, the hailstones will make numerous cycles, up and down, increasing in size until they might fall to earth as big as tennis balls.

While the thunderstorm is in its developing stages, it can be an extremely dangerous place for an aircraft to be, in or near this boiling mass of destructiveness. Within these clouds can be found ice, lightning, severe vertical currents (no such thing as an air pocket), hail, and by far the worst thunderstorm phenomenon, turbulence.

While lightning has set many a forest on fire and damaged property, it usually causes little damage to aircraft. Lightning strikes on aircraft are usually the cause of very small holes in the skin and perhaps a problem with the radios. During 1994, there were over 30 aircraft that were hit by lightning. In 1995, we did a little better; only 24 planes were spiked.

On August l, 1983, the strongest microburst ever recorded swept across the runways at Andrews Air Force Base, Maryland. The force uprooted trees and tore the roofs off several of the base buildings. A scant six minutes earlier, Air Force One landed safely with the President and his party. No aircraft could safely traverse such a perilous storm. While microbursts have always been a weather phenomenon, they were not identified until 1977.

On July 9, 1982, Pan American World Airways Flight 759, a Boeing 727 on a regularly scheduled flight from Miami, Florida, to Las Vegas, Nevada, was boarding passengers at its intermediate stop in New Orleans, Louisiana. The crew's weight and size resembled that of the players on a pro-football team. Captain Kenneth L. McCullus, age 45, was a strapping 6 foot one inch tall and he weighed 190 pounds. Nearly all of his hours of airline time were in the Boeing 727. First Officer Donald G. Pierce, age 32, was 6 feet 2 inches tall and tipped the scales at 225 pounds. Second Officer Leo B. Noon, age 60, out of his 19,904 total hours, amassed 10,508 hours in the 727.

The entire crew formerly flew for National Airlines before the company was purchased by Pan Am, so there was definitely animosity in the cockpit. I say that because whenever a carrier merges with another, there often is a certain amount of resentment among the crews. Each one thinks that his airline is the best. I certainly never felt that way when Mohawk Airlines, the world's worst, merged with USAir, one of the best.

The weather at New Orleans was typical for a hot sultry July day. The ceiling was a measured 4,000 feet, overcast, visibility ... 2 miles, heavy rain showers, haze, wind 070 degrees at 14 knots gusting to 20 knots, and cumulonimbus overhead (thunderstorm). With 137 passengers and a crew of 8, the aircraft grossed out at 71,139 pounds, just 861 pounds under maximum allowable weight for runway 10. Critical engine speed (VI) and rotate speed (VR) were calculated at 138 knots, and safety speed of 151 knots would be (V2) speed. The doors were secured and the engines started. With a wave-off from the ground crew, Co-pilot Pierce keyed his mike: "Clipper 759 taxi, and we need runway 10."

"Clipper 759, roger. Taxi to runway one zero amend initial altitude 4,000 ah, departure frequency will be 120.6."

"20.6 and 4,000 Clipper 759 what is your wind now?"

"Wind zero four zero at eighteen."

Captain McCullus released the parking brake and Pan Am 759 started to taxi out to runway 10. While underway, Captain Ken ran through the pre-takeoff briefing. "I'll be a heavy, ah, take-off so, ah, if we have to take, ah, if we have to abort for any reason, you'll have the throttles, get all we can out of 'em now so if we bust one (lose an engine) before VI, we'll stop and we'll, ah, stand on the brakes, Don.

Co-pilot: "Yes, sir."

Captain: "If it's, ah, past VI, go ahead and start dumping, Leo."

When the tower's ground controller found a break in the radio chatter, he broadcast the following pertinent message. "Winds 080 degrees at 17 and, ah, peak gusts that was, ah, 23 and we have, ah, low level wind shear alerts, all quadrants appears, the frontal passage overhead, right now we're right in the middle of everything."

At 2105:20, Captain McCullus picked up the PA microphone and said, "Ah, good afternoon ladies and gentlemen. We would like to welcome our New Orleans passengers aboard the continuation of, the continuation of Flight 759 to Las Vegas and San Diego. We'll be ready for takeoff momentarily. We'd like to ask you to please ensure that your seat belts are all buckled up. We'll be cruising at 31,000 feet to Las Vegas and estimated flying time is 3 hours and 10 minutes. After takeoff, we'll be maneuvering around, circumnavigating some, ah, some little thundershowers out there, so we would like to ask you folks to please remain in your seats. We thank you. Flight attendants, please secure the cabin."

The storm was now directly over the airport and the rain was extremely heavy. Don Pierce made this transmission to the tower. "Clipper 759—is ready."

Tower: "Clipper 759 maintain 2,000, fly runway heading, cleared for takeoff, Runway One Zero."

Co-pilot: "Maintain 2,000, runway heading, cleared for takeoff, Runway One Zero, Clipper 759."

Captain McCullus released the parking brake and taxied Clipper 759 onto the rain-swept, 10,000-foot runway.

Captain: "Takeoff checklist"

Co-pilot: "Takeoff check, transponders and DME on, cabin notification and lights."

Captain: "We got 'em."

Co-pilot: "Engineer's check."

Engineer: "Complete"

Co-pilot: "Configuration check."

Engineer: "Antiskid."

Captain: "Skid is on."

Engineer: "Speed brake."

Captain: "Forward"

Engineer: "Stabilizer trim."

Captain: "It's set."

Aircraft frequencies are similar to a telephone party-line system; all aircraft on the same channel can hear each other's conversation.

The tower contacted an Eastern Airliner and gave him a weather report. "And, ah, Eastern the wind, zero seven zero on seven heavy DC eight, er, ah, heavy, Boeing just landed, said a ten-knot wind shear at about a hundred feet on the final."

The Pan Am crew must have been in another world. The crew heard that there was a wind shear reported by the tower. There was a thunderstorm over the field and that made a takeoff against company policy. There was simply no reason to go, and with three men up front, you would think one of them would have mentioned it.

Now Pan Am 759 was in position and poised for takeoff.

Engineer: "Takeoff check complete."

Captain: "Okay, spooling up" (throttles going forward).

The co-pilot would be flying this leg, and it would be Captain McCullus' turn to act as the first officer. This is a standard airline practice to split every leg of the trip.

Captain: "Lights are on, engines spooling up, Leo."

Engineer: "Looking good."

Co-pilot: "Need the wipers (told the captain to turn on the windshield wipers).

Captain: "Eighty knots (this is a standard air speed callout to check any differences in their readings; also a check of all other instruments).

The aircraft was now well on its way down the storm-soaked runway and accelerating past 80 knots. The next call would be to commit to flight speed because there was insufficient runway left to stop the aircraft if an abort became necessary.

Captain: "VR positive climb."

Co-pilot: "Gear-up."

Captain: "V2."

She lifted-off 7,000 feet down a 10,228 foot runway, but seemed very reluctant to climb and wasn't even happy about maintaining altitude. All the engines were running perfectly, the crew was highly experienced, everything was done by the book, yet she didn't want to stay in the air. Why?

Captain McCullus shouted to his co-pilot: "Come on back, you're sinking Don.... Come on back,"

The sound of the ground proximity warning system activated with a loud "Whoop ... Whoop ... pull up."

At 2109:00, just two minutes after the takeoff was initiated, Pan Am Flight 759 had reached its highest altitude, a scant 95 feet. It started dropping lower and lower, and contacted a row of trees at 2,376 feet beyond the airport boundary, clipping them off at the 50-foot level.

Three hundred feet past the first contact, she hit another group of trees, shredding parts as she reached for the ground. The left wing struck the ground and ripped off. The remainder of the plane slammed into a group of 16 houses where it exploded and burned in a resounding tremor, killing all on board and 28 unsuspecting people on the ground.

The total in lawsuits exceeded the $4.5 billion mark. That would pay for all the Doppler radars needed to modernize all the airline airports in America.

"The NTSB determined that the probable cause of the accident was the airplane's encounter during the liftoff and initial climb phase of flight with a microburst-induced wind shear. This imposed a downdraft and a decreasing headwind, the effects of which the pilot would have had difficulty recognizing and reacting to it in time for the airplane's decent to be arrested before its impact with the trees. Contributing to the accident was the limited capabilities of current ground-base, low-level wind shear detection technology to provide definitive guidance for controllers and pilots for use in avoiding low-level wind shear encounters."

At the time of the accident, the control positions in the tower were operated by developmental (trainee) controllers. The radar screen in the radar room and the BRITE display in the tower could not accurately depict the outline of the thunderstorms because their radar is designed to display aircraft targets, not weather. The ground controller stated that he was aware of a wind shear condition, but it was not his job to disseminate such information. This job belonged to the tower's local controller (the man that issues takeoff and landing clearances).

Just prior to the crash, a Republic Flight 632 reported to the departure controller: "We had a wind shear on the runway." The departure controller acknowledged this important message but failed to alert the tower controllers. The Pan Am AOM (aircraft operating manual), the pilots' bible, stated, "When significant thunderstorm activity is approaching within 15 miles of the airport, the captain should consider conducting the departure or arrival from a different direction or delaying the takeoff or landing."

There is always pressure from the company to make schedule. Airlines, as a rule, aren't interested in how many regulations the pilots break. If the captain should decide to land when the weather is below limited, the company is most grateful just so long as there is no incident.

I have seen times when the weather was so bad you could barely see down the runway, and another company aircraft (Mohawk) took off and made it okay. In five minutes, I got a call over the company radio telling me that Flight 22 just took off and what was I waiting for? You can imagine what I had to say in answer to such a stupid question. I am not suggesting that Pan Am took off because of company pressure, but it's there, believe me.

To prove that the aviation industry is really still in its infancy, the NASA Contractor Report No. 156885 had some startling information concerning the effects of rain on aircraft aerodynamics. During the past few years, two research scientists of the University of Dayton Research Institute have developed a theory concerning the results of how heavy rain impacting an aircraft can penalize performance in three distinct ways:

1. A certain amount of rain adheres to the aircraft and thereby increases its weight.

2. The raindrops striking the aircraft take on the velocity of the aircraft and the exchange of momentum retards the velocity of the plane.

3. The rain forms a thick water film on the wings that roughens the wing's surface, thereby lessening the aerodynamic efficiency of the wing.

Number 3 is the most significant of the three penalties, not unlike snow or frost adhering to the wings. It was estimated that the added roughness to the wing surface can increase drag in the range of 10 to 20 percent, and decrease lift up to 10 percent. The higher the angle of attack (angle of wing to the relative wind) in taking off or landing, the greater the loss of lift.

After the accident, the FAA once again was awakened to an ongoing problem: wind shear. They began running tests on a wind shear plus Doppler microwave radar. They decided that this system is the best one for further development for the Next Generation Radar (NEXRAD). I wonder how many more people will die before some sort of efficient wind shear warning system is devised?

Presently, 70 of the major airports in the country have wind shear detectors. This system consists of five or more poles strategically placed around the perimeter of an airport. Each pole is equipped with a wind velocity and direction device that registers in the cab of the control tower. It is rather a complicated readout to decipher, especially when the traffic is building and the tower personnel are extremely busy. However, when the wind velocity at one pole differs by 15 or more knots from the center pole, it supposedly is brought to the attention of the flight crews. Even when the wind shear detectors located on the airport are operating normally, they are by no means infallible. At Dallas/Fort Worth Airport, the site of the worst wind shear accident in America where 136 people died on a Delta L-1011, there was no wind shear warning until five minutes after the crash. This is a good stop-gap system because it only tells you about wind shear close to the ground. What might be happening on final approach could be an entirely different story.

If you feel uneasy when flying through rough weather, it's a legitimate fear. During the past 20 years, crashes related to thunderstorm activity have killed more passengers than any other causes. Perhaps there are some of you that "haven't the foggiest" as to exactly what a wind shear is all about. Wind shear is an abrupt change in wind velocity, direction, or a combination of the two. In extreme cases, direction can change as much as 180 degrees and wind velocities as high as 100 mph have been recorded.

The phenomenon takes place in a very small area, perhaps less than one-half mile. A well-developed thunderstorm will propel a downward column of air and rain that will strike the ground at a great speed. As an aircraft enters the outer limits of the microburst, the air that bounces off the ground will cause the aircraft to climb. As the plane approaches the center of the downdraft, the intensity of the rain hits its peak and the aircraft is forced toward the ground. At this point in the microburst, there will be a loss of altitude and air speed. If the pilot is quick, he can apply maximum power and pull back on the yoke until he is near a stall (stick shaker reacts). With a lot of luck, he may keep from hitting the ground. But if the pilot has no idea he is in such a dangerous predicament, it might be his and your last flight.

Wind shear is not something that you can see; when the rain is pounding your aircraft, you just hope it will stop soon and be past the noisy area.

Airliners all are equipped with weather radar; however, it is not capable of pointing out minute microbursts. But you are far too busy on final approach to spend time checking your radar.

What's the big deal about wind shear? Well, I will tell you. If a captain does not take immediate evasive action in a microburst, there is no way that he can fly through the horrendous downdraft. Try as he may, he's going to crash. I am not trying to scare you, but I do want you to realize that the FAA is definitely not trying to keep you alive. The only way to outsmart the wind shear phenomenon is to do one of two things: first, do not land or take off at an airport when there is a thunderstorm in the vicinity; and second, heed the advise of the air traffic controller when he tells you that his radar is showing wind shear at the airport. But what is a person to do if there is no state-of-the-art Doppler radar at your airport?

I am sure you are thinking, why in the world are airlines operating into substandard airports that lack the safety of Doppler radar? Doppler has been around for a decade but it wasn't perfected for wind shear spotting until April of 1993. The FAA contracted the Raytheon Corporation to supply them with this state-of-the-art, life-saving equipment. In 1986, a government brief made this statement: The FAA fully intends to have Doppler radar operational and installed in over 10 airports by the 1990s. Another FAA joke.

As of 1995, the Raytheon Corporation had delivered 24 units to the "feds." In 1993, the first unit was commissioned at the FAA Oklahoma City training school. Surely, the other 23 units must be installed at the major airports throughout the United States? Wrong. Houston, Memphis, St. Louis, Denver, Kansas City, and Wichita are the only airports where Doppler radar has been commissioned. If you are wondering about the other 18 units that are sitting gathering dust, here's the answer. The FAA claims that they lack sufficient funding to install the rest of the units. Talking about funds, the FAA has been playing with a new system to enhance the radar equipment at all of the major facilities called the Advanced Automation System (ASS), a system that has plagued the FAA since they first started developing it over a decade ago.

The "feds" have decided that the lion's share of the technology would be scrapped at a loss of $1.8 billion dollars. And they say they have no funds for a life-saving, proven system such as Doppler. Well, that $1.8 billion would pay for the installation of about 375 Doppler radars, putting one at every major air carrier airport.

How does that make you feel about the FAA, the people that you trust for your safety in the air? Some airlines are stressing wind shear survival in their simulators during the six-month captain's checks. Co-pilots may or may not receive this training, even though they fly as much as the captain does.

From the very beginning of aviation, pilots have been instructed in the way to increase air speed when it starts to deteriorate. The standard method is to lower the nose and add some power. Pilots caught in a shear must forget this fundamental of flight. When a shear is encountered, it pulls the aircraft down. Therefore, it becomes mandatory to add full power, put sufficient backpressure on the yoke, and fly it out just below stalling speed.

It would be far more appropriate to instruct pilots how to avoid the treacherous wind shear and keep a safe distance away. If the FAA would stop sleeping with the airlines, they could inaugurate a regulation that would close an airport when thunderstorms and wind shears are in progress. It might inconvenience a lot of passengers but it's far better to miss an appointment than the rest of your life.

Since 1964, there were 149 aircraft accidents causing 450 fatalities. There were 27 transport category aircraft takeoff, approach, and landing accidents in which wind shear was a factor. And from 1970 to 1995, there were an alarming 20 airlines that documented wind shear accidents. Here are a few of the major ones compiled by my friend, David B. Gwinn, who conducts wind shear seminars for many of the airlines.

ACCIDENTS INVOLVING TRANSPORT CATEGORY AIRPLANES WITH WIND SHEAR AS A FACTOR

July 27, 1970	Flying Tigers DC-8; Okinawa, Japan; 4 fatalities—approach encounter with heavy rain.
May 18, 1972	Eastern Airlines DC-9; Ft. Lauderdale, Florida; non-fatal—Hard touchdown after encounter with heavy rain.
December 12, 1972	Trans World Airlines B-707; New York, New York; non-fatal—Descent below ILS glideslope; struck approach lights.
July 23, 1973	Ozark Air Lines FH-227-B; St. Louis, Missouri; 38 fatalities—Crashed 2 miles short on ILS; heavy rain and strong winds.
October 28, 1973	Piedmont B-737; Greensboro, North Carolina; non-fatal—Long, fast touchdown in heavy rain.
November 27, 1973	Delta Air Lines DC-9; Chattanooga, Tennessee; non-fatal—Struck short of runway; heavy rain.
December 17, 1973	Iberia Airlines DC-10; Boston, Massachusetts; non-fatal—Struck approach lights and sea wall after frontal wind shear.
January 30, 1974	Pan American B-707; Pago Pago, American Samoa; 96 fatalities—Struck short of airport; heavy rain and wind shear.
June 24, 1975	Eastern Airlines B-727; New York, New York; 112 fatalities—Struck short of airport; heavy rain and wind shear.
August 7, 1975	Continental B-727; Denver, Colorado; non-fatal; Crashed after encounter with microburst on takeoff.
November 12, 1975	Eastern Airlines B-727; Raleigh, North Carolina; non-fatal—Crashed short of runway during ILS approach; heavy rain.
April 27, 1976	American Airlines B-727; St. Thomas, Virgin Islands; 37 fatalities—Long, fast touchdown; terrain wind shear at flare.
June 23, 1976	Allegheny Airlines DC-9; Philadelphia, Pennsylvania; non-fatal—Crashed on runway during go-around encounter with thunderstorm.
June 3, 1977	Continental B-727; Tucson, Arizona; non-fatal—Struck power lines and poles after take-off wind shear.
July 9, 1982	Pan American B-727; Kenner, Louisiana; 153 fatalities; Crashed after take-off encounter with heavy rain and wind shear.
June 13, 1984	USAir DC-9-31; Detroit, Michigan; non-fatal—Crashed on runway after encountering a thunderstorm on approach.
May 31, 1984	United Airlines, B-727, Denver, CO
August 2, 1985	Delta Airlines, L-1011, DFW, Texas

Sept. 14, 1993   Lufthansa Air bus A320 Warsaw; 65 fatalities—Approach over-
                        ran runway.

July 2, 1994   USAir DC-9-31; 37 fatalities; Crashed on go-around.

In fiscal year 1994, the "feds" decided not to request funding for the all-important LLWAS and that future funding also would not be requested. This means that the units presently in use will not be repaired or replaced. This system is presently installed in 110 of the major airline airports. Thirteen million air carrier operations annually rely on LLWAS for real-time, reliable wind shear information, but the "feds" choose to wait until the latest technology called Doppler radar is installed.

The following organizations all have written letters to David R. Hinson, the past FAA Administrator, requesting that the present LLWAS be continued until they can be replaced with Doppler radar. These people know more about air safety than the FAA will ever know.

Aircraft Owners and Pilots Association

National Air Traffic Controller Association

Air Line Pilots Association

Helicopter Association, Inc.

National Air Traffic controllers Association

National Business Aircraft Association.

In discussing weather-related problems, we have started at ground level and will gradually work our way up to higher altitudes. We have seen the devastating effects that can be encountered near the ground. Let's climb up to the middle altitudes and investigate the damages your aircraft is subjected to by an unfriendly cloud.

Precipitation

On April 4, 1977, the National Weather Service weather chart depicted a low-pressure system over most of the southeastern states. A warm front occupied a line from southwestern Indiana to North Carolina. A squall line (an active line of thunderstorms) extended from Meridian, Mississippi, through northern Alabama and northwestern Georgia. Numerous tornadoes were recorded here during the past three years.

Southern Airways Flight 242, a Douglas DC-9, was in the process of
boarding passengers at their intermediate stop at Huntsville, Alabama. The
crew was on the final leg of the trip, and when reaching their destination,
Atlanta, Georgia, they would all have a few days off. Fifty-four-year-old
Captain William W. McKenzie had accumulated an impressive 19,380
hours. However, he was a relatively new captain on the 9, having been
checked out for a scant 39 days. His co-pilot, 34-year-old First Officer
Layman W. Keeler, had extensive military training and was a carrier qualified fighter jock in the U.S. Navy. The cabin crew consisted of two flight
attendants. Twenty-six-year-old Anne M. Lemoine who would be the boss
of the cabin or flight attendant A and the B position at the rear of the aircraft would be under the guidance of Sandy M. Ward, a 22-year-old who
had a scant three months seniority with Southern Airlines.

There was a thunderstorm overheading the airport as Southern Airways
Flight 242 taxied out for takeoff. First Officer Keeler would be flying this leg
of the trip and Captain McKenzie would be handling the radios. They were
cleared directly to a navigation facility at Rome to maintain 17,000 feet.
The company flight dispatcher was derelict in his duties by not alerting the
pilots about the dangerous weather ahead. The crew received no warning
pertinent to the treacherous weather buildups that were presently boiling
over the Rome VOR. The takeoff and climb were normal with only an
occasional nibble (slight turbulence).

At 20:56, Huntsville Departure radar control called: "Southern 242, I'm
painting (radar is depicting) a line of weather which appears to be moderate to, uh, possibly heavy precipitation starting about, uh, five miles ahead
and its ..."

Captain: "Okay, we're in the rain right now and it doesn't look much
heavier than what we're in, does it?"

Departure control: "It's painting ... I got weather cutting devices on
which is cutting out the, uh, precip that you're in now, this, uh, showing
up on radar, however, it doesn't ... it's not a solid mass it, uh, appears to be
a little bit heavier than what you're in now."

Captain: "Okay, thank you."

Since the air traffic controller's primary job is to keep airplanes separated from each other, their radar screens are tuned for this function. If a controller adjusts his screen to show weather, the traffic display deteriorates and the weather tends to block out the targets. When the scope is set for normal traffic functions, the weather picture is not present. You would think in this day and age technicians could come up with a scope that would perform both functions at the same time.

Unfortunately, pilots know little about the workings of ATC and most of them have no knowledge concerning the lack of storms on the controller screens. They are under the assumption that a controller would never steer him into a storm. True, a controller would never intentionally do such a thing, but when he is not painting weather, he can't very well steer you around something he can't see. It's a very poor system but that's the way it is.

Captain McKenzie was busily adjusting his radar set, trying to find a hole in the wall of towering cumulus clouds. "I believe right straight ahead, uh, there the next few miles is about the best way we can go."

The turbulence intensity started to increase.

"Here we go ... hold 'em cowboy. I think we'd better slow it up right here in this, uh ..." was Captain McKenzie's advise to his co-pilot. After a tilt adjustment to his radar, Captain Bill believed he had found a soft spot in the boiling turbulence ahead.

"See that?" he said.

Co-pilot Keeler answered: "That's a hole, isn't it? Do you want to go around that right now?"

The jolts were increasing in both occurrence and intensity. A radio transmission from a TWA flight just beyond the clouds stated that they were in the clear. This call led the Southern crew to believe that smoother air was just around the bend.

The cockpit speakers crackled and ATC spoke: "Southern 242 descend and maintain one four thousand at this time."

Captain: "242 down to 14."

Flight 242 was now in the heart of the storm. The turbulent rain and hail were showing their true colors. It was as though they teamed together to seek vengeance on the sleek silver intruder who dared to venture into their territory.

Up to this point, the passengers were bearing up quite well under such trying conditions. Some of them were beginning to show their fears by crying aloud. With no word from the cockpit, the plucky little newly hired flight attendant made a cool clear announcement: "Keep your seat belts on and securely fastened. There's nothing to be alarmed about. Relax, we should be out of it shortly."

Now, the intensity of the hail increased and cracked the pilot's windshield, turning it nearly white with craze marks. To coincide with this development, the engines started to seize and stall. B Flight Attendant Sandy Ward knew there was real trouble brewing. Being the professional that she was, she picked up the PA mike and pressed the talk button: "… check to see that all carry-on baggage is stowed completely underneath the seat in front of you, all carry-on baggage … put all carry-on baggage underneath the seat in front of you. In the unlikely event there is a need for an emergency landing, we ask that you please grab your ankles. There is nothing to be alarmed about, but we have lost temporary PA power so in the event there is an unlikely need for an emergency landing, you will hear us holler, 'please grab your ankles.' Thank you for your cooperation and just relax. These are precautionary measures only."

At 2109:36, No. 2 engine quit. There was still one engine left that could easily carry the plane to a safe landing. Thirty-six seconds later, the second engine flamed out.

Co-pilot Keeler, who was hand-flying the craft at the reduced turbulence speed of 285 knots, told his captain: "My No…. the other engine's going too … alright, Bill, get us a vector to a clear area."

Atlanta Center: "Southern 242, say again"

Captain: "Stand by … we lost both engines. Get us a vector (direction) to a clear area."

With the power gone, the instruments began to tumble, and the radar and transponder both became inoperative. Atlanta Center saw the target drop off the radar screen as it went into a coast. The life of an airline pilot has aptly been described as months of boredom interrupted by moments of stark terror. This situation most certainly depicts the latter. For nearly three minutes, the crew was totally consumed by their immediate tasks. First Officer Keeler was trying to keep her straight and lose as little precious altitude as possible. Captain Bill was rapidly going through the engine relight procedure. Unbeknownst to him, both engines were nothing but solid molten metal. Now, the life-saving altitude had dropped to a scant 7,000 feet. The electric power returned and after a two-minute radio silence, Captain McKenzie pressed his mike button. In a clear, commanding voice, he stated a situation that no pilot ever wants to be in: "Uh, we've lost both engines. How about giving us a vector to the nearest place. We're at 7,000 feet."

This startling transmission made little or no impression on the controller. Here's an airliner with no engines, descending at the rate of 56 feet per second with no immediate landing facility below, and what does he do? He issues the crew a heading to Dobbins Air Force Base and then goes about his routine business of giving instructions to other aircraft on his frequency. He made six transmissions to other planes before returning to Southern.

You might expect this kind of stupidity from a new controller, but this fellow was a 21-year veteran. He should have gone out of his way to hand-off his remaining traffic to another controller. Then he could have devoted full time to the fate of 92 people whose lives were solely dependent on him and the actions of the flight crew. His first and last transmissions were all in the same calm, laconic voice. This controller should have been horse-whipped for the disgraceful manner in which he controlled Southern 242.

The cabin crew was having their problems calming the fearful passengers. Once again, Sandy gave them instructions: "Ladies and gentlemen, please check that seat belts are securely, again, across your pelvis area on your hips."

Captain McKenzie was indeed a patient fellow. If I were in his shoes, I would have told the controller to devote his entire attention to me and get rid of his other traffic. After all, they have operating engines. Captain Bill calmly spoke to the Atlanta controller, although he was disturbed by this fellow's lack of interest: "Alright, listen, we've lost both engines, and, uh, I can't, uh, tell you the implications of this, uh, we uh, only got two engines and how far is Dobbins?"

"Southern, uh, 242, uh, nineteen miles."

"Okay, we're out of, uh, fifty-eight hundred, two hundred knots."

Atlanta Approach: "Roger, and you're approximately, uh, seventeen miles west of Dobbins at this time."

Captain Bill: "I don't know whether we can make that or not."

Atlanta Approach: "Roger, well there is Cartersville; you're approximately ten miles south of Cartersville, fifteen miles west of Dobbins."

By now the flight was so low it was committed to any open field. The crew was fully aware that all their skill and concentration were a lost cause. As the scrub pines got closer and closer, Co-pilot Keeler spoke to his skipper: "Like, we are, I'm picking out a clear field. Keeler, you've got to find me a highway."

"Let's take the next open field."

"No, damn it."

"See a highway over ... no cars."

"Right there, is the straight?"

"No."

"We'll have to take it."

Less than 500 feet remained before the moment of truth would arrive. Captain Bill McKenzie makes his final transmission to Atlanta Approach. His commanding voice had not changed throughout the entire emergency, but now there is an unmistaken tone of disgust. "Uh, we're putting it down on a highway ... we're down to nothing."

Co-pilot Keeler has landed on a carrier many times, but the highway that he had picked out was much narrower than a carrier and lined with unwanted arresting gear, consisting of trees and poles. One lone car was in the way as Keeler leveled out and started to flare.

From the cabin, Flight Attendant Ward saw trees outside her window that prompted her to yell to her passengers ... "Grab your ankles."

The A flight attendant, Anne Lemaine, repeated the same command from her forward jumpseat. These girls did a superhuman job, especially since they received no instructions from the busy flight crew.

"I've got it, Bill ... I've got it now ... We got it." chanted Keeler.

Captain McKenzie replied: "Okay, don't stall it."

"We're going to do it, right here."

With the wheels now only a few feet over the highway, the 130-knot speed started to decay. The aircraft's left wing was the first part of the airliner to make ground contact, slicing through two trees. About a half-mile further down the highway, the left wing again contacted another tree adjacent to the highway and within the town limits of New Hope, Georgia. She continued down the road, snapping trees and utility poles like toothpicks. The left main wheel contacted the road and now the speed had diminished to 100 mph. Simultaneously, the left wing tip struck an embankment and veered to the left. She continued on, striking signs, fences, trees, utility poles, five cars, and a truck, finally coming to rest after shearing off the gas pump in front of a general store.

After the first contact, a fireball erupted in the cabin and traveled along the ceiling to the rear of the aircraft. It then shot downward and set some passengers on fire. This all happened before the plane had stopped its destructive path. The fuselage broke into five sections. The cockpit came to rest inverted and both pilots were ejected to their deaths. The aft flight attendant, Sandy was relatively intact. After using her apron to grasp the hot seat belt release buckle, she went forward to assist her passengers, but was confronted with a wall of fire. She left the aircraft only to continue her professional efforts to pull passengers to safety until an explosion forced her away.

The forward flight attendant, Anne Lemaine, found herself hanging inverted in her seat, restrained only by her belt. She released her lap belt and fell to the ground atop debris from the galley. She tried to open the main door but it was jammed. She climbed through a gaping hole in the belly and jumped to the ground. Still thinking of her passengers, this courageous girl ran to a nearby house to summon help.

Of the 85 persons on-board, 62 were killed outright, 22 were seriously injured, and 8 people on the ground were killed in the wake of the 90,000-pound hulk.

Once again, the airline company manual states: "Flights shall not intentionally be conducted through thunderstorms or clear air turbulence."

After the engines were lost, the crew did a magnificent job. The cabin crew deserved the highest praise possible. Those girls performed in an outstanding, professional manner, and they clearly depicted the role of heroines, not just food servers that the public fails to realize.

The NTSB's Probably Cause states: "The National Transportation Safety Board determines that the probable cause of this accident was the total and unique loss of thrust from both engines while the aircraft was penetrating an area of severe thunderstorms, and the loss of thrust was caused by the ingestion of massive amounts of water and hail which, in combination with thrust lever movement, induced severe stalling in and major damage to the engine compressors."

The engines were JT-80s.

In March of 1998, the FAA printed their criteria for testing turbine engines: "Ingestion of extreme quantities of rain or hail through the engine case may ultimately produce a number of engine anomalies, including surging, power loss, and engine flameout."

The airworthiness standards regarding operation during rain and hail testing are as follows: The engine must be capable of withstanding a beating in rain for three minutes. And after ingesting three small pieces of hail, it must do okay for thirty seconds.

Nothing short of a joke. The crew on Southern Airlines was buffeted by heavy rain for many minutes, and as for three small hail pellets, they had their windshield shattered by large holes for numerous minutes. Thirty seconds is nothing short of ludicrous. Engines should obviously be tested in the environment that nature produces and not on some factory test stand.

Turbulence

An explosion and intense fireball was seen in the clear midnight skies over Falls City, Nebraska. It wasn't lightning, although there was an intense line of thunderstorms only a few miles from the town limits. Moments after the first sighting, another explosion rocked the rolling farmland and awakened farmers on the outskirts of town.

When investigators reached the site, they saw the remains of an aircraft being rapidly consumed by an intense fire. Inside were the bodies of 38 passengers and a crew of 4. What had caused the destruction of one of the finest aircraft ever produced is going to be difficult to believe.

Braniff Airlines flight 250 departed Kansas City, Missouri, on its final leg of a short flight to its destination airport in Omaha, Nebraska. On board an airworthy aircraft sat a qualified aircrew. Forty-seven-year-old Captain Donald G. Pauly had accumulated 20,767 hours of experience in the air; however, his time in the BAC 111 aircraft (a British built aircraft similar to the DC-9, only far superior) was limited to only 549 hours.

The departure was normal and the climb to their assigned altitude of 20,000 feet was interrupted by the Captain's request to stop at 5,000 feet. Once again, the crew was placing too much confidence in their weather radar to find them a soft spot in the line squall that traversed their course only ten miles ahead.

When you're fighting the turbulence and rain, the lightning is flashing in all quadrants, and your radar is showing that the clouds are only a few miles thick, it's very difficult not to press on, even though you know the only completely safe plan of action would be to fly miles out of your way to parallel the front, or make a "180" and go back and land.

What would the company say if the flight before you and the trip behind you both punched through the same storm and landed on schedule? Would you receive a call from dispatch or the director of flying? On many airlines, management has the crew under their thumb, and it takes a lot of guts to fight them.

The aircraft was now level at 5,000 feet and the thrust was reduced to give them the turbulent penetration speed of 280 knots. The main thrust of the squall-line was laying in wait a mere five miles ahead. Numerous ground observers stated that the aircraft was clear of the central storm area. A squall line is one of nature's most devastating meteorological phenomenon and probably on a par with the dreaded microburst.

The crew of Braniff decided that their radar was painting a relatively clear shot through the storm. The autopilot was engaged and the altitude hold switch was purposely left disengaged, as per company requirements. With the altitude hold engaged, it would put too much strain on the aircraft in its quest to stay at one level. Far better to ride with the flow and reduce the potential caused by severe vertical currents. While maintaining straight and level flight, the aircraft was suddenly subjected to extreme forces that caused it to roll to the left. The vertical fin and the right tailplane tore from the fuselage. Following this, she pitched down and exceeded the structural limits of the right wing that caused it to be torn from the fuselage and tumble to the ground. The rupture of the fuel tank in the wing released a great quantity of fuel that ignited, creating the ball of fire observed by the ground witnesses. The remainder of the aircraft plummeted to earth and burned out of control for nearly two hours. Once the aircraft "break-up" started, it was completed in less than five seconds.

The flight recorder was recovered and it showed that vertical excursions of +3.2 to -1.3 "Gs" were recorded. The manufacturer of this fine aircraft put the maximum limits permissible at +2.5 to -1.0 "G's," so it's easy to see that it doesn't take much past the limits before it breaks up.

In spite of the necessity to know precisely how much stress has been placed on an aircraft, there is no instrument in the cockpit that a pilot might check to see if his aircraft is overstressed. Yes, there is a record kept of most of the parameters of flight, but it is a sealed unit that is used only after a crash.

The price of a "G" meter, which could be positioned in the instrument panel, would cost about $300 and would take approximately one hour of labor to install. It's a very simple device that when activated, causes a tiny weight to operate a pointer whenever the aircraft encounters more than one "G" negative or positive force.

You are probably wondering why on earth the airlines don't install such an important and inexpensive device. The answer is quite simple. Whenever a pilot reports that his "G" meter reading exceeded the aircraft limits, the aircraft would have to undergo an extreme turbulence check which might mean that the most dreaded word in the airline industry would rear its ugly head: DELAY. In this case, what the pilots don't see might hurt them.

Another source of potential structural problems can be derived from pilots making hard landings. These kinds of touchdowns require a notation in the logbook, but it will be a cold day in hell before a pilot will deliberately announce the fact that he hit the runway just a "tad" too hard.

A hard landing can be just as detrimental to the airframe as turbulence, and to check the structure for a hard landing is more time consuming than a turbulence check. The USAF has "G" meters on all of their fighters and most of their transports. They don't run the risk of sending out broken aircraft just to make schedule.

Once again, the dispatch at Braniff failed to accurately brief the crew. The company forecast was not accurate with respect to the intensity and number of thunderstorms, and the danger of the accompanying turbulence in the system.

The NTSB's final statement was: "The probable cause of this accident was in-flight structural failure caused by extreme turbulence during operation of the aircraft in an area of avoidable hazardous weather."

NASA's latest test data for all turbine-powered commercial aircraft was based on 10 million miles of experience. They stated that an airliner would have to fly 2.78 million miles before encountering turbulence that could cause structural damage.

While we are on the subject of turbulence, I would like to share some information with you. How many times have you heard people talking about a rough flight that they had on a certain airline? Or that they would never fly on that airline again? The turbulence encountered on one airline is the same rough area for every other flight in the vicinity. Please don't blame the carrier on whose airplane you are flying. If you were on another airline in the same area, you would be jostled just as much. Pilots do their best to keep the trip smooth, and often are busy checking with ATC, trying to find a better level of flight. But this is not always possible, especially when traversing a large, turbulent air mass.

Whirlwinds

Much of the following is taken from a paper written by Carl A. Posey. Pilots flying in mountainous terrain must be vigilant for rotors caused by wind that is forced up the side of a mountain and spills over the slopes beyond. On the ground, the breaking waves are strong gusts of wind that are hazardous to trees, power lines, and roofs. But high in the sky, they can be extremely dangerous to aircraft.

An Air Force B-52 had nearly all of its vertical fin ripped off by 95-mph gusts at 14,000 feet. In March of 1996, a BOAC Boeing 707 blew apart as it traversed Mount Fujiyama. In 1968, a Fairchild F-27B encountered a mountain wave that tore off a wing. In December 1992, a cargo DC-8 was flying near Denver at 33,000 feet when an engine was torn off by treacherous winds. A glider pilot was caught in a wave cloud and it ripped the wings from the glider. The pilot was thrown through the cockpit. His parachute opened, and he was traveling down one minute but the next thing he knew, he was being thrust upward rapidly.

A GAO (General Accounting Office) report in 1993 found that from 1983 to 1992, the aircraft accident statistics showed 40 percent higher in the mountainous terrain in eleven western states than for the other 39.

In 1995, I was watching a TV talk show that was devoted entirely to flying. The name of the show was "Marilu" (I believe it has now been taken off the air). At any rate, there was an experienced American Airlines check captain who was one of the participants. His latest job was to run seminars for those who are afraid to fly. He made at least one mistake when he said that turbulence was something that no one liked, but it was definitely something that the crew could cope with and that there was nothing to worry about. Perhaps he would like to tell that to the relatives of the people on board the airliners that disintegrated in flight because of turbulence. Even though there hasn't been an in-flight break-up since 1992, the turbulence is still out there, waiting.

Clear-Air Turbulence

It is quite evident that at certain times, the air space adjacent to the ground and middle altitudes can produce aerial disasters. Surely, the higher altitudes above the storm level must be the safest altitudes of all.

Clear-air Turbulence, or CAT, is defined as all air disturbances occurring about 15,000 feet and not associated with low-level temperature inversions, thermals, wake turbulence, or local terrain features. The flow of air is quite similar to the way a river flows rapidly down stream. Rocks on the river bottom impede the flow of water and cause it to become choppy in some areas and smooth in others. The sky currents in many ways are very similar to the river. At the higher altitudes, areas of dense, cold air form mounds which act like the large rocks in a river.

Meteorologists have a difficult time forecasting CAT. It occurs more frequently in the winter when the airborne river of air known as the jet stream flows the fastest. It is usually encountered at about 30,000 feet as it usually flows out of western Canada and crosses the United States in a southeasterly direction. Wind speeds of 200 knots are common and its dimensions may vary, but it is usually only a few hundred miles wide and averages about 5,000 feet thick. The stream itself is relatively smooth; it's the edges of it that harbor all the bumps.

On November 4, 1970, a Pan Am Boeing 747 was cruising at 28,000 feet en route to Orly Airport, Paris, France. As it passed Nantucket, Massachusetts, it encountered severe turbulence. The seat belt sign had been on since the departure from JFK, and the cabin crew had instructed the passengers to remain seated but they failed to heed the warning. Twenty-one passengers and two flight attendants incurred injuries during the three minutes of severe turbulence. Six passengers and one hostess were hospitalized. Two of the passengers stated that they both struck the ceiling with their heads and then fell back into their seats. When the aircraft traversed the initial jolt, the flight attendant was bounced to the ceiling where she struck her head and fell back hard to the floor. Throughout the remainder of the bumps, she stayed on the floor clutching a seat leg to prevent further injuries. She suffered a cerebral concussion and a severely sprained back. The turbulence opened several of the overhead storage bins and their contents rained down on the passengers below. During the three minutes of turbulence, the aircraft dropped from an altitude of 27,850 feet to 22,800 feet. The aircraft returned to Kennedy and landed without further incident.

On April 12, 1972, a Northwest Boeing 747 was climbing to 33,000 feet after departing Tokyo, Japan, for Honolulu, Hawaii. Passengers were instructed to keep their belts fastened even though the sign was off. At 29,000 feet and in clear air, a light chop was encountered. After leveling at 33,000 feet, severe turbulence was encountered for a period of 55 seconds. The passengers who had failed to strap in were the ones who were injured. The two most severely injured passengers were a young girl who dislocated her shoulder and a boy who sustained a fractured left arm. The turbulent encounter was near an upper level depression adjacent to the jet stream. The trip continued on to Hawaii and there was no damage to the aircraft.

On November 24, 1983, Air Canada's Flight 965, a wide-bodied Lockheed 1011 with 15 crewmembers and 145 passengers had just departed Trinidad for its flight to Toronto, Canada. The air was clear of clouds and the visibility was excellent as the jet leveled out at the assigned altitude of 37,000 feet. About eight minutes later in the vicinity of Charleston, South Carolina, a few light nibbles were encountered. The captain switched on the seat belt sign and announced to his passengers: "We are encountering unexpected light turbulence. Please remain seated and fasten your seat belt as a precautionary measure."

Back in the cabin, the attendants had completed a beverage service and were about to dispense some food when the flight began to shutter and plunge. Loose articles were projected about the cabin, and three of the 100-pound serving carts were hurled against the ceiling. Several passengers screamed and many more were frightened by the encounter.

The altimeter displayed a loss of 500 feet and then an abrupt gain. The encounter lasted a little over two minutes but during that time, 24 people were injured. One flight attendant was in the lower gallery and was trying desperately to strap into one of the crew seats. As the craft dropped, she hit the floor, seriously injuring her back. When the main jolt struck the craft, it registered an increase in altitude of 250 feet in two seconds. During the next two seconds, the aircraft lost 100 feet. The aircraft landed safely at its destination and was immediately examined for post-turbulence damage. A five-eighths-inch crack was detected in both horizontal stabilizers.

On March 31, 1993, a Japanese Airline's 747 had just departed Anchorage International Airport. While on climb-out, CAT struck again, tearing the No. 2 engine from the wing and depositing it next to a shopping center.

On April 6, 1993, a China Eastern Airlines MD-11 was cruising at 33,000 feet over the Pacific Ocean. The flight plan called for stop at Shanghai before landing in Los Angeles. A poorly designed flap/slat handle in the cockpit was inadvertently moved, causing an abrupt 5,000-foot dive. The aircraft was in smooth air and the majority of the passengers neglected the F/A warning: "While seated, please keep your seat belt fastened."

Well, there are two passengers who will never have to worry about those instructions again because they were thrown from their seats and killed. One hundred sixty passengers were injured, some severely.

On October 22, 1993, a United Airlines Boeing 767-300 encountered moderate turbulence at flight level 350. The airliner was approximately 400 miles southwest of Miami, flying in smooth, clear air. The crew related that they flew through about 20 to 30 seconds of light turbulence. This was followed by 30 seconds of moderate turbulence. The seat belt sign was immediately turned on. The weather radar was operating and was showing nothing but clear blue sky. They encountered severe turbulence that caused two passengers to sustain minor injuries. One passenger was seriously injured.

A month later, another United flight, this time a Boeing 757, was descending over Barbados in the West Indies. They were descending from F1290 when they rammed into CAT. All passengers were seated with their lap belts fastened, but one of the flight attendants was seriously injured.

When a pilot's radar shows a large thunderstorm or a line of them directly ahead, it is not his prerogative to turn off course without first consulting ATC. When a flight crew requests a turn to miss turbulence, it usually requires the ATC to do some fast coordinating.

The turn that the crew requests could necessitate coordination from a controller in an adjoining air space, clearance from the authority that controls restricted air space. There could be traffic in the vicinity of the requested turn, or the controller could be so busy because of the storm that he might not be able to immediately answer the crew's radio transmission. The controller, in a case such as this, may be so inundated with requests for vector changes from aircraft that proper spacing could be jeopardized. It is true that the captain is solely responsible for the safety of his flight and may want a turn immediately, but it is not always possible. It would be a great benefit to pilots if controllers were taught that deviation requests are not always initiated so that the passengers will not spill their martinis but instead to keep the aircraft from structural damage.

From 1975 to 1981, 44 air carrier accidents were caused by turbulence. These encounters left the aircraft with minor damages, but 70 persons sustained serious injuries and 80 persons received major injuries.

Concerning weather, the vast majority of the time you are perfectly safe in an aircraft. But then there are times when you can encounter problems from the ground extending upward to as high as man can fly.

CHAPTER 16

▼

DANGEROUS ENCOUNTERS

Captain Gregory Engelbreit was one of the numerous military "weekend warriors," an experienced combat pilot with over 60 missions in Vietnam. In civilian life, the 35-year-old family man was a marketing engineer. His love for flying was still evident; much of his free time was utilized in flying the RF-4C. This proven fighter weighs over 20 tons and in level flight, can fly faster than the speed of sound.

The night of April 8, 1982, was a night that neither Greg nor his navigator Fred Wilson would ever forget. The flight would be a low-level radar mission to locate and engage four prearranged targets. The weather at the Idaho Air National Guard's 124th Tactical Reconnaissance base was perfect for the mission; a clear, cool night with unlimited visibility. Greg gave the crew chief the start signal and the powerful jet engines screeched to life. As they approached the active runway, Greg asked: "Fred, are you ready to do it?"

"All set, Greg."

Capt. Engelbreit selected the tower channel and made his call. "Gowen Tower Tango 45 ready."

The tower replied. "Tango 45, you're cleared for take off."

Greg ran up the power. Once again Greg asked: "Fred, ready to launch?"

"Let her rip."

With the brakes released, it was nothing but rapid acceleration from now on. As the takeoff speed registered, Greg eased back on the stick. The Phantom lifted off and rapidly climbed to altitude. Fred had always wanted to be a pilot, but because he was overage, the Air Force would not accept him. He loved flying and figured that he was better off being in the back seat than on the ground. Soon they were abeam of King Mountain level at 1,000 feet and approximately 100 miles west of Boise. Within seconds, they would be up on their first target. Suddenly, a deafening explosion interrupted the peaceful flight. The left side of the pilot's canopy was gone and the shrieking air blast of over 480 knots filled the cockpit.

"I knew instantly what had happened," Captain Engelbreit said. "I also knew there was something drastically wrong with me, that I didn't have the ability to fly the airplane. The last thing I remembered was thinking, Fred it's up to you to fly this thing."

The explosion was the result of a 20-pound whistling swan crashing through the left quarter panel of the windscreen. It hit with the force of a 37mm cannon shell, spreading razor-sharp pieces of the windshield all over the cockpit. The main carcass of the bird lodged in Greg's left shoulder, leaving a hole as large as a baseball. His left arm was nearly severed and his face and neck were peppered with glass. The cold air cauterized the pilot's wounds and kept him from bleeding to death.

Lt. Wilson knew immediately they encountered a bird strike. The Phantom was most erratic and he knew he had better take control and fast. He climbed to 7,000 feet in order to clear the mountains and slowed to a more comfortable speed of 240 knots.

"Greg! Greg, can you hear me?" There was no answer. Fred knew he was in serious trouble. He did have some of the pilot's flight controls in the back cockpit, but not the gear or flaps. These must be controlled from the front seat. Fred thought about ejecting, but he saw his pilot's parachute was damaged by the bird. His limited visibility from the rear seat was another concern. The left side of the canopy was covered in bird guts; the right side had a few inches of clear vision. Fred did what he was told to do in numerous briefings: he got to a safe altitude, slowed the plane, and checked for controllability. He had always wanted to be an Air Force pilot, but this was not what he had in mind. He tried to contact his pilot again. "Greg, can you hear me?"

No answer was forthcoming. Deeply religious, Wilson began to pray. He asked God, "Help us make it." He kept calling his pilot, and finally his prayers were answered. Greg moved to the right side of the cockpit. However, it was only a momentary shift. Fred held the plane steady as he headed for home. He watched his pilot drift in and out of consciousness as he raced along the evening sky.

"Mayday! Mayday! Mayday! Tango 45 at 6,000 feet on the 265-degree radial. We hit a bird and the cockpit is badly damaged. Mayday! Mayday! Mayday! Does anybody read?"

The call was received by Major Bill Miller and Captain Michael McGeath, who were up in their F4 on another mission. "Tango 45, we're on our way to assist. Is the aircraft controllable?"

Fred replied, "She's okay so far."

"Hang in there. We are getting a vector to you."

Even though the other plane could only offer advice, it still remained Fred's job to fly this jet. He scanned the sky for a glimpse of his friends. It seemed to Fred that it had been hours since his last transmissions; in reality it was only a few minutes. Off to his left he saw some lights closing rapidly. He heard the radio crackle to life again.

"Tango 45, this is Tango 44, we have you in sight. Do you read?"

Fred answered, "I have you closing in at eight o'clock. My pilot is seriously hurt and is unable to assist me. It looks like I will have to land this beast from the back seat."

"Hang in there. Is the plane working okay, no control problems? What's your fuel state?"

"It's okay, but I don't know about getting the gear down. I don't relish a wheels-up landing."

Tango 44 answered "You're doing fine. We're going to lead you for an approach at Mountain Home Runway 30. It's longer than home base and their equipment is better."

"Roger 44", Wilson answered.

The air was smoother and the presence of the other plane just off the wing gave him a renewed lift.

"Greg, can you hear me?"

Fred saw some signs of life in the front seat and he tried again to make contact.

"Greg, can you hear me? Please try your best to lower the gear. Please lower the gear."

Fred said a few more silent prayers. This time they were really answered. As if by magic, the gear and flaps extended, the emergency transponder was on, and the landing lights were on.

Fred's lead aircraft exclaimed, "You got three wheels, flaps, and a hook. You are in great shape. Stay on my wing. I will lead you to the runway. It will be a 14-mile straight in. Ease off on the power, and drop your nose, maintain 140."

Fred replied, "Okay, stay with me." He could hear his lead calling the tower and getting clearance for a two-ship landing.

"Tango 45, I will be guiding you for a straight in. Keep close and maintain 140. You're doing a great job. Just fly that angle of attack until you touch down, then chop the power."

"Okay, I'll try it", replied Fred.

Now the runway lights were clearly visible.

"You are about three miles out, doing okay. Keep that speed, and your sink rate is good. No need to answer me, just fly her. You are about one mile out now and in the groove. You're over the threshold, ease her down and when she's on, chop the throttle."

Fred said a quick prayer as he felt a hard ground contact. He rolled 1,000 feet and the hook caught the arresting gear and slammed him hard in the straps to an abrupt stop. He had done a fantastic job. The Air Force awarded him the Distinguished Flying Cross, the nation's second highest peacetime medal for valor. Fred's pilot is alive today because of his skill and unbelievable courage.

A few years after this incident, Lt. Fred Wilson's aircraft hit another bird. This time very minor damage resulted. Lightning isn't supposed to strike twice in the same place, but birds don't adhere to any rules. For years, birds have dominated the skies without competition. Early aviators who flew balloons and gliders posed little threat to our feathered friends until the Wright Brothers invented the airplane. In fact, it wasn't until 1912 when the first official bird strike was reported. A young aviator named Calbraith P. Rodgers was flying his Wright EX biplane over Long Beach, California, when a seagull became snarled in his control wires causing a crash that killed him.

Bird migration is the movement of birds between wintering grounds and summer breeding grounds. In the fall, birds fly south and return home in the spring. There are many factors influencing the flyways (specific paths flown by migrant birds). Both coasts of the United States have the largest flyways, although large flocks have been seen over the Mississippi River. In addition, there are numerous smaller flyways going west and east. At various times along these routes, swarms of insects have been detected as high as 10,000 feet. This is why some species of birds prefer to fly high over mountains instead of in the valleys where they can feed en route. The longest migratory route for a bird is that of the Arctic Tern which flies 12,000 miles from the Arctic to Antarctica. The largest flocks are starlings that number 15 to 20 million. Ducks fly up to 5,000 feet, geese between 2,000 and 7,000 feet, and songbirds from the ground to 3,000 feet. The vast majority of birds are found at the lower altitudes. That is why 90 percent of all bird strikes occur at or below 3,000 feet.

In recent years, the incidence of an actual high-altitude bird strike has increased. An RAF aircraft struck an eagle at 17,500 feet over the Indian Ocean. A military jet fighter took a hit at 21,000 feet. The highest altitude record was a strike at 37,000 feet.

Birds range in size from hummingbirds at two inches long to the large albatross with a wingspan of twelve feet. Their speed varies greatly. Small birds fly at half the speed of ducks which have been clocked at 60 mph. Pilots of light aircraft have reported being passed by falcons and sandpipers.

On October 4, 1960, fifty-nine-year-old Captain Curtis W. Fitts was in command of one of the newest four-engine turboprop aircraft, the Lockheed Electra. Captain Fitts was a highly qualified pilot with over 23,000 hours, over 1,000 of which were in the Electra. At 1735, Eastern

Airlines Flight #444 was ready to taxi away from its gate at Boston's Logan Airport for its destination in Philadelphia.

First Officer Calloway keyed his mike. "Logan ground Eastern 444 ready to taxi."

The ground controller replied, "Eastern triple four cleared to runway nine via the outer follow the Twin Beech."

"Runway nine, Roger."

The weather was good with 15 miles visibility. As they taxied into the block of runway nine, there were only a few remaining items to complete on the before-takeoff check.

As the flight engineer completed the check, First Office Martin J. Calloway was already talking to the tower. "Logan Eastern triple four is ready."

The local controller replied, "Eastern triple four maintain runway heading for two minutes cleared for takeoff."

Captain Fitts advanced the throttle and four giant turbines screamed to life as various instrument needles started their arc to the proper setting. The air speed indicator started its sweep up the dial, and as it hit one of the call-out speeds, the first officer said, "80 knots." A few seconds later, he again called out, "V1" and finally at 116 knots, "V2".

Captain Fitts applied some back pressure to the control column and after a roll of 2,500 feet, Eastern triple four was airborne. Moments later the crew felt a jolt and the No. 1 engine (engines are numbered from left to right) auto feathered. Whenever the throttle is past 75 percent and the autofeather switch is on, a propeller will go to the feather position; it will knife-edge if an engine fails to produce 50 percent of rated power. The aircraft started a bank to the left and the faltering engines on the left side produced sufficient drag to force the left wing down. At an altitude of 200 feet, the angle of climb and the roll rapidly increased. The nose then fell through and she started toward Winthrop Bay. Twenty-seven and one-half seconds after takeoff, 97,987 pounds of aircraft slammed vertically into the water. Of the 72 passengers and crew on board, only 10 survived. The aircraft was totally destroyed.

Everybody knows that a sparrow is a small bundle of feathers and certainly no match for a gigantic engine; but when a flock of them are scared to death by a giant, they really don't know which way to turn. Crash investigators discovered the carcasses of 75 sparrows on the takeoff runway. All four engines were recovered and tests were performed on them. They all showed no malfunctions except for bird damage. Engines one and two had the brunt of the bird impact with three and four showing less bird injections. By piecing the evidence of eyewitnesses, on board, on the ground, and from another aircraft, the investigators concluded the following: No. 1 engine received that most strikes and shut down automatically. No. 2 started to shut down, but relit. The relatively undisturbed power from No. 3 and No. 4 caused a tremendous pull to the left. This power asymmetry was responsible for the crash. With only a few hundred feet of altitude, recovery was not possible. The aircraft manufacturer and FAA ran bird ingestion tests at the Lockheed Factory. When up to two starlings were shot into the engines, over 50 percent of the power was still available. When 4 starlings were ingested, power fell to below 50 percent, causing an automatic engine shut down. If these tests were performed by the FAA, as they should have been, during initial aircraft certification, we would have been more cognizant of the potential bird danger.

On November 23, 1962, a United Airlines four-engine turboprop Vickers Viscount was cruising over Maryland at 6,000 feet. The tail section hit a whistling swan and was nearly ripped from the fuselage, causing the aircraft to go out of control and crash, killing all occupants.

On November 7, 1967, a United DC-8 had just taken off from Cleveland and was climbing through 5,000 feet when an explosive noise was heard and the co-pilot's windshield was shattered by a bird. The first officer was injured by the intruder when it came into the cockpit and hit the captain on the left shoulder, coming to rest on the captain's side window. The aircraft was flown to a successful landing by the captain alone because the co-pilot was too badly injured to be of any assistance. Once safely on the ground, the damage was surveyed. There were at least eight bird strikes: five in the cockpit windshield area, one on the tail, and one on the left wing. This time, the crew was lucky. No one received any permanent injuries.

When a military crew briefs before a flight, they discuss what each member is to do if they should encounter a bird strike. The roar of the wind coming through a shattered windshield is deafening, making conversation even over the intercom impossible.

The crew of the United DC-8 was lucky that the noise level was all right because airline pilots never ever discuss what is to be done after a strike. I don't know of any airline that has any pages in their operating manual concerning the ever-present bird hazard.

Birds also do extensive damage to aircraft that are parked on the ramp or in the hanger. Birds have been discovered in engine housings with extensive amounts of nesting material. When the engines are started, these nests have caused numerous fires. Clogged intakes, as well as static and rotor blades on jet engines, can be significantly damaged by nesting material. Bird droppings also have a corrosive affect on wiring and have caused expensive electrical shorts.

On December 15, 1972, a Northwest Airlines Boeing 747 ran off the end of runway 27L while involved in an emergency landing at Miami International Airport in Florida, from which the plane had just taken off. There were 149 passengers and 11 in the crew. No one was seriously injured. This incident was caused by the ingestion of birds into the No. 3 engine while on takeoff roll. During the climbout, the crew noticed the vibration meter for No. 4 was showing full-scale deflection, so it was shut down. This, combined with the malfunctions caused by the bird strike on No. 3 rendered reverse thrust inoperable on the right side. As the crew turned for a landing, the wind component was indicating a downwind landing on runway 27. As they touched down, the reverse was not available on the right side, and on a slick, newly paved runway, they could not stop without going off the end. They hit a cement slab at the far end of the strip. After the incident, the concrete slab was hastily removed and the runway was grooved.

On February 6, 1973, Captain Ernest F. Sellfare was the pilot of Learjet N454RN, a business jet owned by the Machinery Buyers Corp. After take-off, the tower made this comment. "Lear 454RN it appears the left engine laid a pretty good layer of smoke out of the left side there for approximately 300 or 400 feet."

The captain replied, "We just hit some birds."

"Roger, you returning to land?"

The flight responded, "Don't believe we're going to make it."

At 300 feet, the aircraft stalled (lost flying speed) and started down. Two miles south of the airport, the jet initially collided with the roof of a three-story apartment building. After shattering some large trees, it came to its final rest in a ravine. It exploded and killed everyone on board.

Crash inspectors revealed that birds had damaged the windshield and severely impaired both engines. Neither engine showed any mechanical failure or malfunction. Turbine blade damage to the left engine revealed 14 individual bird strikes and the right engine showed five. Fifteen cow bird carcasses were found within 150 feet of the departure end of the runway. A municipal garbage dump is located adjacent to the airport. Investigations revealed large flocks of birds were seen on the airport and thousands of birds swarming over the dump area.

In 1960, Dekalb-Peachtree Airport was returned to Dekalb County after serving as a Naval Air Station. The County gave the FAA assurance that it would not construct anything detrimental to air safety: "The County will ... take action to restrict the use of land adjacent to or in the immediate vicinity of the airport to activities and purposes compatible with normal airport operations including landing and takeoff aircraft."

Two years later in 1962, the County broke its promise to the FAA and erected a garbage dump. Nobody hit any birds for over ten years so perhaps the County would luck out.

In 1970, the ever-forceful FAA advised the County of the hazards to aviation associated with the dump. In February of 1971, the County advised the FAA that the dump would be closed in August 1972. Six months later, the accident happened. To my knowledge, that dump is still feeding birds. Since this airport was improved with government funds, the NTSB concluded in their report: "The following-up on the compliance requirements for airports developed or improved with Federal funds, the FAA did not take adequate measures, in accordance with existing statutes, to assure that the hazard was removed from the vicinity of the airport." The FAA had struck again.

Fifty-five-year-old Captain Henry R. Davis was employed with Overseas National Airways on May 21, 1951. His logbook showed over 25,000 hours, 2,000 of them in the DC-10. The flight from JFK to Frankfurt, Germany, on November 12, 1975, was to have been an enjoyable one because there were only company employees on board. Ferry flights without paying passengers are always more fun than scheduled trips because there's nobody to cater to. The DC-10 was loaded with 235,000 pounds of fuel and 139 employees that brought the gross weight up to 555,000, just 1,000 pounds short of the maximum allowable.

Captain Davis wisely selected the longest runway at Kennedy, 31 Right that extended for 14,572 feet. This runway borders a marsh, a beach, and tidal water, all great places for birds to congregate. During the takeoff roll, everything was fine until reaching 100 knots. At this time, a large flock of seagulls lifted off the runway and were sucked in by the No. 3 engine, causing it to disintegrate and shed various parts down the length of the runway. The captain shouted: "Watch the EGT" (exhaust gas temperature).

At this time, takeoff rejection procedures were put into effect. As the engines were placed in reverse, the engineer stated, "We have lost No. 3."

No. 1 and No. 2 engines attained normal reverse.

The engineer advised the Captain, "Brake pressure is Okay."

Within seconds, the Captain's instrument panel showed that No. 3 engine fire light and fuel control lever both were illuminated. Because of the wet runway and the loss of No. 3, reverse deceleration was not up to par and the end of the runway was rapidly approaching. The engineer attempted to shut down No. 3 by closing the fuel shutoff, but the lever could not be moved. The tower noticed that there was a fire on the right side of the aircraft, but did nothing to alert the flight crew. It seemed to the crew that they were going to stop before clobbering the blast fence at the end of the runway, but it would be close. They were still doing about forty knots with the runway end still too close for comfort. Captain Davis made a fast decision to turn left onto taxiway "Z". As they came to a stop just off the taxiway, the cockpit was shaking violently. They believed the right gear collapsed, which it had, as well as three blown tires. The wing could not be seen from the cockpit so they still had no idea that they were on fire. As a precautionary measure, the engineer pulled the fire handles for one and two. The Captain had already shut off the fuel cocks. As the crew attempted to exit through the cabin, they saw dense black smoke before them. They retreated and quickly evacuated through the right cockpit window and down the escape rope. The ship was evacuated in an orderly fashion, and the crew performed a "text book" emergency rescue.

The NTSB report stated that there were at least six bird strikes to the No. 3 engine. Fire erupted as the engine separated. The probable ignition source was the fuel released from a fuel line onto the hot engine at the rate of 160 gallons per minute. As the aircraft was turned just short of the blast fence, the right gear collapsed. The transfer of the aircraft weight to the wing cracked the spar and ruptured the skin in the vicinity of the No. 3 fuel tank. This fuel fed the fire that eventually gutted the aircraft. Although airport firemen were on the scene within 60 seconds, they were unable to extinguish the fire for over 34 hours. The NTSB's probable cause for this accident was once again the neglect of the FAA. The board stated that the two main causes for this accident were:

"1. The bird-control program at JFK did not effectively control the bird hazard. 2. The FAA and the General Electric Co. failed to consider the effects of rotor imbalance on the abeadable epoxy shroud material when the engine was tested for certification."

The engines on this aircraft were new CF-6 bypass turbo fan type engines, ones that had never gone through the prescribed testing for bird ingestion. So the FAA, being the "good old boys" that they are, allowed the manufacturer to utilize a test for a previous engine that was, ALMOST, similar to the CF-6.

The control of the bird population at JFK has been under scrutiny for years. Kennedy does have a man with a shotgun who patrols the airport and they utilize explosive devices to scare the birds, but the gulls get immune to these blasts and they have little effect. The bird patrol was not 24 hours a day, 7 days a week, but rather when the mood struck them. There were no bird patrols after sundown and most of the bird strikes occur after dark.

One man in a truck with a gun is not nearly enough protection for an airport as vast as Kennedy. London's Heathrow Airport boasts of 4 vehicles that patrol continuously 24 hours a day. Military bases curtail flying when birds are reported. No chance for the money hungry airlines to follow suit.

The bird strike problem greatly increased during the months preceding the Overseas DC-10 National accident. In July, there was one strike, two in August, one in September, and as many as seven in October, only a month before the mishap. The last seven bird strikes were all against jumbo jets that caused five engines to be changed at better than two million per copy.

There are two ways to reduce bird strikes: (1) reduce the number of birds at the airport, and (2) make aircraft that can withstand bird hits. FAR 33.77 states: "Ingestion of a four-pound bird striking a critical area of engine operating at maximum cruise power at maximum climb speed may cause an engine to (1) catch fire (2) burst (penetrate its case) (3) generate loads greater than specified, or (4) lose the capability of being shut down."

We have seen all of these requirements shattered during the DC-10 accident at JFK. At least so it would seem. On closer examination of the above poorly written rule, we find that the aircraft in question was on takeoff roll. This is not covered by the regulation. In fact, I find it nearly impossible to make an aircraft perform as the regulation states. When you are at cruise power, you are cruising and when you are at maximum climb speed you have climb power set. Criteria for foreign object testing is also found in FAA Advisory Circular 33-1 B, page 1: "The typical object being ingestion tested are normally introduced by dropping them into the inlet." I can't imagine how a bird could drop itself into an engine. They usually impact on takeoff roll or during approach.

Page 8 of the same circular states in paragraph 5: "Bird injection tests using freshly killed birds and gun injectors are "preferable" as actual strikes are closely simulated." The gun injector is to propel the bird into the engine at over "drop in speeds." As the name implies, at the beginning of the circular, it is only advisory in nature, which means the engine manufacturers can do whatever the hell they want. And they do.

On December 15, 1980, a Pan American 747 was on takeoff roll at San Francisco International Airport when the Captain felt a strange vibration just prior to liftoff. He aborted the takeoff and taxied back to the gate. It was discovered that a single bird had caused the following damage to the No. 4 engine. Extensive damage to most of the fan blades, damage to the cowling honeycomb, and all of the tail cone attach bolts were gone.

On April 7, 1981, Learjet N400PG was poised on the active runway, number 20L, at Lunken Field in Cincinnati, Ohio. The weather was perfect, the ATC clearance was copied, the various checklists were completed, and all that was left was the takeoff clearance.

"Lear Papa Golf your clear for takeoff. Climb to 2,500 on runway heading."

The crew acknowledged the message and started their takeoff roll. At 2,500 feet, First Officer Kent Woodworth keyed the mike and said: "Cincinnati departure Lear 400 Papa Golf Lunken at twenty-five hundred."

Departure "Four hundred Papa Golf climb and maintain one zero thousand and at turn left, left turn heading 360 direct Dayton on course."

The pilot responded, "Papa Golf."

Little did First Officer Ken Woodworth realize that he had made his last radio transmission. In 19 seconds, he would be dead. Captain Jim Griesshaber goosed the power and started a climbing left turn. He was warned by the controller of traffic at ten o'clock, two miles. Unfortunately, he was not warned of far more lethal traffic that was not being painted on radar. Halfway through the turn, a loud bang was heard as a 12-pound loon came crashing through the co-pilot's windshield, killing him instantly and causing the right engine to shut down. A turn back to the field was made, and on the downwind leg (heading opposite to landing), the gear was extended. The flaps would not go down. The captain had his hands full with an engine out, no flaps, and a dead co-pilot. Captain Griesshaber was doing a superb job, but there were more problems awaiting him on the ground. He had no brakes. He hastily applied the emergency brake system and it worked as advertised.

Post-flight inspection of the aircraft showed the extensive damage that the bird had caused. After its entry through the windscreen, it struck the co-pilot and managed to ricochet off the ceiling, tearing out 50 square inches of the ceiling fabric that ended up in the right engine, causing a blockage. There was a trail of blood and guts as far back as the aft bulkhead of the aircraft.

Captain Griesshaber had nearly everything against him. His good friend sitting in the right seat dead, one engine out, no flaps, no brakes, and an air blast through the cockpit that was deafening. A job well done.

To be a USAF Thunderbird pilot is the dream of most pilots who enjoy flying fighters. Hundreds of applications are submitted each year for a chance to fly with the greatest military flight demonstration team of them all. Only one or two are accepted and they may not be skilled enough to complete the course. Lt. Col. David F. Smith was on the team and was their leader.

On September 9, 1981, the Thunderbirds had put on one of their flawless shows at Burke Lakefront Airport in Cleveland, Ohio. The next day, they were deployed to Scott Field for another show. The weather in Cleveland was 1000-foot overcast and three mile visibility with light rain. Lt. Col. Smith would be flying with a passenger today. His back seat would be occupied by his crew chief, Staff Sergeant Dwight Caldwell Roberts. The aircraft they were flying was a T-38 Talon trainer used almost exclusively for advanced pilot training. This little beauty could hit Mach 1 in straight and level flight, and was a gem to fly.

After strapping into the Talon, Lt. Col. Smith fired up the two powerful engines and proceeded to contact the towers ground controller. T-Bird: 1 "Lakefront ground, Thunderbird 1, taxi with two, put our clearance on request."

Ground Control: "Thunderbird 1, turn left, taxi to 24 right, via taxiway Bravo intersection 6 right, wind 240 at 8, altimeter 29.75."

Throttles were advanced and the aircraft moved from its parking spot. Fighter pilots don't have the luxury of a co-pilot, so they handle everything themselves. The T-Bird leader also would be leading one of his teammates who would be flying on his wing. In the block of runway 24 he performed his before-takeoff check.

Flight controls—check.

Zero delay and parachute arming.

Lanyards—connected.

Helmet visor—as required.

Takeoff data—review.

Anticollision beacon—on.

Navigation lights—strobe position lights.

Pitot heat, defrosters and cockpit temperature—as required

Canopy—closed lock (check lightout)

With this check out of the way, Lt. Col. Smith called the tower: T-Bird 1: "Lakefront Tower, Thunderbird 1 is ready for departure with two" (meaning two aircraft since the lead makes the radio calls for the formation).

Tower: "T-Bird 1 make right turn after takeoff, cleared for takeoff, winds 230/10, caution the birds, and you can make your right turn just off the end of the airport if you will, please."

"T-Bird 1 cut loose."

As the two Talons lined up for takeoff, Lt. Col. Smith locked the brakes and ran through his lineup check (when both aircraft are aligned with the runway).

Heading indicator—check.

Altitude indicators—check.

IFF—as required.

Throttles instruments—checked

Loadmeters—check.

Warning lights—check off.

All was well so he gave his wingman the circular motion with his index finger signifying max power runup is next. The leader leaned his head back and touched his headrest. This was the signal to the wingman to be ready to release brakes. Lt. Col. Smith gave a final check to his backseat man and then rapidly nodded his head forward, signifying brake release time. The afterburner (added thrust used for takeoff) came to life with a deafening roar and two of the USAF's finest were on their way.

At 2,000 feet down the runway, the acceleration check looked good (a pre-takeoff calculated speed that must be reached at this time). The air speed indicator was showing 150 knots, backpressure was applied to the stick, and the Talon leaped into the air. Unfortunately, the T-38s were not the only ones to get airborne because a flock of over 50 sea gulls also were in the takeoff mode. As the lead ship approached the gulls, its powerful engines sucked the birds in, causing an instant flameout. The wingman watched the tragedy unfold. There was insufficient runway to land again, and they only had 75 feet of altitude. Time and proper decisions would mean the difference between life and death. The arming handles were raised to the full "up" position, exposing the cocking triggers. The trigger was squeezed initiating the ejection procedure. First the cockpit canopy was blown off; three-tenths of a second later, the rocket catapult was ignited and the occupant and seat started up the tracks and overboard at the rate of 45 feet a second. The backseat ejects first because if the pilot were to go first, his rocket-propelled seat would severely burn the man in the rear cockpit. Meanwhile, the stricken aircraft fell to the runway and nosed over. It became airborne again, then struck the runway once more, sliding off the end into Lake Erie.

Two thousand feet is the minimum safe altitude for ejection; however, if everything is performed flawlessly, ejection is possible at ground level with a minimum speed of 50 knots. It was Sergeant Roberts lucky day. He landed with only minimal injuries. The pilot was not so fortunate. His chute failed to open until ground impact. Once again, the birds had scored. This time, a million dollar aircraft was destroyed along with a superb pilot who will never be replaced.

The first few months of 1981 produced two potentially dangerous encounters with birds for the world's biggest operational bomber, the B-52. On January 28, 1981, the bomber had just become airborne when at approximately 200 feet, the pilot noticed a large flock of birds flying from right to left. He took evasive action and dove under one flock but was unable to miss a second. After the collision, the crew checked for damage. All engine instruments were in the green (normal) except for number 5EGT that was higher than the others. Observers on the ground noticed a trail of fire from No. 3 pod that housed engines 5 and 6. The pilot was advised of this and he shut these engines down as a precautionary measure. After flying in the local area for a time to reduce the fuel load they landed.

Immediately after the incident, a visual inspection of the aircraft revealed that No. 5 engine rotors, combustion chamber, and turbines were heavily damaged. Engines 1 and 6 were also in need of repair. The remains of 75 birds were recovered from the runway.

As expected, the bigger the bird, the worse the damage. The eagle may be the proud symbol of America, but to Captain Trottier, this bird is not placed in such high esteem. While flying at 350 knots at an altitude of 800 feet, the crew of a B-52 bomber encountered a strike by a giant eagle. The bird came crashing through the skin of the left wing. On its destructive journey through the wing, it cut several generator cables. From here, it penetrated the fuselage. It slammed into a junction of throttle cables, severing two and completely shutting those engines down.

Captain Trottier kept his cool and landed without further incident. He had this to say about his harrowing accident. "If the bird had impacted six inches lower, it would have severed all my throttle cables, immediately shutting down all my engines, leaving us no recourse but to eject."

We have seen the destructive force of a bird on various types of aircraft: mach two fighters, mach one trainers, jumbo jets, and giant bombers. Perhaps the world's largest aircraft, the USAF C5A can keep these intruders from spoiling a pilot's day.

The C5A transport is 247.8 feet long, has a wing span of 222.8 feet and features a cargo compartment 13.5 feet high and 144.6 feet long-, large enough to hold an M1 tank, helicopters, two 18-wheel trailer trucks, and 75 troops. No bird would dare to try and enter such a giant. But on January 23, 1983, the weather at Dover AFB in Delaware was poor. The ceiling was down to 300 feet with visibility varying at one mile with rain. Dover is situated close to the water and the pilots there are well aware of bird problems. The cockpit crew of the C5A was busily scanning for birds as they taxied out. None could be seen on the ground and they hoped the bad weather would stop the birds from flying. All checklists were completed and a clearance for takeoff was received.

After takeoff the Aircraft Commander called, "Gear up."

Just as his co-pilot was positioning the gear handle to the "up" position, the aircraft encountered a flock of snow geese. Sixty of the birds struck the aircraft in numerous places. The impacts were pronounced and followed by burning odors and heavy airframe vibrations. The pilot and engineer's panel were both showing an overheat condition for No. 2 engine. The Aircraft Commander retarded the No. 2 throttle and the overheat extinguisher. The scanner was sent to the cargo compartment to check for damage to the wings and engines. No. 2 engine was vibrating noticeably. He also noted that engines 3 and 4 had taken some hits, and that four was on fire. He reported this to the flight crew who immediately shut down No. 4. They fired the engine extinguisher and the fire was reported out. From this time on, until they were vectored to runway 1 ILS final approach course they dumped over 60,000 pounds of fuel. This would prevent an overweight landing. The crew performed nobly and the landing was uneventful.

Post-flight inspection revealed that all engines were damaged, but No. 2 and No. 4 received a major share to the fan rotor assembly. Holes torn through the sheet metal skin were noted in the following places: No. 4 engine 10x10 inch hole in the thrust reverse panel and the nose landing gear bulkhead broken; damage to both left and right main landing gear doors, and a 5x5 inch hole in the slot panel. Due to the skills of a well-trained crew, a major disaster was averted. It is interesting to note the different tactics taken between military airports and civilian.

After the crash of a DC-10 at Kennedy, there were various meetings with the FAA and bird control parties. There were many promises made but nothing concrete was ever accomplished. Here are a few excerpts from the new rules adopted by the powers to be at Dover AFB: "Transition training" (pilot checkouts) "will not be conducted in the local area pending further notice regardless of weather conditions. All Dover C-5 training and airlift missions are being rescheduled to avoid arrival and departures during the hours of peak bird activity."

To the Air Force, their mission is just as important to them as the movement of passengers is to the airlines. The only difference is that the Air Force is definitely more safety conscious. From 1983 to 1987, the Air Force lost three aircraft at a cost of $235 million. The most expensive loss was in 1987 when a $215 million B1B bomber crashed caused by a 16-pound pelican that penetrated the airframe. While there are tests performed on engines, there are no bird ingestion tests on airframes (all of the aircraft other than engines) even though over half the bird collisions were with this section of the plane.

To get an idea of the exact destruction force of a bird, some common physics is necessary. If, for example, you hit a bird weighing one pound at 100 knots, the impact force would be 880 pounds. If the same bird is struck at 300 knots, its 7,928 pounds; and at 600 knots, that one-pound feathered beauty would generate a force of 63,000 pounds. Canada geese weigh an average of eight pounds, so this gives you some idea of the speed versus weight ratio.

Prior to the jet era, aircraft flew at much slower speeds, and their rugged internal combustion engines could better withstand bird strikes. The jet engine is considerably more reliable but infinitely more vulnerable to bird ingestion. Since the front of a jet engine has tremendous suction power, is it any wonder that these large diameter engines on the jumbos invite more birds than the smaller prop predecessors?

There are numerous ways that man has used to combat our feathered friends but none are regarded as foolproof. Pyrotechnics is the name given to devices that produce loud noises such as miniature cannons that fire by a set timer. Broancoustics is the name given to the broadcasting of recorded bird distress calls. Even radio-controlled model airplanes have shown some effective results. The models are fashioned after falcons, birds natural enemy. By far the best method of dispersing is a man with a shotgun. Kennedy airport boasts of paying $500,000.000 per year for bird patrols. Obviously this is not enough.

Land adjacent to airport runways are ideal places for rodents and birds to congregate. The field itself is rarely visited by humans, and the birds grow accustomed to the jet noises. It has been proven that water, whether salt or fresh, is a desirous place for birds to roost. The three New York airports are all guilty of harboring great feeding grounds for birds. LaGuardia was built on a garbage dump, and JFK and Newark grew out of marshlands. O'Hare

Airport in Chicago has a pond between the runways larger than some lakes, and the ponds near the chapels at Kennedy are alive with birds.

Kirtland AFB in New Mexico is the home of an energetic group of officers and men known as the BASH team (Bird and Aircraft Strike Hazard). This organization is fed reports of bird strikes throughout the world and they conduct seminars on how to beat the Bird Strike Problem.

Some of the following material is taken from the August 10, 1995, meeting of Bird Strike Committee-USAA at Dallas International Airport. This whirlwind committee was formed in 1991 to facilitate the exchange of information concerning the bird strike problem. I am deeply indebted to Dr. Richard A. Dolbeer who is the top man at the Denver Wildlife Research Center in Sandusky, Ohio.

The USAF has averaged 2,666 bird/wildlife strikes annually over the past ten years. In 1994, the total cost of these strikes was over $15 million. Nineteen percent occurred during low level, 73 percent on or near the airport, and 8 percent while en route. The lion's share of the strikes was recorded during September and October. All Air Force bases reported at least one strike, with Little Rock AFB reporting the highest number of 106, Barksdale 101, Luke 90, Kirtland 76, Hurlbust 75, Randolph 74, Castle 67, Incirlik 63, Reese 56, and McConnell 52. The three most frequently struck planes were the KC-135 with 316, C-130 with 263, and the F-16 fighter with 210. The birds with the highest strikes were hawks and sparrows. The cost to the USAF per year averages between $50 and $80 million. The cost to civil aircraft worldwide is between $1 to $2 billion each year.

The FAA has been collecting bird strike data since 1968 but little analysis has ever been done. Now that the "feds" have requested the U.S. Department of Agriculture to organize, manage, and edit all reports on bird strikes, we are at last getting some action.

It seems that a different species of birds are more prone to hitting civil aircraft as compared to the military. The most hits are received from gulls; next are waterfowl, and last, birds of prey. Deer were involved in 57 reported strikes, mostly in Pennsylvania.

We have previously touched on the serious problem at JFK airport. Now with the new aggressive work guided by the Department of Agriculture, we are seeing an improvement at Kennedy. A bird that is no laughing matter is the laughing gull (Larus articilla). From 1988 to 1990, these birds were hitting aircraft at the rate of 170 strikes a year. It is estimated that there are over 7,500 nest colonies adjacent to the JFK airport.

From 1991 to 1993, a new experimental program was undertaken to try and reduce the Kennedy strikes. Now there would be between two and five gunners stationed at the airport boundaries to shoot the gulls that traverse the airport. In 3,401 hours of shooting, 35,692 gulls were killed, 13,866 in 1991, 13,466 in 1992, and 7,340 in 1993. The majority, 32,534, were laughing gulls and 3,158 were other gulls. In 1991, strikes were reduced by 66 percent, 89 percent in 1992, and 90 percent in 1993. It seems as though they are on the right track but the main problem is trying to reduce the nesting colonies adjacent to Jamaica Bay. These breeding grounds have only declined by 20 percent. While I hate to see all those beautiful birds killed, better them than us. From 1979 to 1993, there were between 100 to 315 aircraft struck by birds each year. These strikes are a significant threat to aircraft as well as to human safety. Laughing gulls strikes resulted in 51 aborted takeoffs in addition to 46 damaged engines.

In May of 1991 and March of 1992, gulls were ingested into the engines of two heavily loaded transports. One Northwest 747 aborted takeoff, and required the replacement of 10 tires and brakes. The other, a Japan Airlines 747, had to dump 90,700 kg. of fuel in order to get down to a legal landing weight.

On the Sand Island, Midway Atoll, the albatross population has increased from 50,000 in 1939 to over 400,000 adults in 1995. This increase causes serious bird strike problem at the Naval Air Facility. There have been as many as 360 birds crossing the runway per minute.

Exxon's Air World Magazine had an interesting paragraph concerning a remedy for bird strikes. In Japan, All Nippon Airways is taking a new approach to combating our feathered friends. The engineering section at Nippon found that the eyesight of many birds is eight times sharper than that of a human and that birds often fear eye-shaped objects. The CF-6 engines have a center spinner that is over thirty inches in diameter, large enough to paint a giant sized eyeball. They painted these eyes on fifteen of their twenty Boeing 767s. During this first year test program, the frequency of bird strike incidents had dramatically declined from 20 a year for the 767 and nine times for the 747. It dropped to only once a year per plane for each type. The airline is so pleased with their project that they have applied for a patent on their new bird repellent.

Here are a few of the latest bird-strike incidents.

September 26, 1993. American Trans Air Lockheed 1011. After liftoff at 50 feet, aircraft had multiple bird-strikes. Birds were ingested in the No. 1 engine and it was shut down. After landing, a visual inspection revealed that the No. 1 and 2 inboard slats were damaged. No. 14 and 15 fan blades were replaced.

October 29, 1993, America West B-727 was climbing out after takeoff when the crew felt a bump on the left side of the aircraft. The flight was continued and on arrival at destination a visual check revealed a bird strike on the fan and nose cowl of the No. 1 engine.

November 7, 1993, Flagship Airlines Jetstream 320, passing 600 feet, the No. 1 engine ingested a bird. EGT (exhaust gas temperature) started to rise with a foul smell from the engine air bleeds. Crew shut down No. 1 and landed, engine replacement was necessary.

November 11, 1993, Continental Micronesia Boeing 727, prior to landing a bird was ingested into the No. 3 engine. First and second fan blades were damaged beyond limits. The No. 3 engine had to be replaced.

December 21, 1993, USAir 737, after takeoff the crew experienced a bird strike. The flight returned to the departure airport and a visual inspection revealed a damaged radome assembly requiring a replacement.

September 23, 1994 Syracuse, New York a United Airlines 737 jet with 55 passengers on board was forced to abort its flight shortly after takeoff. Over 100 starlings were sucked into the plane's two engines, causing one to shut down. The plane landed safely with no injuries.

October 18, 1994 a Beechcraft Baron slammed into the rear wall of a Sam's Club. The pilot had just taken off from Smith Field near Fort Wayne, Indiana, when he ran into a flock of geese. Three of them came through the windshield. The pilot escaped with no injuries but his passenger required surgery.

December 23, 1994, Tampa, Florida, a TWA 727 had just taken off when it made contact with a pair of large birds. The first bird hit the nose and glanced off. The second became embedded in the nose of the aircraft. The radome had a two-foot hole in it. Inside was a bird with a six-foot wingspan. The aircraft made a safe landing with no injuries.

May 31, 1995, an American Airlines B-757 had just departed San Francisco when a passenger spotted a hole as large as a football on the left wing. The hole was caused by a bird strike. The aircraft landed safely.

August 22, 1995 Continental Flight 129 contacted a flock of geese while landing at Seattle-Tacoma International Airport. The damage was a large hole in the nose radar cone. The aircraft landed safely.

October 2, 1995, Kansas City, two ducks crashed into the windshield of a medic helicopter. The pilot received minor cuts from flying fiberglass but managed to land safely.

Not all strikes are birds. Some are quite a bit larger. An Alaska Airlines Boeing 727 was landing in Cordova, Alaska. Just after touchdown, the crew was alerted to some-thing about 500 feet ahead of them. As they got nearer, they could see it was a large moose standing in the middle of the runway in defiance to the giant bird rapidly bearing down on him. There was no way to avoid the collision. Chalk up one dead moose and one very expensive broken nose gear. The only injury was to the moose who will not be able to play "chicken" again.

Famous Planes and People

Birds show little regard for the planes they hit or the famous people that they scare.

On January 21, 1995, at Le Burger, France, a Mysteae Falcon jet had just departed Le Bourse airport when it suddenly crashed and burned. All ten people on board perished in the flaming wreckage. One of them was the head of a leading French Food Company. Bird ingestion was discovered in one of the engines.

In April 1995, at Andrews Air Force Base in Camp Springs, Maryland, Air Force One was practicing landings when it struck between 200 to 500 birds. The strikes caused extensive damage but the craft was safely landed. President Clinton was obviously not on board.

On June 4, 1995, at Kennedy International Airport, New York an Air France Concord was landing when two of its four engines sucked in a number of Canada geese. No one was injured. The plane made a safe landing. Mr. Marches, an Air France spokesman said: "Flames and smoke could be seen coming from the number three and four engines beneath the right wing. We have a running battle out there with the birds. This could have been serious." Repairs cost over $5 million. Air France received a settlement from the Port Authority of New York and New Jersey for $5.1 million to cover the cost of the bird damage.

On July 9, 1995, rocker Rod Stewart had just finished performing for 30,000 fans in Gateborg, Sweden. He boarded his Hawker Siddely 125 jet for a short flight to London, England. Moments after liftoff, one of the engines ingested some birds. The captain returned to the airport and made an uneventful landing.

On September 22, 1995, at Elmendorf Air Force Base, Alaska, a huge AWACS transport, similar to the ones used in the Persian Gulf War, was poised at the end of the runway awaiting clearance for a training mission. There were 24 crewmembers on board: 22 were Americans and 2 were Canadians. The four-engine jet was fueled to 125,000 pounds, enabling it to remain aloft for over nine hours. Tower clearance was received and as the thrust levers were advanced, all engines started their high-pitched whine on their way to takeoff thrust. Captain Clay Wallace, an Air National Guard Captain who was watching the takeoff had this to say: "Just as he got the wheels up, the left engine started popping and I could see fire shooting out the end. I said, Where the hell did they go? And all of a sudden down he went in a huge fireball."

The aircraft mowed down 200 birch trees when it hit the ground. It left a swath 300 yards long by 150 yards wide. The only recognizable piece was the shell of one engine and a six-foot piece of the fuselage. The aircraft was a highly modified B-707 with sophisticated radar system that could identify, detect, and monitor the field of battle. It cost us well over $180 million. What could possibly have caused a warplane, one that has seen combat and never been damaged, a plane that has been flying for decades without an incident, to crash and take the lives of 24 good men? You guessed it, birds. The runway was strewn with dozens of dead Canada Geese.

On October 8, 1996, HUD Secretary, Henry Cisneros was not injured when his Delta Boeing 727 was struck by a flock of birds. The captain shut down the No. 2 engine and the stench from the ingested birds was eliminated. An uneventful precautionary landing was executed at Washington, D.C. Mr. Cisneros had this to say: "I have logged quite a lot of flying hours, have flown through several incidents, but nothing quite like this one."

On September 25, 1995, in Mackinac Island, Michigan, House Speaker Newt Gingrich and his wife were unharmed when their Cessna Citation jet had an encounter with some birds. Two birds were sucked into the right engine and another pair slammed into the left wing leading edge causing a 14-inch dent. No one was hurt as the aircraft skidded to a stop, 25 feet off the end of the runway. According to the Associated Press, Speaker Gingrich said: "We were very lucky. The pilots were very shaken. Another three or four seconds and we would have had a real problem."

Believe it or not, there is a comical side to the serious business of birds. The citizens of a small town in Arkansas were astounded when a number of frozen ducks fell from the sky. It seemed that these birds were flying too close to a thunderstorm, were caught in an updraft, and were frozen to death. They fell to earth 100 strong.

Birds and bats are not the only creatures that have hit airplanes. Planes have been struck by various other animals. There are pilot reports of colliding with a chicken at 800 feet, a snake at 3,000, a squirrel at 5,000 feet, and a mouse at 8,000 feet. No one knows for sure how these animals got there, but speculation has it that they were all dropped by a bird of prey as it tried to miss being hit by an aircraft.

This one is strictly "for the birds."

An F4 Phantom struck a vulture while on a low-level mission. The pilot of the jet was Lt. Mark S. Bird. His backseat weapons officer was Captain Ralph M. Crow, Jr. The aircraft was nicknamed Gonzo in honor of its crew chief. Two more of the ground personnel answer to the name of Sergeant James B. Mallard and Tech. Sergeant Floyd D. Birdsong.

Delta captain Ed Sobota, an alternate member of ALPA's National Airport Standards Committee had this to say regarding bird strikes: "All parties—pilots, air traffic control, and airport managers—need training on bird hazards. We need to apply the same standards to the hazards as we due to wind shear and icing.

Birds have ruled the skies long before man could fathom how to get off the ground. Pilots try their best to avoid striking them, and I am sure that birds have no interest in being ground up in a jet engine. Hopefully, some day someone will figure a way for us both to keep from killing each other.

CHAPTER 17

▼

DANGER UNDER YOUR FEET

Pan American Clipper Flight 160, a Boeing 707 cargo liner, was just leveling at 31,000 feet. This would be their cruising altitude from their departure point in New York to their destination point, Frankfurt, Germany. On board was 59,912 pounds of cargo, of which 15,360 pounds were toxic chemicals. The seasoned crew consisted of 53-year old Captain John J. Zammett, 34-year-old First Officer Gene W. Ritter, and 37-year-old Flight Engineer Davis Melvin.

The weather was great for aviating and the crew was settling in for a nice, uneventful trip across the pond. These thoughts were soon forgotten when smoke was detected coming up through the floor of the cockpit. They were now 100 miles east of Montreal, Canada. Captain Zammett looked across the cockpit and spoke to his co-pilot: "Tell them we wanna get down and head for Boston."

"Right, Boston 160 please give me a heading direct Boston at this time."

"One sixty pick up a heading of, ah, one seven zero and when able, proceed direct to Boston."

"Thank you very much."

The three crewmembers all donned their oxygen masks and had their smoke goggles in readiness. The smoke was now so intense that they had to depressurize and open the cockpit window.

Boston ATC called "Will you accept a vector for a visual approach to a five-mile final for runway 33 left, or do you want to be extended out further?"

"Negative, we want to get it on the ground as soon as possible."

Ground observers at the airport saw the stricken craft with smoke billowing out the cockpit window. The crew could not see their instruments and the deadly smoke was unbearable. She started banking one way and then the other. People on the airport said a silent prayer and held their breath. Clipper 160 was barely a mile from safety of the airport. The gallant crew was nearly home free.

A sudden burst of power was applied, perhaps for a go-around. The speed on final was faster than normal, and the rolling and yawing continued to intensify. She pitched up violently and at the top of the stall, headed down. The nose and left wing struck the ground simultaneously. The horrendous crash snuffed out the lives of three valiant pilots and scattered parts and cargo into Boston's harbor.

Score one more for the FAA! Here are just a few of the reasons why this tragedy occurred. Of course, after the accident, things began to happen. The dogged NTSB started to build a fire under the "feds." They went back to the original certification of the Boeing 707 and came up with some brilliant discrepancies. As a rule, most fires on an aircraft originate somewhere in the "hell hole" (electronics section). If a faulty electric system can be isolated, the fire usually subsides. When this airplane was tested for smoke evacuation in flight, the test was not realistic. A smoke bomb was set off, but when it was deprived of oxygen, the smoke stopped. This craft was never tested for a sustained fire that could produce its own oxygen such as some of the hazardous materials that would one day be in its belly. Boeing Airplane Company started to run some extensive tests on the Boeing 707. A Mr. R.C. Curtiss discussed smoke prevention in his letter to the FAA: "If the procedure is followed a continuous source of smoke will not exist as the fire will be smothered EXCEPT IN THE RARE CASE WHERE

A HAZARDOUS MATERIAL IS CARRIED WHICH IS PACKAGED AND HANDLED SUCH THAT IT IS RELEASED, GENERATES HEAT AND PROVIDES ITS OWN SOURCE OF OXYGEN" (capitals mine).

Mr. Curtiss goes on to say: "However, design studies will be initiated to establish if any airplane procedure or configuration improvements can handle isolation of continuous source of smoke."

In essence, the Boeing people were saying that they were going to run tests that should have been performed long before the aircraft was used to haul hazardous cargo.

The Pan Am flight was loaded with material that could produce a continuous stream of smoke: hydrofluoric acid 50 gallons, nitric acid 100 gallons, hydrogen peroxide 60 gallons, sulfuric acid 60 gallons, isopropyl alcohol 80 gallons, and acetic acid 50 gallons. These are just a few of the 15,360 pounds of chemicals on board.

It is bad enough to have to fly this potentially dangerous cargo, but when it isn't shipped or loaded properly, things can happen. The investigators zeroed in on the nitric acid and the way it was packed. There were five one-pint plastic-capped glass bottles packaged inside wooden boxes cushioned with highly combustible material similar to sawdust. The boxes were improperly labeled and failed to have the specified markings, "This End Up." If one of these bottles had an insecure cap and it was laid on its side, it could easily penetrate the flammable packing material.

Very few of the cargo handlers were ever briefed on dangerous cargo, and this is against FAA regulations. I have seen "baggage smashers" loading a plane with complete disregard for the markings on a box. "This End Up" means nothing to them. After all, they don't have to fly with their dangerously loaded cargo. Any time hazardous material is loaded on a plane, the captain must be informed in writing as to the nature of the cargo and where it will be stored. This was not done on the Pan Am flight.

I remember my trips through Newark when USAirways was known as Allegheny Airlines. I made a point of refusing to carry any restricted articles on my flight. Of course, if it was for medical needs, I would take it, but that was my only exception. The ramp agent at Newark contacted my chief pilot and told him that I was refusing to carry hazardous cargo. I received a letter from Captain Harvey M. Thompson, at that time the vice president of flying, stating in length how everything was being done to ensure that packaging and shipping of hazardous cargo was all above board. Captain Thompson's letter is as follows: "If you want to inspect them, go ahead and do it, there is no reason why you shouldn't. On the other hand, those items that have been cleared by ALPA and other experts that have been requested to assist them, I THINK THEY SHOULD BE CARRIED ON YOUR AIRCRAFT. WE WILL EXPECT YOU TO COMPLY WITH THE PROGRAM" (capitals mine).

It makes you wonder who's in charge of the flight; me or a man behind a desk hundreds of miles away.

We have examined the faulty testing of the aircraft, the dangerous way the cargo is crated, and the incorrect method of loading and notification. Let's now check on the adequacy of the crew's oxygen equipment.

The Captain's medical records revealed that he was required to wear glasses while flying. Smoke goggles, to be effective, must obviously eliminate smoke from getting to your eyes. The NTSB examined several masks and goggles from Pan Am and several other carriers, and found the majority of them to be faulty. These smoke goggles do not adequately protect the flight crew from smoke when worn either with or without corrective glasses. Other smoke goggles in use restrict the wearer's vision appreciably. It looks like it's a case of let's not bother to perfect something that will probably never be used.

To bolster the NTSB report in 1983, ten years after the Pan Am disaster, the Congressional Subcommittee on Investigations and Oversight revealed some startling facts in their report. After the Pan Am tragedy, the FAA decided it might be time to check into the operation of the oxygen masks used by the flight desk crews. Chairman of the subcommittee, Congressman Elliott H. Levitas, was questioning Mr. Don deSteiger, an expert on smoke goggles and oxygen masks. "Following the Boston accident in November, 1973, in which the function of the protective breathing equipment was questioned, the FAA held two meetings with the industry, one on the west coast and one here in Washington. The problem being that there was no proof of performance requirement for equipment of this type." He goes on to say: "We received from the industry 137 different kinds of protective breathing equipment intended for use on the flight deck. Of the 137 items that were tested, only 22 passed the proposed acceptance criteria. This basically points out that we have a lot of junk on the flight deck."

The FAA did finally publish a ruling concerning "future equipment," but no requirement to replace the existing masks.

Brace yourself before you read this. Mr. deSteiger continues: "An example of indifference on the part of some elements within the FAA is the certification of the Boeing 757 and 767 series aircraft with protective breathing equipment that will not function. At the request of ALPA, CAMI tested these devices demonstrating that they would not provide proper protection for the crewmembers. The FAA was apparently embarrassed when the results were released and consequently HAVE FORBIDDEN CAMI TO CONTINUE TESTING OF PROTECTIVE BREATHING DEVICES" (capitals mine).

That's the way to go "feds." Stick your heads in the sand.

It was determined that over half of the 15,000 pounds of chemicals aboard the Pan Am flight were improperly packaged and nearly all of the packages were improperly labeled. We can all be grateful to Captain's Donald Dunn and James Eckols, both line captains and co-chairmen of the ALPA Hazardous Materials Committee. Nearly two frustrating years after the accident, these two captains and ALPA inaugurated STOP, short for Safe Transportation of People. Since the government wasn't interested in the safety of the travelers, the Air Line Pilot Association was. Crews were briefed, manuals were distributed, and a hotline was established at the ALPA head office in Washington D.C. Pressure from the pilot group finally got some government action. President Ford signed a Hazardous Materials Transportation Act. Now any violation in shipping or packaging would carry a fine of $10,000. This was a step in the right direction but it was not the answer. There are just too many unscrupulous shippers to contend with.

A shipment of nitric acid stored in half-gallon bottles and packaged in cardboard boxes was shipped from Los Angeles to Atlanta. The boxes were labeled "electrical appliances." This cargo was loaded aboard an Aero Mexico DC-9, along with 75 passengers. The boxes were discovered leaking in the cargo bin.

On December 31, 1971, a Delta jet was loaded with passengers and two packages of radioactive materials. The packaging was faulty and the dangerous material contaminated the aircraft and its passengers. This accident was not discovered until days later. By this time, the aircraft had carried 917 passengers who had to be alerted by Delta, and told that a physical examination might be in their best interest. In 1974, another leaky package of highly radioactive material accompanied unwary passengers of two flights from Washington to Atlanta and then to Baton Rouge. This time, about 200 passengers and crewmembers were subject to enormous doses of radiation, ranging over 100 times more than the recommended maximum exposure limit for an entire year. Effects from this exposure may not be known for many years.

What makes shippers package improperly? Money. When a customer wants hazardous material shipped, he has to pay extra for the packaging and handling. So here's a chance for the shoddy operator to reap a "bundle." He charges the high rate for the packaging, but pockets the money and sends the freight out as a unrestricted cargo.

In 1973, it was estimated that 800,000 packages of radioactive materials were transported in the United States. Seventy five percent of those packages were carried on passenger aircraft. Throughout the United States, there were a total of 44 government inspectors to oversee the millions of shipments.

The maximum dosage of radiation that an individual can tolerate a year is 500 millirems. The average chest X-ray exposure ranges from 20 to 500 millirems. The passengers of one DC-9 were exposed to 120,000 millirems in just one flight. Pregnant women and children are more prone to the effects of radiation than others. Perhaps the effects of radiation may not show up for generations. Flight Attendants who regularly fly trips that carry hazardous cargo have a much higher percentage of birth defects than the flight attendants who fly trips without the questionable cargo.

In April of 1979, a Mr. John Stone, President of American Jet Aviation, contracted to carry a shipment of bromine trifluoride from the U.S. to Australia. This chemical is highly toxic and will explode on contact with water. Its primary use is to dissolve drill bits that have failed while drilling for oil. It is never to be allowed in the cargo hold of an aircraft. Mr. Stone repacked the bromine, marked it as well-drilling equipment, and shipped it aboard a Qantas Airlines 747 from Los Angeles to Australia. Mr. Stone and the American Jet Aviation Corporation were brought to trial and convicted.

Postal bags may contain a lot more than mail. On September 5, 1982, it became necessary to evacuate the Hilo, Hawaii, Post Office. Toxic fumes were released when a 15-ounce bottle of undisclosed flammable fingernail solution ruptured. Hazardous materials are often concealed in postal bags, and sealed and placed aboard aircraft as first class mail.

Smoke was observed coming from the baggage compartment of an Aeromexico DC-10 that was about to take off from Mexico to Los Angeles. The cargo doors were opened and a leaking jar of nitric acid was discovered. It had already eaten through the floor, and investigators said that if the discovery was not made, the plane could have exploded in mid-air.

On February 3, 1988, American Airlines flight 132, a Douglas DC-9-83, departed Dallas for Nashville Metropolitan Airport, Tennessee. In addition to the passengers' luggage in the cargo compartment, there was a undisclosed and improperly packaged hazardous material in the form of five gallons of hydrogen peroxide solution and 25 pounds of sodium orthosilicate-based mixture. During the flight, the floor above the cargo compartment began emitting smoke (not unlike Valujet). The floor became warm and soft to walk on, and passengers were moved to other seats in the cabin. No emergency was declared (why I don't know) and a normal landing was made at Nashville. It was determined that the 50 percent hydrogen peroxide containers in the cargo hold was far too dangerous a mixture to be shipped by air, even in an all cargo flight, let alone a passenger flight. The NTSB final report stated: "The NTSB determines the probable cause of the in-flight fire to be a chemical reaction resulting from a hydrogen peroxide solution in concentration PROHIBITED FOR

AIR TRANSPORTATION (capitals mine) which leaked and combined with sodium orthosilicate-based mixture from an UNDECLARED AND IMPROPERLY PREPARED CONTAINER" (capitals mine).

On September 5, 1996, Controller James C. Schultz was working a Federal Express DC-10 cargo trip. The aircraft reported smoke in the cockpit and the crew was declaring an emergency. Descending out of 33,000 feet with a rate of decent of over 7,000 feet per minute, the captain was mistakenly keying his microphone even when he was talking to his crew. "This sucks, don't slow down! We've got [to get] this thing on the ground."

Controller Schultz knew that the DC-10 was in big trouble, and to add to his problems, he did not have the approach plate for the Newburgh, New York, Airport. Schultz was experienced enough that he was able to recite the instructions from a letdown chart that he had on hand (God bless the controllers). The weather was marginal but the DC-10 broke out of the clouds and made a perfect landing. After landing, controller Schultz transmitted the following: "Contact Stewart tower when able."

As the co-pilot began to read back the frequency I could hear the captain scream, "Forget it! We've got to get out of here."

Three minutes after the crew evacuated the cargo flight, it burst into flames. It continued to burn for over three hours. The aircraft was loaded with hazardous material.

Hazardous materials, as defined by the U.S. Department of Transportation, are substances capable of posing an unreasonable hazard to safety, health, and property when transported in commerce. There are roughly 500,000 hazardous materials shipments every day. Luckily for the airline passenger, only very small amounts are shipped by air. The FAA is the inspecting authority of hazardous shipment on both foreign and domestic carriers.

Out of 50 states, only eleven have any hazardous material regulations for air transportation. However, NONE of these states actively enforces the regulations. The eleven safety-conscious states are Arkansas, Delaware, Hawaii, Idaho, Louisiana, New Hampshire, Oregon, South Dakota, Vermont, Virginia, and Wyoming.

Airlines take no responsibility for the contents of the tons of mail that they fly. This is left to the post office to accomplish. With over 630 million pieces handled daily, the post office admits that only a very small fraction ever gets screened.

Ironically, much of the dangerous cargo carried on aircraft may not, by law, be conveyed on other types of passenger transportation. When trains and trucks carry material that is corrosive, explosive, radioactive, or otherwise dangerous, they must display the hazardous material symbol so that you can keep your distance. Ralph Nader's Aviation Action Project petitioned the FAA to warn all airline passengers that they may be sitting a few feet from disaster. The "feds" rejected the petition saying that a notice to passengers of the hazards "Would be misleading in that it would foster an unwarranted apprehension without imparting any information of value to the average passenger."

Would you like the FAA to make this decision for you?

What goes into the luggage compartment is not the only problem that passengers have to endure. Travelers themselves are potential trouble-makers. Unknowingly, passengers pack various hazardous items in their luggage and briefcases without realizing it. Items as seemingly harmless as a book of matches or as potentially deadly as an explosive device have been carried aboard airliners. Last summer, for example, a number of explosions perforated a briefcase being unloaded in Miami, Florida, causing injury to a baggage handler. Investigators discovered that the owner of the brief-case had stored ten hand grenades and a smoke bomb in an old coffee container.

More than once, matchbook covers have popped open, permitting the head of a match in one book to contact the striking strip of another. This may seem rather unlikely, but the FAA claims it happens "several times a month."

Other potentially dangerous items passengers have put in their luggage are mace sprays, gunpowder, model airplane glue, automotive flares, gasoline, and butane lighter fluid. One person who can be singled out is the traveling salesman who carries samples of chemicals in his suitcase that occasionally rupture and emit smoke, odors, or other effects.

In December of 1999, the FAA completed a two-year hazardous cargo investigation concerning American Airlines. American was fined $8 million and pleaded guilty to a felony for their handling of combustible chemicals at Miami International Airport. Investigators found that a Miami shipper was paying passengers to carry his shipments as excess baggage. American has raised their prices on hazardous shipments to aid in the cost of a new safety program.

In 1998, Continental Airlines was fined $25,000 after a shipment of uncovered safety matches. The government said that the boxes of matches weighed 1,319 pounds, 1,264 over the legal limit. I have seen numerous highway signs that state "No HASMAT materials allowed in Tunnel." It's too dangerous to drive a truck carrying HASMAT materials, but it's perfectly legal to fly them on passenger flights.

Nearly all airlines carry hazardous material. They receive triple the payment for flying this type of material as they do for normal cargo. So money, as usual, is the answer. There are, however, two carriers that refuse to carry the dangerous cargo: Southwest and America West. For this they should be highly commended. During an 11-year period, 2,260 HASMAT incidents were filed with the DOT. If the FAA were really safety conscious, they would ban all HASMAT on any aircraft, cargo or otherwise. Here is a statement made by FAA's former chief David R. Hinson after the Valujet crash in 1996. "Our objective is to keep chemicals and other substances that can feed or start a fire out of cargo compartments."

Well, Mr. Hinson, that can be accomplished easily. Simply write a regulation banning such cargo and your objective will be fulfilled.

Airport Security

The weather over the Ionia Sea was beautiful with a few scattered clouds between three and six thousand feet with a visibility of over 15 miles. The crew of a Pan Am 707 was cruising at 33,000 feet on an easterly heading.

The First Officer was flying this leg and was sharing his time with the autopilot. The captain was working the radios and scanning the horizon to keep clear of any other aircraft. At the eleven o'clock position (just to the left of straight ahead, or twelve o'clock) he noticed a 707 aircraft about 4,000 feet below, and approximately five miles away, heading toward him. The traffic was in level flight so there was little concern about a collision. As he continued watching, he saw the aircraft in a steep climbing altitude that kept increasing. He believed that he saw an object just behind the left wing, and when the aircraft reached the same altitude as Pan Am 110, it started to spiral to the left. The Captain watched it until it disappeared from view. He noticed that No. 2 engine was missing and speculated the object he first saw behind the plane was most likely the missing engine. He noticed an abundance of debris at a lower altitude trailing the stricken aircraft. The Flight Engineer left his saddle and pressed his face against the left side window. The aircraft passed within a mile of Pan Am and he could plainly see pieces of shiny metal fluttering earthward. No one saw the aircraft strike the water and there were no reports of military aircraft or missile firing in the area.

The flotsam was initially spotted by a Greek Air Force C-47 that guided the ten surface vessels, including the aircraft carrier, *Independence*, to the crash site. The accident aircraft was identified as TWA's Flight 841 from Athens to Rome, Italy. There were 79 passengers and a crew of 9. No one survived.

The search continued until September 10, 1974, just two days after the accident. Twenty-four bodies were recovered along with 2,500 pounds of debris and luggage. Various pieces of the aircraft were selected and sent to the FBI in Washington. The selection of the pieces were based on the similarity to flotsam collected after a De Haviland Comet jet exploded in mid-air a few years earlier.

Investigators from the NTSB aided by the United Kingdom's Accident Investigation Branch all agreed to the cause of the disaster: "An explosive device was detonated within the aft cargo compartment while the aircraft was cruising at 28,000 feet."

A Ground Agent at the Rome Airport noticed smoke emitting from the rear cargo door on another TWA jet. The smoke was rapidly suppressed by the airport firefighters and all luggage was removed to be identified by each passenger. The contents revealed that the batteries of a tape recorder were leaking on some lighter fluid and caused it to ignite. The aircraft was not damaged and the passengers continued on to their destination. When the suitcase was examined by the FBI, they discovered small particles of unconsumed C-4, a high explosive and sufficient evidence of an "Improvised explosive device or bomb which malfunctioned, resulting in a fire, rather than the intended explosion."

How is it possible for the devices to be placed on board aircraft? Well, you are readily aware of the metal detectors that abound at most airports. These machines screen passengers and their carry-on luggage, but what sort of scrutiny does your checked luggage receive? None! Yes that's right, zero. Air freight and checked bags go merrily down the conveyor belt into a loading cart and onto the aircraft without ever being checked. Sure, if something looks suspicious in the freight room it will be examined, but flight movements are so rapid the "baggage smasher" barely has time to load the aircraft.

Perhaps you have noticed the minimal security at commuter terminals or where the less-than-thirty-seat aircraft are boarded. That's the way the FAA dictates.

On June 23, 1985, an Air India Boeing 747 crashed into the Atlantic about 100 miles southwest of Ireland. There were 329 passengers on board. So far, they have retrieved 131 bodies. While the data and voice recorder could probably solve the mystery, they remain 7,000 feet below the surface. Investigators believe that an explosive device was placed on board before it left Montreal, its last stop in North America. Wreckage and bodies were found in an area five miles wide that would indicate an in-flight breakup.

On October 30, 1985, at Dallas/Fort Worth Airport, an American Airlines 727 had just landed and was heading for Gate 18 in Terminal 2E. Thirty seconds after parking and opening the passenger door, an explosion was heard in the belly. Smoke was discovered and was quickly extinguished by the base fireman. Inside, the pad showed evidence of burning. A woman's overnight cosmetic bag was nearly consumed but there was enough of it left to tell that it contained an explosive device. The passengers and crew evacuated in an orderly fashion and no one was injured.

Just after the tragic TWA bombing over the Ionia Sea, the FAA decided to make airport security one of their most important priorities. They had a number of ways for detecting explosives and as Richard F. Tally, director of the agency's Civil Aviation Security Service stated: "It is still our biggest problem and it has our highest priority."

I am sorry to report that little or nothing has been accomplished since the 1974 accident.

The people who work the metal detector equipment at the various airports throughout the country have literally no screening before they are put to work, and they learn on the job. Their pay is usually less than the people who clean the terminal. If a terrorist group wanted to smuggle arms or explosives on board an airliner, the easiest way for them to operate is for one of them to obtain a job as a security guard. When you are issued your I.D., there is nowhere on the airport grounds that is off limits. The people who clean the cabins of the various airlines have a similar screening check to those in the security program.

It is true that they do fingerprint the new applicants and ask the usual pre-hiring questions, but you can apply for a security position one day and be hired the next. It normally takes at least two weeks for fingerprints to be checked at the various law enforcement agencies. Until this process is completed, there is no way to determine if they are hiring a guard with a criminal record.

There have been a number of independent surveys completed by newspapers and TV stations to determine the adequacies of the system. In 1979, Chicago's O'Hare International Airport was the focal point of a *Chicago Sun Times* expose. A reporter applied to one firm and was put on the job the next day without a reference check. "I once had more trouble getting a job at Burger King," she remarked. After this and other revelations were printed in the Chicago Sun Times, the FAA felt embarrassed, once again, and launched a full-blown investigation into O'Hare's security. Evidently, they discovered nothing because in 1985, the television program "60 Minutes" did another survey at O'Hare Airport and found the security situation to be infiltrated with inefficient personnel. When you only pay a person a minimum wage, you can't expect to get the greatest employees.

Most of the tests that "60 Minutes" exposed were similar to the ones utilized by the *Chicago Sun Times*.

Their reporter was hired with no background check and some of the guards were observed smoking pot on the job. One guard fell asleep while operating the X-ray machine, and 16 out of 23 personnel failed to discover dynamite bombs in luggage at it went through the detecting devices. The equipment, when it functions properly, is designed to detect metal. There are numerous explosive devices that are devoid of metal such as plastic, gasoline, and many pure liquids.

The Federal Aviation Administration has fined 29 airlines a total of 1.7 million dollars for their failure to detect 238 dummy weapons carried through airport security checkpoints by FAA inspectors posing as passengers.

There are numerous gates and doors that are accessible to the public and are seldom guarded. I can't think of an airport in the country where I could not have boarded practically any aircraft without being challenged, and I am not talking about when I was wearing my airline uniform.

The year 1985 proved to be the worst year, not only for airline safety but also for terrorist attacks. Worldwide, there were 20 incidents consisting of five bombings, 15 hijackings, and at one airport, the airliners were fired on while taxing out for takeoff.

On January 1, 1985, at Cleveland Airport, an armed woman demanded that she be flown to South America. She shot an airline agent, found her way onto a Pan American jet, and took seven hostages. When she threatened to harm an eight-month-old baby, police boarded the aircraft and shot her.

On January 18, 1985, the crew of an Eastern Airlines jet really got the best of a would-be hijacker. The culprit demanded to be flown to Cuba. It was nighttime, so the hijacker had no way of knowing that the crew had purposely landed at Orlando, Florida. When the passengers were evacuated, the hijacker was taken into custody.

On February 2, 1985, a Lebanese immigration security officer stationed at the Beirut Airport commandeered a Middle East Airlines jet. He forced the pilot to fly to Cypress and back. He held the crew and passengers captive for five hours and then escaped into Beirut. During evacuation, one passenger was killed and seven were injured.

On April 4, 1985, a Royal Jordanian Airlines jet was taxing out for take-off with a full crew and 75 passengers. An unidentified man took careful aim and fired a bazooka at the aircraft, causing extensive damage. Luckily, no one was injured. The marksman escaped.

On June 14, 1985, TWA Flight 847 departed Athens for Rome, Italy. The plane was taken over by two Shiite extremists and the pilot was ordered to fly to Beirut, Algiers, Beirut, Algiers, and then back to Beirut. There were 104 Americans on board and they were all released except for one who was shot and killed. The hijackers were captured.

On June 6, 1985, a disgruntled Turk, whose working permit was canceled, tried to hijack a Turkish Airliner jet. The flight was mid-way between Frankfurt and Istanbul when the 25-year-old man burst onto the flight deck and sprayed the crew and cockpit with foam from a cabin fire extinguisher. He was overpowered by the crew and the passengers.

On November 23, 1985, Egyptian Flight 648 was airborne from Athens to Cairo when three hijackers took charge of the aircraft. The terrorists began shooting passengers from Israel. The plane landed at Malta and 11 female passengers were released along with six wounded and one dead. Later, Egyptian commandos stormed the aircraft and detonated a bomb that killed 57 persons including eight children and one of the hijackers.

On December 27, 1985, terrorist action at Rome and Vienna Airports killed 25 and wounded 117 people in the two terminals. Machine guns and grenades were used in an area that encompassed the ticket counters of Pan Am, TWA, and El Al.

In September of 1989 an in-flight bomb exploded on a French UTA McDonnell Douglas DC-10 over Africa. That killed 171 passengers and crewmembers. The blast occurred in the underfloor baggage/cargo hold where a bomb inside checked baggage may have been hidden.

The most famous of all bombings was Pan Am Flight 103, a 747 that exploded over Lockerbie, Scotland. That killed 259 people on board and eleven on the ground.

Probably one of the most despicable incidents relating to this bombing is that Pan Am management knew there was a bomb threat potential at Frankfort but neglected to tell the captain of Flight 103. The captain is the one person who must decide if it is safe for his flight to depart. He cannot do this without being consulted on such a grave matter as a bomb threat. Luckily, new FAA rules mandate that the crew must be advised of any bomb threats that might concern that safety of their flight.

Isaac Yeffet was the director of security for El Al, the Israeli national airline. In 1986, Yeffet was part of a security team commissioned by Pan Am to survey 20 of their world airports and six in the United States. He stated: "No airports in the U.S. are safe."

Mr. Yeffet visited a few airports in the States and drew the following conclusions: At LaGuardia he was able to place his suitcase on a United flight to Chicago without showing his ticket or even getting on the plane.

During the last few years there have been numerous explosions aboard commercial aircraft while parked at the gate. The preferred explosive material is plastique, a powerful explosive invented by the British in WWII. Plastique is 30 percent more powerful than TNT. A few pounds strategically placed on an airplane could easily remove it from the sky. The worrisome part of this deadly substance is that it can be molded to fit inside a camera or radio, and it is virtually undetected by the airport's X-ray machines.

I have been flying on airliners for many years, and it never ceases to amaze me the degree of the detection qualities at the various airline gates. The money clip in my pocket has triggered the alarm in one concourse, but in the next checkpoint I went right through. It really depends on the sensitivity level of the metal detector. Some are set too high and some much too low. At any rate, these machines detect metal, not plastic, so I might be stopped for a money clip and the passenger ahead of me gets through with a pound of plastique in his pocket.

The executive of the Lockerbie commission made the following statements concerning Pan Am security before the tragedy. He cited an FAA inspector's report that security was "Totally Unsatisfactory. All passengers flying out of Frankfurt on Pan Am are flying at great risk."

According to the FAA, funding for security has increased from 16.9 million in 1990 to about 36 million in fiscal year 1993, a 113 percent increase.

What is the latest on the terrorist scene? Well, how about shipping plutonium by air. Believe it or not, this practice has been going on for some time. About eleven ounces of 239 was concealed in a checked baggage suitcase. Officials got a tip, and when a Lufthansa 737 from Moscow landed in Munich, Germany, the suitcase was seized and indeed contained plutonium. Many of Russia's airports have little or no screening, even of passengers and their carry-on luggage. However, the passenger screening at most of the other foreign countries far exceeds that of the United States.

The FAA has recently announced certification of CTX-5000, the first explosive checking system for checked baggage. It has been seven years since the bombing of Pan Am Flight 103 and the "feds" are still testing this new device. This new system uses computer topography for the detection of various types of explosives. Two of these units were field-tested in Los Angeles and San Francisco Airports, but as stated before, the device is still in the testing state.

Currently, there are 70 vivid explosive detecting devices in service worldwide at 35 airports such as Zurich, Switzerland, Amsterdam, Schiphal, Heathrow, Gatwick, and Glascow. The vivid system costs between $300,000 and $600,000 depending on the model. The CTX-5000 is over $1 million per copy.

So far, the "feds" have invested over $90 million in explosive detection and over $8.5 million in the CTX-5000 system. Since it is clear that terrorism in the U.S. is on the rise, we can no longer sit back and say it won't happen here.

CHAPTER 18

▼

AIR RAGE

Over thirty years ago, United Airlines coined the phrase "Fly The Friendly Skies." Today, airline officials are asking the federal government to try to keep passenger conduct aboard airlines merely civil. The following are some examples of new phenomena called "air rage."

The cabin PA system was turned on and the captain tried to direct your attention to the right side of the aircraft by saying "… you will get an excellent view of the Grand Canyon." At this time, passengers were far more interested in what was taking place in the forward cabin. A man and woman were trying to enter the cockpit by furiously banging and kicking the cockpit door. The woman began screaming that she had a gun. She kicked the door with such force that she managed to put a hole in it. The man grabbed a pot of hot coffee and threw it at a female flight attendant, severely scalding her. Both passengers were under the influence of drugs and are now facing federal charges of interfering with a flight crewmember.

Football player Dean William Trammil, 21, of Silver Springs, Maryland, was arrested for assaulting a flight attendant on a USAirways plane just before landing at Baltimore Washington Airport. He could receive up to twenty years in prison and a fine of $250,000.

Reverend Robert Schuller, 70, allegedly grabbed a United flight attendant and vigorously shook him. The dispute began when the attendant refused to hang up a robe that Reverend Schuller planned to wear at a memorial service. The flight attendant was treated for injuries at the JFK Airport infirmary. Reverend Schuller apologized in the misdemeanor assault case and agreed to pay a $1,100 fine.

Eric Douglas, 38, youngest son of actor Kirk Douglas, was arrested in Los Angeles on federal charges of disrupting an airline flight. He refused to put his dog in a cage during a flight from Los Angeles to Newark. He also was charged with verbally abusing crewmembers and tossing rolled-up blankets at them. He pleaded guilty to a misdemeanor, paid a $5,000 fine, and spent a month in jail.

Marcelle Becker, wife of the late insurance magnate Martin Becker, was traveling in first class along with her dog who was enjoying a seat next to her. The dog became a nuisance and the pilot was summoned to quell the disruptive behavior of the dog and Mrs. Becker. The pilot found it necessary to restrain Mrs. Becker's hands behind her back, using her dog's leash. This case has not yet come to trial.

Federal assault charges were lodged against Usman Anthony Abdallah, 27, a resident of Scotland. During the flight, he had consumed a large amount of alcohol, and became abusive to his friend and other passengers. Abdallah hurled a traveling companion into the galley wall. With the help of a passenger and an off-duty KLM pilot, they managed to wrestle Abdallah to the floor and cuff him with plastic restraints.

Investment broker Gerard Finneran of Greenwich, Connecticut, was fined $50,000 and a two-year probation. He was obviously drunk and becoming unmanageable. When the attendants refused to serve him any more drinks in full view of the passengers, he defecated on the flight attendant's serving cart.

A passenger on an American Airlines flight from Madrid to Miami, Sally Ann Stein, 57, was arrested and charged with interfering with the duties of a flight attendant and a flight engineer. When refused permission to smoke on a nonsmoking flight, she became abusive, shoving two attendants and the captain. She allegedly said that she was a terrorist that she was going to blow up the plane. She called the flight attendants "American fascists," and said she was going to gun one of them down.

Frank Lopez, Jr., 28, of New Orleans handed a flight attendant a note threatening to blow up the aircraft. Southwest Airlines had to make an unscheduled landing to discharge the passenger and have the plane thoroughly checked, causing a three-and-one-half-hour delay.

A Japanese woman flying on a China Airlines flight berated a Taiwanese flight attendant for accidentally spilling water on her. The passenger demanded that the attendant and her supervisor both get on their knees and bow in apology. She retaliated by throwing water on both of them.

A flight attendant on an American Airlines flight was kicked in the back by a male passenger who was traveling economy class. He was refused the use of a business-class toilet.

On one flight, baseball star Wade Boggs drank himself into a big law case. Boggs was seated two rows from the back galley as Continental Airlines flight attendant, Karen H. Plympton, was trying her best to keep her cool. Boggs had already consumed at least eight beers during the two-hour trip. There was growing friction between Boggs and Plympton. It came to a head when she threw down some baseball cards that the pilot wanted him to sign. Plympton stated that he threatened to "kick her fat lips in" and that he "should have thrown her out at 30,000 feet." Boggs continued to subject her to vulgar terms and sexual slurs. In a deposition, Plympton said the case was worth up to $10 million, but plaintiff attorney John T. Byrd suggested that Boggs be hit with a $250,000 damage suit.

In another incident, the aircraft had just taxied away from the gate. A passenger stood up and was asked by the flight attendant to please sit down. He said, "If you don't get out of my way, I'm going to blow up the airplane." The captain was advised and he immediately returned to the gate where the passenger was arrested.

A Northwest pilot was behind the ticket counter picking up his paperwork. A passenger came up and wanted to check in for his flight. He said, "I can't do that. You have to wait for the gate agent." The passenger became so angered that he punched the captain and knocked him to the ground.

A bricklayer on a flight from London to Washington got into some real trouble. He decided that he wanted to smoke so he locked himself in the toilet. A flight attendant noticed the smoke coming from the john, and asked him to stop smoking and come out. He became abusive and unruly, and injured the attendant. The flight crew finally restrained him. On arrival, he was arrested and eventually sentenced to thirty months in jail.

Canadian Airlines flight attendant Karen Hegland feels lucky that she didn't get her head bashed in. During a flight from Norita, Japan, to Vancouver, she asked a passenger to please stop drinking from his own liquor bottle. She had to make this request numerous times. Karen stopped him from entering the washroom and asked him to put his bottle away. The irate passenger raised his bottle over her head. Her arms shot up to block the hit. A male attendant saw the bizarre actions and tackled the passenger to the floor.

On a United flight from Frankfurt to Dulles, a German tourist complained that the cabin attendant had bumped him with the food cart. The flight attendant said that he was sorry, but the irate passenger pushed him against an emergency exit and proceeded to punch him out. Passengers came to the rescue. The tourist was prosecuted and got off with six months' probation.

In one incident, an aircraft started to taxi out from the gate as a passenger began eating his bag of peanuts. He rang the call button and demanded a Coke. The attendant told him, "Once we get in the air, we'll get you a Coke." He became irate, so she contacted the head attendant. They both returned to the passenger to offer an explanation as to why he could not be served. He spit his chewed-up peanuts in her face, and the mess ran down her chin and onto the head of another passenger.

On another flight from Chicago to New York, a passenger became violent and knocked down a flight attendant, laid on top of her, and violently punched her.

On a trip from Hong Kong to Heathrow, a man masturbated and ejaculated on a sleeping female passenger. He was arrested on arrival and was fined $650.

On an American West flight from Las Vegas to Chicago, a female passenger became so enraged when informed that there were no extra sandwiches she proceeded to pummel a cabin attendant and knock her to the floor, clawed a male flight attendant, and punched the pilot in the face.

A flight attendant for a major carrier sued a young couple for physically attacking her. The flight was delayed and the couple was afraid that they would miss their connecting flight. As the cabin attendant tried to calm the man down, she was spiked in the back by the lady's shoe, and had to be removed from her flight and rushed to the hospital.

A ticket agent at O'Hare International Airport in Chicago had a suitcase hurled at her by an irate passenger. Agent Karen Brennan was eight months pregnant at the time of the incident.

One pilot hurried to the aid of his cabin crew to quell an unruly passenger, only to retreat with a broken nose and achieving nothing. His performance as a pilot became clearly impaired.

An American Airlines flight from Los Angeles to Dallas had an unruly passenger on board. His main problem was that there was no fruit on his meal tray. The flight attendant was unable to fulfill the passenger's request so the passenger struck the attendant and threw him to the ground.

On a flight from Miami to Madrid, a passenger became uncontrollable in flight. He tried to open the door of the MD-11, screaming that he wanted to commit suicide and was going to take the plane down with him. Fortunately, he was unable to open the door.

A drunk and disorderly passenger on board a flight from Frankfurt to Philadelphia was prosecuted in a federal court in Greensboro, North Carolina, for making obscene gestures, using profanity, kicking a pregnant passenger's seat, causing her to fall out, and urinating in the aircraft's aisle. He was sentenced to nineteen months in jail.

Actress Elizabeth Ashley was fined $2,000 for tampering with a restroom smoke detector.

A flight attendant asked a passenger to please unplug her laptop computer. The passenger was Saliva Oahanti, a Saudi princess who never took orders, only gave them. She jumped up from her seat, and scratched and choked the unsuspecting flight attendant. The princess was fined $500 and sentenced to six months probation.

An All Nippon Airways captain was murdered by a deranged passenger who used a flight attendant as a hostage to gain admission to the flight deck. The passenger plunged a knife into the neck of the captain who bled to death before the co-pilot could make an emergency landing. The passenger stated that he just wanted to fly the airplane.

A six-foot, two-inch, 250-pound passenger recently broke into the cockpit of an Alaska Airlines jet. He attacked the crew and made a lunge for the controls, screaming, "I'm going to kill you!" He was grabbing for the throttle when he was subdued by a passenger who was alerted by a PA call from the captain. The co-pilot required eight stitches in his hand.

I'll finish these stories with one that happened to me. We were on final approach to Kennedy when the attendant came up and said that there was a man in the back that would not fasten his seat belt. We were about five miles out on final and I told my co-pilot to go around while I went in the back to try and fix the problem. This gentleman was in the first row so I didn't have far to go. I told him that it was a regulation that all seat belts must be securely fastened before landing. He made no motion to comply so I fastened it for him. By now, the nearby passengers were beginning to enjoy the show. He unfastened his belt again and I quickly buckled it up. He was obviously feeling no pain and I made one last effort to close his belt that he promptly opened. I told him "If you want trouble I can easily arrange it." He said, "Yeah I want trouble." I went back to the cockpit and we landed. On the way in, I called the company to have a state trooper meet the aircraft. I let no one off until the trooper was on board. As the parking brake was set and the jetway moved in, I saw the trooper waiting at the door. I went back to Mr. Obnoxious just as the trooper boarded the aircraft. I confronted the passenger and stated, "You know that trouble that you wanted? Well, here it is." The burly trooper hovered over his seat. The passengers all applauded and the show was over. It was amazing how quickly he sobered up. I had him deplaned before his final destination so that his luggage would continue but he wouldn't. I told the trooper to detain him until we took off, then they could do what they wanted with him.

On the lighter side, this one should give you a chuckle. We were at the gate at O'Hare, and the passengers were all seated and ready for the flight. That is, all but one. The flight attendant entered the cockpit and was very flustered. "There's a man in the rear of the cabin who is completely nude and he is parading up and down the aisles."

I got out of my seat to investigate this strange happening. Sure enough, he was out there, "bumping and grinding" away. I told the flight attendant to try and throw a blanket over him and that I would call for airport security.

The streaker must have been under the influence of drugs because when the security officers came into the cabin, the man hugged and kissed them as they covered him with a large blanket. The last I saw of him, he was walking down the jetway with his arms around both of the guards.

I could relate many more intriguing anecdotes, but the interesting question is, why do some airline passengers do the disruptive and dangerous things they do?

Doctor Jerald Post is the director of the political psychology program at George Washington University. He is a recognized expert in the field of psychology of terrorism and political violence. According to Dr. Post, most of the incidents are related to alcohol use. Many of the more violent ones suggest a syndrome called pathological intoxication in which a small amount of alcohol can produce an extreme reaction. Because of airline delays, many passengers frequent the numerous airport bars. As a result, they are well on their way to inebriation before they board their flights. These passengers in first and business class are barely in their seats before an attendant is taking their order for more alcohol. Alcohol on an empty stomach can produce extreme reactions and it is clear that when airlines dispense drinks early in the flight, problems can result among certain passengers.

Alcohol is the catalyst for many people to become unruly, but when combined with other psychological traits, it can turn a normal person into a monster. The stress of flying, overcrowded cabins, delays, and the no-smoking problem all magnify the three leading personality traits which can lead to aggressive behavior: entitlement, opposition to authority, and fear of loss of control.

A good example of entitlement is the anecdote involving the Saudi princess above who was told to do something and flew into a rage, attacking the attendant and saying "I have never been told by anyone to do anything" or words to that effect. Opposition to authority is demonstrated by executives who are used to being in control of others, and resent the most minor kinds of requests by cabin attendants. Important executives resent being instructed by some person, clearly beneath his rank, to be ordered to do something. The fear of loss of control also is a problem. The experience of sitting in a giant aluminum tube, your destiny clearly in the hands of others, is aggression-provoking for some people.

Deportees

Prisoners from one country are often flown to another where they will be imprisoned or executed. These people are, at times, flown on commercial passenger airliners where the flight attendant also assumes guard duty. Many of these prisoners have not bathed for an extended period of time. Some have lice that are deposited in the seats you will occupy eventually. It is believed that some deportees may be infected with TB.

Many times, individuals are escorted and handcuffed by armed guards. When the person reaches the aircraft, his cuffs are removed and the attendant is told to treat him as he would any normal passenger. Now the attendants have the added worry of fugitives storming the cockpit and demanding to be flown to a neutral country where they could evade prison or execution.

In one case, a group of deportees were being flown from their adopted country to a third country. These individuals were not familiar with western toilets. Instead of defecating into the toilet, they left their calling card on top of the lid.

On an Air France charted flight from Paris to Benaco, Mali, with no flight attendants on board, a guard was bitten by one of the deportees. During disembarkation, the prisoners swarmed about the aircraft, damaging it severely on both the inside and outside, and injured local police during a twenty-minute rampage.

Another deportee flight was en route to the runway when a prisoner opened an over-wing emergency vent, climbed out onto the wing, and jumped off.

An aircraft was parked overnight and some of the deportees crawled into the tail section and hung their clothes on the control cables.

On another flight from Vietnam, the interpreter spoke in one dialect and the prisoners in another. Proper communication was nearly impossible. The food served during the flight was unlike the food the prisoners normally ate. Virtually every deportee became sick in the cabin, on each other, and on the crew.

MADD (Mothers Against Drunk Drivers)

Katherine Prescott, the National President of MADD, made some interesting comments as she spoke to the 1997 ALPA (Air Line Pilots Association) Conference on Disruptive Airline Passengers.

You are probably wondering what in the world have drunk drivers got to do with airline safety? You will soon see.

It is against federal regulations to allow a visibly intoxicated person to board an airliner. It may be difficult, in some cases, to be able to spot a drunk. Many of them are experts at hiding their condition. In fourteen states, a person is considered intoxicated if his or her blood alcohol limit (BAC) is .08 or more. BAC can be estimated by the weight of the person and the number of drinks that have been consumed. A 120-pound woman who consumes three drinks in one hour would also reach the threshold.

Flying is now an excuse to get drunk, especially in first class. While the luxuries of first class are many, the unlimited free liquor is like a red flag to a bull. Most first class seats cost double the price of those in coach. It seems that normal drinkers drink excessively when they try to get their first class fare out of the bar.

As an airline passenger myself, I have seen people order as many as six drinks before the plane even leaves the ground. They order doubles. Many passengers ask the attendants to give them extra bottles so that they can consume them at home or worse, on the way.

[I have] arrived at seven interesting solutions to alcohol-related problems on the aircraft:

1. Flight attendants must get special training to identify impairment caused by alcohol.

2. Limit the number of drinks that can be consumed on a flight based on actual flight time. A person can digest a maximum of one drink per hour. This policy should be combined with the no-smoking announcements and should be printed in the in-flight magazine.

3. Do not begin serving alcohol until after the airplane has taken off. Long ATC (air traffic control) delays or mechanicals can use a lot of time, and time for some passengers means more drinks.

4. Only serve one drink at a time. Do not allow the flight attendants to serve doubles.

5. Try to keep track of the number of alcoholic beverages a person is served, although this solution requires a little more work. This practice would be fairly easy in first class.

6. Management training is essential. None of these policies can be effective without the staunch support of management. MADD has numerous complaints from flight attendants who have been disciplined, suspended, and even terminated because they have refused service to an individual who is intoxicated.

7. Safe driving messages should be used at the beginning of the flight and at the conclusion, such as: If you choose to drink alcohol, please remember to use a designated driver on your way home.

In October of 1998, a case involving a major airline and a drunk driving victim was settled out of court. Just after disembarking from a flight, a man drove his car from the airport and hit an 18-year-old man and his girlfriend, causing life-threatening injuries to the teenaged man. As a first class passenger, the drunk driver had been served eleven drinks on a one-and-a-half-hour flight.

This major airline involved in this lawsuit spent millions of dollars fighting this case that lasted over five years. The airline's main contention was that it is impossible that one of their crewmembers would serve eleven drinks in a one-and-a-half-hour flight. To refute this claim, the lawyer for the injured man hired a private investigator to fly from Dallas to Chicago, the same flight pattern and time period as the previous passenger in the first-class cabin, to see how many drinks he would be served. It turned out the airline was wrong. The private investigator was not only served eleven drinks in an hour and a half; he was served twelve.

The victims of this tragedy have already incurred over $2 million in medical costs. The settlement between the airline and the injured man has not been made public.

I really think that it is only a matter of time before airlines are held responsible for damages done by one of their liquored-up passengers. Dram shop laws have been passed that will hold bar owners responsible for over-serving patrons who get out on the road and kill or harm someone.

[I receive] approximately fifteen complaints each month from flight attendants who have been disciplined for refusing alcohol service to passengers. I am sure this would never happen on Southwest Airlines, a carrier that treats its employees with respect.

Southwest cabin crews now have an official document to give to unruly passengers.

NOTICE OF U.S. FEDERAL REGULATION VIOLATION

Your behavior appears to be in violation of federal law.

If you fail to control your actions, federal authorities will be notified and requested to meet this flight.

THIS IS A WARNING THAT FEDERAL LAW PROHIBITS THE FOLLOWING:

Assaults, threats, intimidation or interference with a crewmember in performance of the crewmembers' duties aboard an aircraft being operated.

Disruptive behavior due to alcohol consumption.

Failure to follow instructions given by a crewmember regarding compliance with passenger safety regulations.

An incident report may be filed with the appropriate federal agency if you do not refrain from this behavior. The Federal Aviation Act provides for fines up to $10,000. In the case of interference with a crewmember in the performance of crewmembers' duties, imprisonment for up to twenty years may be imposed in addition to the fine.

Of course, in some violent cases, it will not be easy for the cabin crew to display the card, especially if they are being punched. But at least it is a step in the right direction.

The Association of Flight Attendants spent a lot of time and money to get Congress to agree to a no-smoking ban on all U.S. flights. While the effects of second-hand smoke are well known and the damage to the body takes years to develop, the effects of alcohol are felt much more quickly. It doesn't take much imagination to picture a drunken passenger who could block exits in an emergency and cause a disaster in a fiery crash.

Ninety-eight percent of all disruptive passenger cases are caused by travelers who are drunk. It was only a few years ago that smoking was banned on all flights. Airlines are mainly interested in making a profit wherever they can. Consider that tiny bottle of liquor that sells for four dollars in the cabin and costs the airline an average of less than fifty cents. The no-smoking ban on airlines was far easier to mandate because airlines did not sell cigarettes. Alcoholic beverages are quite another story.

Those of us who do not drink alcoholic beverages would be well served if the Association of Flight Attendants would champion this latest cause: to ban alcohol on all flights. The attendants have been abused for too long by inebriated passengers, and it is high time the abuse comes to a halt.

Many flight attendants are under the impression that, since an assault happened while they were performing their duties, it was the company's responsibility to seek prosecution of the culprit. This is incorrect. The assault is on an individual, not a company. Any complaint must be filed by the individual involved in the incident. Thank goodness for organizations such as The Association of Flight Attendants. They have in-house lawyers that do not charge their members for representation.

If the airlines expect their cabin crews to go out on a limb, the least they can do is back them in any way possible.

Within the space of two years, one major carrier went from 162 incidents to over 285. Most airlines carry plastic handcuffs, similar to wire ties used by electricians. Cathy Pacific has a veritable arsenal of restraints. On each aircraft, you will find two sets of metal handcuffs and eight sets of flexible cuffs. Does that sound like the friendly skies?

It is interesting to note the stance taken by various law enforcement agencies and their jurisdictions. As long as the passenger door is open, any disturbance is quelled by local authorities. As soon as the cabin door is closed, the case belongs to the FBI.

In the United States, Australia, and Canada, a passenger found guilty of disrupting a flight crew in their duties can expect to spend twenty years in a federal penitentiary. In the United Kingdom, however, unless a passenger is actually a hijacker or commits such an act in British air space, they'll simply walk away scot-free. That certainly is not proper.

It wasn't long ago that sky marshals were on board to stop any person from hijacking the aircraft. Perhaps it would be a good move to reinstate these people to intervene in any dispute on board. Sure, a pilot can be asked to help in a cabin confrontation, but his primary duties require him to be in the cockpit. The flight engineer would have been a good prospect to leave the flight deck and help the cabin crew. Unfortunately for us, all the engineer positions have been eliminated. Modern jets, regardless of their size or complexity, are manned by only two pilots. And if the airline has its way, you might soon be flown by a crew of one, a pilot with an oil can to keep everything moving freely.

Flight attendants are on board for one reason: to help save your life in an emergency. Whether or not they serve you food and soft drinks is something that has little to do with safety. In fact, we will never know the number of lives that have been lost in an emergency because of alcoholic drinks served to inebriated passengers who may have blocked egress of a fellow traveler.

When you purchase an airline ticket, you are paying for a safe ride to your destination. Any other amenities are at the discretion of the carrier.

It's amazing the way people's habits change as soon as they get aboard an airline. Folks at home do not eat or drink every few hours, but as soon as they get in that airline seat, they turn into demanding, ravenous gourmets. The passengers who sit adjacent to emergency exits can consume as much alcohol as any other person on the aircraft. And in an emergency, that drunk sitting in a vital emergency exit aisle could cost you your life. Think about it.

All members of the ATA should agree that they would no longer dispense alcohol on any of their flights. The FAA should demand this restriction.

In 1997, a conference concerning disruptive airline passengers was held at the Marriott Hotel in Washington, D.C. The president of the Air Line Pilots Association, Captain Babbitt, cited alarming statistics that indicate a huge rise in disruptive passenger incidents can be expected in the future. "With implanments as high as 925 million over the next decade, we can expect double the number of such incidents by the year 2015. This is intolerable."

I want to thank Jerry Wright, an ALPA safety expert, and Ms. Ann Tongas of the Association of Flight Attendants for sending me information on disruptive passengers.

CHAPTER 19

▼

THE MASTER RACE

On October 26, 1993, the weather at Winchester Regional Airport, Virginia, was not conducive to VFR flying. A moist, easterly flow of air covered Maryland and Virginia. A widespread low ceiling with light rain and fog prevailed over the area.

A Beech Super King aircraft, owned and operated by the FAA, was about to leave to perform its mission of inspecting airway facilities at Norfolk, Virginia. There were three crewmembers on board: the Captain, First Officer, and an electronics technician (ET) whose duty was to perform the checks required on the ground-based navigation equipment. The Winchester Airport was not equipped with a control tower, but a remote communication outlet was in operation. This radio unit was installed so that flights could contact Dulles Airport to received vital instrument clearances. The captain of the FAA aircraft used poor judgment in not obtaining his instrument clearance before leaving the ground, a mistake he will never forget. Instead, he chose to take off in marginal weather and pick up his clearance in the air. The first transmission from the FAA aircraft was received at 1541: "Just off Winchester, see if you got ... anything you can give us heading on down towards Harcum."

The Dulles arrival controller advised "Maintain VFR for right now, it's going to be about five minutes before I can get to you, I'm extremely busy at the moment."

Now the crew was required to stay clear of the clouds, and the mountains, and circle in a dangerous environment. If the captain had received his clearance, as he should have, while safely on the ground, I would not be writing about this particular flight.

There was obvious apprehension in the cockpit. Here is a master race crew trying desperately to keep clear of the clouds and the rock piles that were shrouded by fog. The FAA does not require cockpit voice or flight data recorders in their aircraft. I am sure that there would have been a few choice words between the First Officer and the Captain. Perhaps the FAA wants to keep their mistakes off the record.

At 1552, eleven minutes after the crew's first transmission, the Dulles controller advised "Maintain VFR please and can you contact Dulles on one two four point six five, you are just about to enter his air space down there."

There was no answer to the controller's transmission for a very good reason. At the precise moment the controller was transmitting to the FAA aircraft, it was plowing through a ridgeline forest at 1770 feet on its way to total destruction and fire. All FAA personnel aboard were killed instantly, and the fate of a captain that was long foreseen became a reality.

If you think I speak harshly about a fellow pilot, read on and see what you think.

In 1983, the captain was hired by the FAA as an air traffic assistant. In 1985, he passed his instrument rating. His first crack at the ATP rating was unsuccessful. On February 15, 1989, he failed the initial phase of his type rating. He received additional training and failed a second time. On April 4, 1989, his third attempt at the BE-300 type rating was successful.

Airline pilots may get two chances to check out on a piece of equipment, but certainly never three. During the NTSB's investigation, the following discrepancies were noted in their October 26, 1993 report on page number eight: "Continued on a VFR positioning flight into IMC."

This is one violation that killed him.

"Conducted VFR flight below clouds at less than 1,000 feet above the ground in marginal weather conditions.

This is another violation that killed him.

"Conducted departures without the flight viewer's knowledge of essential flight planning information such as IFR/VFR/in route filing/weather/ultimate destination or routing. Departed on positioning flights without informing other crewmembers whether he had attained weather information or filed an appropriate flight plan. Disregarded checklist discipline on numerous occasions. Refused to accept responsibilities that his failure to adhere to a checklist had caused an engine damage incident in January 1993. Performed a 'below glide path check' in IMC when VMC conditions were required by FIAO regiments, and refused to answer SIC query regarding the reason for his alleged violation of VFR requirements in an incident two weeks before the accident."

There were eleven first officers assigned to the deceased captain's organization. Eight of the eleven co-pilots formally requested that they not be assigned to the deceased captain's crew. Does this start to tell you something? Evidently it made no impression on the captain's superiors. The Flight Operations Supervisor (FO/ISS) had this to say regarding the co-pilot's formal complaints: "Following some of these complaints, the FO/ISS, in the most recent performance appraisal period, rated the PIC [the deceased pilot in command] 'proficient' on his interpersonal skills and complimented him on his productivity and ability to 'get along with his fellow workers'."

Here is a quote from the NTSB report page 77: "Moreover, it appears that conflicts between crewmembers resulted in preferential scheduling by the FO/ISS to ensure that the PIC involved in the accident under investigation flew only with SIC who were tolerant of his behavior. Lack of action by the FO/ISS reportedly discouraged crewmembers from further expressing concerns or complaints or reporting additional incidents."

That line of thinking would not be tolerated on today's airlines.

Perhaps the above statement will give you some insight as to how the FAA operates. After eight out of eleven co-pilots had written formal complaints to their boss about not wanting to jeopardize their lives by having to fly with this person, the boss gives the potential killer a clean bill of health. To say that the FAA takes care of its own is putting it mildly. But wait, there is much more to come.

Since there is an abundance of substance abuse today, the FAA requires that all airmen must report any DUI incidents to the FAA within sixty days of their occurrence.

Here is a review of the diseased captain's driving records. He received two convictions for driving under the influence. The most recent event occurred in May 1991. At this time, his New Jersey driver's license was suspended. In January of 1993, his New Jersey license was suspended once again. It was suspended again in March of 1993 because he failed to comply with the state drug and alcohol countermeasure at the time of the accident.

The diseased captain had not resided in Mississippi for over twenty years but he still maintained a Mississippi driver's license. It was renewed on July 29, 1993. The law in New Jersey requires that all out-of-state licenses must be relinquished when a New Jersey license is issued.

If a non-FAA pilot committed any of the above discrepancies, there would be a hearing concerning his medical qualifications.

The FAA operates a fleet of about fifty publicly owned aircraft. Let us remember that the term publicly owned aircraft means that their operation and maintenance procedures do not have to comply with the regulations that govern General Aviation or Airlines. Sure, the FAA does comply with many of their own regulations, but the salient point here is that they are not required to.

Problems similar to this accident were identified after a 1988 crash that destroyed a FAA Jet Commander. The aircraft was flying in air that was extremely conducive to icing conditions and their ice detection system was not operating one hundred percent. They remained in a holding pattern while the icing continued to intensify. Ice began to break loose and entered both engine intakes, causing instant flameouts. The aircraft crashed, killing both FAA pilots and the electronics technician.

The night before the accident, both pilots were seen drinking in a local bar. The co-pilot had recently lost his drivers license for DUI. Where have we heard that before?

The NTSB stated that the problems, however, "were not corrected because management action was ineffective and oversight by senior executives was insufficient."

The board also stated: "Both fatally injured flight crews were supervised by the same FO/ISS. Both fatal accidents involved questions of PIC judgment and decision-making related to weather factors."

The NTSB probable cause follows: "The National Transportation Safety Board determines that the probable causes of this accident was the failure of the pilot-in-command to ensure that the airplane remained in visual meteorological conditions over mountainous terrain, and the failure of Federal Aviation Administration executives and manager responsible for the FAA program to:

1. Establish effective and accountable leadership and oversight of flying operations;

2. Establish minimum mission and operational performance standards;

3. Recognize and address performance related problems among organized pilots, and

4. Remove from flight operations duty pilots who were not performing to standards."

I would add the following to this fine NTSB report.

1. Do not allow nonpilots to supervise pilots. There are no chief pilots in the airlines today who were not pilots at some phase of their careers.

2. Establish manuals for maintenance and flight operations. I would like to see an airline pass an FAA inspection if their manuals were not up to date. The master race is so good they don't need them.

3. Install cockpit and flight data recorders on all FAA aircraft. Also a Ground Proximity Warning System that sounds an alarm when getting close to terrain. This unit might have averted the crash.

We have had a look at the numerous dangerous procedures that the FAA follows in their daily operation. Now, let's take a look at what the wrath of the Master Race can impose on a non-FAA pilot. Please try to remember the myriad rules and regulations that are broken by the FAA crews. Also keep in mind the cover-ups that the pilot supervisors put into effect to keep their "good old boys" flying.

On August 25, 1994, an FAA owned and operated Beech King Air was taxiing for takeoff at Alaska's Iliamna's 4,800-foot gravel strip airport. All was well until the right main landing gear got stuck in loose gravel near the ramp. The pilot, who was in the left seat, revved up the engine in order to give some added thrust to the mired-down wheel. Well, as to be expected, when an excessive amount of power is applied in the vicinity of loose stones, they will be propelled through the air and cause damage to the aircraft. The right-hand propeller suffered severe damage to all four blades, and the props threw stones that damaged the rubber deicing boots and put numerous dents and dings in the fuselage.

Who do you suppose was responsible for all this extensive damage? The pilot, of course, who was none other than the former director of the FAA, Administrator David Hinson. What kind of example does this set for the rest of us ordinary pilots in the United States?

After the engines were shut down, the aircraft was towed to the runway where both engines were started and the plane taxied back to the parking area where the damages were evaluated. Maintenance officials in Anchorage were contacted, and they faxed back propeller blade specifications, along with authorization for a specific mechanic in Iliamna to perform the repairs. The propeller was so severely damaged that field repairs were not possible. When the "feds" decide to break maintenance laws, they do so at will.

Aircraft mechanics are not allowed to perform any extensive maintenance to aircraft propellers. The only people authorized to work on props are authorized propeller shops. According to the FAA incident report, the mechanic who was singled out to repair the damages declined "Because he believed the damages to be too extensive to be repaired in the field with hand tools." Here we have a mechanic with "gonads." It takes a lot to turn down repairs to an FAA aircraft, especially one piloted by their chief.

After the first mechanic refused to do the work, Peter Dula, an FAA aviation safety inspector from the Anchorage Flight Standard District Office and co-pilot of the Beech, solicited the assistance of another mechanic who was a member of an airline flight crew on the ground at Iliamna. He said, "he would field dress the right propeller blades, at no charge, and signed the log approving the aircraft for return to service."

Now we have two direct FAA violations. The first was authorizing a specific mechanic to repair the prop blades, and the second mechanic who backed the FAA illegal authorization for work he never should have attempted. The second mechanic who thought he was doing the FAA a favor got bitten by the ever-present fangs of the "feds." He was required to undergo "counseling" by FAA officials on proper techniques and practices relative to propeller repairs, and use of technical data.

After only a two-hour delay, Hinson and his acting co-pilot, Dula, were on their way to continue the inspection tour/vacation of Alaska. Can you imagine how two supposedly experienced and qualified pilots on the King Air would dare to fly it in its present state of unairworthiness? Well, there is more trouble for these two just around the bend.

Twenty minutes after takeoff from Iliamna, a five warning light activated on the left engine. Hinson and Dula shut it down and shot the fire bottle to it. They declared an in-flight emergency and landed 10 minutes later at King Salmon Airport. There was no fire in the left engine, only a faulty warning. Where have we heard this one before? Try Chapter 1.

The proceeding comedy of errors only goes to show you the high experience level of some of the "feds" finest pilots. They had no business trying to field repair a badly damaged propeller. They certainly should never have tried to fly an unairworthy aircraft, and believe me it was unairworthy, regardless of the second mechanic's write-off. The propeller in question was shipped to an authorized repair station in Oklahoma City where it was determined to be not worth repairing.

Do you suppose that the Administrator requested some remedial training or how to pre-flight a propeller before flight? Not on your life. Administrator Hinson deferred all decisions and repair processes to Dula, his co-pilot, and the unnamed mechanic. The administrator caused a lot of trouble by his actions, not to mention the many thousands of dollars in repair bills that you and I had to pay.

While the incident investigation was in progress, David Hinson characterized it to a reporter in Washington D.C., as "much ado about nothing." When the "feds" break regulations and airplanes, it's really not a problem, but if an ordinary pilot had violated so many FARs, I know he would have been subjected to severe certificate action.

Let's Get Hoover

In June of 1992, thousands of spectators at the Aerospace America Air Show at Wiley Post Airport in Oklahoma City were patiently waiting to be entertained by the greatest pilot of all times, Robert A. Hoover. He skillfully climbed his stock Shrike Commander to air show center and cut both engines. In essence, Bob was piloting a glider. He would perform loops, point rolls, and various other maneuvers with both engines shut down. This highly skilled aviator could do things in an airplane without power that high-time pilots would not attempt with both engines running. He is truly a master at what he does. Bob has performed in hundreds of air shows throughout the world but on this day, he would be considered unfit to pilot an aircraft by the FAA.

Bob was born in 1922. He grew up loving airplanes and when war broke out, he joined the Air Force. He got his wings and was assigned as a test pilot at Wright Patterson testing facilities in Dayton, Ohio. He tested nearly all the aircraft that the Air Force had to offer, both fighters and bombers. He yearned for combat and managed to sweet-talk a general into getting assigned to a fighter outfit. He flew 59 combat missions in a Spitfire in the European theater. One day he encountered five German fighters. He managed to down two of them before one shot him down. He bailed out, was captured by the Germans, and remained a POW for 15 months.

During the XI testing at Murdock, California, Hoover was the backup pilot for Chuck Yeager, the man who first broke the sound barrier.

In 1948, he retired from the Air Force and joined the great North American Aviation Company. There, he test flew the F-86 and F-100 super saber (I was also privileged to fly this great aircraft). He tested the Navy version of the F-86 and also was designated as a Navy test pilot. He has been flying air shows for over forty years. He has used the P-51, T-28, F-86, and the Shrike Commander as his aerobatics mounts. He is the official pace pilot who starts the Reno Air Races each year and assists any of the race planes when in trouble. Bob has received numerous awards and medals such as the Distinguished Flying Cross, the Air Medal, and the Purple Heart. For two years, he was President of the Society of Test Pilots and in 1988, he was inducted into the Aviation Hall of Fame. But in June of 1992, after his stellar performance at an Oklahoma City Air Show, Bob A. Hoover was treading on dangerous ground. No, he didn't get killed and he didn't retire. He was going to be grounded. You might ask what in the world would cause the FAA to contemplate grounding such a superb pilot? Well, two of the Master Race inspectors from the local Flight Service District Office (FSDO), the FAA's local police station, observed Bob's show and did not like the way he performed. They wouldn't know a good maneuver from a bad one. The combined experience of these characters, Clint Boehler and James Klein, might equal the time that Bob Hoover has spent passing over the outer marker (a radio aid you pass over on final approach). FAA management stated that, THEIR INSPECTORS ARE NOT QUALIFIED TO JUDGE AEROBATIC PERFORMANCES. But when the FAA is after you, they usually catch you.

Another inspector, Norbert Nestor, who witnessed the show stated that he thought Hoover did a good job. Nestar, who is over six feet tall, is in a class with Hoover when it comes to height. Inspector Clint Boehler told Nestar, "I hate people like you because you are … tall and skinny. I don't like being short and paunchy." Nestar, the good inspector, stated that he overheard Boehler say he was after Hoover because "the old bastard has been around for a long time." Nestar put his job on the line by telling the truth, something the FAA has yet to learn.

It is quite obvious that FAA inspector Boehler was jealous of Hoover's flying skills and he was going to show off the mighty power of the FAA. Believe me, they have unlimited powers and literally no one else to answer to. If Bob was such a threat to the public safety, why was he allowed to fly 33 more air shows AFTER the FAA claimed he was medically unfit to fly?

Bob Hoover's medical certificate was voluntarily given to the FAA. They claimed his flying was flawed and that he should be neurologically tested. Bob played their game and was tested by a team of FAA doctors. Hoover came through with flying colors. When the report came to the office of Dr. Pakull the FAA's chief psychiatrist, he decided to overturn his colleagues' findings and continued to ground Bob. A second FAA test was requested by Bob, and once again, he passed, but was turned down by Dr. Pakull. One of the neurologists was intrigued by Bob's "bulbous red nose." Perhaps they could now try to get him for drinking because we all know that people with red noses are "drunks."

Hoover calls the FAA's tests "nutty." He says, "If they'd done their homework, they'd know he's had numerous surgeries on my nose to remove skin cancer."

F. Lee Bailey and John Yodice, two prominent lawyers, came on board to aid Bob in his fight to get back in the air. The case was appealed to the NTSB and a hearing was held on January 13, 1994, before Judge William R. Mullins. The lead witness for the FAA was Dr. Elliott, the neurophysiologist, who was a member of the first team to find Bob's tests okay. It looked like somebody got to him because he revised his original findings and said Bob was not fit to fly.

Bob Hoover was allowed to fly his routine again with American Airlines Captain Leo Loudenslager who was a seven-time national aerobatics champion. After the aerial demonstration, Loudenslager stated that Bob's flying was superb. Leo was watching at Hoover's ill-fated Oklahoma Air Show and had this to say regarding the 1992 exhibition: "as usual, flawless."

Now, we have an FAA designated Air Show Certification Evaluator who stated that Bob's flying was flawless. How in the world did two FAA inspectors who knew nothing about aerobatics have the audacity to ground the great Bob A. Hoover?

It only goes to show you the awesome power that the FAA has at their command. The FAA has seen fit to keep Bob from making a very lucrative living, at least in the United States. Bob has passed any and all flight and physical standards that other countries require. He has performed in Canada, South America, and Australia. All these countries are clambering for a look at Hoover's Aerial Artistry, but the government that he was willing to die for refuses to allow him to make a living.

Aviation writer J.R. Campbell sums up this case nicely: "Bob is a victim of a good old fashioned con-job, maybe even a 'hit,' on the part of some persons whose motives are not clear but certainly suspect. I don't know what it is … Maybe they're prejudice against those who have lived beyond a certain age. Maybe they are jealous of his skills. Maybe they wanted to bring down a modern American aviation figurehead … or maybe they just wanted to prove that they were the biggest jerks anyone in aviation (and maybe the known universe) has ever seen. Personally, I think they may be guilty of all counts."

A reliable source has informed me that the mood within the OKC FSDO was one of "smug joy" at having ruined Hoover's career.

Bob intended to take his case to the Supreme Court, if need be. He was fighting a great battle, not just for himself, but for every pilot out there. If the Gestapo can nail Bob Hoover, what chance do the rest of us mere mortals have?

In October of 1995, Bob Hoover's diligence finally paid off. After two and a half years of misery, he was awarded a second-class physical that permitted him to perform his flawless routine in the United States. Bob Hoover was thoroughly tested at the Mayo Clinic, UCLA, and Johns Hopkins. He passed all tests with flying colors. I wonder if the fact that all the tests were performed at non-FAA facilities could have had anything to do with his reinstatement.

Bob Hoover spent over $100,000 on legal and medical expenses, not to mention the sale of two of his aerobatic mounts: a Saberline and a T-28. Bob's grounding cost him close to $2 million in cancelled U.S. Air Shows.

While Bob was performing in Australia, government officials received a call from the FAA. They related to Bob, "They told me that the FAA had called them and complained that they were embarrassing the U.S. government by letting me fly in Australia." Hoover said, "Can you believe they'd do something like that? I certainly can. When the FAA finally issued Hoover his physical in October of 1995, they did so without one word of apology.

I would like to tell you another FAA horror story that happened to my best friend. He has an impeccable career as a pilot and ran a small flight school from a private strip behind his home. One day, one of his students arrived to put an hour of solo flight time in his logbook. This student, Bob "Weasel" Wetzel, is a retired engineer with about ten hours solo to his credit. At the time of Wetzel's arrival, my friend was busy briefing another student and neglected to check that Weasel had not flown for over ninety days. To be legal to fly, a pilot must make three takeoffs and landings every ninety days. It just so happened that the student my friend was briefing, Jerry Emrick, was building an airplane with Wetzel so Jerry and the instructor went out to watch Weasel Wetzel start up and taxi out. They were standing just short of the wing tip when the engine came to life in the full throttle position. Weasel went by them, wiped out a gas pump, and finally stopped about fifty yards away. It was obvious to all but the Weasel, "a person who has never made a mistake," that the checklist had not been followed. It plainly states, "throttle in one-quarter inch," not full throttle. The instructor asked the astonished pilot why he failed to use the checklist? Wetzel stated that he must have skipped that part.

That incident cost my friend a new engine and propeller, worth over $10,800, not to mention other damages to the gas pump and airframe. Weasel never said he was sorry for his damaging mistake, and to this day, has never called my friend to make restitution. However, he did manage a call to the local FAA police station and told them that he was allowed to fly without the prescribed ninety-day checkout. Now, he thought he could put all the blame on the instructor. My friend found out, the hard way, that Weasel was the kind of person who has never made a mistake. He told the FAA that the throttle stuck open. Well, his partner Jerry, who flew the plane first, said there was no problem with it at all. A mechanic checked the throttle after the accident and said it was fine. The FAA promptly notified my friend that he was being considered for enforcement action. My friend visited the FAA where he voluntarily gave them his instructor's license. The two pompous inspectors involved in this case were better known as "Let's get him Galo" and a "Mr. Jealous Klipa." Mr. Galo was a former state trooper so he was used to giving people a hard time. My friend had so many different type ratings that it required two licenses to list all of them. Mr. Klipa was quite taken with this, but at the same time, did not act like he was really that impressed. It was more of an "I could have done that if I had the chance" attitude. Another case of FAA jealousy.

About three months had elapsed and my friend was required to visit the FAA for the return of his certificate. There was no enforcement action taken for the incident, if you don't count not being able to instruct for three months, but an FAA "slap in the face" that my friend will never forget.

There are pilots who get thirty-day suspensions for flying into restricted airspace. Pilots that crash and kill dozens of people do not lose their ticket. Sure, they get a new check ride, but their license is not taken away unless they fail the ride.

After waiting two years for the court case to be called, the case was decided in favor of my friend and he was fully reimbursed. Mr. Robert Wetzel was extremely nervous on the stand, mainly because he was lying under oath. I don't believe it helped his case to be so unsure of himself. My friend previously had written numerous books condemning shoddy FAA operations. I suppose this was the "feds" way of getting even with a person who dared to criticize them.

Passenger Power

USAirways Captain Kenneth Bodner was preparing to take his scheduled trip out of Philadelphia. He picked up his flight documents at the check-in counter. He glanced at the flight release papers and a passenger said, "It's a warm night in Columbus. It should be a nice night." No other discussion occurred. He went down the jetway into his aircraft. His professional career was about to be trashed.

The passenger now made a statement to the gate agent: "Maybe he should take a breatholyzer test before flying," then boarded the aircraft that was about to be flown by the pilot whom he has accused of being "under the influence."

At departure time, the agent working the flight stood by the cockpit door and informed the captain that she had contacted her supervisor. Two men appeared and escorted the captain into the terminal. He passed another captain who said he had been ordered to take the flight. Neither captain had any idea of what was going on, except that it was not good.

Captain Bodner was escorted to a room where he would be tested for alcohol. Tests showed 000. Captain Bodner thought it was over, but there was more. They couldn't nail him for alcohol so they tested him for drugs. The test results were disclosed in a few days and showed the spurious attacks on his character were without merit. The tests were all negative.

Captain Bodner says, "You get the impression as the accusing people file out of the room that they are disappointed they didn't get their trophy pilot this time, but there will be other opportunities for them as their 'policy' and the great Oz lay waiting in the shadows for their next innocent victim."

Captain Bodner is presently seeking legal action against his airline. It only goes to show you how a statement from an unknown passenger can cause such disruption to an innocent pilot's life. As I said before, in aviation matters, you are always guilty until proven innocent.

Jealousy versus the FAA

This is a story that you will find hard to believe. Colonel Steve Goodman is a fighter pilot with the United States Air Force. In civil life, he flies an aerobatic plane at contests and air shows. At his daughter's wedding, he met his son-in-law's brother, Michael Bollinger. Michael was a private pilot with a burning desire to fly high-performance aircraft. However, this was not to be. He is presently driving nails for the Bollinger Roofing Company in Abington, Maryland. He had always been envious of Steve, and on this day, he had his chance to finally nail him.

He was helping his brother hang a garage door when the conversation turned to a medical condition that Colonel Steve Goodman had suffered. It was brought out that Steve had momentarily blacked out. Michael Bollinger could not wait to contact the FAA medical department in Oklahoma City, Oklahoma. He called them on the telephone and said that he thought they should know that pilot Steve Goodman was having blackouts. The FAA sprang into action. What a great chance to show their vast power. Without even contacting Colonel Goodman first, Dr. Michael J. Antunano of the Aeronautical Certification Division of the FAA sent a letter to Colonel Goodman. At the same time, a copy was sent to Steve's FAA medical examiner.

This proves that the FAA will accept any crank call concerning an airman and condemn him before hearing the whole story. In this case, they were dead wrong. Yes, it was true that Colonel Goodman blacked out, but the reason for this was the fact that he had a severe case of food poisoning that caused the blackout. The FAA did not have the decency to learn the complete story before condemning an airman with his FAA doctor.

The following is a quote from the FAA's Dr. Lomangino's letter to Colonel Goodman: "Although this letter does not constitute, nor should it be construed as an order or demand for the return of your medical certificate, you may wish to voluntarily surrender it for cancellation." The last paragraph states: "If we do not hear from you within 30 days, this matter will be referred to our legal department for appropriate action." All this because of a crank telephone call from a very shallow person.

Now Colonel Goodman is a criminal.

Nearly two years of misery were caused by Michael Bollinger, a jealous pilot who did a good job of grounding an innocent pilot.

Steve Goodman hired a lawyer who did him more harm than good. The outcome of this case is still pending. Luckily, Colonel Goodman was medically tested by the USAF. The only restriction on Colonel Goodman is that he not fly his own private aircraft. It is shocking the way the FAA can ground a pilot without hearing anything from the pilot in question.

If there is a pilot out there that you don't like, call up the FAA. They will be glad to ground him.

A Kinder, Gentler FAA

Joseph M. Bellino is one of the best controllers at O'Hare Airport in Chicago. He frequently contributes timely stories to his union's quarterly publication, The Voice. Listen to the events and remember they are all true.

There was a handicapped receptionist, a wheelchair-bound woman, employed by the FAA. Her handicap was the result of Multiple Sclerosis (MS). The Chicago Center had no handicap access lavatory. Federal law does not require a federal installation conversion to accommodate handicapped employees as federal law requires of the private sector. Volunteers assisted the receptionist to the toilet, into the toilet, and from the toilet. Remember that the wheelchair could not fit into any stall.

The friendly FAA decided to force the woman out of the agency. The FAA actions were swift and brief. Mr. Ralph Dais, FAA manager, put out a letter forbidding any assistance to her. She was forced to wear a diaper while she worked. The case went to court. The judge who heard the case was appalled with the FAA and "advised" them to settle immediately. And settle they did; for 100 percent of the lady's claim.

Don't Fool with the Boss

An air traffic controller at Chicago Center (ZAU) was attacked when he chose to challenge the immoral and illegal activity of a supervisor. The supervisor was a long-standing problem to the FAA involving criminal as well as FAA issues. The FAA promptly removed the air traffic controller from his control position and assigned him to the center's loading dock, loading and unloading freight that came to the facility. This case went on for years. The controller was soon to be medically retired. It took over three years for the agency to destroy this controller's career because he filed a complaint against a supervisor.

Controller Joe Bellino, who has worked for the FAA for over 30 years, had this to say concerning the demoted controller: "He became accustomed to FAA administrators who do nothing, see nothing, and say nothing."

Jane Garvey is the FAA administrator who continues in the tradition of being a "do-nothing."

What kind of person does it take to be an FAA Operations Inspector? Well, to start with, there are very few inspectors who would not jump at the chance to be an airline pilot. Large air carriers pay their pilots over three times the yearly salary of an inspector, and an air carrier pilot only works a total of about seven months a year. Civilian and military pilots are held in high esteem by the rest of the aviation industry whereas the FAA is looked down on by nearly everybody. With that broad variance, why would a pilot choose to join the FAA? That is easy to figure out. They were denied service with the military or airlines because they were too short, not experienced enough, too old, in poor physical condition, or just plain stupid.

I found an interesting requirement for FAA inspectors in their FAA book AS1-006. It seems the last line of their requirement states: "Not more than two flying accidents in the last five years." An accident, compared to an incident, is where a nearly total destruction to the aircraft, or hospitalization or death of the occupants occurs. There are very, very few airline pilots who have ever crashed or injured any of their passengers, and that might include a time interval of over thirty years. Yet the FAA inspectors can be hired by the government to oversee people who are better and safer pilots, and have no incidents on their records.

Following a fatal crash of an FAA aircraft in California, the San Jose Mercury News listed 409 FAR violations discovered by seventeen of their own inspectors. "Flying with expired licenses, uninspected repairs, incomplete and outdated manuals, unlabeled spare parts, and pilots deferring mandatory training."

A few years ago, another FAA owned and operated King Air met with tragedy near Pittsburgh, Pennsylvania. The aircraft crashed into a wooded area because of severe wing icing. The NTSB determined that the three dead crewmembers were not in the best shape to be flying. The pilot had been drinking, and the co-pilot had recently lost his license for driving under the influence and was inadequately trained.

You would think that high profile people such as Bruce Springsteen, Tom Cruise, Gerald Ford, Ronald Reagan, George Bush, and Billy Joel would make sure that they were being flown by a reputable operator. In the case of Northeast Jet, run by Earl Holtz, you were taking your life in your hands on nearly every flight. Holtz was convicted in federal court of illegally modifying his jets and hiding the safety violations from the "feds." Northeast Jet was a worldwide charter service that catered mainly to celebrities. Holtz ordered his pilots to fly unairworthy and overloaded planes. They did this because they feared losing their jobs. Two former FAA safety inspectors pleaded guilty to aiding Holtz cover up safety violations. Inspectors John Doster and Steve Klidonas admitted to conspiring with Holtz to falsify documents and conceal violations. Two more "good old boys" face a maximum of five years in jail and fines up to $25,000.

In 1995, according to Edward H. Phillips of Aviation Week, the FAA intensified its probe of 29 pilots, including at least four FAA safety inspectors and 12 designated pilot examiners for allegedly falsifying flight records and issuing invalid type ratings for vintage World War II aircraft as well as business jets. So far, four of the six aviation safety inspectors employed by the FAA were fired and two more resigned.

The following comments are from James R. Campbell, editor of U.S. Aviator. I think you will find them interesting.

"You're going to love this one. These days the FAA grounds a pilot (quite justifiable) for one year if he/she gets caught drinking and flying. However, let that same pilot not break the law, but instead do the smart thing and submit himself for treatment for alcohol abuse, get professional help, and admit same to the FAA. Then, he has to stay on the ground for two years, twice as much as if he or she gets caught breaking the law! Yeah ... this really breaks respect for the law and promotes safety, doesn't it?"

Campbell's second story continues concerning the Master Race at work and play. "A homosexual male was harassed repeatedly (and now I understand that he is not the only one so afflicted) by FAA officials who disagree with his sexual preferences.... Bothering him at home, ramp checking his aircraft (while making antigay statements), and then speaking to others, indicating that he was gay and under the scrutiny of the FAA. While you or I may not approve of this guy's lifestyle choices, it sure isn't the FAA's business what we do in our bedrooms."

Congressman Wolf Says it All

Congressman Frank R. Wolf is the former Chairman of the Transportation Appropriations Subcommittee. I have taken the liberty of extracting some of what Congressman Wolf's thoughts are concerning the FAA: "The lack of leadership at the Federal Aviation Administration (FAA) has now reached a crisis point.... When poor decisions are made, they try to cover it up or 'ride out the storm.' No one is ever fired. No one is ever punished.... One year after the terrible Valujet and TWA 800 tragedies, the FAA is lifeless and adrift.... The FAA does not have a funding crisis. They have a crisis of management. They have an organizational culture, built up over many years which is secretive and cagey, self-interested rather than public-spirited, and resistant to change."

Who do you suppose was the second ranking official in the FAA's hierarchy? Her name is Linda Hall Daschle and here are her qualifications that enable her to know all about aviation. She has served as vice president in charge of federal and environmental affairs for the American Association of Airport Executives. She was general manager of the associates' new business television network and training network. She is also a former beauty queen. Her real claim to fame is the fact that she is the wife of Senator Tom Daschle, Minority Leader.

To get back to a good quote from James Campbell's U.S. Aviator concerning Mrs. Daschle and her husband: "What about the fact that a well-known senator succeeded in getting a friend out of hot water with the FAA after a series of known/reported safety problems culminated in a fatal accident killing several doctors? This senator, mind you, just happens to be married to the FAA's Linda Daschle. Yup ... THE FEDS TAKE CARE OF THEIR OWN" (capitals mine).

In 1996, FAA administrator David Hinson left the agency in shame. His handling of the ValuJet crash in Miami was his swan song. At least Hinson was a qualified pilot and an airline executive. His government post went vacant while a search went on for a person who could manage the largest government aviation administration in the world. President Clinton nominated Jane Garvey and the Senate approved her as Director of the Federal Aviation Administration. She would be the first director to serve a five-year term. During the first three years, Garvey did nothing to improve the plight of the FAA. Her only claim to fame was her two-year stint as a director of Boston's Logan International Airport. Prior to the Logan job, she served as a commissioner of public works in Massachusetts where she was responsible for the new Boston Harbor Tunnel.

The project estimates incurred from 2 billion to an excess of over 10 billion. The FAA knows all about the budget projections. The following is a quote from the president of the largest pilot organization in the United States: the aircraft owners and pilots association: "It seems inconceivable that, in this vast country, the president couldn't find an experienced manager who has the ability to innovate and motivate positive traits attributed to Garvey—and who is also a pilot or has more than Garvey's limited aviation experience."

Just Take Their License

You are speeding down the highway and you spot a patrol car closing in on you. You know you were way over the speed limit so you will just have to bear with the officer as he writes out a citation. Instead of a ticket, the officer confiscates your driver's license. You say that could never happen. Well, it's happening all the time in the FAA. One thing we can all thank Jane Garvey for is a blatant use of the "emergency revocation."

Emergency revocation has been around for many years, but lately the FAA has been using it much more frequently. The number of emergency revocations has doubled since 1989. An FAA inspector has the power to tell you he or she is going to revoke your pilot's or mechanic's license. Just like that, it's gone, and you are guilty until proven innocent.

FAA Sex Seminars

A few years ago, the "feds" decided it would be a good idea if their male controllers were subjected to the same sexual harassment that they bestowed on female controllers. The seminars were called "Cultural Diversity Training," but you might have another name for it.

Some of the shocking behavior included the following:

1. Allegedly, men were forced to walk naked between a gauntlet of prodding women where they were fondled and subjected to distasteful remarks from the opposite sex.

2. Government employees were tied together (similar to handcuffing criminals) for a period of 24 hours. Some pairs consisted of the same sex, but when they ran out of like sexes, males and females were shackled together. This included using the toilet facilities.

3. Male/female couples were required to sleep together, not for love, but as a condition of their employment.

Joseph M. Ballino, the former vice president of NATCA, had this to say in a letter to the Associate FAA Administrator, William Pollard: "It is NATCA's belief that the FAA now enters the world of the mind. Trauma long since forgotten, horrors, rapes, beatings, loneliness, to mention only a few … for years properly stored and categorized within the mind of an FAA employee allowing this individual to function quite well within the FAA and society. This employee then volunteers to attend a two- or three-day CD training seminar that is designed to probe for exactly these memories. While at the CD class, no participant may sit on the sidelines. All must reach within the recesses of their mind and find 'something'." How the "feds" believed that publicly airing one's past misery would make him or her a better person is more than I can see. Some controllers suffered physical and psychological damage as a result of these seminars, and some were unable to work after attending one of these meetings.

Here is a statement from the Chicago Tribune 9-23-94 written by Andrew Gottesman: "The same issue was highlighted recently by a separate lawsuit filed in federal court by controller Douglas Hartman. After Hartman and several colleagues walked the gauntlet at a 1992 diversity seminar, he said, 'the women rated the men's penis sizes on a scale of 1 through 10'. Hartman is presently suing the FAA for $300,000 for psychological damage related to the cultural training program.

Another controller will receive $75,000 for the above reasons.

The FAA claims that Cultural Diversity Training is purely a voluntary program. The only problem is that if you don't volunteer to undergo this nonsense, you have no possibility for a promotion to supervisor.

The "feds" improperly funded the diversity training through the use of Task Orders and elected not to use the competitive bid process. Task Orders have a cap of $25,000. So far, the FAA has used more than $1.5 million through multiple Task Orders.

Joseph M. Ballino states: "Had the FAA not abused the money provided to them by the United States Congress and the American people to provide perverted sport for themselves, our members would not have been harmed.

The controllers' union NATCA has, for years, been battling the FAA concerning Diversity Training. And on September 22, 1994, the FAA agreed to allow NATCA to establish some of the ground rules concerning the warped FAA testing. NATCA has never objected to Cultural Diversity Training; they simply want the opportunity to provide input to enhance the government seminars. Perhaps then these meetings will benefit the workers instead of causing the numerous traumas of the past.

The person who administered these FAA seminars was Gregory May, a clinical psychologist. He was recently sentenced to six months in jail and $5,000 in fines after he pleaded guilty to one count of mail fraud. Hopefully, NATCA will be successful in putting a stop to some of this nonsensical training.

Oops! I Goofed!

This one takes the cake. An FAA Inspector was making a routine ramp check examination of parked aircraft and finding "nitpicking" discrepancies.

Henry H. Polchow left the following note on his 8620-1 form and attached it to a 414 Cessna: "No. 1 engine needs to be inspected due to all three prop blades being bent at tips." He also stated: "No. 2 engine needs to be inspected due to all three prop blades tip bent ... this must not fly until it meets all requirements of FAR Part 43.

It would not take a genius to see that the props were not bent because of a ground strike; there was no jagged metal and the paint was perfect. The manufacturer of the prop, Hartzell, made the prop with bent tips to decrease noise and vibration, and to shorten the radius reducing vortice effects.

The FAA scrambled to rectify its stupid mistake and informed the owner of the aircraft that there would be no further enforcement action and it would not become part of the owner's FAA file. They also mentioned that the inspector who filed the discrepancy would be sent to school for more training. He was probably never trained in the first place.

FAA Operations Inspectors are required to receive flight checks every six months. The General Accounting Office did a survey concerning FAA inspectors. They found that 63 percent of the total inspecting force failed to receive the prescribed check rides, but they continued giving illegal check rides to airline pilots.

Airline pilots may be checked by their own company check pilots who know what they are doing, or by FAA inspectors who usually don't know what they are doing. I would say that 50 percent of the FAA check pilots who have ridden with me are decent people who know their job. The rest are a pain in the backside. When they get on your flight, they must show you their credentials and the fact that they are assigned the jump seat. The inspector is supposed to sit there, observe, and take notes. But this is not always the case. At times, all their questions and remarks are a safety hazard. You know that this person is jealous of your job, and if he gets a chance to rub it in, he will.

These inspectors have the power to ground you if they spot any operation not to their individual satisfaction. Most of the time, they conduct themselves as they should but the odd balls give the rest of the group a bad name.

I remember the frequency of my FAA route checks, before and after my first air safety book. Prior to the book's publication, I might see an FAA inspector once every couple of years. After the publication, it was quite another story. I could expect an FAA Inspector at least once a month. Do you think the publication of my book had anything to do with it?

There is a strange code among check pilots. If you give them a perfect ride, they seldom tell you so. Instead, they will nitpick the most minute discrepancy. It's always "It was a good ride, but, …" That's the way the Master Race operates.

I learned one thing the hard way. You never, ever surrender your license, medical, or airplane airworthiness certificate simply because the Master Race requests you do so. Bob Hoover voluntarily relinquished his medical certificate, simply because an FAA inspector asked for it. I now find that if you relinquish any certificate to the FAA, you may never get it back. They simply state that you gave it to them to keep so it belongs to them. The FAA has no authority to request any of your certificates without a formal hearing. The average airman doesn't know this and the "feds," as sneaky as they are, would never tell you. You should never go to an FAA hearing without a lawyer. The "feds" will have one, perhaps two, in order to drive home their one-sided accusations.

FAR (Federal Aviation Regulations) or FARces?

The FAA has two assigned missions to perform: to promote and regulate aviation. There is very little to be said about their promotion of aviation, but a lot to say regarding regulating.

Following are just a very few of their mandates that are not only stupid but also potentially dangerous.

Money Talks

FAR 121.311 Seat and Safety Belts. (a) No person may operate an airplane unless there are available during the takeoff, en route flight, and landing:

(1) An approved seat of berth for each person on board the airplane who has not reached his second birthday.

Most passengers like the idea of being able to fly with their babies without having to buy a ticket. I will admit that it is tempting to fly infants for free, and besides, there must be a good reason for this. You would think the

FAA has researched this matter thoroughly and they have decided that it is perfectly safe. Wrong on all counts.

This regulation has been in effect for decades and it should never have been allowed. Ms. Dee Maki, who was my former flight attendant and the past president of the Association of Flight Attendants, has, on numerous occasions, petitioned the FAA to cancel this potentially dangerous regulation. This is one of the few times that the FAA shows any credence to their mandate to regulate and promote aviation. The airlines would lose a tidy sum if passengers were forced to strap their infants into car seats rather than hold them on their laps. This would necessitate buying another seat. So being "good old boys," the FAA turns their head to keep airlines happy.

By now you are probably wondering why I am fussing over such a minor discrepancy. Every year, hundreds of infants are killed when the car they are riding in is involved in a fatal accident. If the infants were secured in proper car seats, many lives could have been saved. According to Newton's third law of motion, once an object is in motion, it remains in motion until a force acts upon it. When a vehicle that is cruising at sixty miles per hour hits a brick wall, any unrestrained occupant will continue forward at 60 miles per hour. Increase that speed to that of a landing aircraft and you get an idea of the tremendous forces involved. The NTSB estimates that airline crash speeds can average 20 to 40 Gs. This means that the gravitational force on a 20-pound child in a 20G accident would be 400 pounds. If you think for an instant that you could contain 400 pounds of weight accelerating forward, you are greatly mistaken.

In July of 1994, USAir Flight 1016 was slammed to the ground by a microburst. Thirty-seven passengers died and fifteen lived. One more could have survived if a proper child restraint system had been used. There were two infants aboard this aircraft but because they were under the age of two, the FAA says, "anything goes."

The following is a direct quote from the NTSB report concerning the infants in the cabin. "The two lap children were seated in 18F and 21C. The 18-month-old female infant was lying across seats 18E and 18F [not even strapped in] (brackets mine). This infant sustained serious injuries, and her mother sustained minor injuries. The other lap-child, a

9-month-old female infant, was being held by her mother in 21C and sustained fatal injuries. According to the mother, SHE WAS UNABLE TO MAINTAIN A SECURE HOLD ON HER CHILD DURING THE IMPACT SEQUENCE" (capitals mine).

Following the crash of United's DC-10 in Sioux City, Iowa, on July 19, 1989, the NTSB issued recommendation A-90-78 to the FAA to revise 14CFR Parts 91,121,135 to require all occupants be restrained during takeoff, landing, and turbulence, and that all infants under 40 pounds be restrained in an approved child restraint system. This crash killed infants who were not properly restrained. This time, the NTSB was 100 percent correct. They recommended that the age criteria be eliminated and replaced with a weight restriction.

In 1994, the "feds" researched a child restrain system aided by the Office of Aviation Medicine Civil Aeromedical Institute (CAMI). Their tests proved that an anthropomorphic test dummy (ATD) representing a child of three restrained by a lap belt would be afforded adequate protection. A child of two in a normal lap belt would have a "marginal" chance for safety. The tests stated that a child below the age of three has very little security in a normal seat belt but that in an approved child seat restraint, his or her chances were excellent.

In this issue, the "feds" were really pushing their mandate of promoting aviation. They didn't want to make the airline passenger pay for an extra seat or use a child restraint system, so at no extra charge, your loved one could be snatched out of your arms and killed before your very eyes. The FAA has proven that they couldn't care less.

NTSB has investigated numerous aviation accidents where children were held on an adult's lap. In every case, these actions contributed to a fatal injury.

When an airplane comes to a sudden stop, everything that is not secured rigidly goes flying forward and stops at the first cabin bulkhead. If the FAA wants to play games with your child, the least they could do is put a criteria on the infant's weight, instead of on the child's age.

My daughter, Laurette, who is a USAirways flight attendant, informs me that in an emergency, parents who occupy the seats just behind the cabin bulkheads are instructed to place their infants on the floor snug against the bulkhead. Why do you suppose this procedure is recommended? That's an easy one. In a crash, that infant is going to hit that wall, like it or not, so it's far better to put the infant there prior to the accident. Passengers seated further back in the aircraft will have to watch in terror as the tremendous power of inertia snatches their loved ones from their arms and propels them against the first obstruction.

Australia's Qantas Airline is more concerned with your infant's safety than most of the American carriers. They have special "belly belts" that go around your infant and attach to your seat belt. This beats trying to restrain inertia by cradling your infant.

In the April 1994 issue of FAA News, an interesting article appeared concerning infant restraints in aircraft. It was written by Phyllis Ann Duncan, Editor, and John M. Wensel, an FAA safety inspector. "Many minor automobile accidents turn tragic when a child not restrained in an approved seat or seat belt is injured or killed by bouncing around the car's interior like some horrific pinball. An otherwise survivable aircraft incident can become just as tragic for the same reason."

This is a quote from an FAA inspector. "Why is it that the faulty regulation concerning seat belts continues to be on the books?"

My suggestion to you is this. If you wouldn't dream of allowing your infant to ride in your car without a proper car seat, don't think about allowing them to fly without the same lifesaving seat. It will cost you a few bucks more, but aren't your children worth it?

What Did He Say?

Part of the criteria for a student pilot to satisfy one of their private pilot requirements (61.107) is that he or she must make three solo landings at an airport with a control tower. This is so minimal that it becomes potentially dangerous. If the student pilot received training at a controlled airport (one with a tower), he or she would probably be safe to operate from a busy airport. But if the student received most of the training at a non-towered airport, three landings is not nearly enough. Some controllers rattle off instructions so fast that the student usually asks, "What did he say?" It takes many hours to be comfortable at a low-traffic controlled field. But at a busy terminal, the student pilot is completely bewildered.

For example, if the low-time private pilot is on final approach at an airline airport, and the tower says: "Cessna 17230 you are cleared to land, turn off at taxiway Tango. Jet traffic following at three miles no delay." The pilot replies, "Roger 17230."

Now the fledgling has a problem. He has a jet airliner three miles behind him and closing fast. The jet is traveling at 140 miles per hour; the student is flying at 80. Things would be less stressful in the cockpit if the neophyte only knew which taxiway is Tango. Sooner than broadcast his ignorance and ask the tower which taxiway is the one in question, the pilot lands his aircraft well past the assigned taxiway. The next available turnoff is at midfield and by the time he taxies to it, that jet is on him. The next transmission he hears from the tower is "USAir 263 take it around (abort the landing). The light plane is still on the runway."

This is only one example of what lies in wait for a pilot who has only three tower landings to his credit. It is hard to say how many landings should be required, but three landings is nothing short of ludicrous.

I Haven't Forgotten a Thing

While we are on the subject of landings, how would you feel about flying with a pilot who has not flown for over a year? Would you feel confident to climb on board with a person who has just completed three questionable solo landings? I think not. Yet the FAR 61.57 (G) (Recent Flight Experience: Pilot In Command) says that it is perfectly legal. Well, it might be legal, but as for safety, that's another story. Flying is like riding a bicycle. You never really forget how to do it, but your flying skills show a downward trend after only a month or so on the ground. It might be prudent for a rusty pilot who has not flown for a long time to find an instructor to requalify him, not only in normal landings but also in gusty crosswinds. Flight time is very expensive but the safe pilot should be requalified by a licensed instructor. The FAR infers, save your money and do it yourself.

Alone and Dangerous

The FARs always have more stringent standards for aircraft that carry thirty or more people. But what about a single-seat airplane?

Well, for starters, if you fly in an aircraft that only has one seat, the "feds" really don't care that much about your safety. For one thing, FAR 91.52 states that an Emergency Locator Transmitter (ELT) is not required to be on board your aircraft. If, however, you fly passengers in anything but a turbojet, you must have an ELT as part of your aircraft's equipment. Should your plane crash, the ELT would automatically activate and send out a distress radio signal that could be received by any aircraft or satellite. This could mean the difference between life and death, but if you are by yourself, the government doesn't care.

Parachute

There is only one salient point to wearing a parachute while piloting an aircraft: to enable you to save your life in an emergency. Should your airplane break up in flight, if you have an uncontrolled fire, or you are involved in a mid-air, a parachute could enable you to live to fly another day. FAR 91.307 (c) states that "chutes" are not required during acrobatic maneuvers which are required by any regulations for any certificate or rating when given by a certified flight instructor. In other words, if you decide to go up in your acrobatic Pitts aircraft and really wring it out and a wing falls off, it's okay to kill yourself, just as long as you don't have a passenger with you.

Legal but Not Safe

Your patience is getting thin because you have been waiting for over 45 minutes for weather conditions to improve so that your airliner can make a legal takeoff. The cabin speakers come to life and the captain states, "Very sorry for the delay. They expect the weather to improve shortly and we will try our best to make up the lost time once we get rolling. Thank you."

You look out your cabin window but because of the fog, you can barely see the end of the wing. Your aircraft is not the only one waiting for weather improvement. The captain announced earlier that, "we were number one and there was a long line of aircraft behind us."

Out of the corner of your eye, you pick up a tiny aircraft that is taxiing by your airliner. What in the world can a tiny airplane be doing here in such foul weather? Your questions are answered as it taxies by you to the active runway and starts his takeoff roll. You sit perplexed. How in the world can a private pilot in his own small plane possibly have more skill than the experienced crew up front?

The answer is simple. While the airline crew probably has far more experience, many thousands of hours compared to the pilot of the tiny aircraft who could have as little time as 300 hours, FAA regulations are what make the difference. FAR 91.175(F) allows a private pilot with an instrument rating to take off when the ceiling and visibility are both zero. Since airlines must fly under the more stringent 121 or 135 regulations, and the general aviation pilots fly under more lenient part 91 rules, nearly anything goes.

Single-Engine Pilot

When a pilot received his first license, it's called a student pilot certificate. This certificate is granted as soon as the pilot solos. The next license could come in as little as forty hours. That one is the private license. Listed under the private pilot certificate might be airplane single-engine land if that was the type of aircraft used to obtain the license. Since the license states single-engine, that enables the pilot to fly any noncomplex aircraft up to 12,500 pounds that is propelled through the air on one engine.

If a pilot decides he would like to check out in a surplus P-51 Mustang that weighs less than 12,500 pounds, he would be qualified to do this providing he passes a check ride in a high-performance aircraft and gets a tail wheel checkout.

FAR 61.31 (e) requires a logbook endorsement by a flight instructor certifying that his student has passed a successful checkout in a high-performance airplane. The P-51 is definitely a high-performance plane but the FAA classifies high performance in the following manner: the aircraft must have more than 200 horsepower, or a retractable landing gear, flaps, and a controllable propeller.

Now the stage is set for excitement. Try to picture a private 45-hour, single-engine pilot who has just checked out in a Beechcraft Bonanza strapping himself into a "fire eating" P-51 Mustang. You don't want to be anywhere near this accident waiting to happen.

Let's take a look at some of the major differences between a tiny Beechcraft and the mighty Mustang.

AIRCRAFT	HORSEPOWER	WEIGHT	SPEED	CEILING
Bonanza	285	3,600lb.	136mph.	16,600ft.
Mustang	1,695	10,100lb.	362mph.	41,900ft.

In a nutshell, you can see the vast differences between the two aircraft. The P-51 has over 1,410 more horsepower, weighs 6,500 pounds more, and is 226 mph faster than the Bonanza.

I speak from experience. I have checked out in both these aircraft and there is absolutely no comparison between them. The military prepares you for the P-51 by requiring time in an AT-6, about the nearest thing you can get to a P-51. This also should be an FAA requirement. There are real high-performance aircraft and then again, there are so-called high-performance planes.

Ice Polishing

I have saved the most unbelievable regulation for last. Elsewhere in this book, I have gone into the requirement for keeping the wings of the aircraft free of ice and snow so I will just skim over the clean wing regulations.

What would you think if, while sitting in the gate area of an airport, you noticed a bazaar sight: mechanics climbing up on an aircraft's wings, not with deicing guns, but with electric buffers. Are they out there polishing the ice? Why in the world would mechanics be polishing ice rather than removing it?

"FAR 91.527 Operating in icing conditions: (a) No pilot may take off in an airplane that has (1) Frost, snow, or ice adhering to any propeller, windshield, or power plant installation or to an airspeed altimeter, rate of climb, or flight altitude instrument system. (2) Snow or ice adhering to the wings or stabilizer or control surfaces; or (3) Any frost adhering to the wings or stabilizing on control surfaces, UNLESS THAT FROST HAS BEEN POLISHED TO MAKE IT SMOOTH" (capitals mine).

Anything adhering to an aircraft's wings will greatly reduce the wings' lifting capabilities. Even dirt or rain will affect the power of a wing to perform as designed. Frost, while it is the lightest of all the icing phenomena, is still something to be reckoned with. When you take off with a wing coated with ice, polished or otherwise, you are flirting with a wing that has not been tested in this condition.

The thought of added weight to an aircraft must not have entered the minds of the Master Race. On a large aircraft, it could increase the weight by hundreds of pounds.

I have never witnessed ice buffing, and you can bet I would not fly the aircraft until it was properly de-iced, not simply polished.

There are many more dangerous regulations that I could tell you about, but I think you have a good idea of what your government is doing to keep you safe.

Your Wasted Money

For decades, the "feds" have been pumping our money into better ways to enhance safety. Some of these projects are fine, but the majority takes far too long, come in way over budget, and then get scrapped.

Over 27 years have elapsed since the Microwave Landing System (MLS) first was initiated. This system took so long to complete it was overtaken by newer and, hopefully, better technology. In three decades, things are bound to change. And while the FAA always moves at a snail's pace, large expenditures are inevitably wasted.

In June of 1994, former director of the FAA, chief David R. Hinson, cancelled the MLS project at a loss of over $400 million. That money would have gone a long way in updating the many substandard airline airports.

In February of 1994, the FAA initiated a new Global Positioning Satellite that should far surpass the now defunct MLS. This new approach system was scheduled to come on line in 1997 at a cost of between $400 and $500 million. Where have we heard those figures before?

In 1981, former President Ronald Reagan flexed his antiunion muscles when he fired 11,000 PATCO air traffic controllers. It takes about 175,000 dollars to completely train a controller until he reaches full performance level. Reagan cost us a vast amount of money just to show his rich friends in industry how to break a union. We have been paying back the $1.4 billion that was wasted by a whim from our leader.

1995

The Advanced Automation System (AAS) has cost us over $3.7 billion so far and the FAA has been experiencing problems with this complicated system. In 1994, Administrator Hinson cancelled most of the program. The restructuring of the voice communication system increased in cost by $46 million because of faults in the AAS. Because of delays, the FAA will be paying an increase of $7.6 million for their Doppler radar. And because of a decision to cancel the initial sector suite system, the voice switching and control system will have an increased price tag of $45.9 million.

In 1996, former FAA administrator Hinson made the following statement concerning the good job he was doing in cutting government expenses. "We've done a lot. We're pretty much on track every place on the air traffic control modernization. We've saved the government a whole lot of money.

1999

The Standard Terminal Automation Replacement System (STARS) is a new unit being developed to replace the radar processing systems at Terminal

Radar Approach Facilities for 172 various airports. This system is long overdue, but does it work?

The following are various quotes from controllers and FAA engineers: "We do not want this equipment as it is currently designed. It does not work. It has less functionality than our current system … On June 8, 1998, the backup software failed 41 out of 58 times."

FAA project engineer Bob Schwartz has some startling things to say about STARS: "STARS displays were 10 to 20 times slower than existing equipment. FAA hides the fact that STARS is not even needed because FAA already solves the problem with CARTS and OLLIE systems!! CART/OLLIE is vastly superior to STARS because CARTS has been optimized for more than 30 years in the intensely busy and intricate environment of U.S. air traffic loads. But FAA officials yanked OLLIE and shipped it back to the factory because OLLIE embarrassed them with its vastly superior performance over STARS. Because STARS was determined to be too dangerous to deploy at Washington, D.C.'s Reagan Airport, FAA is now shipping STARS systems to Syracuse, New York, and to El Paso, Texas.

How much money has the government spent on STARS? A system that FAA engineers, controllers, and PASS people all thoroughly despise? Would you believe that $6 billion has been spent on a system that is not completely functional?

Changes in Cost for Five Major Projects

	1983	**1995**	
ASDE-3	83.2 mil	247.3 mil	40 radars
AWOS	16.7 mil	255.3 mil	737 units
FSAS	35.1 mil	394.2 mil	61 stations
ITWS	138.9 mil	250.7 mil	37 systems
OAP	169.1 mil	236.5 mil	3 systems

These figures come from a GAO report. They really do a great job when it comes to watching the money that our government wastes.

The GAO has stated, in many of their reports, that the FAA needs help in many ways, especially in managing projects and money. The scenario goes something like this:

A. The FAA gets an idea for a new piece of equipment.

B. They put out bids and, of course, the lowest one gets it. Not necessarily the best but the lowest.

C. Contracts are signed and the "games begin."

D. The contractor says it needs more money and will have to move the completion date forward a number of years.

E. The FAA starts to get friendly eyes for another manufacturer and cancels the contract with the initial supplier.

F. The FAA project manager is just about to get a handle on what he is overseeing when the "feds" assign a new manager to the project who takes months to acquire the knowledge of the first manager.

G. The FAA changes its concept of the project after spending years and millions on a new piece of equipment. FAA decides to scrap the whole project and wait for a better idea.

If a civilian corporation were run the way the FAA conducts business, they would be bankrupt in short order. Probably one of the most important aspects of updating our air traffic control system is listening to what the working controllers have to say. There is no group in the FAA who knows more about the day-to-day operation of the air traffic control system. The workers could save millions of dollars if they were consulted about what is really needed to produce a good, efficient, safe system but their input is set aside while management prevails.

Controllers are sick and tired of having to work with new equipment that is riddled with faults that they are expected to "make work."

The FAA has numerous divisions but only a very few are worthy of being in existence such as Air Traffic Control, Airways Technicians, Flight Service Stations, and Research and Development. Many of the remaining 25,000 positions could be consolidated or eliminated.

Nearly every state has at least one Flight Service District Office (FSDO) where you could go and sit for various aviation written exams. The "feds" gradually have been phasing out most of the written tests. Now they don't allow applicants a chance to be tested at a facility where there is no charge for exams. One must go to an FAA-designated examiner (one who does the FAA's work) who will charge you for administering the various written exams.

Just a personal note concerning the FAA FSDO. The one in my state administers written tests for an aircraft mechanic only one day a month. I arrived for my exam and the secretary checked to be sure that I had the appropriate certificates to take the aircraft mechanic exam. She had the task of looking at my credentials, issuing me the exams, and telling me where to sit. This only took her a matter of minutes but the FAA claims they are overworked and that is the reason for assigning the testing to non-government facilities.

The FAA office was run as though they had very important secret papers there. You can't enter the office of the inspector without going through a door that is electronically locked. The secretary, who sits behind a glass partition, has controls over the door. When you enter the office you are continuously watched. What are they afraid of?

After completing my exams, I was told that an inspector would have to verify my qualifications, something he should have done before starting the tests. I asked where the inspector was. I was told that he was out of the office for the day and could I come back another day? Well, I promptly told them that since the tests were only given one day a month, the least the inspector could do was be there on the assigned day. They eventually managed to find a person with the authority to sign off my application. Can you imagine they couldn't do their assigned work just one day a month? Well, that's water under the bridge. A month later, I took my practical and got my mechanic's license.

Cars—Aren't Us

No wonder the FAA cannot manage its sophisticated Advanced Automation System, a program that is more than $1 billion over budget and years late. According to the Transpiration Department's Office of the Inspector General, the FAA cannot even manage something as simple as a fleet of cars. The agency wastes about $4.4 million annually through mismanagement of its more than 4,000 leased vehicles. In fiscal 1992, 64 percent of vehicles leased were underutilized. The OIG found that FAA employees preferred to use their own cars for government business, even when agency vehicles were readily available. The problem may be a blessing in disguise for taxpayers: a Washington insider suggested "money saved from car leases could be applied to AAS."

When the FAA wants to change or inaugurate new rules, they do so by printing their Notice Proposed Rule Making (NPRM) that eventually becomes part of the Federal Register. The vast majority of pilots have no idea what an NPRM means, and the FAA likes it that way. Before the "feds" change a regulation, they must allow a certain amount of time between the date an NPRM is printed and when it becomes a law. Obviously, the less time allowed produces the least amount of opposing comments, and it seems the FAA thrives on short reply time. Proposed NPRM 94-31 will have drastic effects on all FAA physical requirements for all pilots. In fact, it will ground many of the older, more experienced aviators. This NPRM is unquestionably the result of the grounding of Bob A. Hoover. The FAA is only covering their behinds after their disgraceful treatment of Mr. Hoover.

It really makes very little difference whether the FAA receives pro or con replies to their NPRMs because they, the FAA, are the final authority concerning the outcome of any of their proposed new regulations.

CHAPTER 20

▼

THE VALUJET TRAGEDY

At first, the pilots of Valujet Flight 592 thought the click they heard was just another electrical problem on their aging plane.

"What was that?" Captain Candace Kubeck asked co-pilot Richard Hayes less than six minutes after the plane took off from Miami, Florida, en route to Atlanta, Georgia, on May 11, 1996. Within thirteen seconds, it was clear to Kubeck that what she felt in the controls was a major problem. "We're losing everything" she said.

The crew told ATC that they wanted to return to Miami. Three seconds later, there were shouts from the cabin: "Fire! Fire! We're on fire!" As Kubeck turned the plane and Hayes radioed their emergency situation, flight attendants, choking on smoke and flames, asked the pilots to deploy oxygen masks for the passengers. "We need oxygen! We can't get oxygen back here!"

Fourteen seconds later, the plane was completely on fire. Two seconds after that, as toxic fumes filled the cabin, everyone had fallen silent.

Captain Kubeck, too, was silent.

Hayes was still trying to fly the plane, calling out their altitude of 9,000 feet and telling the controller he needed the "closest airport available." Almost three minutes after the fire was discovered, the cockpit voice recorder picked up only tones, and clicks, and the sound of rushing air.

At this point, the intense smoke had overcome the crew and their flight controls were probably not functioning.

The DC-9 was now aiming straight down from 7,000 feet, and at a tremendous speed, dug a deep crater in the Florida Everglades. All 110 people on board died. (Many of the previous statements were taken from Robert Davies of USA Today.)

While much of the controversy concerning the crash is still going on, I would like to offer a few suggestions as to the real culprit of this disaster.

Valujet was the fastest growing airline in the United States. Its stock was the darling of Wall Street and many people grew rich because of it. The history of the airline was something else.

1993—On October 26, Valujet began service with two DC-9s to three cites. Within twelve months, they had acquired 30 more jets and served over 123 cities.

1994—On June 8, a DC-9 caught fire on the runway in Atlanta, causing one injury. The aircraft was completely gutted by the fire. In August, the Defense Department rejected Valujet as a military contractor because of its lack of maintenance expertise. And in September, the FAA launched an inspection of all airlines and found many discrepancies at Valujet.

1996—On January 12, a DC-9 skidded into a snow bank at Dulles International Airport outside of Washington, D.C. On January 26, a DC-9 slid off the runway in Atlanta. On February 1, a tire blew at Atlanta, causing an evacuation of crew and passengers. On February 14, the FAA in Washington was critical of their Atlanta office for lax inspections of Valujet and stated that the airline might have to be recertified. On February 29, the FAA tells Valujet that, "… it is not meeting its duty to provide service with the highest possible degree of safety in the public interest." On April 23, the Department of Transportation Secretary, Federico Pena, released a study depicting how low-cost carriers such as Valujet saved passengers $6.3 million in 1995. On May 2, Secretary Pena said that low-cost airlines were as safe as the major carriers. Talk about pulling the wool over the public's eyes. At this time, there an was extensive safety inspection in progress at Valujet and the airline's safety record proved to be four times worse than any other "no frills" airlines. On May 6, the FAA discovered over 100 discrepancies. And on May 11, Valujet flight 592 crashed into the Florida Everglades.

After the crash, both FAA Administrator Hinson and Transportation Chief Pena appeared on numerous television shows stating that Valujet was still a safe airline. A TV anchor asked Mr. Hinson why he made such a statement knowing the carrier was under scrutiny for months before the crash. He stated: "I'll never say it again, because I'm not stupid. What I should have said was they are compliant."

Semantics is the name of this game. On June 17, 1996, after pressure from the FAA, Valujet voluntarily agreed to suspend service.

So far in this chapter, you have been reading about the discrepancies at Valujet. Now it's time to get started on the real culprit: the FAA.

There have been numerous crashes caused by fires in the baggage compartments of airliners, killing hundreds of people. The Valujet cargo compartments were all considered class D that requires no smoke or fire detection, or extinguishing systems. This type of compartment depends solely on the limited availability of oxygen to suppress a potential fire. It is obvious that these compartments were never tested with the hazardous materials that are capable of producing heat over 3,000 degrees F such as the 150 oxygen generators found in the forward cargo hold. Such intense heat could easily have destroyed the vital engine and flight controls above it, leaving the aircraft at the mercy of gravity.

In 1980, a Riyadh, Saudi Arabia, Lockheed L-1011 experienced a fire in the class D cargo compartment while in flight. There was a smoke detector on board but no fire extinguishing system. Three hundred and one people were burned to death.

In 1988, an American DC-9 experienced an in-flight belly fire. Luckily, the crew was not far from their destination so a safe landing was accomplished. No fire detection warning system or extinguisher was on board, and none was required.

In 1991, a USAir DC-9 experienced a fire in the belly. It went undetected until the plane made a safe landing in Greensboro, North Carolina. No fire warning or detection units were on board.

On February 10, 1981, the NTSB issued safety recommendation A1-81-12 that in essence stated that class D compartments should have fire warning or detection, or be made more flame resistant. The FAA did nothing. This was SEVEN years before the Valujet crash.

In August of 1993, five years after the American Airlines cargo fire, the NTSB recommended that the FAA make smoke detection and extinguishers mandatory on all class D compartments. The Acting Administrator's reply stated that it would cost the airlines $350 million to retrofit their aircraft and had this to say about the new proposal: "The proposal rule would not have provided a significant degree of protection to the occupants from the extremely severe fire that resulted from the illegal shipment of powerful oxidizer in the American incident."

This is a direct lie. The crew on the American DC-9 had no way of knowing the intensity of the fire and no way to extinguish it.

In 1993, the NTSB sent their final salvo to the FAA Administrator: "The safety board continues to believe that a fire should not be allowed to persist in any state of intensity in an airplane without the knowledge of the flight crew. Further, the safety board is concerned that the FAA failed to consider the effects of hazardous materials (declared or undeclared) in cargo compartment fires when it approved burn-thru test requirements for cargo compartment liners in 1988 in lieu of fire detection and extinguishment systems." Safety Recommendations A-188-122 and 123 are classified as 'closed, UNACCEPTABLE action'" (capitals mine).

Twenty-six hundred airliners in service today have class D cargo bays. That means a raging fire might not be detected until it is too late. And still there would be no way to extinguish it because these compartments are not accessible in flight.

In December of 1996, the chief executives of all the major airlines held a meeting in Washington, D.C. to discuss safety problems. It was mutually decided that the carriers would voluntarily begin to install fire-detection systems in cargo holds that were not equipped with them.

Well, that may sound like a great idea, but there might be some divine dealings when an airline voluntarily spends money. If they were to wait for the FAA to issue explicit instructions, they might require far more expenditures than the airlines wanted so it would be cheaper in the long run to install a quick fix on their own. So now the carriers are going to install detecting systems voluntarily, but nothing has been mentioned concerning extinguishing systems.

There was little or nothing wrong with the Valujet aircraft. The crew was qualified and the weather was good. The hazardous material that was not supposed to be on board ignited, causing an intense fire. This fire easily could have started when the aircraft made the first turn on the taxiway or it could have been raging during the takeoff roll. The crew had no warning until a few minutes after takeoff when dense smoke filled the cabin. If they had a warning system in place, this whole mess could have been prevented on the ground.

The FAA has been badgered for decades to put the warning and extinguishers on board. After 110 people died, they decided to put their "tombstone philosophy" to work. The FAA proposed a rule that by the year 2000, all passenger-carrying airlines had to be equipped with smoke detectors and suppressants.

The following is a quote from Kenneth P. Quinn, the former FAA chief council: "Remember that after the Valujet crash, the NTSB held these parties accountable: Saber Tech, Valujet, and the FAA. Of course, the prosecutors could not pursue criminal sanctions against their sister agency—the FAA. Yet one could argue that the FAA was reckless—perhaps criminally so—in failing to mandate smoke detection and fire suppression systems in class D cargo compartments. But at bottom, it was just a terrible mistake, a fatal judgment that cost many lives."

CHAPTER 21

▼

WHAT ARE MY CHANCES?

Flight attendants have been working flights in this country since 1930, marking 71 years of safety and service. In the early days, flight attendants did little more than be sure the wicker passengers' seats were bolted to the floor of the aircraft.

On May 15, 1930, Ellen Church climbed aboard a United Boeing 80 tri-motor to start her flight between San Francisco and Chicago. This trip took a total of 20 hours, and included thirteen scheduled en route landings. Little did she know at the time, but the flight would be the start of the flight attendant profession. There are now over 90,000 professional "skygirls" as they were commonly called in the early 1930s.

The need for a skygirl became evident when many passengers who flew under severe conditions experienced some apprehension and frequent bouts of airsickness. The attendants were paid $125 a month for 100 hours of flight time. Besides being nurses, these skygirls had to be under 25 years of age, less than 5'4", weigh less than 115 pounds, and single.

The tri-motored airplane they worked held between 12 and 20 seats, and flew at an altitude of 2,000' at a speed of 125 mph. There was no heat, no air conditioning, and no pressurization. If all seats were taken, including the one assigned to the skygirl, she found herself sitting on a suitcase or on mailbags. The food service consisted of a box lunch. Other duties included looking for fuel leaks in the cabin, answering questions about the terrain, and making sure that the exit door was not mistaken for the lavatory. They also were required to carry the passengers' luggage and to help the crew push the plane into its hanger.

The 1930 work rules consisted of the following:

- Maintain the respectful reserve of the well-trained servant when on duty.
- Treat captains and pilots with strict formality while in uniform. A rigid military salute will be rendered as they go aboard and deplane. Check their personal luggage and place it on board promptly.
- Warn passengers against throwing cigarette and cigar butts out of the window, particularly over populated areas.
- Wind the clocks and altimeters mounted in the cabin.
- Swat flies before takeoff.
- Offer to remove passengers' shoes and put on slippers. Clean shoes thoroughly before returning them.

Boy, have things changed!

The other airlines soon realized that United's skygirls were here to stay so they all followed suit. In the beginning, these girls were on board for esthetic reasons. In 1952, the Civil Aeronautics Administration passed a ruling that aircraft with ten or more seats would require at least one attendant for safety reasons. In 1974, this regulation was updated by the FAA to require one attendant for every 50 passenger seats. Today's flight attendants are trained professionals. The following, well-publicized crashes will give you an insight of how these gallant crewmembers have given their lives to save yours.

Aloha Airlines B-737

Aloha Airlines Flight 243 was level at 24,000 feet en route from Hilo to Honolulu, Hawaii. Without warning, 18 feet of the cabin roof and sides exploded, leaving the passengers sitting in an airborne convertible.

The following story was written by Mary Anne Forbes, the editor of the AFA Association of Flight Attendants' newsletter:

When Aloha Flight 243 left Hilo April 28, everything seemed routine. The Hilo-to-Honolulu run mostly carried local islanders who were familiar with the flight attendant crew. This was the eighth flight of the day for senior flight attendant C. B. Lansing and flight attendants Michelle Honda and Jane Sato-Tomita.

After completing the beverage service, the flight attendants normally took a break, but Lansing, a 37-year veteran was on board. She had a reputation for running her flights "by the book." She set the tone for the trip, insisting that once the drinks were served the flight attendants maintain their stations.

For some reason, the pilot had decided not to shut off the seat belt sign after takeoff, so all of the passengers were secured in their seats. The flight attendants were concluding the beverage service.

Honda was helping to collect empty glasses when, suddenly, a thunderous blast knocked her out of her shoes and slammed her onto her back. She grabbed for the metal bars under the seats and a passenger helped hold her to the floor so she would not be thrown around the cabin.

There were screams. Then silence. Lansing was gone.

About 20 feet of the Boeing 737s roof had been torn from the plane's ruptured fuselage, exposing 89 terrified passengers and the flight attendants to open sky and gale force winds. They were 24,000 feet over the Pacific.

Michelle Honda had been flying for 14 years. Her training and experience told her the cabin had undergone rapid decompression. She knew what to do.

"I had to keep my breathing shallow. I couldn't get to an oxygen mask. It was important that I not pass out."

A blizzard of vapor, debris, and large pieces of the aircraft tore through the cabin. Honda tried to stand but could barely move against the wind.

"As I crawled up the aisle clutching the seat rungs, passengers were reaching out and holding me as I helped them locate and put on life vests. The closer I came to the hole, the more intense the wind was. I didn't know if I would stay in the aircraft if I let go."

Jane Sato-Tomita, a flight attendant for 18 years, was unconscious. She had been struck on the head and lay bleeding on the floor.

"The first time I saw her I was worried she was dead. She was lying near the hole. Her head was split open and she was under debris. I wanted to get Jane to the back of the aircraft. I tried to move her—drag her back, but I couldn't." Her feet were tangled in the cables from the piece of the ceiling that blew away.

Honda, the only flight attendant left in charge, crept down the aisle to calm and assist passengers.

Amy Jones-Brown, with less than two years experience as an Aloha flight attendant was also on board. She was returning from her honeymoon. Even though she was not on active flight duty status as the time, she assisted Honda by encouraging the passengers around her to put on their life vests, keep their heads down, and stay calm.

Two huge ceiling panels landed on several passengers and Honda dragged the pieces to empty seats in the back. "I would take things to move them and they would disappear."

One man asked Honda to help remove a strip of fuselage from his face. "I was trying to pull it away. But I realized it was stapled into the side of his face. I told him I couldn't help. I heard a passenger say, 'I'll help' but I knew from my first aid training to leave that kind of stuff in."

Honda carefully worked through her mental emergency checklist. When she was finally able, she crawled to the rear of the plane and tried to call the pilots but the line was dead. She could tell, however, the plane was turning to land on Maui.

In the cockpit, pilot Robert Schornstheimer and first officer Mimi Tompkins tried to restart a stalled engine and steady the plane. They soon realized they would have to overcome structural damage, make an emergency descent, and attempt a single-engine landing with potential landing gear problems. They contacted Kahului airport to prepare for an emergency landing.

As the jet prepared to land, Honda crawled back up the aisle and lay next to Sato-Tomita to protect her. I grabbed her waist and held tightly to the metal retainer bars."

After the plane came to a stop on the runway, Sato-Tomita came to and went with Honda who opened the right aft service door and deployed the slide. Some passengers were able to deploy the left forward entry door and slide. The other forward door was jammed.

Jones-Brown and her husband struggled free from their seats and opened the left aft entry door to extend the air stairs. They helped Honda evacuate the passengers as Sato-Tomita was taken to the hospital by rescue personnel who were waiting at the scene.

"Jane, despite her adverse situation and being badly hurt, did not panic and asked repeatedly about the welfare and safety of C. B. and her passengers. Once discharged from the hospital, she continued to seek out the welfare of her crew, passengers and family, forgetting about herself and her injuries."

Not until the plane was emptied did Honda learn that Lansing was gone.

"I know that I am alive today because of C. B. and the standards she set."

The evacuation was efficient. Thirteen passengers near the damaged roof, however, were seriously injured. Fifty-two passengers received minor injuries. Honda and Jones-Brown continued to assist the medical teams with the injured passengers.

Honda took a head count and worked to keep all the passengers together. She and Jones-Brown comforted and supported the passengers until each one was safely in an ambulance on the way to the hospital.

United Airlines DC-10

Among the 185 survivors of the UAL Flight 232 crash on July 19 1989, were eight flight attendants. Among the 112 dead was flight attendant Rene LeBeau who was several months short of completing her first year of service, and deadheading pilots Paul Burnham, J. F. Kirk, and J. L. Kennedy. The Chicago-based cabin crewmembers aboard Flight 232 were on the final leg of a long, four-day trip. Their morning departure from Philadelphia to

Denver had to be pushed back slightly to give them a contractual ten-hour minimum rest period.

About halfway through the two-hour flight, there was a loud explosion. "We heard a loud sound … we felt the plane shudder to a certain degree," said flight attendant Donna McGrady. The captain announced over the PA that engine No. 2 had to be shut down but that he could still fly the airplane. Lead flight attendant Jan Brown was called to the cockpit.

"My highest priority was to keep everything as calm as possible. When I opened up the cockpit door, nobody needed to tell me that we had a real problem," recalled Brown in an interview with Flightlog. "There was superhuman strength being used to control the plane. I could see through the window that we were banking to the right. I knew there was the possibility we could spiral out and crash right then." "The captain told me we had lost all hydraulics and that the cabin had to be secured for an emergency landing."

"When I came out of the cockpit I had a lot of confidence. I felt this is what we're trained to do and now we have to do it." Brown went immediately to the forward service center to inform first class flight attendants Barbara Gillespie and LeBeau that the cabin had to be picked up as quickly as possible. Deadheading flight attendant Kathy Shen came up to offer assistance. Then Brown walked to the back to inform flight attendants Timothy Owens, Jan Murray, Susan White, Georgeann Del Castillo, and McGrady.

There were more than 280 passengers aboard the plane. Some 150 still had meal trays in front of them. Numerous children, including infants and unaccompanied minors, were on board. The crew picked up in record time and began preparing for a planned emergency. "There were several passengers we had to move," said McGrady. "In my case, there were two children that were sitting together. I replaced one of the children with an adult … and I moved the child closer to his mother."

White noticed a man with a blanket over a baby on his lap. From her training she knew the baby could be crushed on impact. "I explained to him that it would be safer if we wrapped the baby up in a blanket and pillows and put him on the floor. He didn't want to let go of his child, but be believed me."

The captain announced the landing would be rough and that passengers should follow the flight attendants' instructions. The flight attendants instructed passengers in the brace positions and on how to exit after the plane stopped. "Jan [Brown] talked to the passengers very calmly and composed," remembered McGrady. "She reminded them to remove sharp objects that could hurt them and to be sure all bags were stowed properly. We were walking around to make sure that everyone felt comfortable doing the brace position and to check if they had any questions."

"It wasn't in the book [emergency manual] but I knew we had infants on-board," said Brown. "So I came on the PA again and I said anyone with infants should place them on the floor now and take their brace positions at this time. My crew had already handed out pillows and blankets to buffer them during the impact." As a final preparation for landing, each flight attendant took his or her seat, and briefed helpers on opening the door and keeping the eight exit areas clear on the ground.

The captain gave a "four minutes to landing" notice. At the back of the aircraft, McGrady was seated at 4R and White at 4L. In between the B and C zones, Owens was seated at 3L. Lead flight attendant Brown was at 2L and Murray was at 2R. First class flight attendants Gillaspie and LeBeau were seated at 1L and 1R. Deadheading flight attendant Shen was at 1L inboard.

The captain announced two minutes to land and said "brace." "We started shouting 'brace, brace' continuously until we stopped," recalled McGrady. "We impacted—it was unbelievable. I don't know if I can adequately describe it," said Brown. The plane cartwheeled to a stop, breaking into three pieces as it rolled. The tail section split from the rest of the plane and the cockpit, first class, and forward service center split away from the main part of the fuselage. When it stopped, Susan [White] and I said: "Release your seat belts and get out; release your seat belts and get out."

"I was in a slant position," remembers McGrady, who was in the tail section of the plane. "I didn't see the door. I didn't see practically anything around me." White was standing outside a hole. McGrady helped a child out before going through the nearest hole herself.

A flash fire raced through the upside-down cabin, passing over Owens at 3L and traveling on to Brown who was at 2L. "I have a clear image of myself two-thirds in a ball of fire. I had no fear, no pain; I thought very calmly, I guess this is the way I'm going to go. But the fire went on beyond me and we stopped." "The man in 9C helped me release my belt. I slid down and stood up. There was a man buried in debris and I pulled him out," Brown continued. "It was dark and there was nothing recognizable. We were upside down. I heard someone say there is an opening here. I turned to my right. There was an opening and everyone was walking through like a normal deplaning. I just stood there and got people out. I later realized we exited where the cockpit, first class and forward service center should have been."

"When I got out [of the aircraft]," remembered Murray, "there was a passenger who I'd asked to be my helper at the door ... and we were running parallel to each other. I said, Are we alive? Are we alive? because it was such a euphoric feeling after that 44 minutes [from the time we knew] until impact."

Owens, who was buried under a pile of carry-on baggage and debris, dug out and found he was one of the last people still inside. He assisted a woman who was having trouble walking, before exiting the aircraft himself.

Georgeann Del Castillo directed passengers away from door 3R because of a fire outside. Flight attendants Gillaspie and Shen, at 1L, were severely injured. Rene LeBeau, at 1R, was dead.

Outside, the six foot high corn was impeding the rescue and firefighting teams who were hard at work. Denver-based flight attendants Becky Larson, Debbie Best, and Kathy Buckley on a layover in Sioux City got to the airport about 15 minutes after the crash. They were asked to set up a room for the survivors in the nearby National Guard dining hall. They washed cuts, comforted people, and tried to reunite families and groups of people who were traveling together. Best took responsibility for two small boys who had lost their mother and brother in the crash. She contacted their father and escorted them back to relatives in Denver. Survivors of the fiery

DC-10 crash credited flight attendants for maintaining calm and helping passengers escape from the wreckage.

From an Associated Press, July 25, wire release: "Her (flight attendant) voice was very soothing. She prevented the passengers from going into complete hysteria."—Survivor

"This crew deserves a lot of credit … because all that we heard from the survivors was: they stayed very calm; they helped us; they made us the calm people we are, and they saved our lives."—Cathy Buckley, UAL 09, who assisted survivors after the crash.

FAR 121.39 states that, "(2) For airplanes having a seating capacity of more than fifty but less than 101 passengers—two flight attendants." For larger aircraft there must be one attendant for every fifty passengers. Nowhere in the regulation does it talk about serving cocktails. The attendants are on board for one salient purpose: SAFETY

All flight crewmembers must meet rigid FAA requirements in order to be licensed. This naturally would include the flight attendants. Wrong. Both the FAA and the airlines treat these people like second-class citizens. They are known as crewmembers compared to the pilots up front who are called flight crew. There are no requirements to maintain their licenses because they don't have licenses. All other members of the crew have specific FAA on-duty times and certain crew rest periods. Union pilots are not allowed to fly more than 85 hours a month and they must be free of all duty at least every seven days. Many passengers consider flight attendants glorified cocktail waitresses whose only duty is to serve food and drinks to hundreds of passengers, at times, in less than an hour.

Let's examine some of their other duties. They must carry luggage to an appropriate hiding place, perform travel agents' duties, assess the seriousness of a sick passenger and administer first aid, help control cabin fires, keep pot smokers out of the rest rooms, tactfully discourage male sexual innuendoes, bear the burden of irate passengers when a trip is running late (the flight crew is safely locked in the cockpit), and oh yes! in an emergency make sure that all the passengers are guided to safety. When the seat belt sign is turned on because of turbulence, the flight attendant is the most vulnerable person in the cabin. She is the one walking down the aisle to make sure that your seat belt is fastened. Many times, the attendants have been thrown to the ceiling sustaining fractures, broken necks, and other crippling injuries. All this to ensure that you are safely tucked in.

A new-hire flight attendant must attend ground school for a minimum of five weeks. Required subjects are responsibilities and duties of the flight attendant, emergency training, passenger handling, the authority of the captain, and a knowledge of each airplane to which they may be assigned. Airlines are required to have flight attendant recurrent training once each year for a minimum of 8 hours. Every year, the flight attendant is required to attend emergency training. Here they are supposed to have hands-on training concerning such important equipment as operation of emergency windows and slides, the discharging of fire extinguishers, and the discussion of various emergencies. I say they are supposed to have hands-on training, but it usually ends up with one person activating the equipment while the others watch. In my 28 years as an airline captain, I have never released an emergency slide or fired off a fire extinguisher. I have opened an emergency window once.

Miss Janis Sarto, the former Director of Safety of the Association of Flight Attendants, the largest flight attendant union in the U.S. with over 42,000 members, had this to say at a congressional hearing concerning aviation safety: "Over the years, we are seeing the skills tested more by true-false, multiple choice and fill in the blank quizzes, than by mock up drills. During the FAA recurrent training for the FAA inspectors last year, it was reported by many of these men that while conducting on-line checks, flight attendants could easily recite the location and operation of a piece of emergency equipment, but when asked to get that equipment piece, an alarming number of flight attendants were unable to unbracket it."

Regarding hands-on operating of fire extinguishers Miss Sarto had this to say: "Surprisingly, book learning is the method used to track how to fight a fire. The majority of carriers do not let flight attendants discharge a fire extinguisher during recurrent training. Instead we are taught to recite, aim the nozzle at the base of the fire, and discharge."

On November 16, 1979, at Denver, Colorado, a DC-9 captain rejected his takeoff. The plane overran the runway, the landing gear broke off, and it came to rest in a ditch with a fire engulfing the left side of the aircraft. The flight attendant opened the door leading to the tail cone exit. She was unable to find the emergency release. A passenger located the handle and successfully deployed the tail cone. Later, when questioned by the authorities, she stated that she had never before been in the tail cone section. Then other flight attendants also stated they had never been in the tail section.

Once a flight attendant is trained on a particular aircraft, she may not fly on it for many years, yet she is still considered qualified. This is nothing short of ludicrous. With the varying complexities of the numerous doors, it only takes a few months away from the equipment before forgetting the correct operating procedure.

All carriers pay their pilots well when they have to undergo their six-month checks. Not so with the flight attendants. They have to train on one of their days off, or in the evening, and many airlines don't pay them a nickel. Luckily, the unions have some stringent requirements regarding pay and on-duty time, but since deregulation, many of the rules that have been in effect for years are being broken. Any time an aircraft is loaded with more passengers than originally planned, there may not be enough attendants on board to properly serve the passengers.

When it comes to seat strength, the flight attendant has to sit in the weakest seat in the plane. Many of them look like afterthoughts, where aircraft companies decided they had better add on some jump seats for the cabin attendants. Add on is correct. Many of the seats are attached to non-rigid structures such as carry-on containers, galleys, and nearly any other place that looks fragile. Most normal landings produce a scurry of bottles and trays that slide across the galley. Many times, flight attendants sitting in the galley have been struck with equipment, those seated in front of the carry-on rack have been pelted with objects, and in the event of a crash, galley, carts and luggage racks have broken loose, injuring the cabin crew and greatly hampering egress.

How is the Air up There?

Outside air enters the engine where the temperature and pressure are increased. Air is then directed through the air-conditioning pack where its temperature is cooled before entering the cabin. There are air inlets in the cabin ceiling and also along the walls. Some air is discharged outside, whereas the remainder is recirculated through charcoal filters into the fuselage where it is mixed with fresh air. This whole process can be run through one or more air-conditioning packs. It is entirely up to the pilot to decide to run all the packs, or just one. When all units are selected on, the cabin is quite healthy as compared to a one-pack aspiration. However, each pack uses more fuel and steals a small amount of power from the engine.

Some airlines tell their crews to run on one pack in order to cut fuel costs. That is not the way the aircraft was designed to operate, but it saves money. The 747 has three packs, but many times, there is only one pack operating. What this means to you is the potential of inhaling viruses that have been brought aboard by infected passengers. Not only is this static air a potential virus carrier but also air that has been breathed in and out by passengers is more likely to have a high concentration of carbon dioxide that may cause dizziness and fatigue.

Two young ladies were sitting in business class aboard a Sabena jet. They were flying from Brussels to New York. When they arrived in the U.S., they felt fine. A few weeks later, Sabena informed them that they could have contracted tuberculosis. Both ladies were tested, and indeed, both were positive. It seems a 20-year-old immigrant who was seated ten rows behind them was a carrier of the dreaded disease. It is believed that the air-conditioning system was the carrier of the TB bacillus.

When you are airborne and all packs are running, the cabin air is at its best, but when delayed on the ground, the air becomes much more stagnant. Pity the passengers who were stuck last year on the ground for five hours while Northwest was blocked by snow and other carriers.

You know how dry you feel on an airliner? Well, that is one of the reasons that you are more prone to infection. Dr. Richard Dawood's Condon Nast Traveler's medical advisory states: "It's the inevitable drying out effect of being on an airplane, which removes the protective film of mucous from the nasal passages."

Cosmic Radiation

Captain Rita Lanney, a United Airlines pilot, was very concerned about cosmic radiation. She had a healthy body and was intent on producing another one. "My airline was changing its maternity policy to allow pilots to fly while pregnant."

She obtained a dosimeter with a digital readout that measured ionized particles. "The amount of radiation doubles between 30,000 and 40,000 feet. We were getting the equivalent of a chest X-ray every month." International crews, flying to Los Angeles at 37,000 feet receive, the equivalent of a chest X-ray (30 macrosieverts) on each leg of the flight. To be on the safe side, Captain Lanney took a year off and stayed on the ground. She is now flying the Boeing 737. She says that she tries to stay at the lower altitudes (below 30,000) as much as possible. If she cannot escape the radiation, perhaps the 737 will end her career.

Because the majority of passengers do not fly nearly as much as flight crews, there is little to worry about. If you fly extensively, however, you could be getting too much radiation.

Emergency Medical Equipment

If you should become ill during a flight, what are your chances of receiving proper medication or landing before it might be too late? This will give you some idea of how the FAA has been taking care of you over the years.

On August 20, 1981, Ralph Nader's Aviation Consumer Action Project petitioned the FAA to improve the medical equipment on air carriers. The petition was denied on May 19, 1982. The reason given by the FAA follows: "The FAA noted that if the proposals presented in the ACAP petition were adopted, air carriers would be required to provide equipment and medicine to handle general health emergencies unrelated to flight or not shown to affect aviation safety.

Nader, fighter that he is, took his case to the United States Court of Appeals for the District of Columbia. The court ruled in favor of Mr. Nader, and now it is up to the FAA to do something. But in their usual good time. Three years went by and on March 14, 1985, the "feds" issued a change to 14CFR parts 11 and 12.

U.S. Carriers board approximately 800 million passengers each year. It is estimated that one passenger per million might necessitate an unscheduled landing. The statistics are not very high, but if you were that one in a million, you would expect the best of service. The FAA takes the attitude that if your medical emergency was not caused by the flight you are on, they don't want to hear from you. It seems plausible that a passenger who trusts his or her life to the skills of the pilot also should expect basic medical care while on board. What would you think if you were turned away from a ship's doctor simply because you came on board with a medical problem and failed to develop your ailment while en route?

The NTSB found that in a four-year period, 57 flight attendants and 84 passengers were seriously injured on U.S. airlines during flight, most of these injuries resulting from turbulence. The American Medical Association's Commission on Emergency Medical Services estimates that 46 to 47 persons die in-flight each year in the U.S. No telling how many could be saved with proper medical gear.

In a number of situations such as heart rhythm abnormalities, heart attacks, allergic reactions, rapid reactions, rapid blood loss, asthmatic attacks, choking, and diabetic coma, rapid medical treatment can make the difference between life and death. A recent survey of doctors showed that 88.9 percent of 300 doctors surveyed believed that airlines should be made to carry basic medication and equipment on board, and that 30 percent of the doctors had offered their services in-flight. The FAA estimates that during a period of four decades, 840 deaths occurred on airliners.

As of 1986, all carriers must equip their fleets with updated medical kits to be used by licensed physicians. They contain syringes, needles, stethoscopes, nitroglycerin tablets, and other prescription drugs. These kits are locked inside the cockpit and will only be released by the captain only after a physician has identified himself. As of 1999, there are nine carriers equipped with heart defibrillators: Qantas, Virgin Atlantic, USAirways, Swissair, Varig, Alaska, Delta, Hawaiian, and American. Attendants on British Airways take four days of medical training. In the U.S., this training is cut down to a few hours.

Air Africa has gone a step further. Their long haul jets have special medical compartments that could be used for patients requiring resuscitation, isolation, and other assistance for seriously ill passengers.

Why is it that all airlines are not carrying defibrillators? Because the FAA has not made it mandatory. In 1996, a study by the ATA discovered that there were 10,471 medical emergencies on board airliners in flight. Carriers also reported 1,020 cardiovascular-related events. Qantas was the first airline to install defibrillators, stating that the device has already saved six lives.

Industry-wide, there are, on average, fifteen in-flight medical emergencies every day. Some of the more caring carriers have signed up with a medical information company called MedLink where there are doctors on call around the clock. In flight, pilots can call MedLink and receive expert information concerning passengers who might need medical help. The doctors on call are thoroughly knowledgeable concerning the in-flight environment. The decision to direct a flight is always up to the discretion of the captain, but with MedLink, the crew can consult an expert before deciding to divert the flight.

Since 1996, USAirways has utilized the MedLink service. It seems to be working. In September of 1998, Flight Safety received 100 medical reports. There were 29 MedLink contacts causing only four diversions.

Flights over the U.S. can land readily if necessary, but for those out over the ocean equipped with only tongue depressor and a band-aid could pose serious trouble for sick or injured passengers. The cost of these new kits is far less than a single diversion of a 747 that could cost thousands in terms of fuel, hotels, rebookings, landing fees, and possible crew replacement.

All crewmembers should be required to take CPR training, and ground schools should spend more time on medical training and less time on "pretty and charming."

Speaking of wasting time, you will find it hard to believe the extent the FAA goes to just so the airlines won't have to spend a buck. They estimate that the improved emergency medical kits will cost about $300 per unit. Now hold onto your hats. Here is a quote from the Federal Register, VOL 50, No. 50, Thursday, March 14, 1985: "Each emergency kit weighs approximately 10 pounds, and each additional pound weight will result in an estimated average fuel consumption of 15 gallons per year per aircraft. Based on a fuel price of 89.4 cents per gallon, each emergency kit will result in an average fuel cost of slightly more than $134 per year."

The Federal Register continues, "For purposes of economic studies, the FAA valued a life at $650,000 in 1983. Now, it is up to $1.5 million. The expected number of lives that could be saved over the 10-year period is 21 to 100. The expected present discounted value of the lives that could be saved over the 10-year period ranges from $8.4 million to $41.9 million. This is derived by discounting the value of life at a 10 percent rate."

It seems rather foolish for the FAA to go to such great lengths to justify ten pounds when the airlines themselves allow passengers to carry on such heavy items as barbells.

The Brace Position, Before Crashing

There is strong evidence to support the fact that the proper brace position can mean the difference between life and death. A few years ago, an aircraft was carrying sixteen passengers and two crewmembers. No warning was given, but a 16-year-old girl, seated near the rear of the plane, noticed how close the aircraft was getting to the top of the trees. She remembered the briefing card, and lowered her head and assumed the brace position. On impact, her seat was torn loose and she suffered a broken arm. She was the only one to live.

The reason for the brace position is to preposition yourself against whatever you are most likely to hit during the crash and to prevent a secondary impact. The seat belt should be located as low on the torso as possible. The tighter the belt is adjusted, the better restraint it will provide. Your feet should be flat on the floor just slightly in front of the edge of the seat.

There are two basic brace positions. One is where you are bent over and your arms are locked around your legs. The other is with your arms crossed in front of you leaning on the seat in front of you. If I had a choice, I would pick the one where you lock your arms around your legs. This way, you are in a nice tight ball, and if your seat doesn't pull loose, you have a chance.

However, I find fault with the other position because of the following. I am sure that most passengers believe that when their seat back is in the upright position their seat is rigid and solid as a rock. Next time you are on an airliner, see how easy it is to push the seat back forward. If space does not allow you to put your head between your legs and you have to lean on the seat ahead of you, think what kind of damage you might be doing to the passenger sitting in front of you.

If you have a small child with you and cannot tighten their seat belt sufficiently, you should put a blanket or a pillow behind the child to fill in the space. Airlines always have allowed children below the age of two to be held in the arms of an adult. This saves you the price of a ticket but in an emergency, it is very poor practice. If you place the seat belt around you and your child, in a crash, your weight against the belt could crush your loved one. The NTSB has long badgered the "feds" to require a child-restraint seat for all children. In September of 1992 the FAA, "stop gap" regulation stated that airlines will permit the use of approved CRS, but does not require its use. If you buy a CRS for your child, be sure that it is acceptable. The label should state that, "This restraint is certified for use in motor vehicles and aircraft."

When an aircraft comes to an abrupt stop, everything in the cabin tries to go forward. You might think that you are strong enough to keep your infant close to your body, but you would be wrong. Gravity will rip your arms apart and that infant will be propelled forward like a missile.

Ditching

A few years ago, a DC-9 with 63 people on board was having a problem landing at an airport near St. Croix in the Virgin Islands. The weather wasn't bad with a ceiling of 1,000 feet and a visibility of two miles in light rain. The weather would not have been a factor had the airport been equipped with ILS instead of a landing aid that gave no vertical guidance while on final approach. With adequate letdown facilities, there would not have been an accident.

After three approaches, Captain Bakey D. DeWitt decided to abandon any further attempts to land at St. Croix. A quick computation of the fuel remaining revealed the fact that he could not reach another airport, so ditching would be imminent. When he took off from JFK, he was aware that the PA system from the cockpit to cabin was inoperable, but he neglected to inform the cabin crew that he would not be able to talk to the passengers. This inoperable piece of equipment was perfectly legal per his company MEL, but it would soon be the cause of more than one death.

Captain DeWitt signaled for the lead cabin attendant to come forward and he told him to prepare the passengers for a possible ditching. The passengers again were briefed by the cabin crew on how to put on their life vests. The initial briefing never mentioned where the life preservers were located, and nobody had read their briefing card. The preservers were stowed in a pocket fastened to the bottom of the seats. These pockets were held closed by a strap-and-snap fastener that had to be pulled down to open. After battling the pocket, the vest could be pulled out, still sealed in a transparent plastic container. There were two different types of vests on board and both fastened differently. However, there was only one type of vest used in the initial briefing.

It should be noted that since the vest is under the seat and the luggage from the person behind you is also under the seat, this makes a very tight fit when you try to remove the life vest.

The following is a most important bit of information. The normal briefing does not mention anything concerning the differences between an adult and a child when it comes to donning the life vest. In the about-to-happen ditching, there was between five to seven minutes time to prepare the cabin and passengers before water contact would be made. All of this time was used by the passengers who were trying to find and don their flotation gear. Passengers experienced difficulty opening the vest storage compartment and the storage cover. One passenger had to use his pocketknife to get into the preserver, and many people were on their hands and knees trying to locate the pocket under the seat. There were four 25-man life rafts on board but no mention of them was made in the briefing.

Prior to water contact, the captain flashed the seat belt and no smoking sign on and off. Bell chimes are supposed to ring each time this switch is activated but they failed to work. As a result, there were a number of passengers and crewmembers standing up when the plane hit. The captain did an excellent job on landing with minimal damage to the aircraft. She stayed afloat for 10 minutes and then sank in 5,000 feet of water.

A life raft was pulled from its storage compartment into the galley but it was accidentally inflated, trapping the first officer against a bulkhead and blocking egress. Most of the passengers exited over the wing and the captain went out through the cockpit window. He swam around to the left wing, and opened that exit, and assisted two more passengers out. In spite of the fact that there were four life rafts on board, none of them ever reached the outside of the aircraft. Twenty-three people died, and the other 40 were picked up by helicopter. The death toll could have been much lower if proper procedures were followed. There was ample time in the air, over six minutes, and the plane floated on the water for 10 minutes.

All aircraft that operate on extended over-water routes must be equipped with life rafts except when they apply for an FAA waiver. At the present time, there are at least 12 airlines that make extended over-water flights that have FAA waivers. The first exemption in 1977 was issued to Braniff Airlines who intended to prove that the weight reduction would make the plane lighter. They went on to add they would be able to carry more cargo and six extra passengers.

Cabin attendants who fly over large bodies of water receive their ditching training in a swimming pool. Monica Kaufman, National Safety Chairperson of the Independent Federation of Flight Attendants, has this to say regarding training: "Ditch training is conducted in a swimming pool. However, it does not in any way simulate what actual ditching is like, and we are all very much aware of it because it is a warm swimming pool that is basically placid, and it turns into sort of a fun afternoon."

Unless your flight extends 50 miles or more from land, you probably do not even have a life preserver on board. That seat cushion that the hostess refers to as a flotation device is nothing more than a large sponge. The Coast Guard says that they are never to be used by children or non-swimmers, and that they will keep you afloat for a maximum of 15 minutes. The FAA has done something about making life vests easier to put on. All vests manufactured after 1985 must be designed so that they can be put on in 15 seconds (I'll believe that when I see it). The bad news is that all the vests in service today can be used until they wear out, sometime at the turn of the century.

I have witnessed numerous cabin briefings but never have I heard any specific instructions for children. Very few cards relate the fact that the lower life vest straps must be placed between the child's legs, not around their waists. Otherwise the vest would float away. FAA Advisory Circular #121-24B, page 7, states Individual Flotation Equipment—"the briefing cards should depict the method of fitting adult life preservers on small children."

It is not a good idea for children to use a seat cushion, but what's the alternative?

Next time you are on an over-water flight, check below your seat to ensure that the last person to use your seat has not walked off with the life preserver. They are very small packages and are fun in swimming pools.

Only 25 percent of today's scheduled airlines have life rafts aboard. The other 75 percent have none. If you are able to get a life vest on properly and to get out of the aircraft, your troubles still are not over. If there is wave action or if you should become unconscious, you still may drown.

We can all thank the Airline Pilots Association for fighting vigorously for new and improved life vests. They got the FAA to up the buoyancy level from the old vest, 23 pounds, to a new standard of 35 pounds of buoyancy. They are also pushing for life vests on all carriers. There are over 200 airports in America that are adjacent to large bodies of water. Who would have thought about drowning in the Potomac River?

Evacuation Slides

In the days of the DC-3, the cabin windows were so near to the ground that in order to escape in an accident, you simply jumped out onto the ground. In the DC-6, the cabin was quite a distance from the ground. In an emergency, two people would have to use a rope to descend to the ground. Then they would get on either side of a fabric chute while the rest of the passengers slid down.

In 1960, the first wide-bodied 747 arrived with a deck level 16' above the surface. This machine necessitated new egress technology so automatic inflatable slides were invented. These slides are constructed of large, inflatable tubes beneath a sliding surface and a tank of compressed gas stored under the slide. The slide and the gas cylinder are kept in a container on the bottom section of the door. Before takeoff, it is the flight attendants duty to "arm" the slides by attaching both of the top ends to the floor of the aircraft. In this position, the emergency slide can be deployed. By opening the cabin door, the slide will drop to the ground and automatically inflate. On some slides, a handle has to be pulled to start the inflation process. These slides stay attached to the aircraft floor until the trip is safely on the ground and taxiing in. Then the crew simply unhooks the straps and stores it back in the door.

A few years ago, a Pan American 747 was taxiing out from San Francisco International Airport with a crew of 19, a full load of fuel, and 191 passengers. The captain never got her high enough on takeoff roll, and at the far end of the runway, he hit some approach lights. These stanchions rammed through the aircraft floor. One fixture badly lacerated the arm of a passenger and nearly took a leg off another. A second structure impaled four unoccupied seats and stopped four inches from a little girl's chest. The craft was flyable and fuel was dumped immediately to make ready for a landing.

The landing was hard and an emergency evacuation was ordered. Unfortunately, four of the ten slides were unusable because of a high wind that blew the slide against the side of the aircraft. The plane began to settle on its tail. This elevated the two front slides so that they were hung straight down. There were 19 minor and 8 major injuries sustained during evacuation on the faulty slides.

When new aircraft are certified by the FAA, they must be evacuated with half the available exits blocked. If the new eight-exit ruling were in effect on this carrier, only four exits would have been available. This points up the fact that many times less than half the exits are usable. It isn't only wind and aircraft position that can disrupt an evacuation: fire also has burned some slides away before they could be used. Consider the accident following the rejected takeoff of a DC-10 at Los Angeles International Airport. The left side of the fuselage became engulfed in flames. The slides were deployed and immediate evacuation was initiated. Because of the fire on the left side, no effort was made to open those doors. The fire was so intense that the radiant heat from the left side of the aircraft began to melt and burn the nylon slides on the right side.

After this accident, the FAA established that if the emergency involves a fire, the emergency escape slides used today are likely to melt. They stated that there are materials available today that would almost double the heat resistance of the slides.

The past chairman of the NTSB Mr. King made this statement before a congressional committee: "What I was concerned about is that everybody in the business knew that nylon slides start to melt at about 300 degrees, whatever the source of the temperature, and it fails absolutely at 360 degrees. They always have known that there has been a number of products around that have a much higher failure rate, double and triple, and you can even move into quadrupling the type of heat before failure would start."

This scenario reminds me of the shocking way that seat belts were tested.

Now let's see what has been done about improving the serviceability of the slides since the DC-10 accident.

Congresswoman Geraldine A. Ferraro was questioning the new Chairman of the NTSB concerning the feasibility of new slides. He answered as follows: "But I think it is important to note that the FAA, after having developed the aluminized slide, has failed to implement any regulation that would mandate updating of slides. These slides have a long life. In fact, unless the FAA decides to change strategy and use a different type of slide, the ones that are in aircraft now will be there for the life of the aircraft."

Fires and Extinguishers

On July 11, 1973, a Varig 707 was approaching Orly field for a routine landing. Just prior to turning on final, an intense fire broke out in the aft lavatory. The fire could not be contained with hand fire extinguishers, and smoke rapidly filled the cabin and cockpit. The captain elected to make an emergency landing short of the airport. It is believed that all passengers survived the landing. However, all but one died from asphyxiation.

A year after this accident, two more airliners experienced similar fires in the rear lavatory. The first incident happened on July 17, 1974, aboard a 747. The next fire occurred aboard a 727 on the 9th of August 1974.

One June 2, 1983, Air Canada Flight 797, a Douglas DC-9, was on a regularly scheduled flight from Dallas to Montreal, Canada, with an en route stop at Toronto. There were 41 passengers on board and a crew of five. While cruising at 33,000 over Ohio the cabin crew discovered a fire in the rear lavatory. They tried in vain to extinguish it by use of hand extinguishers, but they proved to be useless. The cabin crew should be highly commended for their heroic work in a smoke-filled cabin. They all had the "Right Stuff" when it came to ingenuity. They distributed damp towels, and instructed the passengers to place them over their nose and mouth to help filter some of the contaminants in the smoke. This smart move saved many lives. Air Canada also should be commended for having an automatic Halon 1301 fire extinguisher in the lavatory. The Halon extinguisher 1301 exceeds the ones in use in America.

The captain elected to make an emergency decent and received a vector (steer) to the Greater Cincinnati International Airport. The cockpit rapidly filled with dense smoke and the instruments became difficult to read. The crash crews were alerted and in position. The landing was uneventful. As soon as the airliner was stopped, the emergency exits were opened and the crash crews were already in place.

What should have been a textbook evacuation turned out to be a disaster. Eighteen passengers and three flight attendants exited the three over-wing exits, and through the forward doors and slides. The pilot and co-pilot left through their respective cockpit windows.

Things were going along relatively smoothly for about the first 90 seconds, then all hell broke loose. The fire in the cabin became a raging inferno because of a phenomenon called "flashover." Between 90 and 150 seconds after a cabin fire originates, a frightening thing can happen. Technicians believe that gases generated by the combustion may reach such a high temperature that they, themselves, ignite and elevate the fire. There is no increase in flames until a given flash point is reached. Then it is just as though a can of gasoline was hurled into the open flames. Anyone who has not escaped from the cabin before the flashover has erupted isn't going to make it. Twenty-three passengers died in this raging inferno.

As you can see, speed is of the essence and any time gained before the oxygen in the cabin is exhausted is a definite plus.

There are available smoke hoods that can greatly increase the chances of survival. Today's carriers have installed these masks within 3' of any on-board fire extinguisher. Unfortunately, their use is for crewmembers, not for passengers. The supply of oxygen in this hood should last between 12 and 15 minutes, longer than the 90-second maximum that the FAA requires to evacuate an aircraft.

What a blessing these hoods would have been in the Air Canada fire; they sure beat damp towels. These hoods already are installed in 100 corporate jets such as those listed in Fortune 500. Mass production would bring the price down to where airlines might be interested, but don't hold your breath. If you would like to acquire a smoke mask, you can a purchase one that will give you an extra five minutes of breathable air. The small plastic bag is no bigger than a bag of frozen food and they can be purchased for $15. Just call Sporty's Pilot Shop at 1-800-LIFT-OFF and they will be glad to explain their product line.

Oxygen Masks

Oxygen masks will deploy automatically for any of the following reasons:

1. The cabin altitude reaches 14,000 feet

2. Decompression

3. Electronically or manually triggered by the flight crew.

In a smoke-filled cabin below 14,000 feet, the majority of the air breathed in through the mask is cabin air and could be contaminated with heavy smoke. On the ground, the oxygen mask is practically useless.

If the aircraft should depressurize for any reason, the following will happen:

In Rapid Decompression, masks will drop down, you will hear a loud bang, and fog or haze will fill the cabin.

In Slow Decompression, your nails and lips become blue, and you will probably feel lethargy, euphoria, and nausea.

Passenger Briefing

What you won't hear or see during the passenger briefing: suppose you are on an aircraft and the oxygen masks have been deployed, but yours fails to drop down. What do you do? There are usually two means of opening that overhead compartment:

1. There is a tiny hole adjacent to the overhead compartment. If you stick a work pen or paperclip into it, the door will open.

2. If there is no hole, the door can be opened by sticking a flat, thin object such as a credit card into the center or crease of the door.

While we are on the subject of oxygen, here is something to consider. The oxygen system used in emergency situations is a very rudimentary system. The mask may fit over your nose and mouth nicely, but there is something that may hinder its functioning properly. Here is what the FAA AC No. 120-43 has to say about passenger oxygen masks efficiency: "The data indicated beards adversely affect efficiency of contiguous flow oxygen masks. The leakage of ambient air caused by beards does not permit an adequate percentage of oxygen to be presented to the lower portion of the respiratory track."

Here are some statistics to ponder concerning the time of useful consciousness at various altitudes:

At 25,000 feet 1–2 minutes

At 30,000 feet 50–60 seconds

At 35.000 feet 30–40 seconds

At 40,000 feet 15–20 seconds

Emergency Lights

The FAA is doing something about trying to keep you alive. They have, since the no smoking ban on U.S. flights, installed smoke detectors in lavatories on all airliners. If any passenger is caught smoking in a lavatory or tampering with the detector, they are breaking a federal regulation. All emergency exit lights must be lowered from the ceiling, where all the smoke gathers, to a position no higher than 4' above the floor. There is no telling how many lives these newly positioned lights will save. This ruling went into effect November 29, 1986 for all part 121 carriers who were certified after January 1, 1958. Since smoke rises, the best place for escape emergency lighting is 0n the floor. A few years ago, all 121 carriers were forced to install these all-important floor lights. The white lights in the aisles go from one end of the cabin floor to the other. There is usually a red light adjacent to each emergency exit. Unfortunately, different carriers have different colored lights.

Cabin Interiors

When the Roof Caves In

On January 8, 1989, a British Midland Airways B-737 jet was experiencing engine vibration problems and fire in one of its engines. The crew shut down the wing engine and elected to make an emergency landing near Keyworth, Leicestershire in England. The aircraft made a hard landing and the fuselage broke into three sections. Of the eight crew and 118 passengers on board, 39 passengers died from impact injuries. One of the greatest deterrents for a rapid escape was the fact that all but one of the 30 overhead bins fell from their attachments, killing and injuring many passengers. The luggage that was expelled from the overheads, as well as the bins themselves, contributed to a large number of severe head injuries and entrapment.

The British Department of Transports Investigating Department had numerous new safety regulations, but this is one of their most important statements concerning aircraft design: "Overhead bins should either be more securely fixed or they should be eliminated. The contents of the bin should be limited and the door latches better designed to prevent contents from falling out."

On December 27, 1991, a Scandinavian Airlines System (SAS) McDonnell-Douglas MD-80 experienced engine failure of both engines at an altitude of 2,000 feet. This happened three minutes after liftoff from Stockholm International Airport, Sweden. The aircraft was crash-landed. It struck several trees and a ditch, and broke into three sections. Eventually, it stopped in a snow-covered field. There were a total of 123 passengers and six crewmembers on board. Thirty-nine persons were only slightly injured. The co-pilot and seven passengers were very seriously injured.

The Swedish Board of Accident Investigation (SHK) stated that nine passengers sustained blunt force trauma injuries. The report had this to say concerning the overhead bins: "The examination revealed that several of the bins had separated from their anchor points along the cabin wall. Additionally, passenger service units (PSU) became detached, striking the heads of passengers. PSUs above overwing emergency exits at rows 18 and 19 were hanging down, partially obstructing access to the exits. About 70 percent of the bin doors had damaged latch plates or plates that were missing from their attachment paints on the bin doors. Passengers stated that the carry-on luggage in the overhead bins was thrown throughout the cabin during the impact sequence."

The NTSB examined 77 airline crashes in which the impact forces were survivable. In two-thirds of the crashes, it was the cabin furnishings that entrapped, injured, or killed passengers. The seats were not properly anchored, the overhead bins came crashing down, and the galley equipment got loose and injured many people.

Recent FAA tests concerning the integrity of overhead bins proved that the current static tests could contain a given amount of weight, but as soon as dynamic tests were performed, with the same weight, the bins fractured.

In the early days of air travel, very little carry-on baggage was allowed. Later, overhead racks were installed without doors. At times, the contents would fly out in rough air so doors were installed to keep the contents inside. However, the latching mechanism was poor and in turbulence or crash landings, the doors would fly open, allowing the contents to injure the passenger below.

On June 25, 1998, the FAA issued an Advisory Circular regarding carry-on baggage. They recommend that all carry-on luggage should be weighed and measured, overhead bins must not be subjected to very heavy objects, and the bin doors must be closed easily without forcing to get them to lock. All very commendable ideas. However, none of them were carried out by the airlines. The FAA should make the rules concerning carry-on baggage, but instead they leave it up to the individual carriers. Since the airline's marketing department controls the lion's share of how an airline should operate, there is always the competition from other carriers that will have to be dealt with.

Each year, more than 4,000 passengers are injured by out-of-control, overhead items.

Airlines Have Poor Records

When it comes to lost luggage, one out of every 200 bags are lost and only a handful are ever found. Foreign carriers have a one-bag carry-on maximum compared to two allowed by most U.S. carriers.

If airlines were more careful with baggage, perhaps people would not try to carry on all that they can get away with. I know of a case where a flight attendant, doing her job, told a passenger that he could not bring a certain item into the cabin. Airlines want to keep passengers happy, so an agent gave this passenger a first-class upgrade on the next flight going to the same destination. This airline rewarded travelers for not obeying the rules.

Just a word on why it takes time to get your luggage to you in the claim area. I believe that airlines, most of the time, do a great job of getting your luggage to you as fast as possible. You must remember that your flight has hundreds of bags that must be handled by the airline. Each luggage tag must be checked because it might be headed for another flight. All luggage must be placed on a cart and driven to the terminal and perhaps access to the conveyor belt is blocked by carts that are working another flight. There is a veritable maze of workers and carts in the bowels of each terminal. It's a wonder you get your baggage as rapidly as you do.

Let's follow the route of a typical airline passenger when he gets to the airport. He gets out of his car or bus at the curbside check-in, but he does not check any bags and continues to be bent over with unwieldy luggage, lap-top computer, and canvas hanging from his tired shoulders. After waiting in line at the ticket counter, he finally gets to the agent and shows his ticket. Here he could check some bags, but no, he still intends to board the plane with his carry-ons.

Next stop is the security checkpoint where he must put all his belongings on a belt so that they can be scanned for any improper items. Through the magnetic detector he goes and picks up his trappings on the other side of the machine.

If every one carried only one bag, think how small the metal detector lines would be!

Now he has to carry all his belongings down numerous walkways until he finally gets to the carrier's gate check-in. Here is where things should start happening, but they don't. Bags are supposed to be checked for size and weight, but they seldom are. His flight is called and he starts out once again for his final march down the jetway into the aircraft. He is supposed to be carrying a maximum of two bags, but now it becomes the flight attendant's job to decide if his luggage will fit in the overhead or under the seat. The gate agent should have done this, but they push their work onto the cabin crew and let them do the arguing with the passenger.

When flights are 70 percent full, that is the time when all the available overhead space is bursting with luggage. As you wait patiently in line to board, you are wondering why the line is barely moving. The people ahead of you are slowly trying to find space in the already full overheads.

Some inconsiderate travelers will place their bags in the first empty overhead they come to rather than put their luggage in a bin by their seat in the rear of the plane. This way, they won't have to carry these things through the cabin when they deplane.

Think how much quicker it would be if there were no overheads and all luggage were stored under the seats. When the overhead is bursting with luggage, the attendant at the rear will come forward and try to find a place for your luggage. If she can't find one, she will have to wait until all the passengers in the aisle are seated, then bring your luggage to a safe hiding place. If she still can't find one, she will have to go to the trouble of checking it and giving it to the gate agent.

If most of the luggage were checked in the first place, everything would run a lot smoother and passengers would be in a much safer environment.

Reasons for Doing Away with Overhead Bins

1. Boarding and deplaning would be much faster.
2. Turbulence or hard landings would not cause baggage to rain down on top of your head.
3. In the event of a crash, you would have a better chance of exiting the aircraft because of the lack of luggage and overheads falling down and trapping your egress.
4. Flying would be safer because of a weight and balance situation. Airlines take an average weight of passengers and carry-ons. Sometimes, the carry-on luggage weight is as much as 15 pounds per passenger. Multiply that by 200 travelers and you have a 3,000-pound overweight figure. Not a healthy situation for a takeoff on a short runway or if your pilot has to abort the takeoff.

5. Aircraft would not cost as much to construct if they were built without overheads and the savings in weight could allow more fuel to be carried, always a safety factor.

6. Even though you might like an aisle seat so you can stretch your legs, it is not a good idea. Why? Because aisle seats do not have the overhead bins to shield you when the contents inside come crashing down on you.

Reasons for Keeping Overhead Bins

None. Unless you count laziness by having to go to baggage claim.

Since 1985, about 16 percent of all US transport aircraft accidents have involved fire. Approximately 22 percent of the fatalities resulted from the effects of fire and smoke. In 1988, the "feds" upgraded their flammability standards for materials used in cabin interiors. These new standards apply to all aircraft manufactured after August 19, 1990. Aircraft that were in-service prior to this date will have to comply with the new standards only when they undertake a complete replacement of the cabin interiors that they may never do.

The January 1993, GAO report made this statement: "At the beginning of 1992, about 11 percent of the 4,200 aircraft in the fleet complied with the standards. As a result, 45 percent of the aircraft fleet is expected to be operating with cabin interiors not meeting the latest flammability standards by the end of the decade. In fact, under the current practice of replacing aircraft, the entire fleet is not expected to comply with the stricter flammability standards until 2018."

Doesn't that want to make you rush out and buy a smoke mask? The "feds" estimate that between 9 and 16 lives could be saved each year if all airliners met the stricter flammability standards. So let's take an FAA casualty average of 12 per year for 24 years; that comes to a minimum of 288 passengers that could be burned to death before the year 2018. At least that is the way I look at it; lives lost, not cost.

The government sees these accidents on strictly a monetary basis. Another GAO quote: "If the DOT (Department of Transportation) current value of $1.5 million for a human life were used to extrapolate a value for the potential fatalities avoided, then up to $110 million could potentially be saved by modifying aircraft to meet the standards."

USAir, American, Delta, and United account for approximately half of the 4,200 aircraft in the U.S. fleet. As of April 1992, the GAO survey indicated that no aircraft had been modified to meet the new flammability standards. Airlines perform maintenance "D" checks every seven to eight years. However, the airlines have no plans to completely replace the cabin interiors when they perform noise or aging aircraft modifications.

If you can't exit a burning aircraft within 90, seconds you may not get out. The toxic plastics in the aircraft interior will produce cyanide that can incapacitate you completely. And as the temperature builds, a flashover is not far away. This phenomenon is caused by the intense heat released by burning interior panels in the upper cabin. Aircraft that are modified will reduce rates of heat release, and will delay or prevent flashover. When flashover takes place, there is no escaping, not even with a smoke mask.

If the "feds" were to make this new retrofit mandatory, we would all be better off. Since it costs about $1 million to modify the cabin of a small jet, there won't be too many airlines that would voluntarily perform such maintenance.

Here is a comment that the FAA made in the 1993 GAO report. Read it and weep: "FAA officials stated that our findings, as well as an internal FAA cost analysis of refurbishing aircraft cabin interiors, indicate that the costs to retrofit the fleet outweighs the POTENTIAL SAFETY BENEFITS (capitals mine); therefore, mandating a retrofit requirement would not be cost-effective."

In November of 1993, a Northwest Airlines B-727 was in the process of pushing back from the gate at Dorvall Airport in Montreal. Smoke began to appear from an overhead baggage compartment. The fire was quickly extinguished by the crew and the culprit was discovered to be an airline blanket that was intentionally set on fire. An NTSB report states, "Blankets identical to those stored in overhead compartments were examined following the incident.... The fabric, 100 percent polyester, ignited easily with a match. Following ignition, the polyester melted and resulted in a molten pool of fire."

The blankets had previously passed an FAA (unclear) flame spread test. NTSB stated: "Allowing the use of highly flammable blankets for passenger comfort is inconsistent with current FAA standards and requirements to reduce the flammability of interior cabin material."

How much more could it cost the carrier to ensure that their passengers are not encased in a blanket that could be a potential danger in a fire? Not only are the blankets flammable but also potentially loaded with germs. Some unscrupulous suppliers do not sanitize the blankets; they simply put them in plastic bags and do nothing to clean them.

The next time you are on a fully loaded airliner, look around and notice how many elderly people are on board. Perhaps some passengers are handicapped. Are there any children or infants? What about the passengers who have been drinking to excess? How many passengers paid attention when the emergency briefing was given? How do you think these passengers would react in an emergency? Picture the cabin after you have crash-landed. It is in a state of shambles. Many of the seats would be torn from their mounts and hurdled forward, perhaps with you attached. Those flimsy overhead compartments would be torn from their perch and the contents strewn in the aisles. There is dense smoke and fire everywhere, and the upholstery is sending out lethal cyanide vapors. People are near hysteria. Only half the emergency exits are useable and your friendly passengers are trampling each other in order to get out as rapidly as possible. Do you think you could exit the cabin within 90 seconds after the crash in this scenario? The FAA says no problem. Remember that in the vast majority of accidents, the crash kills relatively few people; it's the post-crash fire that kills the majority of the passengers.

You have just read what it could be like in a real airline crash. Now you will see how the FAA goes through the motions to simulate the evacuation of a downed airliner.

Evacuation Tests

Are evacuation test standards rigid enough? I think not, and after you read this I believe you will agree with me.

When a newly designed airliner is undergoing its series of evaluation tests, one of the most cavalier of them all is the initial mandatory emergency evacuation procedures. In essence, this test is made to determine if a fully loaded aircraft can be evacuated in 90 seconds or less with half the emergency exits purposely not used. The exit doors to be used are not made known until the drill begins. The following evacuation information is taken from numerous tests throughout the years, both at FAA facilities and at manufacturer plants.

There are 20 separate criteria that must be strictly adhered to. If any one is broken, the test is null and void, according to the FAA. Let's just count the number of their own regulations that they watch being broken during the course of one of these exercises in futility. I will only comment on the regulations that are not properly followed.

The aircraft used for these tests is supposed to be a standard model, the kind that will soon be in service. The tests are usually performed in a hangar at the manufacturer's airport. It is supposed to be performed at night with only the cabin emergency lights in use. This is simulated in daylight by closing the hangar doors, turning off the lights, and sealing off all the aircraft windows (there is always light that gets through the cracks between the hangar doors). The tests are photographed from the inside and outside of the aircraft. These photographs are used to record the mockery but they also let out an FAA secret.

> Fault #1—All aircraft windows were not covered and the hangar was not completely dark. A representative passenger load must be used. Thirty percent must be female, 57 percent over age 60, and 5 percent must be children under 12 years of age (three life-size dolls). Crewmembers and people who maintain or operate the airplane in the normal course of their duties may not be used as passengers for this test.

Fault #2—On the original tests for the newest Boeing 757, tests were conducted with passengers who ranged in age between 20 to 40 years of age, there were no children or dolls used, and the participants had two full days in which to practice. Seat belts and shoulder harnesses had to be fastened.

Fault #3—Seat belts and shoulder harnesses were not provided for the cabin attendants. On the initial tests of the Boeing 747, there were not enough seats on the aircraft to hold the 550 passengers needed for the test so a platform was erected outside the plane and extra participants were used. When the signal for evacuation was given, these people ran in one side of the plane and out the other. In 1973, when the Lockheed 1011 was certified, kitchen chairs were taped to the floor simply because there weren't enough standard airline seats. Each crewmember must be a member of a regular scheduled airline. The crew must be seated in the normally assigned seat and remain there until the signal is given.

Fault #4—The cabin attendants were allowed to stand adjacent to open the known exit to be used in the demonstration. No crewmember or passenger may be given prior knowledge of the emergency exits available for the demonstration.

Fault #5—Passengers and crew were all aware of the emergency exits to be used. The certificate holder may not practice or rehearse the demonstration for the participants nor may any participants have taken part in this type of demonstration within the preceding six months.

Fault #6—The demonstration was described to participants before being conducted. The same group of people was used for four demonstrations in the first day. If stands are used to help evacuees off the wings, the official timing will not stop until the last passenger is on the ground.

Fault #7—Evacuation time for the over-wing exits was timed to when the last passenger was on the wing, not on the ground, stand or ramp. If the evacuation is not completed in less than 90 seconds, they must keep going until they get it right.

There is little similarity between these tests and the real world. The participants are usually younger than the average airline passenger, and they are dressed in the proper clothing and sneakers. The element of surprise or panic is not present, and there is certainly no danger of losing one's life. There are no fires or smoke, and no real debris similar to what would be found on the floor of a crashed airliner. Only one side of the aircraft is used for egress opposed to the possibility of the aircraft breaking in half. The PA is functioning normally, and there are no drunks or handicapped people to slow down the process. Everybody is "up" for this evacuation because the crews want to fly the aircraft and the manufacturers' employees, who are on board, want to sell their product.

The vast majority of the narrow-bodied (smaller) jets have a unique arrangement for emergency window exits. Over 50 years ago, the Douglas DC-3 had six emergency window exits for an aircraft that only held 21 passengers. Today's jets that carry five times that many people have only two window exits on each side of the cabin. Both of the exits are only a few feet from each other. These exits are strategically placed over the wings. We all know what is in the wings: thousands of gallons of fuel.

Placing two exits only a few feet apart is ludicrous. It would be far better to have them strategically located where it would not require both ends of the cabin to converge in the center of the fuselage. The Boeing 747 is constructed so that all exits are equal distant from each other. That is a definite step on the plus side of safety.

In the real world, the occupants of a crashed airliner only get one chance to get out, they can't go back and try it again. In reality, most evacuation time exceeds 90 seconds. A few years ago, a new airliner was being tested. It took five minutes to evacuate a Delta 880 with only 92 people on board. While testing another airliner a Northwest 747 with only 160 on board, it took two minutes to empty the aircraft completely.

During the congressional subcommittee hearings concerning aviation safety, there were some startling statements made by Monica Kaufman, Independent Federation of Flight Attendants, and Bonnie Harris McKenna, Union of Flight Attendants: "In the Lockheed certification, the participating crewmembers were admonished time and again both Lockheed officials and FAA personnel that each day the airplane remained without a certificate both Lockheed and the airlines which ordered the 1011's were losing big money."

I believe Congressman Elliott H. Levitas, the Chairman of the Subcommittee of Investigation and Oversight, summarizes the situation amicably in his closing statement to the committee: "In closing these hearings today, I wish that I had used a term other than disappointing to describe the FAA regulation of air safety. Perhaps the word "disgraceful" would be more appropriate. And I have no intention of ignoring the complacent attitude, both of airframe manufacturers and of air carriers. Some good share of the failure of the FAA to have promulgated more stringent standards lies with the persuasive arguments of these industries on the economic factors."

------------------------▼------------------------

CHAPTER 22

SOME HELPFUL HINTS

So far, you have been reading about tragedies and disasters. Now it is time to offer some suggestions concerning the various ingredients of your next flight. My wife, Kay, who was my former flight attendant and a pilot, and who is presently a travel consultant, has many useful bits of information pertinent to the traveler.

Ticketing

Once you decide on the date and time you want to start your trip, getting reservations and tickets is relatively simple. You can get your tickets from the airlines ticket office, or if it is more convenient, use a travel agent. You pay no more at an agency than you would at an airline, so don't be hesitant using their services. And today, you can go online and book your flight yourself.

If your travel plans fall at holiday time, you had better make reservations weeks, or at times, months prior to your departure. When you make a reservation, be sure to get the name of the agent, regardless of whether you make the reservation by telephone or in person. Be sure your ticket is filled out properly as to correct spelling of name, destination, and dates, and be certain that the status box on your ticket is marked OK. If this box is not checked, you are not confirmed and you are only wait-listed which means you are waiting for a confirmation.

When a reservation agent requests that you purchase your tickets by a certain time, you had better do it or you will lose your reservation. It's prudent to reconfirm your reservation before you leave for the airport. If you plan to pay for your ticket with a credit card, you will need a driver's license and another ID. If you should lose your ticket, you could be in a real fix. It's always best to copy all ticket numbers and be sure that you have the name of the agent who sold you the ticket. With this information at hand, your refund becomes a much easier transaction. The time required for a refund may vary greatly from carrier to carrier. Some airlines may refund your lost ticket money on the spot; others take as long as six months.

When you are booking your flight, be sure to ask the agent if you will be flying with a smaller carrier that has code-sharing privileges. Here is a quote from USAirways' In Flight magazine: "The U.S. Department of Transportation regulations that require disclosure regarding code-share flights. On our own reservations system, as well as on other computerized reservations systems, code-sharing flights are flagged with an asterisk or another symbol and the code-share airline is indicated so when you make your reservation the agent can tell you what part of your journey is a code-share flight."

Packing

Be sure to pack a small carry-on bag that contains all your necessities for a day or two in case your checked luggage gets lost. Don't pack full-size bottles of shampoo, moisturizers, and the like; pour the contents into smaller plastic bottles. You will be amazed at the space you will save. Buy film mailers so your exposed film can be sent home, and thereby eliminating the worry of losing them. Take just a few changes of underwear; they can be washed nightly. Don't wear high heels when traveling. If you should have to use an emergency chute or a life raft, your heels probably will puncture the thin plastic from which they are made. Invest in a light nylon tote bag so that your vacation purchases can be carried easily. Try to wear clothing that is not made of nylon or polyester because these materials can melt onto your skin if there is a fire. During landing and takeoff, keep as much of your body covered as possible. This will lessen your chances of severe burns in case of a landing mishap. Never pack any valuable items in your checked luggage. If you want to be sure of them arriving when you do, carry them with you. All luggage should have your name and address, inside and out. And last but by no means least, purchase a lightweight smoke mask, one that easily will fold up into the same size as a plastic raincoat. Their cost is only thirty dollars ($30.00), cheap enough to possibly save your life in a smoke-filled cabin. If you would like information about purchasing a mask, call 1-800-LIFTOFF.

Baggage

Be sure and remove all your old airline luggage tags before you check your bags at the airline counter. Many a bag has gone to the destination of a previous trip. When your bags are checked at the counter, be sure that the agent has the proper destination tags and that you have a claim check for each item. Here is a quote from USAirways' In Flight magazine: "No more than two carry-on items are allowed. Purses, cameras, reading material, and overcoats do not count in the allotment.... For under the seat, the carry-on item may be no larger than 8x16x21 inches and the overhead item must be no larger than 10x16x24 inches. The overhead compartment may accommodate a folded standard-size garment bag that is no thicker than 8 inches when folded."

Most carriers have a box in the boarding area that is the exact dimensions of the underseat area. If your luggage fits in this box, you can carry it on with you. If not, it will have to be checked. If your bags are lost, damaged, or delayed, the airline may compensate you up to a maximum of $1,250. On international flights, the Warsaw Convention Treaty sets the liability limits. Damaged luggage will be paid for by the carrier and it's up to the passenger to negotiate the proper reimbursement. If your luggage is declared lost officially, you will be required to submit a claim. Airlines are confronted with many dishonest people and they are wary of paying for items that may or may not have been part of the luggage contents. Once again, this is a debatable situation, and I wish you good luck.

Delays and Cancelled Flights

Airlines cannot guarantee their flight schedules. Weather, equipment failure, and ATC and crew problems can all cause a delay in departure. If the delay is going to be extensive, you might consider using another airline; that is, if your ticketed carrier will endorse your ticket so that you can fly on the competition. They may charge a fee for this service so it's best to check first.

Please be patient if you are delayed because your aircraft is unairworthy. It takes a good captain to cause a delay, especially with the pressure from management and the passengers. Sure, you have a business appointment or perhaps Aunt Minnie will be stuck at the destination airport for a few extra hours, but that is far better than to fly in an unsafe machine.

If the flight is delayed, pilots do not endear themselves to management. In fact, the delay could bite into the pilot's pay. If the flight fails to land close to schedule, another crew may fly the next part of the trip. That means the original crew may have to "dead head" home. If the trip series are scheduled to end in two days, your crew may have to make up that time, possibly on their days off. So you can see passengers are not the only ones to suffer because of a delay.

If you are sitting in an airliner on the runway and there are other planes taking off into a thunderstorm, thank your lucky stars that a real captain is flying, not one who is afraid of company wrath. Sometimes, you are far safer flying with an airline that is having a problem negotiating a new contract with their pilots. The disgruntled crews are far more likely to cancel a flight for maintenance or weather problems than a crew who is extremely happy with management. The latter group will carry a broken airplane on their backs for days, sooner than do the job right.

Rule 240

Next time your flight is delayed or cancelled, you have been waiting in line for an endless period, or you finally get to the ticket counter and are not treated in a friendly manner, you can mention Rule 240. Just the fact that you are aware of 240 will probably get action from airline personnel that you have not seen before.

Rule 240 is not really a rule: it's a term. Before deregulation, it most definitely was a rule. Today, most of the airlines still honor this rule even though they don't have to because it's good for passenger relations.

Rule 240 states that a carrier must get you to your destination within two hours of the originally scheduled flight time. If they cannot accommodate you on their airline, they must put you on another airline. Other perks of the rule include a voucher for a meal, free telephone call, and lounge pass request.

If your flight is cancelled, don't wait in line at the counter. You will get quicker results from a call to the airlines' reservation center. Better still, use your lap-top to get a rapid response.

Force Majeure

Remember this term because an agent may confront you with it. It refers to any condition that is not under the control of the airline and includes labor problems, lockouts, slowdowns, weather, hostilities, and wars. If you are confronted with any of the above conditions, the airlines' only obligation is to refund the price of your ticket. This is dependent on the individual airlines' policy and its agreements with other carriers.

With ever-increasing delays, the term force majeure will become far more commonplace in the airline industry.

Overbooking

If you are "bumped" (left behind) by the carrier, it is probably the fault of your fellow passengers. Many travelers book seats on two or three airlines at the same time. This is to ensure that they will get a seat on at least one of them. This inconsiderate practice is so prevalent in the airline industry that it causes another dilemma. Airlines are fully aware of passengers with multiple bookings who fail to cancel with the airlines they are not using. So in order to counteract this practice, they "overbook" every flight. In this way, they will not be stuck with a lot of empty seats. What happens when 200 passengers arrive to board a plane with 150 seats? Fifty people are going to be left in the terminal. Now the airline has the problem of asking for volunteers to depart on a later flight. For this, the passenger may receive some form of compensation. Here's how it works.

If you aren't in a hurry to get to your destination, you can sell back your seat to the carrier. If the agent says that they will book you on a later flight, be certain that it is a confirmed seat, not a standby. Most domestic airlines will gladly give you a round-trip ticket to any of the cities on their routes. If you see overbooking troubles brewing and you have time to kill, get to the boarding counter, give the agent your business card, and tell him or her that you would not mind going on a later flight. That way, you will be the first to receive the free round-trip flight. If you have to wait a long period before your new flight, you might want to check and see if the airline will give you a meal chit, money for telephone calls, or a hotel room. These items are all negotiable. If, on the other hand, you resent being bumped and want to get on the original flight, the airline must make some compensation. If the carrier can get you on a flight that will arrive within one hour of your original scheduled arrival time, there is no compensation. If your carrier arranges substitute transportation that will get you to your destination more than one hour but less than two (4 hours international) hours past your original time of original time of arrival, the carrier must reimburse the price of your one-way ticket or a maximum of $200. If the new flight will land you over two hours late (4 hours international), the compensation doubles to a maximum of $400.

Each airline has its own rules that govern compensation. You must have a confirmed reservation and you must have purchased your ticket within the time allotted. Some carriers have a 10-minute check-in time, others as much as 90 minutes. There also is a separate time for a ticketing deadline. Most carriers require passengers who have no tickets to be at the airline counter at least 30 minutes before departure. If these criteria are not fulfilled, you would probably lose your reservation and any rights to compensation if your are bumped.

Anytime the carrier substitutes a smaller aircraft for the one it originally planned to use, the airline isn't required to pay anything to people who are bumped. These rules do not apply to any charter flights, or to scheduled trips utilizing aircraft that have less than sixty seats. These regulations only apply in the United States; foreign carriers may or may not abide by them.

Ears Were Not Meant for Flying

Your eardrum sits between the ear canal, the passage that leads to the outside air, and the middle ear. Your ear is most comfortable when the air pressure on either side of the eardrum is equal. The eustachian tube supplies air from the nasal cavity to the middle ear. During flight, the eustachian tube sometimes is unable to cope with the rapid pressure changes.

All modern airline aircraft are pressurized, but I have never flown on one where the pressure changes aren't noticeable. After takeoff and during the climb to cruise, your ears usually experience crackling noises. The higher you climb, the lesser the air pressure outside the ear than in the middle ear. If you experience crackling noises on the climb, they will be much more intense on descent. When you reach cruising altitude, your ears get a chance for the pressure to equalize. However, when the descent is started, it is very difficult for the eustachian tubes to equalize the strong outside pressure and often needs help. To trigger the muscular activation in the tubes, simply yawn or swallow. Chewing gum or sucking on a hard candy increases the swallowing frequency that is how the pressure becomes equalized. If you have a cold or allergy, you will have a much greater problem trying to equalize the pressure. Swollen nasal membranes can block the eustachian tubes. If you can't clear them on descent and the pressure is allowed to build, it may result in a punctured eardrum.

The best way to equalize the pressure is to pinch the nostrils closed and steadily force air into the back of your nose. This should clear the tubes and all should be well. If you have a bad cold and are planning to fly, please try the nose pinching method before you go. If you cannot clear your ears on the ground, forget about flying.

Cabin Courtesies

I would like to introduce you to my daughter, Laurette Power-Waters Bollinger. She is a private pilot and a senior flight attendant with USAirways. She has made a partial list of courtesies and tips that all passengers should follow.

1. Try to bring just one piece of carry-on luggage aboard instead of two. One piece means a quicker boarding and it is a lot less danger-ous weight-wise in the cabin overhead.

2. Don't bring anything on board that you can't carry and stow your-self. If flight attendants lifted bags on every flight, there would be an incredible increase in back injuries. Airlines don't want their flight attendants lifting bags for obvious medical reasons.

3. The maximum for carry-on luggage is two pieces per ticketed passenger with a total weight not exceeding 40 pounds. Briefcases are considered carry-on items. The following is a list of items not considered carry-on items: handbag, pocketbook, camera with case not exceeding 18"x12"x4", coat, umbrella, infant/child safety seat, crutches, or canes.

4. When you get to your assigned row, step out of the aisle and load the overhead bin WHILE IN THE CONFINES OF YOUR ROW. To stand in the aisle and do this is not courteous. There are other people behind you that have to wait while you stow your luggage.

5. Sit only in your assigned seat or you probably will be asked to move. The time to move to a better seat is after you are airborne and the seat belt sign is turned off.

6. Each passenger has paid a lot of money for a certain seat and that seat belongs to its purchaser. This means you have no right to touch it other than to extend your tray. Some people are nervous when

they fly. Please don't let your children thump the seat in front of them, or spend the best part of the trip opening and closing the service tray. Do not use the seat in front of you as a means to pull yourself up out of your seat. When you release the grip on the front seat, that passenger will think that he or she is in a fighter ejection seat because that passenger will be propelled forward at a good rate.

7. Don't be an armrest hog. That armrest must be shared by the person sitting next to you so don't continually elbow-wrestle with them.

8. Sit down and buckle up when the sign is on and the cabin crew tells you to do so.

9. Don't get up and start moving around the cabin after pushback from the gate. Any ground movement by an aircraft is the wrong time to be up and about, and it is potentially dangerous.

10. Realize that this plane is not your living room. Have some respect for those around you.

11. All aircraft are supplied with emergency cards in Braille for blind passengers. If you are one, just ask your flight attendant.

12. Flight attendants must move about the cabin when the seat belt sign is lit. It is their job. However, a vast majority of passengers completely disregard this important sign. If you should encounter turbulence while roaming around the cabin, you could be severely injured. Your seat belt should always be fastened except for a trip to the rest room.

13. Passengers need to realize that the aircraft is not a restaurant. The meals and beverages are complimentary. Passengers only pay for a ride from one point to another. It is very rude to complain because we don't have just what you feel like eating or drinking. When in doubt, bring a sandwich and/or whatever you want to drink. Then you won't be disappointed.

14. If you have diabetes or any medical condition that warrants special foods or beverages, bring what you need; don't rely on the airline to

provide it. Mix-ups do occur and it is possible that the special meal that was ordered may not have been put aboard. Passengers need to take responsibility for themselves and their needs.

15. If you are going to have a cocktail on board, make sure that you board the aircraft with the correct change. Giving a flight attendant a $20 or $50 bill for a $4 drink is ridiculous. They have no change on board. It is difficult and time consuming for the flight attendants to have to ask other passengers if they can make change.

16. The time to visit the rest room is prior to the meal service. The flight attendants are busy serving and you may have to stand behind one for quite sometime before they know you are there. Moving their cart to let you pass will lead to a pleasant smile combined with a few choice words under their breath.

17. If you are nervous and feel that you must talk to the passenger next to you, that's fine, but be sure they are responsive. If they are not, you will only make their trip miserable.

18. Please don't let your children race up and down the aisle and bother other passengers. You might believe that your children are perfect but that thought might not be shared by the rest of the passengers.

19. If you have a child with you, bring everything you will need during the flight. This includes diapers, food, and toys. The flight attendants are not there to diaper, feed, or play with your child. The child is the guardian's responsibility and that individual needs to control the child.

20. If a decompression should occur and the panel above the passenger seats that house the oxygen masks does not open, the passenger has to get it open. For the compartments that have the "pinhole" style, a small sharp object must be inserted into the pinhole to open the panel. Paper clips, stir sticks, or even jewelry pins are effective. The planes that don't have the pinhole can be released by inserting a thin flat object such as a seat pocket card or credit card into the slot and running it from the window toward the aisle to trip the latching mechanism.

21. It is an excellent idea to review your emergency card before landing. All landings are not picture perfect and it behooves you to check out the nearest emergency exit.

22. When you taxi into the gate and the captain has given the two-bell signal to deplane, there is no need to leap out of your seat and try to be the first one off.

23. Please realize that when flight attendants enforce the FAA rules, they are not doing it to be mean and they don't make up the rules as they go along. All rules are for passenger and crew safety. They must be obeyed.

24. If all passengers would use common sense, good manners, and have respect for one another, they would enjoy their flight more and enable the flight attendants to concentrate on their job of safety and service. We love to see that you have an enjoyable and safe flight.

25. The most important thing a passenger can do is to be attentive during the safety demonstration given by the flight attendants. It only takes a few minutes and it may save your life. You never know when an accident may occur and you need to be as prepared as possible at all times. People need to stop having the attitude "nothing will happen on my flight, I'll be fine." Chances are that's what most crash victims think right before their accidents. Wouldn't you want to be as prepared as possible for the worst?

If you really are bent on injury, try standing up before the aircraft has completely stopped. Many times, the plane might have to come to a stop because of another aircraft in front, or because of an order from the tower. If the captain is required to apply hard breaking, you could be thrown to the floor easily. After the aircraft has stopped at the gate, it takes a few minutes to maneuver the jetway up to the cabin door. Then the door must be opened and stowed. All those passengers ahead of you will have to start moving toward the door before you will get a chance to do the same. If you have a close connection, you probably will feel better if you stand in the aisle, but if there is no real hurry, remain in your seat until the coast is clear.

Complaining

When passengers complain about anything, airlines listen. I can vouch for that myself. I was reprimanded by my chief pilot because of a passenger's complaint. It seems a traveler who boarded my flight at Chicago was really "bent out of shape" because I was reading a Playboy magazine in the cockpit. He wrote to the company and I was guilty without ever being consulted. But if you have a complaint and the carrier's response fails to satisfy you, here are two agencies you can contact:

> Office of Community and Consumer Affairs
>
> U.S. Department of Transportation
>
> 400 7th Street, S.W.
>
> Room 10405
>
> Washington D.C. 20590
>
> Phone: 202-755-2220

If your complaint is something you feel is a safety hazard, write to:

> Community and Consumer Liaison Division
>
> APA-400
>
> Federal Aviation Administration
>
> 800 Independence Avenue, S.W.
>
> Washington D.C. 20591
>
> Phone: 1-800-322-7873

Airline passengers can check the safety record of every airline through the Federal Aviation Administration's (FAA) web site at www.faa.gov/agc/enforcement/index.htm. If the airline has a history of fines for improper maintenance, this suggests that the airline may not be as safe as it should be.

How to Survive a Crash

Don't put heavy items in the overhead bins and keep your smoke mask where it is readily accessible. If your aircraft has life vests under the seat, reach down there and be sure you have one. The seats just aft (behind) of the leading edge of the wings should give you the smoothest ride. However, if there are any rear-facing seats, they are the ones to use. It would be nice if you could sit next to an emergency window but you don't want to be next to any of the aircraft's engines in case they should blow. When you settle into your seat, operate your seat belt a number of times so that you are fully acquainted with its function. Many aircraft have different belts so its best to be ready. Count the rows of seats to the nearest exit. In a smoke-filled cabin, you won't have the luxury of sight. Listen to the cabin attendants briefing and STUDY the emergency evacuation card, especially as to how to open doors and windows. In an emergency, there just may not be a flight attendant there to open them for you.

It is advisable to wear your seat belt at all times during flight. Clear air turbulence is unpredictable. Before an emergency landing, be sure that all sharp objects are removed from your person. If you are wearing dentures, remove them. In a crash situation, any sharp objects could puncture your body. When instructed to assume the brace position for a crash, stay tucked up until the aircraft comes to a complete stop. The first jolt is just that; there are usually more to follow. Believe it or not, there are people who are concerned about getting their overhead luggage before departing the aircraft after an emergency or crash landing. This is a definite "no-no." When that aircraft stops moving, there should be only one thought in your mind: GETTING OUT!

Before you open any door, be sure there is no fire in front of it. Opening it only would fill the cabin with smoke. When you do get out, don't go back; get as far away from the aircraft as possible. There is always a danger of fuel igniting by leaking over the hot engines.

Anytime you see a possible safety discrepancy, whether when boarding or sitting in your seat, please bring it to the attention of an airline employee. If you look out at the wing and see something loose or leaking, notify the cabin attendant as soon as possible.

And now we come to the all-important item of wing cleanliness. I don't mean free from dirt, but I do mean free from frost, snow, ice, or slush. If at any time you see any of these forms of precipitation adhering to the wings, immediately alert a crewmember. To attempt takeoff under these conditions is against federal law.

CHAPTER 23

▼

WHAT'S TO BE DONE?

In my first book, *Safety Last*, printed in 1972, I ended the book with the same chapter title. Let's take a look at some of my safety suggestions and see what has transpired in the last 29 years.

Airline Airports

Runways should be at least 6,500 feet in length. There should be ample underrun and overshoot extensions at both ends of the runways. They should be grooved and runway-remaining signs installed.
NOT ACCOMPLISHED

Main runways should have approach lights, centerline lights, high-intensity runway lights, runway-end identification lights, and a visual approach slope indicator.
NOT ACCOMPLISHED

Essential is a control tower equipped with radar monitoring.
NOT ACCOMPLISHED

Sufficient firefighting equipment to handle the largest aircraft that frequents the airport, and backup electric power for all navigation aids, communication, and lights.
NOT ACCOMPLISHED

Airport security that was practically nonexistent should be rectified.
PARTIALLY ACCOMPLISHED

All large airports should be equipped with airport surface detection radar (ASDI II), and Doppler radar. Controllers should not have to work combine positions. This would necessitate the hiring of more controllers. There should be at least one ILS at every airport.
NOT ACCOMPLISHED

Aircraft

Strobe lights should be required on all airliners, as well as "G" meters.
NOT ACCOMPLISHED

The killer three-point altimeter should be eliminated on airliners.
ACCOMPLISHED

A collision avoidance system that always works as advertised.
NOT ACCOMPLISHED

All airliners should be equipped with on-board wind shear detectors that are reliable.
NOT ACCOMPLISHED

Federal Air Regulations

61.47—Three landings in 90 days is insufficient.
NOT ACCOMPLISHED

121.105 Each airline must have adequate maintenance and spare parts available at certain points along their route of flight. A good regulation but one that is not enforced. Airliners fly for weeks on minimum equipment lists before the faulty components are replaced.

NOT ACCOMPLISHED

121.155—When an airline knows of hazardous runway conditions, it should suspend operations. Most airliners are too busy making money to really scrutinize hazardous runways. Airport conditions should be the responsibility of the FAA, not the airline or the airport authority.

NOT ACCOMPLISHED

The following ludicrous regulations were discussed in the chapter on the Master Race.

FAR 121.311	Seat and Safety Belts
FAR 61.107	Controlled Airports
FAR 61.57	Recent Flight Experience
FAR 91.52	Emergency Locator Beacons
FAR 91.103	Parachutes
FAR 91.175	(F) Take off Visibility
FAR 91.527	Icing Conditions

All of the above regulations, and many more, need revising. As you can see, nearly all of my 29-year complaints concerning ways to enhance safety have fallen on deaf ears. The FAA is finally doing something about the vast safety differences between large and small airlines. We have the Air Line Pilots Association to thank for any new safety regulations concerning the part 135 carriers.

The real key to airline safety is certainly not the "Lip Service" Federal Aviation Administration where safety sometimes manages to prevail. Safety is not achieved because of the FAA, but in spite of them. The real key to airline safety is found among the men and women who know aviation best: The Airline Pilot Association, National Air Traffic Controllers Association, The International Association of Machinists (Mechanics), The Professional Airways System Specialists, and last but not least, The Association of Flight

Attendants. Without these dedicated groups working together for a common cause, commercial aviation would be far less safe than it is today.

I thank you for the chance to discuss the pros and cons of commercial aviation with you and I am sure that, by now, you have a fair idea what the answer to my title is.

Is It Safe?

To land at an airport without a control tower?

To land at an airport without an operable Doppler system and no proper wind shear warnings?

To fly from an airport without ASDI (ground radar)?

To fly with a crew who has been on duty for 16 hours?

To fly from an airport where the runway is so short a decision to abort the takeoff could be dangerous?

To fly on an airliner that contains hazardous materials in the hold?

To land at an airport, in instrument conditions, without the aid of an ILS (75 percent of all airline approach accidents occur when there is no ILS)?

To fly an airliner with many of its components inoperative?

To fly in an airliner that lacks proper fire detection and suppression devices?

To fly in an air traffic control system where the equipment is older than many of its operators?

To fly with disruptive passengers who are trying to crash your plane?

To fly in a system that lacks the FAA minimum number of controllers?

To taxi out for takeoff with ice or frost adhering to the wings?

To fly in a system that allows unairworthy aircraft to be signed off by supervisory mechanics?

To fly on a new model airliner that was inspected, 95 percent by the manufacturer's people and only 5 percent by the FAA inspectors?

To fly on an airliner whose crews are not trained to react properly when the aircraft is in certain unusual positions?

To fly on an aircraft that may have unairworthy hardware components on board?

To fly from an airport that has potentially dangerous structures in close proximity to the runway?

To fly from an airport with ancient metal detectors that can't detect plastic bombs?

And last, but not least, to fly with a captain who is so scared of his company that he or she would take off or land in dangerously high winds, go through horrendous thunderstorms simply to make schedules, or fly a broken aircraft just to keep in good with the company? Believe me, they are out there!

How does the aviation safety record of the United States compare with other countries? Over the last ten years, the accident rate in Europe is over three times higher than ours, and in Asia and the Pacific Rim countries, it is over fifteen times higher. In 1993, large U.S. carriers were three times safer than commuters, nineteen times safer than air taxies, and over fifty times safer than privately operated general aviation aircraft (according to the GAO). It is somewhat comforting to know that your country's accident statistics are better than somebody else's, but we are still killing too many people.

At a recent FAA Aviation Safety Conference in Washington D.C., Mr. Hinson, the former administrator of the FAA, cited a Boeing Corporation study that projected that: "Given the forecast growth in air travel—if worldwide aviation maintains the same level of safety that it has had for the past five years, by the year 2013, we can expect to lose one aircraft worldwide about every eight days."

Some of what you have read in this book has probably shocked you. If you are a representative or a senator, please come to the aid of the traveling public. If you are not affiliated with the government, a quick note to your legislator will definitely help the course. You should not have to be called upon to make the skies safe, but in reality, you are the one who can turn the tide.

Perhaps between the two of us, we can save a few lives.

Author Biography

Captain Brian Power-Waters XIII has flown for two air forces and two scheduled airlines over his long career in aviation. He has over 3,000 hours in the air and holds most of the FAA ratings. He flew as a commercial airline pilot for 28 years and has written three other books on airline safety: *Safety Last, Margin for Error: None*, and *93 Seconds to Disaster*. Visit his website at www.brianpowerwaters.com

978-0-595-49015-8
0-595-49015-8